Mark Your Calendar!

SO-DJF-962

Important Due Dates for 1996

January 16, 1996	Final installment of 1995 estimated tax (Form 1040-ES) due.
January 31	Last chance to file income tax return (Forms 1040, 1040A, 1040EZ) for 1995 and avoid penalty for last quarter if you missed your January 15 estimated payment.
January 31	All W-2 forms and 1099 forms should be in the mail on the way to you by now: Check your mailbox and don't throw anything out!
April 15	File your tax return today and forever hold your peace.
April 15	Oops! Don't forget to send in your 1st quarter estimated payment for 1996 today as well. But don't mail it with your tax return. It goes to a different address.
April 15	Filing an extension (Form 4868) for your income tax return? Today's the day it must be mailed—don't forget to include a payment for any tax that's due to reduce a possible penalty.
April 15	One more thing. Your state income tax return is probably due today, too. Check the rules for your state.
June 17	Second quarter estimated payment for 1996 due today.
August 15	If you extended the due date on your 1995 income tax return with Form 4868, it's due NOW!
September 16	Third quarter estimated payment for 1996 due today.
January 15, 1997	I know this isn't a 1996 date. It's still an important one. Fourth quarter estimated payment for 1996 is due today.

Your Filing Status (a Primer)

STATUS	DOES THIS DESCRIBE YOU?
Married Filing Jointly	You're married as of December 31, 1995. You file a combined tax return with your spouse, and no one else can claim you as a dependent.
Single	You're not married as of December 31, 1995. (That was easy.)
Head of Household	You're single as of December 31, 1995. You maintain a household for a dependent who is lineally related to you (it's all explained in the book...). You live in the same household with the person you support.
Married Filing Separately	You're married as of December 31, 1995. You and your spouse each file your own tax return.
Qualifying Widow(er)	Your spouse passed away sometime during 1993 or 1994. You were entitled to file a joint return with your late spouse in the year of death. You had not remarried before December 31, 1995. You have a child who qualifies as your dependent.

Extra! Extra! Get Your Tax Forms Right Here!

Order blank tax forms: 1-800-TAX-FORM
Order transcript of prior year tax return: 1-800-829-1040

alpha
books

10 Cool Tricks for Avoiding an Audit

1. **Don't deal in huge cash transactions.** Pass out cash in the tens of thousands of dollars and you tend to call attention to yourself.

2. **Stay legal.** Getting involved in illegal activities is an easier way to trigger an audit than calling up the IRS and saying, "Hey, c'mon over and audit me!"

3. **Choose your friends wisely.** The IRS pays a bounty to people who turn in others who may have "accidentally" omitted income items from their tax returns.

4. **Choose your friends wisely, Part 2.** Hang out with nefarious tax-cheaters and you may find yourself under IRS scrutiny.

5. **Try not to earn so much money.** That's right. The more you earn, the more likely the chance of an audit.

6. **If you do have to earn a lot of money, ease off on the deductions.** Well, don't really, not if you are entitled to take legitimate deductions. Just be aware of the fact that the higher the percentage of your income that gets reduced by deductions, the more likely the chance of receiving a friendly letter from the IRS.

7. **Check your tax preparer's credentials.** If you use a professional tax preparer and that preparer is on the IRS's most wanted list, chances are all of his or her clients, including you, will be subject to an audit. How do you find out if your tax preparer is on the hit list? That's a tough one. Try to get the names of the preparer's former clients and ask them if they've been subjected to audits.

8. **Get it right the first time.** Amending your income tax return isn't a sure way to trigger an audit, but it does call attention to you and your tax return, making an audit a bit more likely.

9. **Don't be in the wrong place at the right time.** Each year the IRS picks a handful of tax returns to audit based on the profession of the taxpayer. The audits are performed so the IRS can gain information about the income and deduction habits of the particular profession.

10. **Get lucky.** Grab your rabbit's foot, walk on the same side of the street as your black cat, stay away from ladders, wish upon a star, whatever you do for lucky vibes. Some audits occur just by chance and no amount of crafty tax return preparation can help you avoid them.

Do I Have to File a Tax Return?

Yes you do, if your income exceeds these amounts:

WHO YOU ARE	HOW MUCH INCOME YOU NEED TO REQUIRE FILING A TAX RETURN
Single, under 65-years-old	$6,400
Single, 65 and up	$7,350
Married, filing jointly	$11,550
Married, joint, one of you is 65+	$12,300
Married, joint, both 65+	$13,050
Married, filing separate return	$2,500
Dependent child with unearned income*	$650
Head of Household, under 65	$8,250
Head of Household, 65+	$9,200
Qualifying Widow(er)	$9,050
Qualifying Widow(er) 65+	$9,800

* unearned income = income such as interest and dividends as opposed to income for which you worked.

What Tax Forms Do I Use for My Income?

YOU'VE GOT THIS KIND OF INCOME	PUT IT HERE
W-2 wages	Form 1040, page 1
Interest	Schedule B
Dividends	Schedule B
Income from self-employment	Schedule C
Sale of stock	Schedule D
Rental property	Schedule E, page 1
Partnership	Schedule E, page 2
S corporation	Schedule E, page 2
Farm	Schedule F
Retirement income	Form 1040, page 1
Unemployment compensation	Form 1040, page 1
State income tax refund	Form 1040, page 1
Gambling income	Form 1040, page 1
Alimony	Form 1040, page 1

The COMPLETE

IDIOT'S
GUIDE TO

Doing Your
Income Taxes
1996

by Gail Perry

**alpha
books**

A Division of Macmillan General Reference
A Simon & Schuster Macmillan Company
1633 Broadway, New York NY 10019-6785

Dedicated to my dear daughters, Georgia and Katherine, who accepted (most of the time) a smile in lieu of an afternoon at the park while mom was writing.

©1995 Alpha Books

International Standard Book Number: 1-56761-586-4
Library of Congress Catalog Card Number: 94-079890

97 96 95   9 8 7 6 5 4 3 2 1

Interpretation of the printing code: the rightmost number of the first series of numbers is the year of the book's printing; the rightmost number of the second series of numbers is the number of the book's printing. For example, a printing code of 95-1 shows that the first printing occurred in 1995.

Printed in the United States of America

Publisher
Theresa H. Murtha

Associate Publisher
Lisa A. Bucki

Manuscript Editor
Judy J. Brunetti

Production Manager
Kelly Dobbs

Designer
Kim Scott

Illustrations
Judd Winick

Manufacturing Coordinator
Paul Gilchrist

Production Team Supervisor
Laurie Casey

Graphic Image Specialists
Jason Hand, Clint Lahnen, Laura Robbins,
Craig Small, Todd Wente

Production Team
Angela Calvert, Heather Butler, Dan Caparo, Kim Cofer,
Jennifer Eberhardt, Kevin Foltz, Aleata Howard,
Erika Millen, Regina Rexrode, Karen Walsh, Robert Wolf

Indexers
Chris Cleveland
Brad Herriman

Contents at a Glance

Contents

Foreword

It's little wonder that tax reform is such a hot political issue. Shortly after each new year begins, the Internal Revenue Service sends every American a tax packet that can cause even the stoutest heart to quake. Included are myriad tax forms and pages of nearly incomprehensible explanations of how to fill out those forms (many of them mandated, oddly enough, by the Paperwork Reduction Act). Also included—perhaps to make you really feel like an idiot—are the estimated times it should take to fill out those forms. After hours spent trying to fill out the forms—and to measure up to those estimated times—the allure of a postcard-sized income tax return must be nearly universal.

Well, another year has come and gone and Uncle Sam's tax packet for this year looks at least as big as last year's. Personally, I'm not holding my breath waiting for reform. And if you're thinking about avoiding the anxiety by having an expert do your taxes this year, consider: Some surveys have shown that one in every eight returns completed by professional tax preparers contains an error in favor of Uncle Sam. If you're like me, you're willing to pay your fair share, but don't really want to give the government a gift.

When it comes right down to it, unless you're H. Ross Perot or William Gates, the best bet is usually doing your taxes yourself. After all, you're the one who cares the most about your financial well-being.

Fortunately, there's hope for the tax-impaired and tax-intimidated. *The Complete Idiot's Guide to Doing Your Income Taxes 1996* can make filling out those IRS forms a lot less taxing than in the past. And paying your tax share—and not a dime more—is what this book is all about.

Like all the books in *The Complete Idiot's Guide* series, this one is written in down-to-earth, everyday language—with just a little humor on the side. A certified public accountant with 15 years' experience in tax accounting, author Gail Perry speaks with a professional's expertise on the knottiest of tax problems. Also an author and computer trainer, Perry knows how to present tricky concepts in easy language. Perry takes you step-by-step through all the twists and turns of your tax return, avoiding jargon and speaking directly to the questions you have, such as:

➤ Is it deductible? Perry helps you find the common and not-so-common expenses that can reduce your income—and your income tax.

➤ What's a tax credit, and how do I get one? Credits are better than deductions, but too many taxpayers don't know if they qualify.

➤ Is my IRA still deductible? Don't assume that it isn't.

➤ Where can I get that last-minute form I need? What do I do if the Post Office doesn't have it?

➤ What happens if I've filed my return and then discover a mistake? There's still time to fix it—and it's easy to do.

There's more. Looking for a way to take advantage of that computer you bought last year? Perry gives you the lowdown on the best software programs for doing your own taxes, and tells you whether the IRS's electronic-filing program makes sense for you.

Best of all, *The Complete Idiot's Guide to Doing Your Income Taxes 1996* can help you with year-round tax planning. You'll discover tax-smart ways to borrow; how to turn your hobby into a tax-deductible business; how to save for your retirement and lower your taxes at the same time; and what to keep track of so you won't miss out on deductions next year. You'll even find out how to handle an IRS audit.

The good news is that keeping taxes to a minimum isn't just a game for the wealthy. But to take advantage of credits, deductions, and other methods of reducing your taxes, you need an easy-to-understand guide. My recommendation? Grab this book when you need easy, painless tax prep help. By the way, the book is tax-deductible.

Tom Siedell

Managing Editor, *Your Money* magazine

Introduction

It's April. You haven't taken any steps toward getting ready to prepare your income tax return. Frantically you begin to wonder where all those little forms that came in the mail throughout the spring are hiding. You had a book of tax forms that came from the IRS, but your toddler got to it with her crayons. Visions of astronomical accounting fees begin clouding your eyesight. Beads of sweat start forming on your forehead as you sit down, head in your hands, and try to catch your breath.

Suddenly, the doorbell rings. A friendly looking stranger is at the door, smiling and holding a hot pizza and a carton of soft drinks. Skeptical, you cautiously let him enter your home. The stranger sits by your side at your table, deftly selecting the tax forms you need to fill out, carefully explaining which items of income get reported on the various forms, pointing the way to deductions you may have overlooked, offering friendly advice about record keeping and computerized methods of filing tax returns. By the end of the evening, the stranger is a stranger no more, but a trusted friend who has guided you through one of the most traumatic annual events of your life. You want to pinch yourself to see if this is all a dream that will vanish with a jolt back to reality, yet you hesitate, hoping the stranger may actually exist.

This book is that stranger at the door. *The Complete Idiot's Guide to Doing Your Income Taxes 1996* is the friend who will take you by the hand and lead you into the abyss of income tax regulations that consumes taxpayers each April. This book is the bearer of pizza and soda pop, smiles, and pats on the back. Step-by-step, this book will guide you as you prepare your own federal income tax return, specifically, the 1040 form. This book will help you prepare now for tax returns to come in the future. This book won't leave your side until your income tax return is in the mail.

What's in It for You?

What's the point, you say? First of all, let me just explain that I think tax laws are unnecessarily complex and that it's unfair to expect millions of people to follow along and understand the tax forms, while the people who make the tax laws probably hire professionals to prepare their tax returns.

Furthermore, most people seem to perceive federal tax agents as being 20 feet tall, towering over taxpayers, while they, like little ants, scurry away, trying to keep from getting underfoot. Ignorance of tax laws and the confusion that surrounds tax return preparation propel that notion. In this book I attempt to dispel some of the mystique that surrounds both the tax laws and the annual April 15 sacrifice unto the tax gods.

The Complete Idiot's Guide to Doing Your Income Taxes 1996 is an attempt to wipe the mud off the shoes of the concept of taxation. You don't have to walk away from this exercise feeling like the next Roscoe Egger (famous historical tax figure), but you do have to file one of those darn tax returns. Keep this guide by your side and watch it perform magical feats of danger and enchantment as it answers your questions and keeps you on track.

But, I'm Not an Idiot...

No, you're certainly not an idiot. Neither am I. But in a way, we all feel like we've lost a few IQ points when we try to prepare our tax returns. The truly idiotic thing about taxes is that otherwise normal people like you and I are expected to master six-inch thick volumes of tax law and regulations, not to mention entire libraries full of case law, in order to properly fill out a silly tax return form.

This tax law nonsense is a monster that has gotten out of control, a giant ape clinging to the side of the Empire State Building, batting airplanes out of the sky. And the worst part is it shows no signs of climbing down.

The best you can hope for is a clearly written handbook that covers the basics:

Income on which you have to pay tax.

Reaping the benefits of tax deductions.

Taking care of a business you operate from your home.

What to do when the IRS says, "Jump."

Moving into the '90s with computerized tax returns.

Organizing your life from a tax point of view.

This is that handbook.

But, I Don't Have to File the Long 1040

This book focuses on the long 1040 form for federal income taxes. If you think you may need to file the 1040A or EZ form, skim Chapter 3 of this book, but don't buy it!

So How Do I Use This Book?

If I were your fairy godmother, I'd tell you to wave this book over your W-2 form and your mortgage statement, stand back, and, presto!, watch a tax return materialize before your eyes. I'm certainly not going to stand in your way if you want to try this.

A more appropriate way in which to use this book, instead of waving it in the air and causing your friends and neighbors to wonder about your sanity, is to use it as a guide and a reference as you make your way through your tax return.

Keep it right by your side, along with a nice bowl of potato chips or a plate of warm cookies, and when you have questions or when you want some assistance or just need some basic assurance that life goes on after the tax return has been prepared, reach in the direction of the good stuff. You'll be satisfied no matter which item your fingers land on first.

This book is divided into logical parts designed to lead you through the preparation of your tax return in a reasonably organized fashion. The theory is that most people start at the top of the first page of their tax form and continue down that page, then to the top of the second, and so on. This book follows that same path.

In Part 1, you'll find some ideas about how to keep track of the things you need for your tax return, how to figure out if you even need to bother filing a tax return and if so, how to get the forms you need, and you can read about new things that have happened in the tax world in the past year. Read or skim this part at your leisure, between loads of laundry, as a reward for cleaning the kitchen, or just sitting up in bed at night after a hard day of work.

Part 2 gets you started on your Form 1040 tax return. Like they say in cookbooks, you can do the things in this part a day in advance. This section includes the preliminary getting-ready stuff that will ensure that you have what you need when you sit down and get ready to dig in on your tax return.

In Part 3 you jump off the diving board. Use this part as a reference as you figure out how to tell the IRS how much money you made this year. Part 4 will help you whittle away at that income and cut it down to size with deductions, in order to lessen your taxes.

The showdown section is Part 5. Here's where, together, you and I figure out what your income tax will be. We check for last minute ways in which to lower the amount you may owe, and then we talk about how to pay your tax bill and what to do if you come up short.

Finally, Part 6 introduces you to the world of using a computer to help with your tax return preparation. Look at various computer programs that can do the job, and learn about the advantages and disadvantages of preparing tax returns in this way.

This book is an instructional guide as well as a general resource, so feel free to use it as a step-by-step, line-by-line companion to the preparation of your tax return. Or, keep it as a reference, turn to it when you have questions or when tax things don't make sense. Use the index, check the table of contents, go to the part that fits your needs, read for awhile, enjoy the attempts at humor at the expense of the IRS and taxes in general, then get back to your tax return with a feeling of confidence that it is in good hands.

Look Out Below!

Expect to see little gray boxes throughout the book that not only break up the text with visual distractions, but that point the way to particular types of information:

Get Down to Brass Tax

This is for hard-core taxaholics who aren't happy just knowing *what* to put on their tax return. They want to know *why* they're doing it. If there were a test at the end of this book, it would be about this stuff. But there isn't. I promise.

OOPS!
Just like a "Road Work Ahead" sign, these boxes signal potential problems and sticky areas. Don't ignore these or you may find yourself off the side of the road in a tax return ditch.

IRSpeak
Scattered throughout the book are tax terms with which you may not be familiar. Look to the IRSpeak boxes to put a plain-English twist on IRS jargon.

By the Way
These include tricks of the trade, tips for novices, and shortcuts for figuring things out. Watch out! When you read these, you'll almost think you're having fun preparing your tax return.

Other Important Uses for This Book

Here are a few things you may not have realized you could do with this book:

➤ Stick miscellaneous tax receipts inside the front cover—it may not be the most sophisticated filing system, but at least you know the receipts will be easy to find when you need them.

➤ Hold the cover up to a mirror while you try to make Paul McCartney's telephone number out of the backwards letters in the title.

➤ Drop it on top of unsuspecting spiders.

➤ Place it strategically on your coffee table so all your friends will see it and want to buy it too (after all, I'm trying to make a living here).

➤ Sell it at your next garage sale (but wait until your tax return is finished).

➤ Send a copy to your congressman with the message, "Why can't the instructions that come with my tax return read like this?"

Acknowledgments

There's no way this book could have been produced without the help of all these extraordinary people. My deepest thanks go out to each of you who helped me with this project:

Lisa Bucki who took over development of this book in the middle of the project, kept it on track, and added priceless suggestions; Judy Brunetti, whose insightful editing lent continuity and clarity to my writing; Tom Godfrey, whose vision I attempted to keep alive on every page; Bill Rogers, a friend from my past who came into my present and, along with Eric Heinemann, kept my tax facts straight; Chuck Stewart, who met me at the crack of dawn one Sunday and pointed this book in the right direction; Matt Wagner, who recommended me as the author of this book, neither of us having a clue where it would lead; and Bob and Thad Perry, who, 20 years ago, send me to school so I could learn how to prepare tax returns.

Thank you also to a great production team at Alpha, hard workers all, who do their work behind the scenes, letting others take the credit. And thank you to Theresa Murtha and Marie Butler-Knight, who put their faith in me.

Pep Talk Time

It's time. We've got to get this tax return prepared and out into the mail. Sooner or later April 15 is going to come (for all I know, it may already be April 15 and you're getting kind of frantic as you read this introduction). Don't say, "There's always tomorrow," and decide now is a good time to clean out the garage. Just face it head on. And think how good you're going to feel when your tax return is a thing of the past. Remember, we're in this together.

Special Thanks from the Publisher to the Technical Reviewers

The Complete Idiot's Guide to Doing Your Income Taxes 1996 was reviewed by experts who not only checked the technical accuracy of what you'll learn here but also provided insight and guidance to help us ensure this book gives you everything you need to know to avoid pitfalls and better manage your taxes. Special thanks are extended to the following two people:

Eric Heinemann, CPA, a Tax Senior at Deloitte & Touche LLP in the Securities Group. He graduated from Bucknell University in 1992 with a B.S.B.A. in Accounting.

Bill Rogers, CPA, who has been with Deloitte & Touche LLP (formerly Deloitte Haskins & Sells) for more than 25 years. He is National Director for Securities and Investment Banking for Deloitte & Touche. A member of the Wall Street Tax Association, the American Institute of CPAs, and the Illinois CPA Society, he received a B.S. in Accounting from Bradley University.

Part 1
How Do You Start?

Death and taxes and childbirth! There's never any convenient time for any of them.

Margaret Mitchell, Gone with the Wind, *1936*

There's nothing quite like a deadline hanging over your head to prod you into action, and April 15 is a big one. I'll bet you can think of all sorts of things you'd rather be doing than preparing a tax return. But, alas, here you are, and you have this project to tackle.

Use this first part as a chance to wiggle your toes in the water without getting the rest wet. Start thinking about your tax return and begin planning how you're actually going to tackle it. I lay the groundwork so that when you are ready to sit down and face the inevitable, you won't have to keep getting up to look for forgotten receipts or tax forms. In addition, in this part you'll find clever ways in which to amass your tax information during the year so that next year and in years thereafter this process might not seem quite so daunting.

WHO'S FICA?

Chapter 1

Why Are We Doing This?

In This Chapter

➤ Where the tax laws came from (and why you can't turn off the faucet)

➤ Where all your money goes

➤ How all your money gets where it's going

Taxes have been around since the beginning of recorded history. Kings and leaders have extracted taxes from their subjects to fund wars and building projects and to provide the rulers with riches. There have been taxes on property, taxes on income, taxes on agriculture production, taxes on prostitution, taxes on importing, taxes on exporting, per-head taxes, taxes on liquor and cigarettes, taxes on hotel rooms, taxes on estates and gifts, and taxes on traffic tolls. It seems inevitable that you are always going to be faced with some sort of tax, even if the current ideas of tax reform in the form of a flat income tax or a national sales tax come to pass.

Whenever people are faced with the necessity of paying taxes, they are apt to attempt to pay the lowest amount of taxes possible, as well they should. As Judge Learned Hand of the U.S. Court of Appeals said in 1934,

> "Anyone may so arrange his affairs that his taxes shall be as low as possible; he is not bound to choose that pattern which will best pay the treasury; there is not even a patriotic duty to increase one's taxes."

And so you are faced with the prospect of keeping your income taxes to a minimum and paying the lowest amount possible. With this book I hope to help you do just that, by providing you with insights as to what types of income are taxable and what types are not taxable, as well as ideas for ways in which you can reduce your income and thus reduce your tax.

A Little Bit of History About U.S. Taxation

If you traveled back in time to 1913, you'd find a lot of interesting things going on. Cracker Jack boxes got their toys for the first time in 1913. The zipper was invented that year too (although it didn't get its name, zipper, until 1923—in 1913 it was known as a "hookless fastener"). Henry Ford inaugurated the idea of using conveyor belts to build his cars. And then there was the income tax.

When the federal income tax got its start in 1913, it was a fluke. President Taft and his conservative cronies, in 1909, were concerned about tariffs getting a little out of hand and, in a convoluted attempt to squash a tariff-raising bill that contained a provision for a personal income tax, slipped an income tax constitutional amendment through Congress, never thinking the amendment would be ratified by the necessary three-quarters of the states.

Their plan succeeded; the tariff bill was killed. Four years later, however, enough states had ratified the income tax amendment to give this country a shiny new 16th amendment to the Constitution, just as the country was on the brink of war and sorely in need of money.

The first income tax form in 1913 was a simple one: four pages, including instructions, and a "normal" tax rate of 1%. Interesting to consider that Americans could fund their involvement in World War I with an income tax rate of 1%.

In addition to federal income tax, you have the added privilege of paying state income taxes. Almost every state collects income tax, although a handful of them (you know who you are) don't. Rest assured, before you pack up and move, that the states without income tax have developed other means by which they can collect their revenue.

> **HUH?**
> **IRSpeak**
> The income tax that you pay to the United States Government is your *federal income tax*. The taxes pay for most of the activities of the government. Believe it or not, taxation is a voluntary system. The government relies on you to willingly send in your tax return and pay your taxes each year.

> **HUH?**
> **IRSpeak**
> The Internal Revenue Service (IRS) is an agency of the U.S. Treasury Department. It's the job of the IRS to collect your income tax as well as other taxes. The IRS also enforces tax laws and offers tax advice.

TO BE FILLED IN BY COLLECTOR	**Form 1040**	TO BE FILLED IN BY INTERNAL REVENUE BUREAU
List No.	**INCOME TAX**	File No..........................
..............District of.............	**THE PENALTY** FOR FAILURE TO HAVE THIS RETURN IN THE HANDS OF THE COLLECTOR OF INTERNAL REVENUE ON OR BE- FOR MARCH 1 IS $20 to $1,000. (See Instructions on Page 4)	Assessment List..................
Date received.............		Page.................. Line..........

UNITED STATES INTERNAL REVENUE

RETURN OF ANNUAL NET INCOME OF INDIVIDUALS
(As provided by Act of Congress, approved October 9, 1913)

RETURN OF NET INCOME RECEIVED OR ACCRUED DURING THE YEAR ENDED DECEMBER 31, 1913
(FOR THE YEAR 1913, FROM MARCH 1, TO DECEMBER 31.)

Filed by (or for)... of ....
(Full name of individual)   (Street and No.)

In the City, Town, or Post Office of....................... State of..............
(Fill in pages 2 and 3 before making entires below.)

1. GROSS INCOME (see page 2, line 12)................................ $...............

2. GENERAL DEDUCTIONS (see page 3, line 7)........................ $...............

3. NET INCOME.. $...............

Deductions and exemptions allowed in computing Income subject to the normal tax of 1%.

4. Dividends and net earnings received or accrued, of corp- orations, etc. subject to like tax. (See pg. 2, line 11).... $...............

5. Amount of income on which the normal tax has been deducted and withheld at the source. (See pg. 2, line 9, column A)...

6. Specific exemption of $3,000 or $4,000, as the case may be. (See Instructions 3 and 19...............................

Total deductions and exemptions. (Items 4, 5, and 6)...... $...............

7. TAXABLE INCOME on which the normal tax of 1% is to be calculated. (See Instruction 3). $...............

8. When the net income shown above on line 3 exceeds $20,000, the additional tax thereon must be calculated as per schedule shown.

	INCOME	TAX
1% on amount over $20,000 and not exceeding $50,000....	$..............	$..............
2% on amount over 50,000 and not exceeding 75,000....		
3% on amount over 75,000 and not exceeding 100,000....		
4% on amount over 100,000 and not exceeding 250,000....		
5% on amount over 250,000 and not exceeding 500,000....		
6% on amount over 500,000.		
Total additional or super tax......................		$..............
Total normal tax (1% of amount entered on line 7)....		$..............
Total tax liability................................		$..............

The tax return of your ancestors—the grandfather of today's complicated forms.

2

GROSS INCOME.

This statement must show in the proper spaces the entire amount of gains, profits, and income received by or accrued to the individual from all sources during the year specified on page 1.

DESCRIPTION OF INCOME.	A. Amount of Income on which tax has been deducted and withheld at the source.	B. Amount of Income on which tax has NOT been deducted and withheld at the source.
1. Total amount derived from salaries, wages, or compensation for personal service of whatever kind and in whatever form paid.	$	$
2. Total amount derived from professions, vocations, businesses, trade, commerce, or sales or dealings in property, whether real or personal, growing out of the ownership or use of or interest in real or personal property, including bonds, stocks, etc.		
3. Total amount derived from rents and from interest on notes, mortgages, and securities (other than reported on lines 5 and 6)		
4. Total amount of gains and profits derived from partnership business, whether the same be divided and distributed or not		
5. Total amount of fixed and determinable annual gains, profits, and income derived from interest upon bonds and mortgages or deeds of trust, or other similar obligations of corporations, joint-stock companies or associations, and insurance companies, whether payable annually or at shorter or longer periods		
6. Total amount of income derived from coupons, checks, or bills of exchange for or in payment of interest upon bonds issued in *foreign countries* and upon *foreign mortgages* or like obligations (not payable in the United States), and also from coupons, checks, or bills of exchange for or in payment of any dividends upon the stock or interest upon the obligations of foreign corporations, associations, and insurance companies engaged in business in foreign countries.		
7. Total amount of income received from fiduciaries		
8. Total amount of income derived from any source whatever, not specified or entered elsewhere on this page		
9. TOTALS	$	$

NOTE – Enter total of Column A on line 5 of first page.

10. AGGREGATE TOTALS OF COLUMNS A AND B		$
11. Total amount of income derived from dividends on the stock or from the net earnings of corporations, joint-stock companies, associations, or insurance companies subject to like tax. (To be entered on line 4 of first page.)		$
12. Total "Gross Income" (to be entered on line 1 of first page)		$

3

GENERAL DEDUCTIONS.

1. The amount of necessary expenses actually paid in carrying on business, but not including business expenses of partnerships, and not including personal, living, or family expenses				
2. All interest paid within the year on personal indebtedness of taxpayer				
3. All national, State, county, school, and municipal taxes paid within the year (not including those assessed against local benefits)				
4. Losses actually sustained during the year incurred in trade or arising from fires, storms, or shipwreck, and not compensated for by insurance or otherwise				
5. Debts due which have been actually ascertained to be worthless and which have been charged off within the year				
6. Amount representing a reasonable allowance for the exhustion, wear, and tear of property arising out of its use or employment in the business, not to exceed, in the case of mines, 5 per cent of the gross value at the mine of the output for the year for which the computation is made, but no deduction shall be made for any amount of expense of restoring property or making good the exhustion thereof, for which an allowance is or has been made				
7. Total "GENERAL DEDUCTIONS" (to be entered on line 2 of first page)				

AFFIDAVIT TO BE EXECUTED BY INDIVIDUAL MAKING HIS OWN RETURN.

I solemnly swear (or affirm) that the foregoing return, to the best of my knowledge and belief, contains a true and complete statement of all gains, profits, and income received by or accrued to me during the year for which the return is made, and that I am entitled to all the deductions and exemptions entered or claimed therein, under the Federal Income-tax Law of October 3, 1913.

Sworn to and subscribed before me this ....

day of .... , 1913

(Signature of individual.)

SEAL OF OFFICER TAKING AFFIDAVIT.	---

	(Official capacity.)

AFFIDAVIT TO BE EXECUTED BY DULY AUTHORIZED AGENT MAKING RETURN FOR INDIVIDUAL.

I solemnly swear (or affirm) that I have sufficient knowledge of the affairs and property of .... to enable me to make a full and complete return thereof, and that the foregoing return, to the best of my knowledge and belief, contains a true and complete statement of all gains, profits, and income received by or accrued to said individual during the year for which the return is made, and that the said individual is entitled, under the Federal Income-tax Law of October 3, 1913, to all the deductions and exemptions entered or claimed therein.

Sworn to and subscribed before me this ....

day of .... , 1913

(Signature of agent.)

SEAL OF OFFICER TAKING AFFIDAVIT.	---	ADDRESS IN FULL {	---
	---		---
	(Official capacity.)		

(SEE INSTRUCTIONS ON BACK OF THIS PAGE.)

4

INSTRUCTIONS

1. This return shall be made by every citizen of the United States, whether residing at home or abroad, and by every person residing in the United States, though not a citizen thereof, having a *net income* of $3,000 or over for the taxable year, and *also* by every *nonresident alien* deriving income from property owned and business, trade, or profession carried on *in the United States* by him.

2. When an individual by reason of minority, sickness or other disability, or absence from the United States, is unable to make his own return, it may be made for him by his *duly authorized* representative.

3. The *normal tax* of 1 per cent shall be assessed on the total net income less the specific exemption of $3,000 or $4,000 as the case may be. (For the year 1913, the specific exemption allowable is $2,500 or $3,333.33, as the case may be.) If, however, the normal tax has been deducted and withheld on any part of the income at the source, or if any part of the income is received as dividends upon the stock or from the net earnings of any corporation, etc., which is taxable upon its net income, such income shall be deducted from the individual's total *net income* for the purpose of calculating the amount of income on which the individual is liable for the normal tax or 1 per cent by virtue of this return (see page 1, line 7.)

4. The *additional or super tax* shall be calculated as stated on page 1.

5. This return shall be filed with the Collector of Internal Revenue for the district in which the individual resides if he has no other place of business, otherwise in the district in which he has his *principal place of business*; or in case the person resides in a foreign country, then with the collector for the district in which his principal business is carried on in the United States.

6. This return must be filed on or before the first day of March succeeding the close of the calander year for which return is made.

7. The *penalty* for *failure to file the return within the time specified by law* is $20 to $1,000. In case of refusal or neglect to render the return within the required time (except in cases of sickness or absence), 50 per cent shall be added to amount of tax assessed. In case of *false or fraudulent return*, 100 per cent shall be added to such tax, and any person required by law to make, render, sign, or verify any return who makes any false or fraudulent return or statement with intent to defeat or evade the assessment required by this section to be made shall be guilty of a misdemeanor, and shall be fined not exceeding $2,000 or be imprisoned not exceeding one year, or both, at the discretion of the court, with the costs of prosecution.

8. When the return is not filed within the required time by reason of sickness or absence of the individual, an extension of time, not exceeding 30 days from March 1, within which to file such return, *may be* granted by the collector, *provided* an application therefor is made by the individual within the period for which such extension is desired.

9. This return properly filled out must be made under oath or affirmation. Affidavits may be made before any officer *authorized by law* to administer oaths. If before a justice of the peace or magistrate, not using a seal, *a certificate of the clerk of the court as to the authority* of such officer to administer oaths should be *attached to the return.*

10. Expense for medical attendance, store accounts, family supplies, wages of domestic servants, cost of board, room, or house rent for family or personal use, *are not expenses that can be deducted from gross income.* In case an individual owns his own residence he can not deduct the estimated value of his rent, neither shall be be required to include such estimated rental of his home as income.

11. The farmer, in computing the net income from his farm for his annual return, shall include all moneys received for produce and animals sold, and for the wool and hides of animals slaughtered, provided such wool and hides are sold, and he shall deduct therefrom the sums actually paid as purchase money for the animals sold or slaughtered during the year.

When animals were raised by the owner and are sold or slaughtered he shall not deduct their value as expenses or loss. He may deduct the amount of money actually paid as expense for producing any farm products, live stock, etc. In deducting expenses for repairs on farm property the amount deducted must not exceed the amount actually expended for such repairs during the year for which the return is made. (See page 3, item 6.) The cost of replacing tools or machinery is a deductible expense to the extent that the cost of the new articles does not exceed the value of the old.

12. In calculating losses, only such losses as shall have been actually sustained and the amount of which has been definitely ascertained during the year covered by the return can be deducted.

13. Persons receiving fees or emoluments for professional or other services, as in the case of physicians or lawyers, should include all actual receipts for services rendered in the year for which return is made, together with all unpaid accounts, charges for services, or contingent income due for that year, if good and collectible.

14. Debts which were contracted during the year for which return is made, but found in said year to be worthless, may be deducted from gross income for said year, but such debts can not be regarded as worthless until after legal proceedings to recover the same have proved fruitless, or it clearly appears that the debtor is insolvent. If debts contracted prior to the year for which return is made were included as income in return for year in which said debts were contracted, and such debts shall subsequently prove to be worthless, they may be deducted under the head of losses in the return for the year in which such debts were charged off as worthless.

15. Amounts due or accrued to the individual members of a partnership from the net earnings of the partnership, whether apportioned and distributed or not, shall be included in the annual return of the individual.

16. United States pensions shall be included as income.

17. Estimated advance in value of real estate is not required to be reported as income, unless the increased value is taken up on the books of the individual as an increase of assets.

18. Costs of suits and other legal proceedings arising from ordinary business may be treated as an expense of such business, and may be deducted from gross income for the year in which such costs were paid.

19. An unmarried individual or a married individual not living with wife or husband shall be allowed an exemption of $3,000. When husband and wife live together they shall be allowed jointly a total exemption of only $4,000 on their aggregate income. They may make a joint return, both subscribing thereto, or if they have separate incomes, they may make separate returns; but in no case shall they jointly claim more than $4,000 exemption on their aggregate income.

20. In computing net income there shall be excluded the compensation of all officers and employees of a State or any political subdivision thereof, except when such compensation is paid by the United States Government.

Where Your Taxes Go

As you probably know, your taxes go to Washington where they are used to perform magical government-type feats. Herewith, a breakdown of all the places your tax dollars go when they are hard at work:

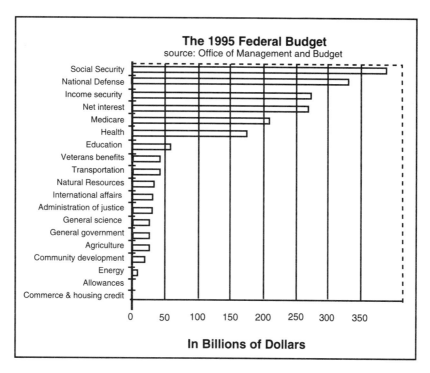

Your tax dollars, hard at work.

How Your Taxes Get Collected

Leave it to the IRS to give you plenty of choices when it comes to getting your taxes to Washington:

➤ Withholding from your paychecks

➤ Withholding from stock dividends

➤ Withholding from prizes and gambling winnings

➤ Withholding from retirement fund payments

➤ Quarterly estimated taxes that you mail to the IRS

➤ Payments with your tax return

➤ Payments when the IRS sends you a bill

IRSpeak
Taxes that are extracted from your pay and sent off to the government are called *withholding*. It is your employer's responsibility to withhold tax from your pay and deposit in an IRS bank account.

IRSpeak
Quarterly estimated payments are tax payments that you mail to the IRS when your withholding is not enough to cover your yearly income tax.

Taxes that are withheld come out of your income before you even see them. You can thank your employer or whomever is withholding the taxes for depositing your tax payment right into an IRS bank account. This method of tax payment is known as *Pay-As-You-Go*. The idea is that you won't even feel the loss if you don't have to actually take the money out of your pocket. Sure it saves you from having to cough up big bucks on April 15. It also creates the illusion of your never having had the money—an illusion that makes the IRS's job of enforcing "voluntary" compliance much easier.

Tax payments that you make yourself—quarterly estimated payments and others—get mailed to the IRS and, again, deposited right into an IRS bank account. The money in the IRS accounts is distributed to various and sundry federal agencies and programs as set out in the graph earlier in this chapter.

The Least You Need to Know

➤ Taxes have been around since the beginning of time: you're not the only lucky one.

➤ Through the system of "voluntary" taxation, part of the money you earn by working at your job or through your wise investments gets channeled to the IRS which then gets disbursed to lots of government agencies and programs as determined by the Federal Budget.

➤ You pay taxes by having the tax withheld at your job or by sending in estimated payments.

Chapter 2

But Do I Have to File a Tax Return?

In This Chapter

➤ Who files tax returns?

➤ What tax return form do you need?

➤ Where do you file?

➤ When do you file?

➤ Electronic filing in the almost 22nd century

➤ Oops! You're late!

Early on, in journalism school, I learned to ask the "W" questions: Who, What, Where, When, Why, and How (<u>H</u>ow?). I find that as I go through life, these questions serve me well. They are great ice breakers at parties where I don't know anyone, they are nice to have in my pocket for those pregnant pauses during job interviews, and they're especially important when quizzing my kids about what they've been up to.

This is the chapter that answers the "W's" about what to do with your tax return—that annoying and much-too-lengthy form you have to send to the government each April 15.

Who Has to File Tax Returns?

Chances are that you must file a tax return if you bought this book. But just to be sure, you should read on.

Look at all your income from 1995. Figuratively, of course. Wouldn't it be nice to just have a big pile on your bed of all the money you earned for 1995 and actually look at it? Okay, *imagine* you're looking at all the income you earned in 1995. When you envision this heap of cash, think of just the amount that is taxable. Don't include gifts and inheritances, interest on state and local municipal bonds, or anything else that you know is not taxable. Now, how much is it?

I can make this easy. If your income is over $13,050 (even if you don't owe any tax), you must file an income tax return, thus you're finished with this section. If your income is less than $13,050, check out these rules about who needs to file:

Who You Are	Minimum Income Requiring You to File a 1995 Tax Return
Single, under 65-years-old	$6,400
Single, 65 and up	$7,350
Married, filing jointly	$11,550
Married, joint, one of you is 65+	$12,300
Married, joint, both 65+	$13,050
Married, filing separate return	$2,500
Dependent child with unearned income*	$650
Dependent, 65+ or blind, with unearned income*	$1,600
Head of Household, under 65	$8,250
Head of Household, 65+	$9,200
Qualifying Widow(er)	$9,050
Qualifying Widow(er) 65+	$9,800

* unearned income = stuff such as interest and dividends as opposed to income you worked for.

Find the entry at the left side of the list that best describes who you are. Then, check the income level in the right column. If your 1995 income equaled or exceeded that amount, you have to file a tax return.

Uncertain about whether you're supposed to be Single or Head of Household? Wondering about the difference between Married Filing Separately and Married Filing Jointly? Check out Chapter 10, "Your Filing Status," for the lowdown on all these fancy terms.

Get Down to Brass Tax

No matter what your income level is, if you had taxes withheld from your paycheck or from some other source of income and you are entitled to a refund, you will have to file a tax return in order to get the refund.

When Tax Returns Are Due

Remember the April 15 target due date when you think "tax return." For 1995 tax returns, the filing date is April 15, 1996. But, as with everything the IRS touches, there are exceptions to this rule.

If April 15 falls on a Saturday or a Sunday, you can wait until Monday (the 16th or 17th as the case may be) to file a timely tax return. You can always check the forms and instructions that come in the mail from the IRS: The correct due dates for your income tax return and your quarterly estimated payments will be printed in that material.

Estimated payments, those nasty checks you send to the IRS when payroll withholding coupled with once-a-year purging of the savings account just isn't quite enough, are due quarterly, they say, but it doesn't quite work out that way. (For more information about who needs to pay estimates and why and when and where—the basic "W" questions again—see "Computing Your Estimated Taxes" in Chapter 26.)

The "1st Quarter" payment for 1996 is due on April 15, along with everything you have to pay for 1995. Even

IRSpeak

Estimated payments, sometimes called *quarterly payments*, are tax payments that you send directly to the IRS. People whose withholding doesn't come close enough to covering their tax for the year send quarterly payment forms to the IRS, accompanying them with money and other sacrificial objects designed to placate the tax gods.

By the Way

If you're really lucky, a federal holiday will creep in when your quarterly payment is due and close the post offices, thus pushing your due date back to Tuesday. Martin Luther King Day in January has a way of doing this pretty frequently.

OOPS!
And what happens if you *don't* make it to the post office by midnight, April 15, hmmmm? The IRS is totally unsympathetic on this matter. When the clock strikes midnight on the tax return due date, your tax return turns into a pumpkin. If you don't owe any tax, you may not be in terribly big trouble. If you have tax to pay, you get to pay a late-filing penalty too. Don't worry about figuring out the penalty. The IRS will kindly send you a notice and tell you what you owe.

though one might think a quarter of a year is three months, the next payment is due in only two months, hence, on June 15. Payment number three clocks in on September 15, and then you get to catch your breath and wait four months until January 15 for the fourth payment. All these payments are subject to the Monday slide, if the 15th falls on a Saturday or Sunday.

Don't forget your state tax return. Most states follow the federal return filing date, but not all of them. Check closely the due date of your state return. In particular, if you've moved to a new state—your state due date may have changed from last year. You will have to send your state tax return to a location different from the one to which you send your federal return. Check with your state for the correct address.

The due date represents the date on which the tax return (or estimated payment) has to be in the mail. As long as you get it postmarked by midnight on the due date, the IRS considers your payment timely. Note, however, that you have to have correct postage on the envelope in order for it to count.

Where to Send the Return

There are IRS clearinghouses around the country, vast football fields full of busy workers, diligently opening envelope after endless envelope, unfolding crinkled tax returns, checking for missing W-2 forms, meticulously recalculating totals and computations, snapping gum to the time of energizing music pouring in over loudspeakers, laboring for the love of their country (I'm just guessing here...).

OOOOH...

By the Way
If you're destined to be selected in a random audit, filing early won't increase or decrease the chance of your tax return being noticed.

It is into one of these football-field-clearinghouses, called *service centers*, that you must catapult your tax return, wondering all the while how it manages to get past the 50-yard-line and into a neat little file with your name on it. You can use the envelope that came with your tax return booklet, if you still have it, or use your own and address it to: INTERNAL REVENUE SERVICE CENTER. Choose the appropriate address from the following table.

If You Live In...	Mail Income Tax Return To:	Mail Estimated Payments To:
Alabama	Memphis, TN 37501	P.O. Box 1219, Charlotte, NC 28201-1219
Alaska	Ogden, UT 84201	P.O. Box 510000, San Francisco, CA 94151-5100
Arizona	Ogden, UT 84201	P.O. Box 510000, San Francisco, CA 94151-5100
Arkansas	Memphis, TN 37501	P.O. Box 1219, Charlotte, NC 28201-1219
California (1)	Ogden, UT 84201	P.O. Box 510000, San Francisco, CA 94151-5100
California (2)	Fresno, CA 93888	P.O. Box 54030, Los Angeles, CA 90054-0030
Colorado	Ogden, UT 84201	P.O. Box 510000, San Francisco, CA 94151-5100
Connecticut	Andover, MA 05501	P.O. Box 371999, Pittsburgh, PA 15250-7999
Delaware	Philadelphia, PA 19255	P.O. Box 8318, Philadelphia, PA 19162-8318
District of Columbia	Philadelphia, PA 19255	P.O. Box 8318, Philadelphia, PA 19162-8318
Florida	Atlanta, GA 39901	P.O. Box 105900, Atlanta, GA 30348-5900
Georgia	Atlanta, GA 39901	P.O. Box 105900, Atlanta, GA 30348-5900

continues

15

continued

If You Live In...	Mail Income Tax Return To:	Mail Estimated Payments To:
Hawaii	Fresno, CA 93888	P.O. Box 54030, Los Angeles, CA 90054-0030
Idaho	Ogden, UT 84201	P.O. Box 510000, San Francisco, CA 94151-5100
Illinois	Kansas City, MO 64999	P.O. Box 970006, St. Louis, MO 63197-0006
Indiana	Cincinnati, OH 45999	P.O. Box 7422, Chicago, IL 60680-7422
Iowa	Kansas City, MO 64999	P.O. Box 970006, St. Louis, MO 63197-0006
Kansas	Austin, TX 73301	P.O. Box 970001, St. Louis, MO 63197-0001
Kentucky	Cincinnati, OH 45999	P.O. Box 7422, Chicago, IL 60680-7422
Louisiana	Memphis, TN 37501	P.O. 1219, Charlotte, NC 28201-1219
Maine	Andover, MA 05501	P.O. Box 371999, Pittsburgh, PA 15250-7999
Maryland	Philadelphia, PA 19255	P.O. Box 8318, Philadelphia, PA 19162-8318
Massachusetts	Andover, MA 05501	P.O. Box 371999, Pittsburgh, PA 15250-7999
Michigan	Cincinnati, OH 45999	P.O. Box 7422, Chicago, IL 60680-7422
Minnesota	Kansas City, MO 64999	P.O. Box 970006, St. Louis, MO 63197-0006

If You Live In...	Mail Income Tax Return To:	Mail Estimated Payments To:
Mississippi	Memphis, TN 37501	P.O. 1219, Charlotte, NC 28201-1219
Missouri	Kansas City, MO 64999	P.O. Box 970006, St. Louis, MO 63197-0006
Montana	Ogden, UT 84201	P.O. Box 510000, San Francisco, CA 94151-5100
Nebraska	Ogden, UT 84201	P.O. Box 510000, San Francisco, CA 94151-5100
Nevada	Ogden, UT 84201	P.O. Box 510000, San Francisco, CA 94151-5100
New Hampshire	Andover, MA 05501	P.O. Box 371999, Pittsburgh, PA 15250-7999
New Jersey	Holtsville, NY 00501	P.O. Box 162, Newark, NJ 07101-0162
New Mexico	Austin, TX 73301	P.O. Box 970001, St. Louis, MO 63197-0001
New York (3)	Holtsville, NY 00501	P.O. Box 162, Newark, NJ 07101-0162
New York (4)	Andover, MA 05501	P.O. Box 371999, Pittsburgh, PA 15250-7999
North Carolina	Memphis, TN 37501	P.O. Box 1219, Charlotte, NC 28201-1219
North Dakota	Ogden, UT 84201	P.O. Box 510000, San Francisco, CA 94151-5100

continues

continued

If You Live In...	Mail Income Tax Return To:	Mail Estimated Payments To:
Ohio	Cincinnati, OH 45999	P.O. Box 7422, Chicago, IL 60680-7422
Oklahoma	Austin, TX 73301	P.O. Box 970001, St. Louis, MO 63197-0001
Oregon	Ogden, UT 84201	P.O. Box 510000, San Francisco, CA 94151-5100
Pennsylvania	Philadelphia, PA 19255	P.O. Box 8318, Philadelphia, PA 19162-8318
Rhode Island	Andover, MA 05501	P.O. Box 371999, Pittsburgh, PA 15250-7999
South Dakota	Ogden, UT 84201	P.O. Box 510000, San Francisco, CA 94151-5100
South Carolina	Atlanta, GA 39901	P.O. Box 105900, Atlanta, GA 30348-5900
Tennessee	Memphis, TN 37501	P.O. Box 1219, Charlotte, NC 28201-1219
Texas	Austin, TX 73301	P.O. Box 970001, St. Louis, MO 63197-0001
Utah	Ogden, UT 84201	P.O. Box 510000, San Francisco, CA 94151-5100
Vermont	Andover, MA 05501	P.O. Box 371999, Pittsburgh, PA 15250-7999
Virginia	Philadelphia, PA 19255	P.O. Box 8318, Philadelphia, PA 19162-8318

If You Live In...	Mail Income Tax Return To:	Mail Estimated Payments To:
Washington	Ogden, UT 84201	P.O. Box 510000, San Francisco, CA 94151-5100
West Virginia	Cincinnati, OH 45999	P.O. Box 7422, Chicago, IL 60680-7422
Wisconsin	Kansas City, MO 64999	P.O. Box 970006, St. Louis, MO 63197-0006
Wyoming	Ogden, UT 84201	P.O. Box 510000, San Francisco, CA 94151-5100

(1) Includes counties of Alpine, Amador, Butte, Calaveras, Colusa, Contra Costa, Del Norte, El Dorado, Glenn, Humboldt, Lake, Lassen, Marin, Mendocino, Modoc, Napa, Nevada, Placer, Plumas, Sacramento, San Joaquin, Shasta, Sierra, Siskiyou, Solano, Sonoma, Sutter, Tehama, Trinity, Yolo, and Yuba

(2) Includes all California counties not listed in (2)

(3) Includes New York City and counties of Nassau, Rockland, Suffolk, and Westchester

(4) Includes all New York counties not listed in (3)

Electronic Filing

In recent years the IRS has been dragged into the 21st century with the advent of *electronic filing*. Still in its Wonder Bread years, electronic filing is a process by which you can send your tax return through a computerized modem hook-up to a big computer at the IRS. Just in case the IRS computer coughs when it receives your information and adds a few odd zeros to your income, hiking your tax bill into the next galaxy, you still have to send in a hard copy (that is, the real tax return).

The theory is that an electronically filed return bypasses the humans (those nice little gum-snapping ladies who

OOPS!
Estimated taxes don't get mailed to the same place as income tax returns; that would be too easy. Make sure that you take the mailing address from the proper column in the preceding table.

OOOOH...

By the Way
If you have moved in the past year, choose the IRS mailing address based on the address where you live now, not the address you lived at last year.

Years ago, some science fiction author probably made up the idea of *electronic filing* and someone at the IRS read the book and thought it was a true story. Wherever the idea came from, it has come to pass that the IRS accepts tax returns filed electronically, from computers with a modem. To communicate with the IRS you have to be an IRS-approved electronic filing center. These places seem to pop up on every street corner after New Year's Eve and disappear into the mist on April 16.

carefully open the envelopes and process the tax returns) and thus saves time. People who expect big refunds (or even little refunds) and who need the money NOW benefit by this process. However, there's no reason to even consider this method if you don't expect a refund.

Electronic filing can't be done directly from your home computer (at least not yet). If you have a modem, however, you may be able to hook up with an approved electronic filing service and dispatch your computer-prepared tax return through an intermediary such as CompuServe.

In addition to paying a fee for the electronic filing service, you must seek out an electronic filing place in order to get the job done. Electronic filing places are pretty easy to spot because they want to be found; they advertise pretty heavily in the spring. Banks and accounting firms and fly-by-night electronic filing places abound. Can't find one on the drive home from work? Let your fingers do the walking and look in the yellow pages under *Tax*. Before you commit, though, be sure to weigh the fee for electronic filing against the benefit of receiving your tax refund a few weeks early.

Quasi-Electronic Filing

In addition to electronic filing, another alternative offers quick refunds and human by-passing at the IRS. You can file your tax return using a Form 1040PC (as opposed to the regular Form 1040). You must prepare a 1040PC on a computer, with special tax preparation software. The 1040PC form is filled with lots of numbers, letters, and secret codes that IRS computers can read. Using a 1040PC speeds up the processing of your tax return because no one has to keypunch your numbers.

For more information about filing one of these secret code tax returns, or if you're interested in other ways in which a computer can help you with your tax obligations, see Part 6, "Automating Tax Preparation with Your (Deductible) Computer."

What to Do if You Miss the Due Dates

Life just keeps sending us these little hurdles to jump over, and one of them is submitting the tax return on time. Probably the best scenario is to file the thing by the first week of February and then spend the rest of the spring making irritating little remarks to your friends, such as, "You're *still* working on your tax return? I got my refund six weeks ago!" and "Look at this cool filing system I've started for *next year's* tax return!"

But if you're more like the rest of us, you wait until it's *almost* too late, then scurry around trying to find all those silly receipts and forms, adding a few gray hairs in the process, and daydream about sandy beaches and days filled with no obligations, while the calendar keeps ticking closer and closer to the middle of April. So what happens if April 15 comes and goes and you're still daydreaming?

➤ Late tax returns, with tax owing, generate a 5%-of-the-tax-due just-to-be-mean penalty per month up to a maximum of 25%. Even if you post-marked your tax return 1 minute after midnight on the due date, you've just incurred one month's penalty. In addition to the just-to-be-mean penalty for filing your tax return late, there is a 1/2%-per-month penalty on any tax that you pay late. (Doesn't this sound a little redundant?)

➤ You'll probably luck out and avoid paying penalties if you don't owe any tax. The IRS has tried to assess penalties on taxpayers who file late returns with no tax owing, but so far have been unsuccessful. This doesn't mean they'll stop trying. Furthermore, just because you don't think you owe anything, the IRS may not agree with you. Then you'll definitely be in a penalty situation. In other words, don't worry too much if you're late but you have a refund due, but don't try to be late intentionally.

Get Down to Brass Tax

Avoid penalties by filing a late tax return the right way. File Form 4868, "Application for Automatic Extension of Time To File U.S. Individual Income Tax Return," to get a four month extension of time until August 15 to file your return. On this form you simply state how much money you think you made last year and figure the tax on that amount. Be sure to pay the amount of tax you think you owe in order to avoid the late tax payment penalty.

Running late and still don't have all the information you need to finish your tax return? You have a couple of sane choices.

First, you can guess the tax, file the extension form (Form 4868), and then hope you come close. If it turns out that you underpaid your tax, the penalty will only be on the part underpaid, not the entire tax liability. When you file an extension, you are given four extra months, until August 15, in which to file your tax return. You are not, however, given an extension of time in which to pay your tax. Pay the tax you owe with the extension form.

Form **4868**	Application for Automatic Extension of Time to File U.S. Individual Income Tax Return	OMB No. 1545-0188

Department of the Treasury
Internal Revenue Service

Please Type or Print

Your first name	MI	Last name	Your Social Security Number
If a joint return, spouse's first name	MI	Last name	Spouse's Social Security Number

Home address (number, street, and apt no. or rural route). If you have a P.O. box, see the instructions

City, town or post office	State	ZIP Code

I request an automatic 4-month extension of time to Aug 15, 1995, to file Form 1040EZ, Form 1040A, or Form 1040 for the calendar year 1994 or to _____, 19___, for the fiscal tax year ending _____, 19___.

Individual Income Tax — You must complete this part.

1 **Total tax liability for 1994.** This is the amount you expect to enter on Form 1040EZ, line 9; Form 1040A, line 27; or Form 1040, line 53. If you do expect this amount to be zero, enter -0- **1**

Caution: *You **must** enter an amount on line 1 or your extension will be denied. You can estimate this amount, but be as exact as you can with the information you have. If we later find that your estimate was not reasonable, the extension will be null and void.*

2 **Total payments for 1994.** This is the amount you expect to enter on Form 1040EZ, line 8; Form 1040A, line 28d; or Form 1040, line 60 (excluding line 57) **2**

3 **Balance Due.** Subtract line 2 from line 1. If line 2 is more than line 1, enter -0-. If you are making a payment, you must use the Form 4868-V. For details on how to pay, including what to write on your payment, see the instructions .... ▶ **3**

Gift or Generation-Skipping Transfer (GST) Tax — Complete this part if you expect to owe either tax.

Caution: *Do not include income tax on lines 5a and 5b. See instructions.*

4 If you or your spouse plan to file a gift tax return (Form 709 or 709-A) for 1994, generally due by April 17, 1995, see the instructions and check here .... **Yourself** .... ▶ / **Spouse** .... ▶

5 a Enter the amount of gift or GST tax **you** are paying with this form. Also, you must use the Form 4868-V **5a**

b Enter the amount of gift or GST tax **your spouse** is paying with this form . Also, you must use the Form 4868-V **5b**

Signature and Verification

Under penalties of perjury, I declare that I have examined this form, including accompanying schedules and statements, and to the best of my knowledge and belief, it is true, correct, and complete; and, if prepared by someone other than the taxpayer, that I am authorized to prepare this form.

▶ Your signature _____ Date _____   ▶ Spouse's Signature, if filing jointly _____ Date _____

▶ Preparer's signature (other than taxpayer) _____ Date _____

If you want correspondence regarding this extension to be sent to you at an address other than that shown above or to an agent acting for you, please enter the name of the agent and/or the address where it should be sent.

Please Type or Print

Name	
Number and street (include suite, room, or apt. no.) or P.O. box number if mail is not delivered to street address	
City, town or post office	State	ZIP Code

D181 **For Paperwork Reduction Act Notice, see separate instructions.** | Form **4868**

This is Form 4868. You must file this form by April 15 and pay the properly estimated amount of tax you owe in order to extend the due date of your income tax return.

Alternatively, you can go ahead and guess the missing parts and actually fill out your tax return and send it in on time. If it turns out that you were right, all is well and you can wipe your hands of the IRS for another year. If the real numbers turn out to be different from those you guessed at, file an *amended tax return*, Form 1040X, to change to the right numbers, and then recalculate your tax. You have three years from the date on which you file your tax return to send in an amended return. If it turns out that you are entitled to a refund, celebrate! You may even get some interest on it because you were such a good taxpayer and sent your return in on time.

The Least You Need to Know

➤ Everyone with income over $13,050 is required to file a tax return. If your income is lower than $13,050, check the list near the beginning of this chapter to see if you have to file.

➤ Tax returns are generally due the 15th of April. When the 15th falls on a Saturday or a Sunday, you get a bonus—you don't have to file until Monday.

➤ It is possible to file your tax return electronically. Electronic filing may speed up receipt of your refund.

➤ File for an extension of time if it looks as if you're going to miss getting your tax return mailed by the due date.

Chapter 3

Where All Those Forms Come From

> **In This Chapter**
>
> ➤ Forms that come in the mail
>
> ➤ Distinguishing one form from another
>
> ➤ Relying on last year's tax return
>
> ➤ Forms in the night

Rest assured that no matter how well organized you are, if you wait until the last minute to prepare your tax return, you will come up short at least one form. You can't do anything to prevent this; it's one of those laws of tax return preparation: You Will Never Have Every Form You Need.

It doesn't matter if you have every form you used on last year's tax return, it doesn't matter if you have the booklet the IRS sent you in the mail, it doesn't matter if you send away for every form the IRS ever printed, it doesn't even matter if you actually have every form you need—when it's time to prepare your tax return: You Will Never Have Every Form You Need. It will be easier on everyone involved if you just accept that as fact right now. This chapter explains how to figure out which forms you need and how to get them.

The Tax Packet That Comes in the Mail

Each year, just when you'd think the holiday mail rush would be enough to send every postal employee looking for a new job, before those folks even have a chance to catch their respective breaths, post offices around the country get inundated with everybody's favorite junk mail item: the 1040 Forms and Instructions packet.

This is the IRS's annual chance to prove it knows who you are and where you live. Over 100,000,000 taxpayers receive Forms and Instructions packets in the mail just in time to celebrate New Year's Eve.

IRSpeak
The U.S. Individual Income Tax Return, known to friends as the *1040*, is the form you send to the IRS each spring. Record your financial events of the past year on the 1040, compute your tax, hope for a refund, or send in a check.

One of the most important things to understand about the 1040 Forms and Instructions packet is that the IRS has carefully customized it for you. There are many different versions of the Forms and Instructions packet, and you get the one that fits your personal tax lifestyle. The IRS takes special care to look at your tax return from last year and see which forms you used; then it selects the Forms and Instructions booklet that includes every form you had in last year's tax return *except for one*. This is just a little IRS trick to help ensure the success of the important tax rule: You Will Never Have Every Form You Need.

But at least you have a good start. Save the tax book you get from the IRS; put it someplace where you're likely to look for it when it comes time to prepare your income tax return.

Figuring Out Which Forms You Need

It's difficult to know in advance which forms you actually need for several reasons:

➤ Each year there are some new forms, just in case you were becoming tired of the old ones. Sometimes the IRS doesn't finish making the new forms until the end of December, at which time all the forms become available to the general public. Therefore, it's difficult to even know what's available until after the beginning of the year.

➤ New forms are not exactly well-publicized. Have you ever seen an IRS agent on Letterman touting the new tax forms? What about magazine ads, radio and television commercials, display ads in your local newspaper? Nope, not a chance. Your only clue to let you know the new forms even exist is printed at the beginning of the Forms and Instructions packet. See "What's New for 1995" near the front of the instruction book to check out the new spring fashions.

➤ Things in life change, not the least of which is your tax situation. As your personal financial picture changes from year to year, the tax forms you choose need to accommodate that change. Look to the pages in this book to guide you to the tax forms you need for each particular tax-related circumstance you face.

> **By the Way**
> When in doubt, go with the more complex form. A problem can arise if you choose a form that is too simplistic for your needs if you don't have space to report everything you are supposed to. In order of complexity, the forms are: 1040EZ (EZest), 1040A (sort of easy), 1040 (the "long form").

OOOOH...

Choosing a Primary Form

If tax returns aren't confusing enough, right from the start you need to determine which 1040 form you need to file. You must choose from the 1040A, the 1040EZ, and of course, the old familiar 1040.

In sending you the Forms and Instructions packet, the IRS has already made an assumption about which form you may want to file. You can accept this decision that the IRS has made on your behalf (and actually that's probably a good idea), or you can take matters into your own hands and choose a form for yourself.

The descriptions that follow will give you a pretty good idea of which form is right for you.

1040EZ

The 1040EZ form takes you back in time to kindergarten. Get out your crayons and fill in the big blanks. In order to use this form, you must meet all of the following requirements:

➤ Your filing status is Single or Married Filing Jointly.

➤ You have no dependents (that you know of).

➤ You are not 65-years-old or older.

➤ You are not blind.

➤ You are not bald, nor do you have a mustache (just kidding).

➤ Your taxable income is under $50,000. (Well, of course you won't know what your taxable income is until you're way past this point of choosing a form. You'll just have to make a guess. If you think your taxable income is around $50,000, plan on using the regular 1040 form.)

➤ The taxable income you have is only from wages, salaries, tips, unemployment compensation, scholarships or fellowships, or taxable interest income not exceeding $400.

Department of the Treasury—Internal Revenue Service

Form 1040EZ

Income Tax Return for Single and Joint Filers With No Dependents   **1995**

OMB No. 1545-0675

Use the IRS label
(See page 12.)
Otherwise, please print.

L A B E L H E R E

Your first name and initial   Last name

If a joint return, spouse's first name and initial   Last name

Home address (number and street). If you have a P.O. box, see page 12.   Apt. no.

City, town or post office, state, and ZIP code. If you have a foreign address, see page 12.

Your social security number

Spouse's social security number

See instructions on back and in Form 1040EZ booklet.

Presidential Election Campaign
(See page 12.)

Note: *Checking "Yes" will not change your tax or reduce your refund.*

Do you want $3 to go to this fund? ▶

If a joint return, does your spouse want $3 to go to this fund? ▶

Yes   No

Dollars   **Cents**

Income

Attach Copy B of Form(s) W-2 here. Enclose, but do not attach, any payment with your return.

1 Total wages, salaries, and tips. This should be shown in box 1 of your W-2 form(s). Attach your W-2 form(s).   **1**

2 Taxable interest income of $400 or less. If the total is over $400, you cannot use Form 1040EZ   **2**

3 Unemployment compensation (see page X).   **3**

4 Add lines 1, 2, and 3 This is your **adjusted gross income.** If less than $9,230, see page 15 to find out if you can claim the earned income credit on line 8.   **4**

Note: *You must check Yes or No.*

5 Can your parents (or someone else) claim you on their return?

☐ **Yes.** Do worksheet on back: enter amount from line G here.

☐ **No.** If **single,** enter 6,400.00. If **married,** enter 11,550.00. For an explanation of these amounts, see back of form.   **5**

6 Subtract line 5 from line 4. If line 5 is larger than line 4, enter 0. This is your **taxable income.** ▶ **6**

Payments and tax

7 Enter your Federal income tax withheld from box 2 of your W-2 form(s).   **7**

8 **Earned income credit** (see page 15). Enter type and amount of nontaxable earned income below.

Type $ **8**

9 Add lines 7 and 8 (don't include nontaxable earned income). These are your **total payments.**   **9**

10 **Tax.** Use the amount on **line 6** to find your tax in the tax table on pages 28–32 of the booklet. Then, enter the tax from the table on this line.   **10**

Refund or amount you owe

11 If line 9 is larger than line 10, subtract line 10 from line 9. This is your **refund.**   **11**

12 If line 10 is larger than line 9, subtract line 9 from line 10. This is the **amount you owe.** See page 20 for details on how to pay and what to write on your payment.   **12**

I have read this return. Under penalties of perjury, I declare that to the best of my knowledge and belief, the return is true, correct, and accurately lists all amounts and sources of income I received during the tax year.

Sign your return

Keep a copy of this form for your records.

Your signature   Spouse's signature if joint return

Date   Your occupation   Date   Spouse's occupation

For IRS Use Only — Please do not write in boxes below.

1   2   3   4   5

6   7   8   9   10

For Privacy Act and Paperwork Reduction Act Notice, see page 4.

Cat. No. 11329W

Form 1040EZ (1995)

The 1040EZ form.

➤ You didn't receive any advance earned income credit payments. (You didn't receive any *WHAT?* Chapter 24, "Cutting Your Tax with Credits," covers earned income credit.)

➤ If you're married and either you or your spouse had more than one employer, the total wages of your spouse from all employers cannot exceed $61,200.

1040A

The original easy form, the 1040A, isn't so easy anymore; but it is still available. You can use this form if:

➤ Your taxable income is under $50,000.

➤ The taxable income you have is only from wages, salaries, tips, scholarships and fellowships, IRA distributions, pensions and annuities, unemployment compensation, and Social Security benefits, dividends or interest.

➤ You do not itemize your deductions.

➤ The only adjustment you make to your income is for a contribution to an IRA. (Other income adjustments are discussed in Chapter 18, "Adjustments to Income.")

➤ Your only tax credits are the child and dependent care credit, the earned income credit, or the credit for the elderly. (These credits are described in Chapter 24.)

1040

The 1040, also called the "long form," is the form that most taxpayers use. If you don't fall into either of the lists for the other two forms, the 1040 is your reward.

IRSpeak

Your *filing status* is kind of like your marital status, but not quite. The IRS uses your filing status as a guide for the rate at which your income tax should be applied. Chapter 10 provides details on the filing status rules.

IRSpeak

Dependents are the people you take care of. I don't mean take care of as in providing a shoulder to cry on or a loan in a pinch, even though these are major ways in which you can take care of the people who are important to you. For someone to qualify as a dependent, you have to provide serious care such as food and shelter. Usually dependents are people who live with you, although not always. See Chapter 11 for information on dependents.

IRSpeak

After all your income is added together and all your tax-related expenses are deducted, after you subtract an amount for each of your dependents, the number you're left with is three times the year in which you were born. Or it might be your *taxable income*. This is the amount on which the IRS wants you to pay income tax.

Form
1040A

Department of the Treasury—Internal Revenue Service

U.S. Individual Income Tax Return

1995

IRS Use Only—Do not write or staple in this space.

OMB No. 1545-0085

Label
(See page 19.)

Use the IRS label. Otherwise, please print or type.

LABEL HERE

Your first name and initial | Last name

If a joint return, spouse's first name and initial | Last name

Home address (number and street). If you have a P.O. box, see page 19. | Apt. no.

City, town or post office, state, and ZIP code. If you have a foreign address, see page 19.

Your social security number

Spouse's social security number

For Privacy Act and Paperwork Reduction Act Notice, see page 8.

Presidential Election Campaign Fund (See page 19.)
Do you want $3 to go to this fund? . . . .
If a joint return, does your spouse want $3 to go to this fund?

Yes | No

Note: Checking "Yes" will not change your tax or reduce your refund.

Check the box for your filing status
(See page 20.)
Check only one box.

1 ☐ Single
2 ☐ Married filing joint return (even if only one had income)
3 ☐ Married filing separate return. Enter spouse's social security number above and full name here. ▶ _____
4 ☐ Head of household (with qualifying person). (See page 21.) If the qualifying person is a child but not your dependent, enter this child's name here. ▶ _____
5 ☐ Qualifying widow(er) with dependent child (year spouse died ▶ 19___). (See page 22.)

Figure your exemptions
(See page 22.)

If more than seven dependents, see page 25.

6a ☐ **Yourself.** If your parent (or someone else) can claim you as a dependent on his or her tax return, **do not** check box 6a. But be sure to check the box on line 18b on page 2.

b ☐ **Spouse**

c **Dependents:**

(1) First name Last name	(2) Dependent's social security number If born in 1995 see page 25.	(3) Dependent's relationship to you	(4) No. of months lived in your home in 1995

No. of boxes checked on 6a and 6b

No. of your children on 6c who:
• lived with you

• didn't live with you due to divorce or separation (see page 26)

Dependents on 6c not entered above

d If your child didn't live with you but is claimed as your dependent under a pre-1985 agreement, check here . . . . ▶ ☐

e Total number of exemptions claimed.

Add numbers entered on lines above

Figure your adjusted gross income

Attach Copy B of your Forms W-2 and 1099-R here.
If you didn't get a W-2, see page 27. Enclose, but do not attach, any payment with your return

7 Wages, salaries, tips, etc. This should be shown in box 1 of your W-2 form(s). Attach Form(s) W-2. | 7

8a **Taxable** interest income (see page 28). If over $400, attach Schedule 1. | 8a

b **Tax-exempt** interest. DO NOT include on line 8a. | 8b

9 Dividends. If over $400, attach Schedule 1. | 9

10a Total IRA distributions. | 10a | 10b Taxable amount (see page 29). | 10b

11a Total pensions and annuities. | 11a | 11b Taxable amount (see page 29). | 11b

12 Unemployment compensation (see page 32). | 12

13a Social security benefits. | 13a | 13b Taxable amount (see page 33). | 13b

14 Add lines 7 through 13b (far right column). This is your **total income.** ▶ | 14

15a Your IRA deduction (see page 36). | 15a

b Spouse's IRA deduction (see page 36). | 15b

c Add lines 15a and 15b. These are your **total adjustments.** | 15c

16 Subtract line 15c from line 14. This is your **adjusted gross income.** If less than $26,673 and a child lived with you (less than $9,230 if a child didn't live with you), see "Earned income credit" on page 47. ▶ | 16

Cat. No. 11327A

1995 Form 1040A page 1

The 1040A form.

1995 Form 1040A page 2

Figure your standard deduction, exemption amount, and taxable income	**17**	Enter the amount from line 16.	**17**

18a Check if: ☐ **You** were 65 or older ☐ Blind
☐ **Spouse** was 65 or older ☐ Blind } **Enter number of boxes checked** ▶ **18a** ☐

b If your parent (or someone else) can claim you as a dependent, check here . . . . ▶ **18b** ☐

c If you are married filing separately and your spouse itemizes deductions, see page 40 and check here. . . . . ▶ **18c** ☐

19 Enter the **standard deduction** shown below for your filing status. **But if you checked any box on line 18a or b,** go to page 40 to find your standard deduction. **If you checked box 18c,** enter -0-.
- Single—$3,900 • Married filing jointly or Qualifying widow(er)—$6,550
- Head of household—$5,750 • Married filing separately—$3,275   **19**

20	Subtract line 19 from line 17. If line 19 is more than line 17, enter -0-.	**20**
21	Multiply $2,500 by the total number of exemptions claimed on line 6e.	**21**
22	Subtract line 21 from line 20. If line 21 is more than line 20, enter -0-. This is your **taxable income.** ▶	**22**

Figure your tax, credits, and payments

If you want the IRS to figure your tax, see the instructions for line 22 on page 41.

23 Find the tax on the amount on line 22. Check if from:
☐ Tax Table (pages 65–70) or ☐ Form 8615 (see page 41).   **23**

24a Credit for child and dependent care expenses. Attach Schedule 2.   **24a**

b Credit for the elderly or the disabled. Attach Schedule 3.   **24b**

c	Add lines 24a and 24b. These are your **total credits.**	**24c**
25	Subtract line 24c from line 23. If line 24c is more than line 23, enter -0-.	**25**
26	Advance earned income credit payments from Form W-2.	**26**
27	Household employment taxes. Attach Schedule H.	**27**
28	Add lines 25, 26 and 27. This is your **total tax.** ▶	**28**

29a Total Federal income tax withheld. If any is from Form(s) 1099, check here ▶ ☐   **29a**

b 1995 estimated tax payments and amount applied from 1994 return.   **29b**

c **Earned income credit.** Attach Schedule EIC if you have a qualifying child.   **29c**
Nontaxable earned income:
amount ▶ | and type ▶

d Add lines 29a, 29b, and 29c (don't include nontaxable earned income). These are your **total payments.** ▶   **29d**

Figure your refund or amount you owe

30 If line 29d is more than line 28, subtract line 28 from line 29d. This is the amount you **overpaid.**   **30**

31	Amount of line 30 you want **refunded to you.**	**31**
32	Amount of line 30 you want **applied to your 1996 estimated tax.**	**32**

33 If line 28 is more than line 29d, subtract line 29d from line 28. This is the **amount you owe.** For details on how to pay, including what to write on your payment, see page 55.   **33**

34 Estimated tax penalty (see page 55). Also, include on line 33.   **34**

Sign your return

Keep a copy of this return for your records.

Under penalties of perjury, I declare that I have examined this return and accompanying schedules and statements, and to the best of my knowledge and belief, they are true, correct, and accurately list all amounts and sources of income I received during the tax year. Declaration of preparer (other than the taxpayer) is based on all information of which the preparer has any knowledge.

Your signature	Date	Your occupation
Spouse's signature. If joint return, BOTH must sign.	Date	Spouse's occupation

Paid preparer's use only

Preparer's signature	Date	Check if self-employed ☐	Preparer's SSN
Firm's name (or yours if self-employed) and address		E.I. No.	
		ZIP code	

Printed on recycled paper

1995 Form 1040A page 2

31

IRSpeak
If you have a lot of expenses such as medical, mortgage interest, taxes, and charitable contributions, you can *itemize* those deductions on Schedule A and try to reduce your income before you figure your tax. Itemizing is discussed in detail in Chapters 19 and 20.

Last Year's Return

One way to figure out which form you need is to follow what you did on last year's tax return. If you're confident that you used the correct form last year and your tax situation hasn't changed this year, there's a good chance you'll need the same form again this year. Be careful though. Take a few minutes to consider the criteria set out previously for choosing a form. Make sure you choose the form that will best meet your needs.

In any case, this is a good time to make sure that you can lay your hands on last year's tax return. It is the single best tool for preparing your 1995 return. In fact, I'm not sure that you should continue reading until you've taken the time to find last year's tax return. Go ahead. I'll be here when you get back.

State Tax Forms

IRSpeak
An *IRA* is an account to which you can make (sometimes) tax-deferred contributions now, and you can withdraw the money in your twilight years and pay tax on it then. Chapter 18 provides more information about IRA accounts.

Although a few states don't have a state income tax, most taxpayers have to file a state tax return as well as the federal return. State tax forms are usually one-page affairs. You should get a little state tax packet in the mail (a junior version of the federal packet), but if you don't, there are places you can go to get state tax forms:

➤ Post offices are notorious hangouts for state income tax forms.

➤ Public libraries abound with state income tax forms.

➤ Your state's tax department can send you a form.

➤ Your friends may have extra forms. Usually the Forms and Instructions packet contains an extra copy of the tax return form in case you goof up on the first one.

Form **1040**	Department of the Treasury—Internal Revenue Service U.S. Individual Income Tax Return	19**95**	IRS Use Only—Do not write or staple in this space.

For the year Jan. 1–Dec. 31, 1995, or other tax year beginning _____ , 1995, ending _____ , 19 ___ | OMB No. 1545-0074

Label
(See instructions on page 12.)
Use the IRS label. Otherwise, please print or type.

L A B E L   H E R E

Your first name and initial | Last name | Your social security number

If a joint return, spouse's first name and initial | Last name | Spouse's social security number

Home address (number and street). If you have a P.O. box, see page 12. | Apt. no.

City, town or post office, state, and ZIP code. If you have a foreign address, see page 12.

For Privacy Act and Paperwork Reduction Act Notice, see page 7.

Presidential Election Campaign ➤ (See page 12.)

Do you want $3 to go to this fund? . . . .
If a joint return, does your spouse want $3 to go to this fund? . . . .

Yes | No | Note: *Checking "Yes" will not change your tax or reduce your refund.*

Filing Status
(See page 12.)
Check only one box.

1 ☐ Single
2 ☐ Married filing joint return (even if only one had income)
3 ☐ Married filing separate return. Enter spouse's social security no. above and full name here. ▶ _____
4 ☐ Head of household (with qualifying person). (See page 12.) If the qualifying person is a child but not your dependent, enter this child's name here. ▶
5 ☐ Qualifying widow(er) with dependent child (year spouse died ▶ 19___). (See page 13.)

Exemptions
(See page 13.)

6a ☐ **Yourself.** If your parent (or someone else) can claim you as a dependent on his or her return, **do not** check box 6a. But be sure to check the box on line 33b on page 2

b ☐ Spouse . . . .

c **Dependents:**	(2) Dependent's social security number If born in 1995 see page 14	(3) Dependent's relationship to you	(4) No. of months lived in your home in 1995
(1) First name Last name			

No. of boxes checked on 6a and 6b ____

No. of your children on 6c who:
• lived with you ____
• didn't live with you due to divorce or separation (see page 14) ____

Dependents on 6c not entered above ____

If more than six dependents, see page 14.

d If your child didn't live with you but is claimed as your dependent under a pre-1985 agreement, check here ▶ ☐
e Total number of exemptions claimed . . . .

Add numbers entered on lines above ▶ ☐

Income

Attach Copy B of your Forms W-2, W-2G, and 1099-R here.

If you did not get a W-2, see page 15.

Enclose, but do not attach, your payment and payment voucher. See page 32.

7 Wages, salaries, tips, etc. Attach Form(s) W-2 . . . . . | 7
8a **Taxable** interest income (see page 15). Attach Schedule B if over $400 . . . . . | 8a
b Tax-exempt interest (see page 16). DON'T include on line 8a | 8b |
9 Dividend income. Attach Schedule B if over $400 . . . . . | 9
10 Taxable refunds, credits, or offsets of state and local income taxes (see page 16) . . | 10
11 Alimony received . . . . | 11
12 Business income or (loss). Attach Schedule C or C-EZ . . . . . | 12
13 Capital gain or (loss). If required, attach Schedule D (see page 16) . . . | 13
14 Other gains or (losses). Attach Form 4797 . . . . . . | 14
15a Total IRA distributions . | 15a | b Taxable amount (see page 17) | 15b
16a Total pensions and annuities | 16a | b Taxable amount (see page 17) | 16b
17 Rental real estate, royalties, partnerships, S corporations, trusts, etc. Attach Schedule E | 17
18 Farm income or (loss). Attach Schedule F . . . . | 18
19 Unemployment compensation (see page 19) . . . . . . | 19
20a Social security benefits | 20a | b Taxable amount (see page 18) | 20b
21 Other income. List type and amount—see page 19 .... | 21
22 Add the amounts in the far right column for lines 7 through 21. This is your **total income** ▶ | 22

Adjustments to Income

23a Your IRA deduction (see page 19) . . . . . . | 23a |
b Spouse's IRA deduction (see page 19) . . . . . | 23b |
24 Moving expenses. Attach Form 3903 or 3903-F . . . | 24 |
25 One-half of self-employment tax . . . . | 25 |
26 Self-employed health insurance deduction (see page 21) | 26 |
27 Keogh & self-employed SEP plans. If SEP, check ▶ ☐ | 27 |
28 Penalty on early withdrawal of savings . . . . . | 28 |
29 Alimony paid. Recipient's SSN ▶ | 29 |
30 Add lines 23a through 29. These are your **total adjustments** . . . . ▶ | 30

Adjusted Gross Income

31 Subtract line 30 from line 22. This is your **adjusted gross income**. If less than $26,673 and a child lived with you (less than $9,230 if a child didn't live with you), see "Earned Income Credit" on page 27 ▶ | 31

Cat. No. 11320B | Form **1040** (1995)

Most people use the 1040 form.

Form 1040 (1995)   Page **2**

Tax Compu-tation

(See page 23.)

32 Amount from line 31 (adjusted gross income) **32**

33a Check if: ☐ **You** were 65 or older, ☐ Blind; ☐ **Spouse** was 65 or older, ☐ Blind.
Add the number of boxes checked above and enter the total here . . . . ▶ **33a**

b If your parent (or someone else) can claim you as a dependent, check here . ▶ **33b** ☐

c If you are married filing separately and your spouse itemizes deductions or
you are a dual-status alien, see page 23 and check here . . . . . . ▶ **33c** ☐

34 Enter the larger of your:
{ **Itemized deductions** from Schedule A, line 28, **OR**
Standard deduction shown below for your filing status. **But if you checked any box on line 33a or b,** go to page 23 to find your standard deduction. If you checked **box 33c,** your standard deduction is zero.
• Single—$3,900 • Married filing jointly or Qualifying widow(er)—$6,550
• Head of household—$5,750 • Married filing separately—$3,275 }   **34**

35 Subtract line 34 from line 32 . . . . **35**

36 If line 32 is $86,025 or less, multiply $2,500 by the total number of exemptions claimed on line 6e. If line 32 is over $86,025, see the worksheet on page 24 for the amount to enter . **36**

If you want the IRS to figure your tax, see page 24.

37 **Taxable income.** Subtract line 36 from line 35. If line 36 is more than line 35, enter -0- **37**

38 Tax. Check if from **a** ☐ Tax Table, **b** ☐ Tax Rate Schedules, **c** ☐ Capital Gain Tax Worksheet, or **d** ☐ Form 8615 (see page 24). Amount from Form(s) 8814 ▶ **e** _____ **38**

39 Additional taxes. Check if from **a** ☐ Form 4970 **b** ☐ Form 4972 . . . . . **39**

40 Add lines 38 and 39 . . . . ▶ **40**

Credits

(See page 24.)

41 Credit for child and dependent care expenses. Attach Form 2441   **41**

42 Credit for the elderly or the disabled. Attach Schedule R . .   **42**

43 Foreign tax credit. Attach Form 1116   **43**

44 Other credits (see page 25). Check if from **a** ☐ Form 3800
b ☐ Form 8396 **c** ☐ Form 8801 **d** ☐ Form (specify) _____   **44**

45 Add lines 41 through 44 . . . . **45**

46 Subtract line 45 from line 40. If line 45 is more than line 40, enter **0** . . . . . ▶ **46**

Other Taxes

(See page 25.)

47 Self-employment tax. Attach Schedule SE **47**

48 Alternative minimum tax. Attach Form 6251 . . . . **48**

49 Recapture taxes. Check if from **a** ☐ Form 4255 **b** ☐ Form 8611 **c** ☐ Form 8828 . . **49**

50 Social security and Medicare tax on tip income not reported to employer. Attach Form 4137 **50**

51 Tax on qualified retirement plans including IRAs. If required, attach Form 5329 . . . . **51**

52 Advance earned income credit payments from Form W-2 . . . . **52**

53 Household employment taxes. Attach Schedule H **53**

54 Add lines 46 through 53 This is your **total tax** . . . . ▶ **54**

Payments

Attach Forms W-2, W-2G, and 1099-R on the front.

55 Federal income tax withheld. If any is from Form(s) 1099, check ▶ ☐   **55**

56 1995 estimated tax payments and amount applied from 1994 return .   **56**

57 **Earned income credit.** Attach Schedule EIC if you have a qualifying child Nontaxable earned income: amount ▶ _____
and type ▶ ----------------------------------   **57**

58 Amount paid with Form 4868 (extension request) **58**

59 Excess social security and RRTA tax withheld (see page 32)   **59**

60 Other payments. Check if from **a** ☐ Form 2439 **b** ☐ Form 4136   **60**

61 Add lines 55 through 60. These are your **total payments** . . . . ▶ **61**

Refund or Amount You Owe

62 If line 61 is more than line 54, subtract line 54 from line 61. This is the amount you **OVERPAID** . ▶ **62**

63 Amount of line 62 you want **REFUNDED TO YOU** . . . . ▶ **63**

64 Amount of line 62 you want **APPLIED TO YOUR 1996 ESTIMATED TAX** ▶ **64**

65 If line 54 is more than line 61 subtract line 61 from line 54. This is the **AMOUNT YOU OWE.**
For details on how to pay including using **Form 1040-V,** Payment Voucher, see page 32   **65**

66 Estimated tax penalty (see page 33). Also include on line 65   **66**

Sign Here

Keep a copy of this return for your records.

Under penalties of perjury, I declare that I have examined this return and accompanying schedules and statements, and to the best of my knowledge and belief, they are true, correct, and complete. Declaration of preparer (other than taxpayer) is based on all information of which preparer has any knowledge.

Your signature	Date	Your occupation
Spouse's signature. If a joint return, BOTH must sign.	Date	Spouse's occupation

Paid Preparer's Use Only

Preparer's signature	Date	Check if self-employed ☐	Preparer's social security no.
Firm's name (or yours if self-employed) and address		E.I. No.	
		ZIP code	

✿ *Printed on recycled paper*

Sending for Forms in the Mail

At some point in the preparation of your tax return, you will realize that you don't have all the forms you need. (Remember: You Will Never Have Every Form You Need.) This is the way it works: You are diligently trying to prepare your tax return, reading this book or trying to make sense of the instruction book the IRS sent you with (most of) your forms, when you see a statement like this: *You **MUST** attach Form 2106 to your tax return.* "Must" is always capitalized and typed with bold letters. So, you page through your Forms and Instructions packet searching for Form 2106, but can't seem to find it. Then you look on the cover of the packet at the part that lists the forms that are inside. Do you see Form 2106 listed? Of course not!

The fact is that on almost every page of the IRS instruction book there is reference to at least half a dozen forms you need to have or publications you need to consult, if particular circumstances apply to you. If the IRS were to include all this stuff in everyone's Forms and Instructions packet, they'd need to hire someone built like Arnold Schwartzenegger to deliver the packet to your door. (Hmmmmmm, interesting possibility.)

Often, this revelation of needing a form you don't have occurs late at night in the vicinity of April 15. If it is already April when you find that you need forms, jump ahead to the next section, "Places Where You Can Get Forms at the Last Minute."

Otherwise, there are three addresses where you can write to the IRS and request tax forms. You should order forms from the location nearest you. Just as a test, to see if they really care where I live when I choose the location from which I order forms, I ordered the following items:

➤ Form 2106, "Employee Business Expenses," from the Eastern Area

➤ Form 3903, "Moving Expenses," from the Central Area

➤ Publication 590, "Individual Retirement Accounts," from the Western Area

The forms and publications all arrived within four days of one another and the longest one took nine days to arrive. The interesting thing is that all three of the deliveries were shipped from the region closest to me. The Eastern and Western offices forwarded my order to the Central office and all materials were shipped from there.

It didn't seem to matter that I was ordering out of my region. On the other hand, I'm probably on some list now for being the sort of person who can't follow directions or who challenges authority. Anyway, the addresses for ordering forms and publications are here, and you should probably choose the one that's closest to you:

Internal Revenue Service
Eastern Area
Distribution Center
P.O. Box 85074
Richmond, VA 23261-5074

OOPS!
The forms that appear in this book were current as of its printing. However, the IRS may have made changes to some forms. Although you can use the forms in Appendix B as worksheets, make sure you use final IRS forms for your tax filing.

Internal Revenue Service
Central Area
Distribution Center
P.O. Box 8903
Bloomington, IL 61702-8903

Internal Revenue Service
Western Area
Distribution Center
Rancho Cordova, CA 95743-0001

When you order forms, include the actual form number or schedule letter (as opposed to a general description such as: "I need a form on which I can list the cost of separating my child's fingers when he got into the crazy glue,") and include your name and address (some say the IRS is clairvoyant, but I think it's a good idea to tell them your address anyway). You don't need to send an envelope, nor do you need to pay postage. If you think about it, you've already paid for this delivery—it's your tax dollars at work!

The IRS also recommends that you call 1-800-TAX-FORM and order forms over the telephone. Form turn-around-time is estimated at between 7 and 15 working days. (All of my days are working days; does the IRS realize this when it makes that claim???) I ordered Form 8283, "Noncash Charitable Contributions," by phone on the same day I mailed in the orders I mentioned earlier. The phone order was the first of all my orders to arrive. It took two "working" days (four real days).

Although the tax forms I ordered arrived pretty quickly, you should know that I was ordering in September. The closer you get to April 15, the more bogged down the order-takers will be. Expect a longer response time as the deadline approaches.

Places Where You Can Get Forms at the Last Minute

All is not lost if it is nearly April 15 when you discover that you don't have all the forms you need. There are still many places that will help you get these forms before it's too late. Check out the following resources:

➤ **Public Library.** Provider of endless important bits of information and a last minute stop for the great tax form search, the library usually has the 1040 and the supporting schedules and some of the major tax forms. But, it is unlikely they will have all the miscellaneous schedules. The library is an excellent place to look if you need a state income tax form.

➤ **Post Office.** Again, count on the P.O. to have the major stuff that everybody uses. More obscure forms require a more industrious search.

➤ **Law Library.** If you are fortunate enough to live in a city with a law school or a courthouse, there will probably be a law library. It's like kids and ice cream wagons: where there are lawyers there are law libraries. Find a law library, then find a kind librarian and ask for a book of reproducible IRS tax forms. Have someone point you in the direction of the copier, bring lots of coins, and you're in business. One nice thing about law libraries is that they keep late hours.

➤ **CPAs and Lawyers.** This time of year, people who prepare tax returns for a living are *rather* busy, so it's not a good idea to walk into their offices as a stranger and beg for tax forms. On the other hand, if you happen to know someone in this business, you can probably call in a personal favor and have your friend bring home a form or two for you.

➤ **IRS.** Don't forget the people who brought you all these forms in the first place. IRS offices are everywhere. Check in your phone book for the nearest location and boogie on down to their office. Step over the bodies of moaning taxpayers waiting for tax advice from harried IRS agents and make your way to the forms counter. They have every form a person could want, if you can only get the attention of someone who will find what you need.

➤ **Computer software programs.** If you have a computer and a tax software program, you probably have all the forms you need at your fingertips. (Some of these programs are discussed in Chapter 32, "Choosing a Software Program.") The program will print your tax return on IRS-type forms, so you don't have to run around town on a tax form scavenger hunt. Alternatively, if you don't have a computer tax program, *but you have a friend who does*, bring your friend a plate of chocolate chip cookies right out of the oven and I bet your friend will run off a couple of blank forms for you.

The Least You Need to Know

➤ Most of the income tax forms you need will arrive in the mail right around New Year's Eve.

➤ The main tax form is the 1040. Simplified variations include the 1040A and the 1040EZ.

➤ Odds are you won't have every form you need, but there are plenty of sources out there for finding additional tax forms.

Chapter 4

What Do You Know? They Changed the Law Again

In This Chapter

➤ Changes such as easier filing and allowable deductions

➤ The Nanny Tax

➤ Changes that are still under consideration

➤ Forms that you can take to the bank (or, at least, to the IRS)

Those folks in Washington just can't keep their fingers out of our tax laws. This year they're at it again. There are some changes in store for 1995 and beyond, most of which are expected to be enacted by Congress, but which were still under debate when this book went to press. Follow these changes in the media if it looks as if they will affect you.

Changes That Affect the Way You Keep Records

In recent years, the IRS has not allowed *club dues* as a deduction, even when membership in the club constituted a bona fide business purpose. Now Congress has changed its mind again. You can take a business expense deduction for dues in Chambers of Commerce, trade associations, civic and public service organizations such as Kiwanis, Lions, and Rotary, and professional groups like medical associations and bar associations. But don't even bother trying to deduct dues for memberships in athletic and country clubs, hotel groups, and airline clubs. The IRS does not accept a business expense deduction for these types of club dues.

At press time, Congress was considering allowing full $2,000 IRA deductions for stay-at-home taxpayers instead of the former $250 limitation for the nonworking spouse. This would restore some of the incentive for saving what was lost when allowable deductions for IRA contributions were cut back several years ago. See Chapter 18, "Adjustments to Income," for more information about the way in which IRA contributions are deducted, and be sure to check reports in the national media to see what Congress decided to do with the deductiblility of IRA contributions.

Changes to Keep You on Your Toes

After a successful test in 10 states last year, the IRS has approved a nationwide telephone tax return filing system that will go into effect in the Spring of 1996 for 1995 income tax returns. Taxpayers filing on Form 1040EZ will be eligible. Instructions that accompany the 1040EZ tax forms will provide information about how to use the telephone call-in system for filing your tax return.

Congress has been considering a tax credit for families with children. At press time, the talk was of a tax credit of as much as $300 per child to parents if the parents' combined adjusted gross income doesn't exceed $95,000 for the year. The bad news is that, if passed, this tax credit will be phased in over several years, beginning no earlier than in (darn!) 1997. This isn't a replacement for the dependent and child care credit, but a credit merely for the sake of giving a break to parents who raise children.

The outrageous 10% penalty for early withdrawal on IRA accounts may be reduced or relieved entirely for withdrawals earmarked for expenditures such as purchase of first homes, medical expenses, or school tuition. This, too, was undecided at press time but was under serious consideration.

Reductions in income tax on capital gains have been proposed for years. Once again this is on the congressional floor and, at press time, it was expected to be one of the most debated issues. Opponents of cuts on capital gains taxes say that it makes the rich get richer; proponents say that it frees up cash to be reinvested in the economy. No matter which side of the fence your representatives and senators are on, all members of Congress seem to be in agreement that a change is due in this area. The possible expectation as this book went to press was that the capital gains tax rate of 28% may be reduced. There was also talk of excluding some portion of capital gains from taxation. In any event, any change in the law that may be passed relating to capital gain taxation probably won't affect sales of assets in 1995.

There is also a possibility that losses on sales of personal residences may start to be treated like losses on sales of other capital assets—taxpayers may finally be able to take a deduction for such a loss.

The Nanny Tax

There is a new tax and a new form to file for 1995 tax returns. Taxpayers who employ domestic servants—maids, nannies, and chauffeurs, for example—will now report the payroll taxes for these employees with their federal income tax return by filling out Schedule H, "Household Employment Taxes" (see the nearby figure).

SCHEDULE H (Form 1040)	Household Employment Taxes	OMB No. 1545-0074
Department of the Treasury Internal Revenue Service	(For Social Security, Medicare, Withheld Income, and Federal Unemployment (FUTA) Taxes) ▶ **Attach to Form 1040, 1040A, 1040NR, 1040NR-EZ, 1040-SS, or 1041.** ▶ **See separate instructions.**	**1995** Attachment Sequence No. **44**

Name of employer (as shown on return)

Social security number

Employer identification number

Before you begin, read **Who Must File** on page 3 of the instructions.

A Did you pay **any one** household employee cash wages of $1,000 or more in 1995?

☐ **Yes.** Skip questions B and C and go to Part I.
☐ **No.** Go to question B.

B Did you withhold Federal income tax during 1995 at the request of any household employee?

☐ **Yes.** Skip question C and go to Part I.
☐ **No.** Go to question C.

C Did you pay **total** cash wages of $1,000 or more in **any** calendar **quarter** of 1994 or 1995 to household employees?

☐ **No.** **Stop.** Do not file this schedule.
☐ **Yes.** Skip Part I and go to Par   on the back.

Part I	Social Security, Medicare, and Income Taxes		
1	Total cash wages subject to social security taxes (see page 3) . .	1	
2	Social security taxes. Multiply line 1 by 12.4% (.124)	2	
3	Total cash wages subject to Medicare taxes (see page 3)	3	
4	Medicare taxes. Multiply line 3 by 2.9% (.029)	4	
5	Federal income tax withheld, if any	5	
6	Add lines 2, 4, and 5	6	
7	Advance earned income credit (EIC) payments, if any	7	
8	**Total social security, Medicare, and income taxes.** Subtract line 7 from line 6	8	

9 Did you pay **total** cash wages of $1,000 or more in **any** calendar **quarter** of 1994 or 1995 to household employees?

☐ **No.** **Stop.** Take the amount from line 8 above and enter it on Form 1040, line 53, or Form 1040A, line 27. If you are not required to file Form 1040 or 1040A, see the line 9 instructions on page 4.

☐ **Yes.** Go to Part II on the back.

For Paperwork Reduction Act Notice, see Form 1040 instructions.	Cat. No. 12187K	Schedule H (Form 1040) 1995

The new tax form for reporting taxes on household employees.

Schedule H (Form 1040) 1995   Page **2**

Part II   Federal Unemployment (FUTA) Tax

		Yes	No
10	Did you pay unemployment contributions to only one state?		
11	Did you pay all state unemployment contributions for 1995 by April 15, 1996? Fiscal year filers, see page 4 . .		
12	Were all wages that are taxable for FUTA tax also taxable for your state's unemployment tax?		

Next: If you answered **"Yes"** to **all** of the questions above, complete Section A.

If you answered **"No"** to **any** of the questions above, skip Section A and complete Section B.

Section A

13	Name of the state where you have to pay unemployment contributions ▶	
14	State reporting number as shown on state unemployment tax return ▶	
15	Contributions paid to your state unemployment fund (see page 4) **15**	
16	Total cash wages subject to FUTA tax (see page 4)	**16**
17	**FUTA tax.** Multiply line 16 by .008. Enter the result here, skip Section B, and go to Part III . .	**17**

Section B

18   Complete all columns below that apply (if you need more space, see page 4):

(a) Name of state	(b) State reporting number as shown on state unemployment tax return	(c) Taxable wages (as defined in state act)	(d) State experience rate period		(e) State experience rate	(f) Multiply col. (c) by .054	(g) Multiply col. (c) by col. (e)	(h) Subtract col. (g) from col. (f). If zero or less, enter -0-.	(i) Contributions paid to state unemployment fund
			From	To					

19	Totals	**19**	
20	Add columns (h) and (i) of line 19 . . . . **20**		
21	Total cash wages subject to FUTA tax (see the line 16 instructions on page 4)	**21**	
22	Multiply line 21 by 6.2% (.062)	**22**	
23	Multiply line 21 by 5.4% (.054) **23**		
24	Enter the **smaller** of line 20 or line 23	**24**	
25	**FUTA tax.** Subtract line 24 from line 22. Enter the result here and go to Part III	**25**	

Part III   Total Household Employment Taxes

26	Enter the amount from line 8	**26**	
27	Add line 17 (or line 25) and line 26	**27**	

28   Are you required to file Form 1040 or 1040A?

☐ **Yes.**   **Stop.** Take the amount from line 27 above and enter it on Form 1040, line 53, or Form 1040A, line 27. **Do not** complete Part IV below.

☐ **No.**   You may have to complete Part IV. See page 5 for details.

Part IV   Address and Signature—Complete this part **only** if required. See page 5.

Address (number and street) or P.O. box if mail is not delivered to street address | Apt., room, or suite no.

City, town or post office, state, and ZIP code

Under penalties of perjury, I declare that I have examined this schedule, including accompanying statements, and to the best of my knowledge and belief, it is true, correct, and complete. No part of any payment made to a state unemployment fund claimed as a credit was, or is to be, deducted from the payments to employees.

▶ _____   ▶ _____
Employer's signature   Date

✸ *Printed on recycled paper*

Taxpayers should file Schedule H if any of the following requirements are met:

➤ Wages of at least $1,000 were paid during 1995 to any one household employee.

➤ Federal income tax was withheld at the request of any household employee, regardless of the amount of wages paid to that employee.

➤ Wages of at least $1,000 were paid during any one quarter of 1995 to household employees.

Fill out Part I of Schedule H by following these steps:

1. List total wages paid to household employees that were subject to Social Security taxes on line 1.

2. Multiply line 1 by 12.4% to calculate Social Security taxes on line 2.

3. List total wages paid to household employees that were subject to Medicare taxes on line 3.

4. Multiply line 3 by 2.9% to calculate Medicare taxes on line 4.

5. Show any federal income tax withheld on line 5.

6. Combine lines 2, 4, and 5 on line 6.

7. Show any advance earned income credit payments on line 7.

8. Reduce total taxes by advance earned income credit payments by deducting line 7 from line 6 and putting the difference on line 8.

If total wages paid to household employees during any one quarter of 1995 exceeded $1,000, go to Part II of the form. If not, enter the amount from line 3 on line 53 of the 1040 (or line 27 of the 1040A) and do not fill out the back side of Schedule H. This amount will be paid as an additional tax with your federal income tax return.

For taxpayers who have to move on to Part II, this part of the form calculates federal unemployment taxes.

Answer the questions at the top of Part II regarding payments of unemployment taxes to your state government.

In Section B, enter the amount of wages and unemployment taxes reported to your state. You will calculate the amount of total unemployment tax due, then reduce the total amount by the amount you paid your state. The difference is the federal unemployment tax due which gets added to the taxes from Part I of Schedule H. The total of the Part I taxes and the federal unemployment tax goes on line 17 of Schedule H. Transfer this amount to line 53 of the 1040 (or line 27 of the 1040A).

Look at the instructions that accompany Schedule H to determine if you are required to sign this form at the bottom of page 2.

The Least You Need to Know

➤ Club dues for certain business-related organizations are once again deductible business expenses.

➤ A telephone tax return filing system is available to all taxpayers filing on Form 1040EZ.

➤ The new Schedule H, "Household Employment Taxes" (lovingly called The Nanny Tax), allows employers of domestic help to report and pay their employees' taxes right on their federal income tax return.

➤ Many other tax law changes are under consideration. Follow the news for tax changes. The weekly tax column on the front page of the Wall Street Journal is a good place to look.

Chapter 5

Collecting the Right Information

In This Chapter

➤ A handy checklist for gathering tax return data

➤ What to do if you can't find the information you need

➤ What to do if you'll never find the information you need

When I prepare my own tax return, I find that more than half the battle is won if I have all my records in order and at arms length before I begin. There is something very discouraging about mustering up the courage to sit down to a project such as this, then realizing you need things you don't have, or that you're not even quite sure what you need. That's usually enough to make me get up and go to the movies.

I would rather spend weeks gathering up every little receipt and form and tax-related slip of paper I can find, than sit down with only part of the stuff. If I have everything together for my tax return, I can glue myself to the chair until I finish the darn thing.

Sometimes though, no matter how prepared you are, the information you need just isn't there. In this chapter, in addition to gaining some common-sense ideas on assembling your tax details, you'll get some pointers about what to do when the data is missing.

The Game Plan

The IRS loves receipts. Save everything you can. Keep it all forever. Well, perhaps that's a bit broad. Let's talk about the things you need in order to get this year's tax return off the ground. Below, you will find a Handy Tax Receipt Checklist that you can use to help you put together your very own pile of important tax receipts.

Handy Tax Receipt Checklist

- ❏ W-2 forms
- ❏ 1099 forms
- ❏ Year-end bank statements
- ❏ Year-end mutual fund statements
- ❏ Expenses for your own business:
  - ❏ Advertising
  - ❏ Auto
  - ❏ Bad debts
  - ❏ Bank service charges
  - ❏ Commissions
  - ❏ Contract, casual labor
  - ❏ Depreciation
  - ❏ Dues
  - ❏ Employee benefits
  - ❏ Freight
  - ❏ Gifts
  - ❏ Interest
  - ❏ Laundry
  - ❏ Legal and other professional fees
  - ❏ Liability insurance
  - ❏ Meals and entertainment
  - ❏ Office expenses
  - ❏ Photocopying
  - ❏ Postage
  - ❏ Rent
  - ❏ Repairs, maintenance
  - ❏ Subscriptions
  - ❏ Supplies
  - ❏ Taxes
  - ❏ Telephone
  - ❏ Transportation other than auto
  - ❏ Travel
  - ❏ Utilities
  - ❏ Wages and salaries
  - ❏ Workers compensation

- ❏ Income earned in your own business
- ❏ Assets currently being depreciated in your business
- ❏ Information from purchases or sales of business assets
- ❏ Auto log
- ❏ Auto (or other vehicle) expenses
  - ❏ Gasoline, oil
  - ❏ Repairs
  - ❏ Tires
  - ❏ Maintenance
  - ❏ Insurance
  - ❏ Interest on auto loan
  - ❏ Parking and tolls
- ❏ Home utilities, maintenance, insurance expenses (if taking office-in-home deduction)
- ❏ Closing statement from purchase or sale of home
- ❏ Improvements to home
- ❏ Statements from brokers
- ❏ Purchases and sales of stocks, bonds or mutual fund shares
- ❏ K-1 forms
- ❏ Income and expenses from rental properties (use list above, Expenses for your own business, to determine expenses of your rental property)
- ❏ Moving expenses
- ❏ Prize winnings and gambling transactions
- ❏ Statements from employers regarding fringe benefits

- ❏ Medical expenses
  - ❏ Doctors, dentists, and nurses
  - ❏ Hospitals, clinics
  - ❏ Laboratory fees
  - ❏ Prescription drugs
  - ❏ Ambulance
  - ❏ Health insurance
  - ❏ Mileage driven for medical purposes
- ❏ Real estate tax statement
- ❏ Estimated taxes paid (both state and federal)
- ❏ Vehicle registration (if you live in a state that charges property tax for registering your wheels)
- ❏ Cash contributions to charitable organizations
- ❏ Documentation for noncash contributions
- ❏ Mileage driven for charitable purposes
- ❏ Insurance documents from casualties
- ❏ Costs of replacement or repairs after casualties
- ❏ Unreimbursed expenses relating to your job
- ❏ Expenses from looking for a job
- ❏ Child or dependent care costs while both parents work
- ❏ Name and Federal ID # for child or dependent care providers

Gather all the records, statements, and receipts (to the extent that you have them and that they relate to your tax return) listed in the Handy Tax Receipt Checklist. Don't worry if you don't understand what some of these things are. Do the best you can to collect these items in advance. When you reach the time to actually use them, you will find a clear description of what each item is.

You may be wondering what the forms listed in the checklist are actually used for. The W-2 form shows how much you earned at your job(s). The 1099 form lists income from interest, dividends, rents, and miscellaneous sources. The K-1 form shows income, and sometimes losses, from partnerships and small business corporations in which you have an ownership interest. All of these forms are explained in more detail later in the book.

The Fall Back Position

While searching for the information listed in the Handy Tax Receipt Checklist, you may discover that you don't have everything you need. Your first reaction may be to decide you don't need to work on your tax return after all and to head for the nearest movie theater—I know that would be my reaction. Alternatively, you may be surprised to find out that there are ways to replicate nearly all of these items.

If you've lost official forms, such as W-2 forms, 1099s, K-1s, and the like, call the company that provided them in the first place. The company has to keep copies of these forms for the company records, so duplicating them can be a fairly simple matter. The same goes for bank statements, and statements from brokers and mutual funds. If they're busy and grouse about giving you the forms, tell them I told you to be persistent.

In the case of missing receipts for expenses you incurred, you may have to spend some time with your checkbook, recreating cash-outflow moments from your past. If you feel you need to recover a particular receipt (that a canceled check won't do), see if you can narrow down the date; then contact the manager of the place that took your money. The manager may be able to re-create a receipt for you. If not, see if you can at least get a written statement detailing the normal cost of the items you purchased.

The Drop Back and Punt Play

Picture these situations: April 15 is fast approaching and you have yet to receive a Form K-1 from a small business in which you are a part-owner. Or you did some work for a company that has yet to provide you with a 1099-MISC

> **IRSpeak**
> The extra money you pay when you pay off a loan, the cost of borrowing money, if you will, is *interest*. This kind of interest is a cost to you. The money you earn on your savings account, the amount the bank pays you to let them use your money, is also *interest*. This kind of interest is income to you. Both kinds of interest are calculated as a percentage of either the amount of your loan or the amount you put in your bank account.

> **OOPS!**
> In the case of the W-2 form, which comes with special pages for the IRS and your state government, your employer will be reproducing the employer copy of the form (Copy D). Although the tax authorities prefer the copies that are made for them (IRS likes Copy B and states like Copy A), they only turn their noses up a little bit at Copy D.

IRSpeak
Money that comes into your possession is *income*. Some income is earned, such as money that you work for at a job or in a business; other income, such as interest and dividends, is a result of savvy investing. Income includes gifts and prizes and pennies that fall from the sky. Most of your income is subject to income tax, but some of it is not.

IRSpeak
Money that you spend is an *expense*. Whether or not it is a *deductible expense*, an amount you can use to reduce your income before you compute income tax, depends on the vagaries of the tax lawmakers.

IRSpeak
The amount of tax you owe, the amount you have to pay, is your *tax liability*. A liability is a debt.

for your services. Or perhaps you paid cash for certain tax-deductible expenses and you don't have the receipt, and you can't remember how much you spent. Before you press the panic button, think about how you can get to the information you need:

➤ **Make a few calls.** The company holding the information may have it ready and just hasn't mailed it yet. See if you can encourage the company to get your information in the mail, or at least see if they will tell you over the telephone what you need to know.

➤ **Check published sources.** If you are waiting on dividend information from a publicly held company, for example, you can go to the library (ask for the book called *Moody's Dividend Record*), or even telephone the library's reference desk, to check 1995 dividend records for the company. Dividends paid by publicly-held companies are a matter of public record.

➤ **Try to calculate amounts you need for your tax return.** You may have statements that give you income or expense activity on a monthly basis, in which case you simply can add 12 months worth of amounts to get to a year-end total. Did you sell some stock this year? Look at how much you received at the time of the sale, and then go back to your earlier records to see what you paid for it. Compare the two amounts to determine a gain or loss. You don't need your broker to tell you the results of the sale.

➤ **Be willing to settle for an estimate.** It may be that the best you can do is make a good guess of the amount that you need. If that's the best you'll ever do, then that's the number you'll have to use on your tax return. Alternatively, if you can get an estimate now with assurances that the real amount will be close on its heels, consider using the number you have to estimate your tax liability and file a request for an extension to file your tax return.

Filing for an Extension

You can get an automatic extension of time in which to file your tax return by filing Form 4868, "Automatic Extension of Time to File U.S. Individual Income Tax Return," and by paying the amount of tax you owe based on the calculation you make on the 4868. Filing this form pushes your tax filing due date from April 15 to August 15, giving you four extra months in which to coerce people into giving you the information you need in order to file your tax return.

Form **4868**	**Application for Automatic Extension of Time to File U.S. Individual Income Tax Return**	OMB No. 1545-0188

Department of the Treasury
Internal Revenue Service

Please Type or Print

Your first name | MI | Last name | Your Social Security Number

If a joint return, spouse's first name | MI | Last name | Spouse's Social Security Number

Home address (number, street, and apt no. or rural route). If you have a P.O. box, see the instructions

City, town or post office | State | ZIP Code

I request an automatic 4-month extension of time to Aug 15, 1995, to file Form 1040EZ, Form 1040A, or Form 1040 for the calendar year 1994 or to _____ , 19 ____ , for the fiscal tax year ending _____ , 19 ____ .

Part I Individual Income Tax — You must complete this part.

1 **Total tax liability for 1994.** This is the amount you expect to enter on Form 1040EZ, line 9; Form 1040A, line 27; or Form 1040, line 53. If you do expect this amount to be zero, enter -0- .... | 1

Caution: You **must** enter an amount on line 1 or your extension will be denied. You can estimate this amount, but be as exact as you can with the information you have. If we later find that your estimate was not reasonable, the extension will be null and void.

2 **Total payments for 1994.** This is the amount you expect to enter on Form 1040EZ, line 8; Form 1040A, line 28d; or Form 1040, line 60 (excluding line 57) .... | 2

3 **Balance Due.** Subtract line 2 from line 1. If line 2 is more than line 1, enter -0-. If you are making a payment, you must use the Form 4868-V. For details on how to pay, including what to write on your payment, see the instructions ▶ | 3

You still have to pay the tax on April 15.

Part II Gift or Generation-Skipping Transfer (GST) Tax — Complete this part if you expect to owe either tax.

Caution: Do not include income tax on lines 5a and 5b. See instructions.

4 If you or your spouse plan to file a gift tax return (Form 709 or 709-A) for 1994, generally due by April 17, 1995, see the instructions and check here .... Yourself ▶ ☐ Spouse ▶ ☐

5 a Enter the amount of gift or GST tax **you** are paying with this form. Also, you must use the Form 4868-V .... | 5a

b Enter the amount of gift or GST tax **your spouse** is paying with this form . Also, you must use the Form 4868-V .... | 5b

Signature and Verification

Under penalties of perjury, I declare that I have examined this form, including accompanying schedules and statements, and to the best of my knowledge and belief, it is true, correct, and complete; and, if prepared by someone other than the taxpayer, that I am authorized to prepare this form.

▶ Your signature _____ Date _____ ▶ Spouse's Signature, if filing jointly _____ Date _____

▶ Preparer's signature (other than taxpayer) _____ Date _____

If you want correspondence regarding this extension to be sent to you at an address other than that shown above or to an agent acting for you, please enter the name of the agent and/or the address where it should be sent.

Please Type or Print

Name

Number and street (include suite, room, or apt. no.) or P.O. box number if mail is not delivered to street address

City, town or post office | State | ZIP Code

D181 For Paperwork Reduction Act Notice, see separate instructions. | Form **4868**

To apply for a four-month automatic extension, use the 4868 form.

To prepare this extension application, estimate your tax liability, figure out how much tax you have already paid (through withholdings, quarterly payments, and a refund from the prior year that may have been carried over to this year), subtract the second amount from the first, and pay the difference, if there is an amount still owing.

OOPS!
Filing Form 4868 by April 15 grants you an automatic extension of time to file your 1040 return *assuming* that you pay your estimated tax liability by April 15. If you just file the 4868 without paying the estimated taxes owed, the form isn't valid, your tax return due date isn't extended, and your tax return will be considered late if it isn't filed by April 15.

The Least You Need to Know

➤ Before sitting down to prepare your tax return, take the time to gather up everything you will need, including a year's worth of tax-related business expenses.

➤ Use the checklist in this chapter to help you gather the receipts and statements you need for your tax return.

➤ Don't give up if you've lost a receipt. There are many ways to re-create information for your tax return.

Chapter 6

Kill Two Birds: Get Ready for Next Year

In This Chapter

➤ Getting your tax act together

➤ Setting up a record-keeping system you can live with

➤ Having a life after this tax return

➤ Tax tasks (try saying that five times quickly...) to do before the end of the year

This chapter is a be-good-to-yourself chapter. What you learn in this chapter will serve you well year-round and into future years, too. Take note. These are the secrets of organizers and planners, tricks of the trade that take people years to learn. Getting yourself organized takes discipline and practice.

Just like a smoker trying to quit, you have to *want* to be organized. It's not going to happen without some effort on your part. And getting organized is only half of the battle. Staying organized is just as important and requires your attention on a year-round basis.

Not for the weak of heart, this chapter is for those of you who are willing to stand up and say, "I'm tired of not knowing where I put receipts when I know I put them 'someplace safe;'" "I'm tired of not being able to find a slip of paper when I know I had it in my hand 24 hours ago;" or, "I'm tired of having chapped lips all winter." (Well, as long as we're wishing for miracles....)

Advantages of Planning and Organizing

I really don't think I need to tell you why it's important to plan and get organized. Deep down, you know you should do it. You don't need reasons; you need an excuse. And here's the best excuse I can offer: If you get audited by the IRS and you are so disorganized that you can't find receipts and other paperwork to back up the deductions on your tax return, the IRS has the right to say that you can't deduct your expenses. Deductions are removed with the magic IRS eraser, taxable income shoots through the roof, and you have to borrow into the next century to pay the taxes, not to mention penalties and interest.

If that's not a good enough excuse, then perhaps you are meant to live the life of chaos and should just move on to the next chapter.

Aha! So you're still with me! Okay, here goes. First of all, believe me when I say that I know about disorganization. Any of my friends who are reading this are wondering right now how I have the nerve to tell anyone else about being organized. They've seen my garage. They've climbed over my piles of books. And they've witnessed me searching in vain for that elusive slip of paper that I know I had yesterday.

All right, so I don't always practice what I preach; at least not at home. But I have spent years showing other people how to be organized, and in my jobs, my work habits have been held out as examples of exceptional organization skills. I may not always put my knowledge in this area to work, but I know that of which I speak. And, in an act of good faith, I'm going to make a deal with you today. Read the rest of this chapter, pick up some pointers on how to organize your life from a tax perspective (at least make an attempt to kick the messy habit), and I promise I'll do the same thing. Agreed? I'm ready to shake on it.

Start with the Basics

First, you need to obtain a goal. Without a goal, a game plan is worthless. You need to strive for something in order to make sense of how to get there. Your goal should have something to do with your tax return preparation. Specifically, you need to achieve the following:

➤ Have a place to put receipts when you get them.

➤ Be able to find those receipts again.

➤ Have receipts sorted so that you don't have to go through the entire collection every time you want one item.

➤ Organize the items in a way that makes sense for tax return preparation.

➤ Keep the system simple.

Record-Keeping Systems for the Neatness-Impaired

I don't know about you, but when I get statements and other papers in the mail that seem important but that I don't need for a while, I set them aside. That's it. I just set them aside. There's no particular "aside" place in my house, just aside from wherever I happen to be standing at the time I open the mail. This nonsystem of saving documents and papers has been the cause of countless hours of searching for things I know came in the mail, important documents I know I didn't throw away but just set aside. It's caused me to miss deadlines because I couldn't find particular documents in time. It's caused a fair number of arguments around the house as well. (Writing a book can be a great psychological release.)

I fully realize the downside of not having an organized record-keeping system in place because I've been there. When something important comes in the mail, and you do not have an established record-keeping system, the item has an excellent chance of getting lost. What's needed instead is a system that is easy to use, makes papers easy to find (an important factor if you live in a cluttered house), and that fits your style of living.

A System You Can Live With

Try to resist the temptation to get too elaborate with your tax record-keeping system. You don't want to go overboard, investing in new filing cabinets, built-in shelving units, or adding on rooms for additional office space. Pull in the reigns and think small. Let's look at the goals listed earlier in this chapter and try to work with them, using the space and the facilities you have at hand.

Have a place to put receipts when you get them. First of all, of course, you need to identify what is and is not a keeper. Most of what comes in the mail isn't stuff you need for your tax return. Some "junk mail" outfits have even gotten to the point of making their mail look official by printing text on the envelope such as "Important Tax Documents Inside," then when you open it thinking you'll find a W-2 form or something you really need, you get a coupon for 10 cents off on some $200 tax self-help guide. It's easy to find a place to put junk mail when it comes in—that round metal container on the floor will do quite nicely.

What you need for storage is something that fits your lifestyle. You need a way in which to store papers unobtrusively, and you need to have a way to break the pile of receipts and forms into small, manageable groups. If you're a filing cabinet sort of person, use file folders. If you like three-ring binders, get one specifically for tax items and get some dividers for it. Shoeboxes are okay, but get several instead of just one. Large mailing envelopes work nicely, as do those colorful pocket folders kids use at school (if you have children, you can probably find some extras in their room). One of those accordion files will work nicely too. You may have some other ideas on this subject. The key is to find something relatively compact, with compartments, that you will enjoy using.

Be able to find those receipts again. After you've chosen a filing system, find a place for it and designate that as the Official Tax Filing Place. Don't keep moving it from one room or one drawer to the next, you'll never keep track of it and it will lose its sense of permanence. You need to find a place that you will be happy with for the long haul—a place that from here on out will always be your Official Tax Filing Place.

Your Official Tax Filing Place doesn't have to be the dining room table centerpiece. It doesn't even have to be in the house—perhaps there is an acceptable spot in the garage or a storage shed that will do, as long as you don't mind going out there with some regularity. Find a hideaway, be it a filing cabinet drawer, a desk drawer, a cardboard box on a shelf, a bookshelf, under your bed, the back of a closet, an abandoned dog cage, whatever. After you choose your place, think of that place only as your Official Tax Filing Place. Brand it on your memory.

Have your receipts sorted so that you don't have to go through the entire collection every time you want one receipt. This is why you have multiple folders, shoeboxes, or dividers in your notebook. Read on.

Organize the tax papers in a way that makes sense for tax return preparation. You need to get out an old tax return or two and look at the kinds of things you reported in past years. You should start one folder (box, divider, whatever) for every type of income and expense you have. Here's a sample list of the kinds of statements and receipts you might have:

➤ W-2 forms

➤ 1099-INT interest income forms

➤ 1099-DIV dividend income forms

➤ Schedule C—income and expenses from your own business

➤ Purchases and sales of stocks or bonds

➤ K-1 forms that list your share of income from a partnership or S corporation in which you participate

➤ Income from other sources

➤ Medical expenses

➤ Tax expenses

➤ Interest expenses

➤ Charitable contributions

➤ Miscellaneous job costs

➤ Child care expenses

I'd be an awfully good guesser if this list exactly fit your needs. It's meant to give you an idea of what you might need. If you don't purchase stocks and bonds, you won't need a folder for that, nor will you need a 1099-DIV folder. If you have your own business and it generates a lot of expenses, you might have a separate folder for each type of business expense, such as advertising, travel, office supplies, purchases of business assets, and so on.

The trick is to not skimp on the number of folders you use. You're talking about a minimal cost for a great organizational tool. If the cost of one folder is 25 cents, how does that compare to the headaches you'll save yourself by being that much better organized?

When you have finished acquiring and labeling your folders or whatever you have decided to use, make yourself set up two more folders: one for the tax returns from the past three years and the other one for "Papers I think go with my tax return but that I can't find a folder for."

Keep the system simple. I know I just told you not to shortchange yourself on the number of folders you choose to use. On the other hand, try not to go overboard. If you use three different baby-sitters, one child care folder will do. A separate file for each doctor and dentist seen by each member of your family is probably a bit of overkill. On the other hand, if you have 100+ prescription receipts, you probably need a separate file for prescriptions, apart from your other medical expenses. You have to be your own judge on this.

After you have this system all set up and ready to meet your organizational needs, you should feel a great weight lifted off your shoulders. Psychic vibrations from me to you.

Year-End Tax Record-Keeping Ideas

Hold on! Before you break open that bottle of champagne, before you exercise your vocal chords on "Auld Lang Syne," before you pucker up for that midnight kiss, there are a few things you ought to do at the end of the year to get yourself ready and off to a running start on January 1.

If you have just read this chapter but haven't chosen the right record-keeping scenario for your needs, then it's not time to celebrate yet. This isn't the sort of subject you think about and never do—this is something you *need* to put in place NOW! The 1995 tax year may be over with and you may or may not have a workable record-keeping system for that year. But 1996 is about to begin and every day you wait is a day you'll regret, come April 15, *1997*. You see, I'm not just talking about helping you with your 1995 taxes here, although that is the year with which this book is most concerned. I'm also talking about tax returns for 1996, 1997, and every year thereafter. A solid, working record-keeping system, once in place, will serve you for years to come. So don't get dressed for the party yet. The stores are still open. Go out and get yourself some file folders, dividers, labels, whatever you need (or raid your closet for shoe boxes), and spend an hour or two now getting ready for the tax years of the future.

If you have a decent record-keeping system already in place, and you use it, you've got a great head-start for this year's tax return preparation. Now you need to think about next year. Right from the start, in January, tax-deductible receipts start coming in that you need to file away and save. If all your file folders are filled with 1995 receipts, neatly organized and ready for your 1995 tax return, you're halfway there—you have a system and you know how to use it. Now you need to start new folders, open up a new binder, empty some new shoeboxes, whatever it takes to get your current system ready to receive 1996 receipts. This is a New Year's Eve job (or maybe New Year's Day, if you don't like football).

Give yourself a running start into 1996 by putting yourself in a tax record-keeping state of mind. No meditation here nor far eastern trances. This is nuts and bolts, sound thinking, planning for the future. Get ready to "think taxes." Every time you collect a little receipt that may be related to your tax return— registration fee for your license plates, receipts for donations to the school fund-raiser, prescription drug receipts (don't spend a lot of time worrying about whether it's deductible or not—if you think it is, then it is) go ahead and file it in the appropriate folder. Whenever some official-looking tax-related document arrives in the mail, in it goes. When you drive your son's Cub Scout troop to the campgrounds or drive yourself to the doctor, write down the mileage and pop the notation in the appropriate folder. Until you make yourself think "taxes" on a daily basis, you won't realize how much of your life belongs in those folders. Wait until April, 1996 to assemble your receipts and your thoughts, and you can count on missing many deductions.

Consider this record-keeping system, the one you customize to meet your needs, a gift to yourself. It's something you will use for years to come and will never regret having spent the time to set up.

The Least You Need to Know

➤ Take the time now to set up a tax-record-keeping system. You'll thank yourself for the rest of your life.

➤ Make your system something you enjoy using.

➤ Don't just set up the system: use it!

Part 2
It's Showtime

"It was as true," said Mr. Barkis, "as turnips is. It was as true," said Mr. Barkis, nodding his nightcap, which was his only means of emphasis, "as taxes is; and nothing's truer than them."

Charles Dickens, David Copperfield, *1849*

No time is really better than any other for starting your tax return, although one could argue that the evening of April 15 is probably a pretty lousy time to begin the darn thing. Basically, you need to remember that you should start early enough so that, if you find you are missing information or tax forms, you will have enough time to go out and find the things you need.

Tax return preparation can seem an intimidating chore, a measure of your patience, and a test of endurance. Instead, I want you to look at this as an opportunity: a chance to get to know your own finances more intimately, a chance to learn some ways in which to save money, and a chance to plan and prepare in advance for next year's tax return.

Over the years, I've found tricks to make tax preparation fun (okay, fun *may be stretching it a bit), and I think I can make the job seem less of a nuisance for you too.*

So come on, choose a nice rainy night when there's nothing good on television, and give it a whirl. Who knows, you may find that you're cut out for this stuff after all.

Chapter 7

The Tax Return Arena

In This Chapter

➤ Making yourself at home with your tax return

➤ Taking the misery out of this job

➤ Planning the tax party

I know you probably think this is going to be awful, and I'm here to tell you that it just doesn't have to be that way. Put a little enthusiasm into your outlook, and this tax stuff can take on a whole new meaning. This chapter helps you try looking at your tax return as a once-a-year cause for celebration. That's right. Celebrate. Why not?

And how long should this celebration last? Plan on spending a few days gathering receipts and documents for your tax return (unless you already have a successful record-keeping system, as described in Chapter 6, "Kill Two Birds: Get Ready for Next Year," in place—in that case, you just need a few minutes to pull out your files and you're ready to begin your tax return!) The preparation time for your tax return, of course, depends on the complexity of the return. Estimate that it will take you three or four hours to actually get numbers onto the income tax forms. And remember that you may need to acquire forms you don't have (but look in Appendix B of this book—you can draft your tax return on these forms while you wait for forms to arrive from the IRS).

A Festive Setting

If you want to ensure that you have a depressing time filling out your tax return, make sure that you have a few burnt-out lightbulbs in the nearby fixtures, leave dirty dinner dishes on the table where you work, let your cup of coffee get cold, send everyone else in the family out to have fun while you sit back in an uncomfortable chair and feel sorry for yourself. That ought to take care of any good mood that you might have been working on.

Alternatively, I suggest the following method for making tax time tolerable, if not downright enjoyable:

➤ **Clear a workspace for yourself that you won't have to use for other purposes for several days.** In other words, don't set up on the kitchen table unless you plan to eat out for a while. Instead, consider setting up a card table or clear a desktop for this purpose.

➤ **Set yourself up in a brightly lit room in pleasant surroundings.** Don't hide yourself away in the basement or the laundry room unless you really like those places. Get out in the open, in a room you spend time in normally, so that you won't feel as if you're being punished when you have to go off and work on your tax return.

➤ **Consider some background music appropriate to your task:**

"Hard Workin' Man"
"Three Coins in a Fountain"
"Take This Job and Shove It"
"I Got Plenty of Nothin'"

➤ **Think about inviting friends.** This is a little touchy because you may not want to share your personal financial situation with the neighborhood, nor they with you. On the other hand, if you promise to not look over each other's shoulders, it can be fun to have a gang over to work on taxes together. (You might even find you have a friend who's experienced with tax preparation and who can help answer questions.) Pool your blank forms and share hard luck stories. Turn what might have been a miserable event into a party.

Get Comfortable

Don't skimp on comfort when approaching this job. If you're physically uncomfortable, you're probably going to be mentally uncomfortable too. Put on your favorite laying-around-the-house casual clothes. Pull up a chair in which you won't mind sitting for a couple of days or evenings. Take occasional breaks to exercise or take a walk so that you don't get stiff or drowsy. Energize yourself for this tax preparation process.

Pizza to Go

Food is really important when preparing your tax return. This is no time to diet. Tax return preparation takes a great deal of energy. Give yourself a food reward for working so hard. Pizza is nice because even if it gets cold while it's sitting on your worktable, it still tastes good.

Don't think about preparing a feast—order out. Let someone else cook since you're going to be working so hard. (Send the bill to the IRS.)

If you've invited friends, you could have a pitch-in, perhaps with a tax-related theme. A menu might include silver dollar pancakes, golden chicken nuggets, penny candy, quarter pounders, millionaire pie, and so on. Be imaginative. Everybody could bring a food that starts with one of the letters: *I, R, S,* or *T, A, X.*

The Least You Need to Know

➤ Set up your tax return operation at a table or desk that you won't need for a few days.

➤ Be sure that you have plenty of light and plenty of space.

➤ Set the mood with music and good food.

➤ Be comfortable.

Tax Tools to Have Before You Sit Down

You have your workspace, you have a healthy feast, you have bright lights, and you even have a group of friends to help share this unforgettable experience. So, what's missing? Let's see…

Tax Return Forms

You need the forms—the paper documents provided at no charge by your friends at the IRS. The forms are the pages on which you translate your life into a pile of numbers. Forms are either numbered (such as 1040, 2106, and 4562) or lettered (such as Schedule A, Schedule B, and Schedule C). And how do you get forms? Refer to Chapter 3, "Where All Those Forms Come From," for the lowdown on finding elusive tax forms.

OOPS!
Last year's blank forms are completely useless to you this year. If you still have some around, don't try to use them for this year's tax return. You can, however, use them for such things as starter in your fireplace or paper for the bottom of your bird cage. Just forget about saving these old forms for future tax returns.

The catch, of course, is figuring out which forms you need. Look at last year's tax return and make a list of each form you used. Make sure that you have all of those forms again, at the very least. Don't forget to check your state income tax return and include those forms on your list too.

Each year the IRS issues new forms and prints the year in the upper-left corner. Make sure that all your forms say 1995 on them.

If you have something new this year that you didn't have last year—maybe you started a new business or maybe you paid for child care for the first time while you worked—you can call the IRS (1-800-TAX-FORM) and ask which forms you will need to report these items. I can't guarantee that they'll tell you every form you'll need (they may tell you that you need a Schedule C for your business, but they may not mention that you need a Schedule SE along with it to compute the self-employment tax), but at least they can help point you in the right direction.

Tax Return Equipment

Here's the stuff you need, the hardware, if you will, to make your tax return preparation go more smoothly:

OOOOH...

By the Way
I don't know about you, but I hate telephone numbers that spell something cute. It takes me forever to find all the letters on my telephone. The worst part is that I'll work through the anagram, figuring out the entire phone number, only to have it be busy. Let me save you the trouble of figuring out *1-800-TAX-FORM*: 1-800-829-3676. You're welcome!

➤ Sharp pencils. Don't write your tax return in ink because the chances of getting the entire thing right the first time are slim.

➤ Pencil sharpener.

➤ Eraser.

➤ Stapler.

➤ Calculator for checking your math.

➤ Stamps for mailing your return (especially if you'll be mailing your return after 5 P.M. on April 15).

➤ File folders, big envelopes, a 3-ring binder with dividers, or some other way of organizing and categorizing your tax receipts.

➤ Change for the local photocopier so you can make a copy of your tax return for your records.

➤ Waste basket.

➤ Blank paper on which to write notes and questions.

If you mail your tax return close to the April 15 deadline, consider taking it to the post office and sending it by certified mail. This way you have a stamped receipt to verify the date on which the tax return was mailed.

Tax Return Records

The Tax Return Records Checklist can help you gather up all the little slips of paper that you need in order to get the correct numbers on your income tax return. For details on what types of receipts make up these major categories included on this checklist, see the complete Handy Tax Receipt Checklist in Chapter 5, "Collecting the Right Information."

Tax Return Records Checklist

Checklist of items to have before beginning to prepare your income tax return.

- ❏ W-2 forms
- ❏ 1099 forms
- ❏ Year-end bank statements
- ❏ K-1 forms
- ❏ Year-end brokers' statements
- ❏ Record of receipts from own business
- ❏ Record of expenditures from business
- ❏ Stock purchase/sale transaction receipts
- ❏ Record of receipts from rental activities
- ❏ Record of expenditures from rental property
- ❏ Record of moving expenses
- ❏ Contributions to retirement plans
- ❏ Amounts spent for child care
- ❏ Social security or Federal ID # of child care providers
- ❏ Medical expenditures
- ❏ Insurance reimbursements for medical expenses
- ❏ Income tax expenses
- ❏ Property tax expenses
- ❏ Annual mortgage statement
- ❏ Charitable contribution amounts (cash)
- ❏ Property donated to charity
- ❏ Documentation of casualty/theft losses
- ❏ Unreimbursed employee business expenses
- ❏ Tax preparation fees

The Most Important Tool

Here it is, the highly technical, top secret information for which you've been waiting. This is the single most important thing you can have with you when prepare your current income tax return:

Last Year's Income Tax Return

By the Way

For noncash contributions, such as donations of clothing and household goods, that you value at $250 or more (see "Charitable Contributions" in Chapter 20 for valuation techniques), be sure you have written documentation to support your contribution. Keep a detailed list of the items you donate and get a signed receipt from the organization accepting the goods.

Don't even attempt to begin this year's tax return without last year's return right by your side.

Can't find last year's 1040? Call 1-800-829-1040. The IRS can send you either a *transcript* of your last year's income tax return at no charge or, for a reasonably small fee, they can send you copies of the actual forms you filed. The transcript isn't as fancy as the actual forms, but it's free, it's fast, and, more importantly, it's all you need.

While you're searching for last year's tax return, poke around and see if you still have tax returns from earlier years. It's a good idea to save your tax returns, keeping them all in a place where they'll be easy to retrieve. Sometime you may need to dig back into an old tax return to correctly report a current tax event. For example, if you sold a home ten years ago and rolled over the gain on the sale (Chapter 14 discusses the tax ramifications of selling your home), when you eventually sell your current home, you will need to look at that old tax return to know how much of the gain on the former sale will be included with the current sale.

The Least You Need to Know

➤ Gather the blank 1995 tax forms you think you'll need in order to prepare this year's income tax return.

➤ Pencils, erasers, trash can, letter opener—mentally put yourself through a dry run of the tax return preparation process and notice the pieces of equipment you will need when you're ready for the real event.

➤ All those little receipts and scraps of paper—now's the time you need them.

➤ DON'T FORGET last year's income tax return!

Chapter 9

The Easy Parts

In This Chapter

➤ Getting started on your tax forms

➤ Filling in all the blanks

➤ Who is the taxpayer? Who is the spouse?

You need to fill out a lot of information on your income tax forms: names, addresses, Social Security numbers, and other miscellaneous stuff that appear on one form or another. Take care of this information up front, and you won't have to worry about it later.

Even if you are still working on figuring out which forms you need for your tax return, you can start with the forms you have gathered together so far. This chapter walks you through the process.

Putting Headings on Your Tax Forms

You must write your name and Social Security number at the top of page 1 of your Form 1040 and on every tax form and schedule you attach to the 1040. If you are married and filing a joint tax return (see Chapter 10, "Your Filing Status," to determine if this applies to you), one of you is the taxpayer and one the spouse. Traditionally speaking, the husband has taken the part of the taxpayer, and the wife has taken the part of the spouse. It doesn't matter, though, who is listed first, just as long as you're consistent from year to year. It creates too much confusion at the IRS if you alternate roles from one year to the next.

Get Down to Brass Tax

Don't underestimate the importance of writing your Social Security number correctly on your income tax forms. The IRS uses your Social Security number to match the income on your tax return with the W-2 forms that your employer has filed, the 1099 forms that the banks and corporations have filed, and other pieces of income that have your Social Security number on them and have trickled into the IRS office. If you put the wrong Social Security number on your tax return, you may find the IRS thinking you are liable for tax on income that was earned by someone else. Check and double-check your Social Security number to make sure that you got it right.

Although both the taxpayer and spouse in a jointly filed tax return put their names on the front of page 1 of the 1040, only the name and Social Security number of the taxpayer appear on the other tax forms.

The taxpayer, the first-named person on page 1 of the 1040 form, is the person whose name appears on nearly every other form in the tax return. The exception to this is when there are forms that specifically relate to the spouse. For example, if the spouse owns a business that is reported on Schedule C, "Profit or Loss from Business," the spouse's name (not the taxpayer's) should appear on the Schedule C as well as any forms related to that Schedule C (such as Schedule SE, "Self-Employment Tax," Form 4562, "Depreciation and Amortization," and others).

Blanks You Can Fill in Without Thinking

By the Way...

If you receive the IRS Forms and Instructions packet in the mail, it will include a sticky label that you can put on top of your tax return. The IRS would prefer that you use this label instead of printing your name and address on page 1 of your 1040. If your address has changed, you can still use this label—just cross out the old address and print the new address right on the label.

In addition to your name and Social Security number, there are other bits of information you can fill out on your tax forms without having to look up anything.

Mailing Address

The address to use on your tax return may seem obvious to you if you receive your mail at your house. But what if you get your mail at a post office box or a business address? The mailing address that goes on your tax return is the address where you receive your mail. This means that if you get your mail at a post office box, or your grandmother's house, or a professional mail service company, that's the address that goes on your tax return. A college student who receives mail at his parents' home should put the parents' address on his tax return.

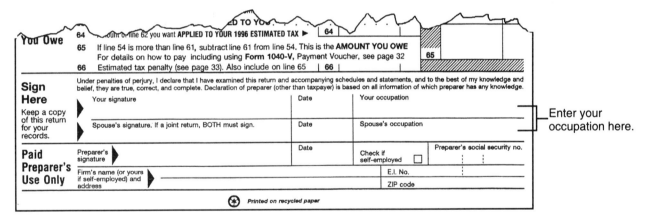

The name and address section of Form 1040. Fill in this section carefully. Mistakes here will slow the processing of your tax return.

Occupation

Down at the bottom of the second page of your Form 1040, at the place where you sign your tax return, you must fill in your occupation. Because there isn't much space here, you may need to abbreviate. Try to describe what you do for a living. You can fill in "student" or "homemaker" or "unemployed" if you don't have a job. It really doesn't matter what you put here. In fact, if you leave it blank, the IRS will still process your tax return.

Your occupation goes at the bottom of page 2 of the 1040. There's no wrong answer here. Use your own words to describe what you do for a living.

Blind, 65 or Over

At the top of page 2 of the Form 1040 you can check a box if you are blind and another box if you are age 65 or over. Checking these boxes can result in a reduced income tax. There's a box to check for each item for the taxpayer and another set for the spouse.

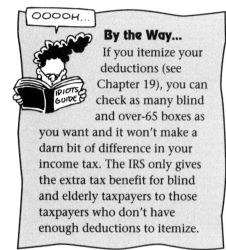

By the Way...

If you itemize your deductions (see Chapter 19), you can check as many blind and over-65 boxes as you want and it won't make a darn bit of difference in your income tax. The IRS only gives the extra tax benefit for blind and elderly taxpayers to those taxpayers who don't have enough deductions to itemize.

The IRS considers you to be blind if your vision in your best eye is no better than 20/200 while wearing glasses or if your field of vision is not more than 20 degrees. You must attach a statement to your tax return from your doctor certifying the condition of your eyesight. If your eyesight is not expected to improve, you do not need to attach the doctor's certification each year—a statement of your own referring back to the first year in which the certification was attached will suffice in future years. If your blindness is expected to be temporary, you must attach a doctor's certification to your tax return each year you claim the deduction for blindness.

Taxpayers who are 65 years old (or older) on January 1, 1996, can claim to be 65 for 1995 and should check the box on page 2 of the Form 1040.

Check these boxes on page 2 of the 1040 if you (and/or your spouse) are blind or at least 65 years old.

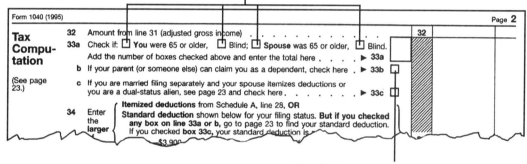

Check this box if someone else has claimed you as a dependent on his or her tax return.

On the second page of the 1040, you specify whether you are over 65 and/or blind, and whether or not someone else (such as a parent) claimed you as a dependent. These choices affect the tax you pay.

Whose Dependent Are You?

If someone else can claim you as a dependent on his or her tax return, then you must check the "If your parent (or someone else) can claim you as a dependent, check here" box at the top of page 2 of your Form 1040. This prevents you from taking an exemption for yourself. Sound like mumbo-jumbo?

Here's an easy example. If you are a student under age 24 and your gross income for the year did not exceed $2,500, and if your parents provide more than half of your living expenses, your parents can probably claim you as a dependent.

The technical definitions of these terms and the precise conditions under which dependency is determined are explained later in this book. Chapter 11, "Dependents," covers the subject of dependents and support. Chapter 22, "Exemptions: Counting the Players," discusses the subject of exemptions.

The Least You Need to Know

➤ Write your name and Social Security number on the top of each tax form.

➤ Write your occupation at the bottom of Form 1040, page 2, taking care not to spend too much time worrying about your job description.

➤ Check appropriate boxes for being blind and over-65 years old in order to qualify for potentially lower taxes if you don't itemize your deductions.

➤ Check the box on the top of page 2 of the 1040 if someone else can claim you as a dependent on his or her tax return.

➤ As you proceed with the preparation of your tax return, each time you find you need a new form, take the time to put your name and Social Security number on the top of the form. Properly headed forms are less likely to look like superfluous extra forms and are more likely to stay with the rest of your tax return.

Chapter 10

Your Filing Status

In This Chapter

➤ Who cares about filing status?

➤ Determining your filing status

➤ Knowing when you have a choice in filing status

➤ Changing your filing status after your tax return is finished

Your *filing status* is similar to your marital status. The purpose of your filing status is to determine which tax rates you will use for computing your income tax, so it's important to know which filing status you are supposed to use. Like all IRS functions, figuring the filing status is just a bit complex. This chapter explains how you can make the best decision for your situation.

Because your filing status is linked to your marital status, it's important to understand that the IRS cares only about your marital status as of the last day of the calendar year.

Not only is your rate of income tax determined by your filing status, but other issues in your tax return can be affected as well. For example, the taxable amount of Social Security and other retirement benefits are determined with the use of your filing status (as discussed in Chapter 15, "Retirement: IRAs and Social Security Benefits"). Some tax credits, such as the earned income credit, the tax credit for the elderly, and the credit for child and dependent care are available to married taxpayers only if they file a joint tax return. (Chapter 24, "Cutting Your Tax with Credits" explains these tax credits.) If you are married, the allowable loss you can take on rental property that you own can be affected by your filing status (see Chapter 16, "Rents, Royalties, and Those Kooky K-1 Forms," for a discussion of rental property).

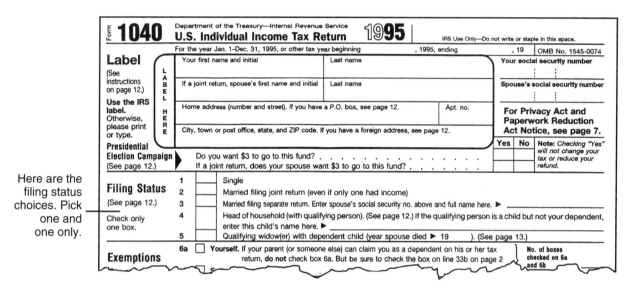

Here are the filing status choices. Pick one and one only.

Choosing a filing status on your primary tax form helps the IRS determine your tax rate.

By the Way

If you and your spouse have been filing jointly and your spouse dies, you may still file a joint return with your deceased spouse for the year of the death. Then, see the "Qualifying Widow or Widower with Dependent Child" section later in this chapter to learn what to do in future years. (Note: If you marry someone else in the same year your spouse dies, you may file a joint return with the new spouse.)

Single

You use the Single filing status if you are unmarried and have no children. You can also use the Single status if you are unmarried and *do* have children, but the Head of Household status, described later in this chapter, might be a better option.

Married Filing Jointly

Most married couples use the Married Filing Jointly filing status. The married couple combines the incomes and deductions of each spouse *on the same tax return*, and one tax is applied to the total. The joint tax rate is lower than the rate for filing separately, so it usually is best to choose the Married Filing Jointly status. However, see the example in the Married Filing Separately section for an occasion when it makes sense for a married couple living together to use the separate rate.

Married Filing Separately

The Married Filing Separately status is used most frequently by separated couples when the husband and wife each want to file his or her own tax returns or in situations where the husband and wife aren't exactly on speaking terms, let alone joint filing terms.

By using the Married Filing Separately filing status, each spouse can file his or her own tax return. The Married Filing Separately tax rates are higher than Single tax rates and attempt to approximate the tax on each person's income that would occur if the couple filed jointly.

Most of the time a couple will save a little money if the Joint status is used instead of the Separate status. Occasionally, however, the Married Filing Separately status can be used advantageously by married couples who are living together, who would normally file jointly, but who have widely divergent levels of income and deductions. Generally speaking, if one spouse incurred most of the deductions, particularly medical and miscellaneous deductions, which are limited by a percentage of adjusted gross income, the tax laws can produce a lower combined tax when the two spouses file separately (these itemized deductions and the ways in which they are limited are discussed in Chapters 19, "Itemized Deductions Most Taxpayers Can Take," and 20, "Counting a Few More Deductions").

If you want to figure out whether it's to your advantage to choose Married Filing Jointly versus Married Filing Separately, here's the trick. If you itemize your deductions (see Chapter 19), the IRS limits your medical, casualty, and miscellaneous deductions based on a percentage of your income. If you file jointly, your income is added to that of your spouse, so the limitation on your deductions is based on a percentage of your combined income.

If one spouse incurred most of the deductions, the couple can file separately and the amount of the limitation on deductions is based on a percentage of the income of the spouse claiming the deductions, rather than the combined income of both spouses. Therefore, a larger amount of deductions can be used to reduce the income before the tax rates are applied. Beware: Both spouses must itemize deductions (as opposed to having one spouse take a standard deduction—see Chapter 21, "The Standard Deduction"), even if one spouse had no deductions with which to itemize.

For example, suppose that a husband had $50,000 in income and his wife had $25,000 in income. Together they had medical expenses of $4,800, and the wife incurred all of them. In addition, they had other itemized deductions of $2,500 in property taxes and $6,400 in mortgage interest—these deductions apply equally to both husband and wife and so are split among the two tax returns. The couple has no children. Tables 10.1 and 10.2 compare the income taxes that this couple would owe if they filed jointly and separately. In Table 10.2, the wife is entitled to the entire deduction for medical expenses, and the rest of the deductions split evenly.

Table 10.1 Tax Computation, Using the Married Filing Jointly Filing Status

Calculation		Joint Income/Deductions
(a)Adjusted Gross Income (AGI)		75,000
(b)Itemized Deductions:		
(c)Medical	4,800	
(d)7.5% AGI Limit	5,625	
(e)Allowable deduction (c – d)	0	
(f)Taxes	2,500	
(g)Interest	6,400	
(h)Total Itemized (e + f + g)	8,900	
(i)Exemptions (2 @ $2,500)	5,000	
(j)Total Reductions to Income (h + i)		13,900
(k)Taxable Income (a – j)		61,100
(l)Income Tax		12,045

Table 10.2 Tax Computation, Using the Married Filing Separately Filing Status

Calculation		Husband	Wife	Total
(a)Adjusted Gross Income		50,000	25,000	75,000
(b)Itemized Deductions:				
(c)Medical	4,800			
(d)7.5% AGI limit	1,875			
(e)Allowable Deduction (c – d)		0	2,925	2,925
(f)Taxes		1,250	1,250	2,500
(g)Interest		3,200	3,200	6,400
(h)Total Itemized (e – g)		4,450	7,375	11,825
(i)Exemptions		2,500	2,500	5,000
(j)Total Reductions to Income		6,950	9,875	16,825
(k)Taxable Income (a – j)		43,050	15,125	58,175
(l)Income Tax		9,526	2,269	11,795

As you can see by comparing Tables 10.1 and 10.2, the change of filing status from Married Filing Jointly to Married Filing Separately saves this couple $250.

If you file a tax return using the Separate status and later decide you wish you had filed with the Joint status, you can prepare an *amended* tax return to change your filing status. (See Chapter 29, "Changing Your Tax Return" for information about amending.) However, if you filed your tax return using the Joint tax status, switching to Separate status is tricky. The IRS will only let you make the switch if you amend the joint return prior to the due date of the return. So, if you file your return in February by using the Joint status, and then realize in March that filing with the Separate status would have saved you some money, you have only until April 15 to amend the joint return and change your status.

> **OOPS!**
> You should carefully consider your situation before switching your filing status from Married Filing Jointly to Married Filing Separately. Most of the time the income tax will be lower if you choose the Joint status.

Head of Household

You can choose to file using the Head of Household filing status if you are not married and have at least one child or relative who can be claimed as your dependent or an unmarried child living with you who can't be claimed as a dependent. What's a dependent? See Chapter 11, "Dependents," for details. Note that your dependent has to be a relative in order for you to qualify for this filing status. Not only that, the dependent has to have lived in your house for at least half of the year. Typically, using this status will result in a lower income tax than using the Single status.

Qualifying Widow or Widower with Dependent Child

For the year your spouse dies, you have the right to file a joint return with your deceased spouse for the year of death that your spouse died, if you did not remarry in that year.

For the years following the year of your spouse's death, you may be able to use joint return rates as a "qualifying widow(er)."

To be considered a "qualifying widow(er)" for your 1995 tax return, you must meet the following conditions:

➤ Your spouse died in 1993 or 1994.

➤ You did not remarry in 1995.

➤ You had the right to file a joint return in the year of your spouse's death.

➤ You have a dependent child who lived in your home for all of 1995 except for temporary absences such as for school or vacations.

➤ You paid for more than half the cost of maintaining your home.

If all the conditions are not satisfied, you may file as a Single taxpayer if you have not remarried or you may qualify to use the Head of Household status.

The Least You Need to Know

➤ The filing status you use is tied closely, though not inextricably, to your marital status. Examine the rules in this chapter if you are uncertain about the best status for yourself.

➤ Single people file with the Single status, but they can consider Head of Household status if they have children. They can also consider Qualifying Widow(er) status if they have children and were recently widowed.

➤ Married people generally file using the Married Filing Jointly status, but sometimes it's advantageous to use the Married Filing Separately status.

➤ If your spouse died during the year, you still may be able to file a joint return for the year of death, and then switch to Qualifying Widow(er) status for the next two years.

➤ If your spouse died and you remarried, choose the status of Married Filing Jointly or Married Filing Separately with your new spouse.

➤ If all this is still confusing, remember to check last year's tax return. Unless your marital or parental standing has changed in the past year, you will probably use the same filing status you used on last year's tax return.

Chapter 11

Dependents

In This Chapter

➤ What is a dependent?

➤ Why should you care about dependents?

➤ Who are your dependents?

You probably take care of lots of people. You might have children in your care, parents or grandparents, cousins, nieces, nephews, maybe you have a foster child, or maybe you've been helping a friend through some hard times.

Usually the IRS cuts you some slack on your income tax if you take care of other people. The people you care for have to qualify as your *dependents* in order for you to list them on page one of your tax return and receive tax benefits for them. This chapter explains how to figure out who qualifies as a dependent, so that you can list all your dependents on your tax returns and count those deductions.

So, What Is a Dependent?

IRSpeak

A *dependent* is a person, usually a relative, for whom you provide at least half of the support. Support includes living expenses such as food, housing, clothing, education, and transportation as well as fun expenses such as movies, trips, ice cream, baseball games, and county fairs. For purposes of your tax return, you can take an *exemption*, a deduction from your income, for each dependent who meets the five tests listed on these pages.

A dependent is someone for whom you provide care. If you provide enough care, by IRS standards, and if the dependent meets certain tests, you can claim an exemption for the dependent and thus reduce your income tax. (See Chapter 22, "Exemptions: Counting the Players," for further discussion of exemptions.) Sounds easy enough, but is it? The IRS has set out a somewhat confusing set of instructions to help you determine who your dependents are for purposes of your income tax return. Herewith, I've layman-ized the rules for your convenience and comprehension. To count as one of your dependents and qualify you to take an exemption, a person must:

➤ Not earn more than $2,500 in total income for the year (but see the following section, "Exception to Rule #1: The Income Test").

➤ Have been supported by you to the tune of at least half of the year's living expenses. Living expenses include such trivial things as food, lodging, medical bills, vacations, books to read, clothes, and so on (but see the following section, "Exception to Rule #2: The Support Test").

➤ Be related to you in at least one of the following ways:

Lineal descendent (child, grandchild, great grandchild, great-great... however many "greats" you need).

Sibling (including step- and half-siblings).

Lineal ancestor (parent, great grandparent, great-great... and on up the trunk of the family tree, step-lineal ancestors included).

Niece, nephew, aunt, or uncle (no relations by marriage allowed— in other words, your mother's brother counts, but not his wife).

In-laws, as opposed to outlaws. (I couldn't resist.)

Anybody else, even if they are not related to you in any way, as long as the person lived in your home for the entire year (this is where your car mechanic and your daughter's boyfriend come under consideration).

➤ Not file a joint tax return and be claimed as your dependent in the same year.

➤ Be a citizen, national, or resident of the United States, a resident of Canada or Mexico, or an alien child whom you have adopted and who lived with you for the entire year.

Exception to Rule #1: The Income Test

When you're figuring out whether someone is your dependent, you can ignore Rule #1 if the person is your child and that child either is under 19 years old by the close of the year or, if the child is a full-time student, under 24 years old by the close of the year. It doesn't matter how much your children earn. They can still be counted as your dependents. (And that makes sense—after all, their income gets taxed at your rates. *"Oh really?"* you say? Check out the Kiddie Tax in Chapter 23, "Figuring the Base Income Tax: Tables and Rates.")

What if a working child who can be claimed as a dependent on his parents' tax return wants to file his own tax return, claim himself as a dependent, and not be claimed as a dependent on the parent's return? Well, too bad. If the parents have the right to claim the child as a dependent, the child cannot claim himself—even if the parents don't claim him. Plain and simple.

Exception to Rule #2: The Support Test

Sometimes more than one taxpayer would have the right to claim someone as a dependent if it weren't for the support test of Rule #2. This happens most often in the case of a child of divorced parents or a relative who is cared for by more than one family member. In these cases there should be a legal document, a *multiple support agreement*, that states who can list the person as a dependent on whose tax return. (Note: A person may be claimed as a dependent on only one tax return, so, for example, if you and your spouse choose the Married Filing Separately filing status, each child and any other dependents you have may only be listed as a dependent on one tax return.)

The general support test rule is that a parent who has custody of a child for most of the year gets to claim the child as a dependent. But, as with seemingly everything in the Land of IRS, there are exceptions to this rule:

➤ A multiple support agreement might be in force. This agreement is a legal document, often developed along with divorce and child custody agreements, that states who claims the child as a dependent.

➤ The parent who has custody of the child can sign away his or her right to the dependency claim. To do this, the parent with custody rights must sign IRS Form 8332, and the parent who doesn't have custody but who is claiming the child as a dependent attaches this form to his or her tax return.

➤ In the old days (before 1985), some divorce decrees included a clause giving the right to claim a child as a dependent to the parent who did not have custody. In return, the parent making the dependent claim was required to provide at least $600 per year for the support of the child ($600 for each child if there is more than one). If this applies to your situation, and you are the parent claiming the child as a dependent, check the box on line 6d of Form 1040.

Check only one box.			Form or... with qualifying person... ...a...or... enter this child's name here. ▶				
	5		Qualifying widow(er) with dependent child (year spouse died ▶ 19). (See page 13.)				

Exemptions

(See page 13.)

If more than six dependents, see page 14.

6a ☐	**Yourself.** If your parent (or someone else) can claim you as a dependent on his or her tax return, **do not** check box 6a. But be sure to check the box on line 33b on page 2
b ☐	**Spouse** . . . .

c	**Dependents:**		**(2)** Dependent's social security number If born in 1995 see page 14	**(3)** Dependent's relationship to you	**(4)** No. of months lived in your home in 1995
	(1) First name	Last name			

d	If your child didn't live with you but is claimed as your dependent under a pre-1985 agreement, check here ▶ ☐	
e	Total number of exemptions claimed	

No. of boxes checked on 6a and 6b

No. of your children on 6c who:
- **lived with you** _____
- **didn't live with you due to divorce or separation (see page 14)** _____

Dependents on 6c not entered above _____

Add numbers entered on lines above ▶ ☐

Income

7	Wages, salaries, tips, etc. Attach Form(s) W-2	
8a	**Taxable** interest income (see page 15). Attach Schedule B if over $400	8a

Check here

Check this box if your right to the dependency claim is a result of a pre-1985 divorce decree.

Why Should You Care About Dependents?

About now, you may be wondering what all the hype is about these dependents. Who cares who gets to claim whom on whose tax return? (I sound like an owl, don't I?) Well, here's the scoop.

HUH?

IRSpeak

An *exemption* reduces your income before you compute income tax (called your *taxable income*). You get one exemption (worth a $2,500 deduction from your taxable income) for yourself, one for your spouse (if you are married and filing jointly), and one for each dependent. You get no exemption for yourself or your spouse if someone else can claim either of you as a dependent.

For each dependent you list on your tax return, you can take an *exemption*. An exemption is a reduction to your taxable income. A reduction in taxable income means a reduction in income tax. That's right—a cash reward from the IRS. A bounty, if you will, in return for supporting friends and family during the year.

For your 1995 tax return, you can reduce your income by $2,500 for each dependent you can claim. You can take an exemption for yourself, your spouse (if you have one), and one for each dependent. So, if you are married and filing a joint return, and you have two dependent children and a mother-in-law you can claim as a dependent because you meet the tests laid out earlier in this chapter, you receive five exemptions. That translates into a reduction of your taxable income of 5×$2,500, or $12,500.

For more information on exemptions, see Chapter 22.

Will the Real Dependents Please Stand Up?

Okay, you've read the rules. But who *really* are your dependents? Determining how many dependents you have may be as simple as checking the nursery and counting heads in the playpen. Sometimes, however, the number of names to list on page 1 of your tax return is a little more involved.

All your dependents get listed in the "Dependents" section of page 1 of the 1040 form. Here are some pointers in figuring out whose names to write down.

Only one exemption is available for each person. If you can be claimed as a dependent on someone else's tax return, you can't take an exemption for yourself on your own tax return. This happens most often in the case of children who work, have income, and file their own income tax returns, but are still claimed as dependents on their parents' tax return.

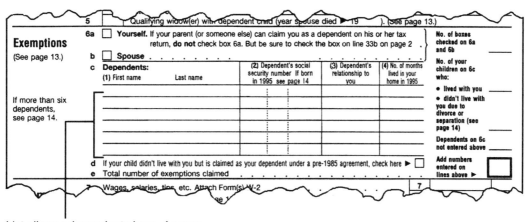

List all your dependents here. Anyone who is one year old or older needs a Social Security number.

The Dependents section of Form 1040.

The Family Head Count

For starters, take care of the easy part. There are boxes on the front of the 1040 form to check for you and your spouse. This is not to say that you are your spouse's dependent (just think of the arguments that might arise from that contention). Checking these boxes enables you to take exemptions for yourself (and possibly your spouse). Check the "Yourself" box (unless someone else is claiming you as a dependent) and the "Spouse" box, if you have a spouse who is not claimed as a dependent on another tax return. Do not check the "Spouse" box if you and your spouse are filing separate income tax returns.

Your children who live with you (under 19 years old) and those who are full-time students (under 24 years old), if they are still in your care, get listed as dependents. Other folks living under your roof count as dependents as long as they meet the tests set out previously in this chapter.

Second Cousins, Three Times Removed

Relatives don't have to live in your house to count as dependents, but some people you might think of as relatives don't necessarily pass muster with the IRS. Remember that to be considered a relative for purposes of dependency, a person must occupy a branch on your family tree. People hanging from the branches because they married into the family rather than being born into it don't count. Step- and half-relatives, however, get automatic family-tree branch status.

Examples of relatives who would count as dependents include

➤ Aunt Isabel, your elderly aunt who lives in a nursing home. You pay for at least half of her living expenses even though she doesn't live with you.

➤ Cousin Miranda who lives in a trailer with 30 cats and hasn't worked a day in her life. You pay for the trailer and other expenses, at least half of her support.

➤ Your dad who lives alone. You split the cost of his care equally with your two brothers and you get to claim him as a dependent due to the terms of a Multiple Support Agreement.

Examples of relatives who would not count as dependents include

➤ Your brother who needed a large loan last year. You made the loan, which was large enough to exceed half of his support for the year, but you expect repayment. You're not providing support as far as the IRS is concerned.

➤ Your daughter, age 22, who lives alone and is not a student. You bought her an expensive car and lots of nice clothing and what thanks do you get? None—at least not from the IRS.

Friends, Neighbors, Romans, Countrymen

You don't have to be related to a person you claim as a dependent, but there is a stricter test to meet if you are not relatives. Nonrelatives must live in your house *all year* in order to achieve dependent status. In addition, the test of providing at least half the support of the person has to be met, and the potential dependent cannot have earned more than $2,500 all year.

Examples of nonrelatives who would count as dependents include

➤ A family friend who lost her job, gave up her home, and moved in with you while getting her life back in order—she lived with you all year and you provided at least half of her support.

➤ Your next-door neighbors move away but their child wants to finish high school in the community. You agree to let the child stay with you and attend school. The child lives with you for an entire calendar year and you provide at least half of the child's support.

Examples of nonrelatives who would not count as dependents include

➤ Your favorite auto mechanic, even if it some days seems as if you must be providing more than half of his support.

➤ An exchange student living with you while participating in an educational exchange program.

The Least You Need to Know

➤ Family members and others for whom you provide care might qualify as dependents.

➤ Dependents must meet five IRS tests in order for you to take an exemption on your tax return.

➤ Exemptions are good! They reduce your income and thus your income tax.

Part 3
What's So Gross About Income?

"'I would,' says Fox, 'a tax devise
That shall not fall on me.'
'Then tax receipts,' Lord North replies,
'For those you never see.'"

Richard Brinsley Sheridan

Almost everybody has income of some sort: income from jobs, income from earnings on savings, income from selling things, income from winning contests, and more. If money comes your way, you can bet that the IRS thinks you have income, and they want to hear about it.

Some income is easy to spot: checks from your place of employment, a pocketful of cash for selling your car, or interest on your savings account. Other income is sneaky; you don't always know where to look for it. Income that's hard to find includes reinvested dividends from mutual funds, income from selling your house (even if you bought another house and never saw any cash), income from benefits you received from your employer, such as retirement contributions and health insurance.

In this part of the book you'll learn about many types of income, if the income is subject to income tax, and how to report the income on your tax return.

AAAAAAHH!!

Chapter 12

W-2 and 1099 Forms

In This Chapter

➤ The W-2 form and how to read it

➤ Sharing your savings account interest with the IRS

➤ Reporting sales of stocks

➤ Receiving change from your withholding

➤ Taxing news for alimony recipients

You wouldn't think it would be so hard to report your income on a tax return. Your friends in Washington have tried, unsuccessfully, to write meaningful and decipherable instructions for reporting income. Now it's my turn to give it a shot.

This chapter explains what are probably the most common forms on income: W-2 wages and interest and dividend income which is reported to you on 1099 forms.

Rounding the Numbers on Your Tax Return

Before you start entering numbers on your tax return, know that you have the option of rounding your numbers to the nearest dollar. It's okay if you want to put cents with your tax return amounts, but the cents are completely optional.

If you choose to round your numbers, round them like this: Any number that contains 50 cents or more gets rounded up to the next dollar. Any number containing less than 50 cents does not get rounded up. For example, if you round the following numbers, here's what you will get:

Number	Gets Rounded To
1,234.75	1,235
1,234.55	1,235
1,234.50	1,235
1,234.49	1,234
1,234.40	1,234
1,234.00	1,234

If you decide to round numbers on your tax return, be consistent. Round *all* the numbers on your tax return. Don't place cents in some places and rounded numbers in others.

Rounding goes for your tax computation too. If you round all the numbers on your tax return, compute your tax and your tax doesn't come out to an even dollar, you should round your tax as well.

Somebody Has to Work for a Living

OOPS!

If you don't receive a W-2 form from one of your employers, call the person who takes care of payroll where you work (or worked). If you can't get the employer to agree to send your W-2 form, and it's past January, call the IRS at 800-829-1040. Be prepared to give the IRS your employer's name and address, and they will contact your employer on your behalf.

If you have a job, chances are you also have a W-2 form. The W-2 form is the three- or four-part piece of paper you get in January or February that tells you how much you earned at your job last year.

If you had more than one job during 1995, you should receive a W-2 form for each job. If you moved during the year, be sure to inform your employer(s) of your new address so that they can send the form to the proper location.

The IRS gets a copy of your W-2 form, just like you do. Not only do they get the form, they actually cross-check the W-2 forms they receive with the tax returns you file. Failure to report W-2 income on your tax return will trigger a "Didn't you forget something?" letter from the IRS. If that happens to you, check the letter the IRS sent you and see if you agree with what they say you should have reported on your tax return. There may be a request for additional payment. If you agree, send in the payment and you won't have to do anything else. If you disagree with the changes the IRS has made to your tax return, you will need to *amend* your income tax return to include the W-2 income you omitted. See Chapter 29, "Changing Your Tax Return," for information on amending tax returns.

Where Do All These Numbers Go?

If you look carefully at your W-2 form, you will notice that each little box on the form has a tiny letter or number in it. (See the nearby sample W-2 form.) Use those letters and numbers as a guide to follow along next as I try to explain what all the W-2 stuff means and where you should put the W-2 numbers on your tax return 1040, 1040A, or 1040EZ form. (Note: Some of the boxes on your W-2 will be blank. Don't think you've been cheated, that just means those particular items don't apply to you.)

a Control number BE45789	22222	Void ☐	For Official Use Only ▶ OMB No. 1545-0008		
b Employer's identification number 17-1717171				1 Wages, tips, other compensation 35,000.00	2 Federal income tax withheld 6540.00
c Employer's name, address, and ZIP code Ridge Top Associates 1035 Ridge Top Road Weyant, PA 54545				3 Social security wages 36,500.00	4 Social security tax withheld 2,263.00
				5 Medicare wages and tips 36,500.00	6 Medicare tax withheld 529.25
				7 Social security tips	8 Allocated tips
d Employee's social security number 444-44-4444				9 Advance EIC payment	10 Dependent care benefits
e Employee's name (first, middle initial, last) Madeline Perry 123 Freedom Way Weyant, PA 54545				11 Nonqualified plans	12 Benefits included in box 1
				13 See Instrs. for box 13	14 Other
				15 Statutory employee ☐ Deceased ☐ Pension plan ☑ Legal rep. ☐ Hshld. emp. ☐ Subtotal ☐ Deferred compensation ☐	
f Employee's address and ZIP code					
16 State Employer's state I.D. No. PA 0015946BB	17 State wages, tips, etc. 35,000.00	18 State income tax 825.00	19 Locality name	20 Local wages, tips, etc.	21 Local income tax

Cat. No. 10134D   Department of the Treasury—Internal Revenue Service

Form **W-2** Wage and Tax Statement **1995**

Copy A For Social Security Administration

For Paperwork Reduction Act Notice, see separate instructions.

The W-2 form.

> **a Control number.** Ignore this; it has nothing to do with you.
>
> **Void.** If this box is checked, you received the wrong W-2 form. Call your employer and ask for another one.
>
> **b Employer's identification number.** Ignore this; it has nothing to do with you.

c Employer's name, address, and ZIP code. Ignore this; it doesn't go anywhere on your income tax form.

d Employee's Social Security number. Check, double-check, and triple-check this number. Make sure that your employer used your correct Social Security number. If there is an error, return the W-2 form to your employer and ask him or her to (1) void this W-2 form and file that void with the IRS and (2) issue a new W-2 form with your correct Social Security number.

e Employee's name. Check the name to make sure that you didn't get a W-2 that belongs to someone else.

f Employee's address and ZIP code. It's not a serious problem if the incorrect address appears here. It's a good idea, however, to notify your employer that his or her records are incorrect. You wouldn't want your big bonus check mailed to the wrong address....

1 Wages, tips, other compensation. This amount should go on line 7 of your 1040 or 1040A (line 1 if you file 1040EZ).

2 Federal income tax withheld. This amount goes on line 55 of your 1040 (line 29a of the 1040A, line 7 of the 1040EZ).

3 Social Security wages. Ignore this; it doesn't go anywhere on your income tax form.

4 Social Security tax withheld. Ignore this; it doesn't go anywhere on your income tax form.

By the Way

If you have more than one W-2 form, combine the dollar amounts on all forms and place the total on your income tax return. For example, suppose that you have three W-2 forms. Add the amounts in box 1 of each W-2 form to come up with a total for wages. This total is the amount that goes on line 7 of your income tax return.

5 Medicare wages and tips. Ignore this; it doesn't go anywhere on your income tax form.

6 Medicare tax withheld. Ignore this; it doesn't go anywhere on your income tax form.

7 Social Security tips. Ignore this; it doesn't go anywhere on your income tax form.

8 Allocated tips. Allocated tips must be reported on line 7 of Form 1040 unless you can prove that you received a smaller amount.

9 Advance EIC payment. This amount goes on line 52 of your Form 1040 (line 26 of the 1040A; you can't use a Form 1040EZ if you received an advance EIC payment). Chapter 24, "Cutting Your Tax with Credits," gives you more detailed information about the Earned Income Credit.

10 Dependent care benefits. Report this amount on line 11 of Part III of Form 2441 (if you file Form 1040A, report this amount on line 11 of part III of Schedule 2; you can't file Form 1040EZ if you have an amount in this box).

11 Nonqualified plans. Ignore this; it doesn't go anywhere on your income tax form.

12 Benefits included in box 1. The amount in this box represents taxable benefits your employer paid to you or provided you with during the year. You don't have to report this as income; it's already included in your total wages. *However*, some of this may not actually be taxable to you. Get a statement from your employer itemizing what makes up this number, then determine if any of this amount is deductible. For example, suppose that your employer provided you with a car. The total value of your automobile usage may be reported here. Only the personal part of your usage is income to you. The business part is a deduction. It's up to you to figure this out. (But I can help! See "Car and Truck Expenses" in Chapter 13 "Do It Yourself on Schedule C.")

13 Coded items. Any amount that appears in this box will have a letter code from A to P listed next to it. Here's what each of those codes means:

A. Add this amount to the total on line 54 of your Form 1040, and write **UNCOLLECTED TAX** in the space to the left of the total on line 54.

B. Add this amount to the total on line 54 of your Form 1040, and write **UNCOLLECTED TAX** in the space to the left of the total on line 54.

C. Ignore this; it doesn't go anywhere on your income tax form.

D. Ignore this; it doesn't go anywhere on your income tax form.

E. Ignore this; it doesn't go anywhere on your income tax form.

F. Ignore this; it doesn't go anywhere on your income tax form.

G. Ignore this; it doesn't go anywhere on your income tax form.

H. Ignore this; it doesn't go anywhere on your income tax form.

I. Fooled you! There is no "I" code.

J. Ignore this; it doesn't go anywhere on your income tax form.

K. The code 'K' amount is an extra tax that must be included on line 54 (total tax) of Form 1040. Write **EPP** in the space to the left of line 54.

OOPS!
The total of amounts coded D through H in box 13 of your W-2 form represents your contributions to tax-deferred retirement plans. If the total of these amounts combined from all your W-2 forms exceeds $9,240, add the excess to your wages on line 7 of your 1040 income tax form. You have to do this yourself. The excess contribution has not been included with your wages in box 1 of the W-2.

OOPS!
There are times when the combined allowable contributions to tax-deferred retirement plans can exceed $9,240 and not cause an increase to your taxable income. If your contribution exceeds $9,240 and you participate in more than one retirement plan, or if you participate in a tax-sheltered annuity plan, or if you're just not sure if the excess contribution is tax-deferred, call an accountant.

L. Ignore this; it doesn't go anywhere on your income tax form.

M. Add this amount to the total on line 54 of your Form 1040, and write **UNCOLLECTED TAX** in the space to the left of the total on line 54.

N. Add this amount to the total on line 54 of your Form 1040, and write **UNCOLLECTED TAX** in the space to the left of the total on line 54.

P. Ignore this; it doesn't go anywhere on your income tax form.

14 Other. Miscellaneous informative messages from your employer. You probably won't see anything such as "Thanks for doing such a nice job!" here. It's more likely your employer will use this space to mention some of the benefits the company paid on your behalf that didn't fit into any of the categories in box 13. Usually this means things that were included in your income in box 1 of the W-2 form but that you can deduct on your income tax return. For example, if your employer paid for your union dues, the amount will already have been added to your income in box 1, and you can take a deduction for this dues amount if you itemize your deductions on Schedule A. If there is something in this box you don't understand, check with your employer.

15 Check boxes. Some of these boxes might be checked on your W-2 form. Information from these boxes doesn't go anywhere on your income tax form.

16 State. The name of the state in which your income is taxable appears here. Unless you live in a state that doesn't require filing a state income tax return (Alaska, Florida, Nevada, South Dakota, Washington, Texas, and Wyoming), you should file a state income tax return for this state. If you have more than one state listed, you may have to file more than one state income tax return.

17 State wages, tips, etc. This is the amount of income you should report on your state income tax return.

18 State income tax. This is the amount of state income tax that was withheld from your wages. If you itemize your deductions on Schedule A of your federal tax return, this amount gets added to line 5 of Schedule A. (See Chapter 19, "Itemized Deductions Most Taxpayers Can Take," for more information about itemizing.) This amount also goes on your state income tax return on the line that asks for your 1995 state tax withholding.

19 Locality name. If you are subject to local taxes (city taxes, county taxes, and so on), the name of the local taxing authority appears here. You may have to prepare a separate income tax return for the locality. In some states the local taxes are paid right along with the state taxes on the state income tax form.

20 Local wages, tips, etc. If you file a local income tax form, this is the amount of income you should report on that tax return.

21 Local income tax. This is the amount of local income tax that was withheld from your wages. If you itemize your deductions on Schedule A of your federal tax return, this amount is added to line 5 of Schedule A. (See Chapter 19 for more information about itemizing.) This amount also goes on your local income tax return (or on your state income tax return, if your local and state taxes are reported on the same form) on the line that asks for your 1995 local tax withholding.

Whew! That's it!

Get Down to Brass Tax

Each year you read about W-2 forms that were prepared and filed with the wrong Social Security number. Two digits were transposed, or the typist had his or her fingers on the wrong keys while typing the Social Security number. No matter how it happens, it happens frequently. When the W-2 form gets to the IRS, the IRS looks at the Social Security number and sees that it belongs to someone named John Templeton in St. Charles, Illinois, even though the name on the form might read Lynne Rock in Rockville, Maryland. It really doesn't matter whose name is on the form. The IRS only reads as far as the Social Security number. Lynne Rock may report the income properly on her income tax return (and that's okay with the IRS), but John Templeton is going to receive a notice from the IRS saying that he forgot to report this income on his tax form. If you double-check your Social Security number on your W-2 forms, you could prevent many of these problems of mistaken income allocation.

What Do You Do if Your W-2 Form Is (Choose One: Wrong, Lost, Illegible, Irreparably Damaged)?

It happens. W-2 forms are chewed up by the dog, swallowed in the vacuum cleaner, thrown out with the junk mail, smeared with whipping cream (I don't think I want to know how that happened...). Don't despair! W-2 forms are remarkably easy to replace.

First of all, if all you lost is, for example, the federal copy (Copy B) of your W-2, just photocopy one of the remaining pages (Copy 2, which goes with your state tax return, or Copy C, the copy for your records). It really doesn't matter which copy is attached to which tax form, so if your W-2 came with an extra copy of Copy 2, you can stick that copy on your federal tax return. If you don't have enough pages of your W-2 to go around to your tax returns, photocopy one of the pages you do have.

a Control number BE45789		OMB No. 1545-0008	This information is being furnished to the Internal Revenue Service. If you are required to file a tax return, a negligence penalty or other sanction may be imposed on you if this income is taxable and you fail to report it.	
b Employer's identification number 17-1717171			1 Wages, tips, other compensation 35,000.00	2 Federal income tax withheld 6,540.00
c Employer's name, address, and ZIP code Ridge Top Associates 1035 Ridge Top Road Weyant, PA 54545			3 Social security wages 36,500.00	4 Social security tax withheld 2,263.00
			5 Medicare wages and tips 36,500.00	6 Medicare tax withheld 529.25
			7 Social security tips	8 Allocated tips
d Employee's social security number 444-44-4444			9 Advance EIC payment	10 Dependent care benefits
e Employee's name, address, and ZIP code Madeline Perry 123 Freedom Way Weyant, PA 54545			11 Nonqualified plans	12 Benefits included in box 1
			13 See Instrs. for box 13	14 Other

15 Statutory employee	Deceased	Pension plan ✕	Legal rep.	Hshld. emp.	Subtotal	Deferred compensation

16 State	Employer's state I.D. No.	17 State wages, tips, etc.	18 State income tax	19 Locality name	20 Local wages, tips, etc.	21 Local income tax
PA	001594688	35,000.00	825.00			

Department of the Treasury—Internal Revenue Service

The copy indicator on the W-2. ➤

Form W-2 Wage and Tax Statement **1995**

Copy C For EMPLOYEE'S RECORDS (See Notice on back.)

This copy goes to the IRS. Attach it to your 1040. (Hmmm, let's see. The customer's copy has to be here somewhere….)

If the W-2 form is completely lost or irretrievably destroyed, call the employer who issued the W-2 form. The employer may either type up a new W-2 form for you or just make a copy of the form the company already gave you. There's really nothing special about the quality of the W-2 form that is attached to your tax return, so it's perfectly all right for your employer to photocopy a copy of your form (the employer keeps a replica of the form sent to you) and give that copy to you. For that matter, if the employer writes out a new W-2 form by hand, that's okay too.

Getting Change from Your W-2

If you have more than one employer, there is a chance that too much Social Security tax has been withheld. The most Social Security tax that can be withheld from all your employers is $3,794.40. If your Social Security withholdings add up to more than this amount, put the excess on line 59 of page 2 of your Form 1040. This amount will go toward any tax you owe, and if you are entitled to a refund, this excess Social Security will increase your refund.

A Neat W-2 Form Trick

The setting: It's the afternoon of April 15, you're putting the final touches on your income tax return before mailing it, and you don't have a clue as to where your W-2 form is hiding.

As long as you know the numbers that were on the W-2 form (and you can call your employer and double-check those amounts), just type or write a simple statement that includes your name and Social Security number, your employer's name and address, and the crucial amounts that were on the form: wages, federal income tax withheld, state income tax withheld, local income tax withheld. Attach this to your tax return and mail everything to the IRS. Don't let yourself miss the April 15 deadline just because you can't find your W-2 form.

Interest and Dividends

You may be fortunate enough to have some cash tucked away, steadily earning interest in a savings account, or regularly generating dividend checks. It's a nice feeling, eleven months out of the year, knowing that your money is earning money of its own, adding to your retirement coffers, or helping you save for your child's college education or a nice vacation.

Then April arrives. What's this? The IRS wants to know how much your investments earned and wants to take a piece of that nest egg? As improper and invasive as that may seem, it's true. No income hides from the IRS.

The Schedule B

If you file the 1040, transfer your interest and dividend income to Schedule B, and then add it all up. If neither total exceeds $400, you are technically free from including this form with your federal income tax return. Does this mean that if you aren't required to file a Schedule B, you are free from reporting the interest and dividend income on your federal income tax return? Never! Even if your total interest or dividend income is only $1 you must still report it on your tax return. You just don't have to document it on Schedule B.

> OOOOH...
>
> **By the Way**
> You might as well fill out the Schedule B even if you don't have enough dividends or interest to get over the $400 hump that requires your filing this form with your tax return. A filled-out Schedule B makes a nice summary of all your dividend and interest income, something you can save as a reference for preparing next year's tax return.

Schedules A&B (Form 1040) 1995 — OMB No. 1545-0074 — Page **2**

Name(s) shown on Form 1040. Do not enter name and social security number if shown on other side. | Your social security number

Schedule B—Interest and Dividend Income
Attachment Sequence No. **08**

Part I
Interest Income

(See pages 15 and B-1.)

Note: If you received a Form 1099-INT, Form 1099-OID, or substitute statement from a brokerage firm, list the firm's name as the payer and enter the total interest shown on that form.

Note: *If you had over $400 in taxable interest income, you must also complete Part III.*

1 List name of payer. If any interest is from a seller-financed mortgage and the buyer used the property as a personal residence, see page B-1 and list this interest first. Also, show that buyer's social security number and address ▶ | **Amount**

1 |

2 Add the amounts on line 1 . . . . | 2 |
3 Excludable interest on **series EE** U.S. savings bonds **issued** after 1989 from Form 8815, line 14 You MUST attach Form 8815 to Form . . . . . . | 3 |
4 Subtract line 3 from line 2. Enter the result here and on Form 1040, line 8a ▶ | 4 |

Part II
Dividend Income

(See pages 16 and B-1.)

Note: If you received a Form 1099-DIV or substitute statement from a brokerage firm, list the firm's name as the payer and enter the total dividends shown on that form.

Note: *If you had over $400 in gross dividends and/or other distributions on stock, you must also complete Part III.*

5 List name of payer. Include gross dividends and/or other distributions on stock here. Any capital gain distributions and nontaxable distributions will be deducted on lines 7 and 8 ▶ | **Amount**

5 |

6 Add the amounts on line 5 . . . . | 6 |
7 Capital gain distributions. Enter here and on Schedule D* . | 7 |
8 Nontaxable distributions. (See the inst. for Form 1040, line 9.) | 8 |
9 Add lines 7 and 8 . . . . | 9 |
10 Subtract line 9 from line 6. Enter the result here and on Form 1040, line 9 . ▶ | 10 |

*If you do not need Schedule D to report any other gains or losses, enter your capital gain distributions on Form 1040, line 13. Write "CGD" on the dotted line next to line 13.

If either of these amounts is at least $400 you must include this form with your federal income tax return.

Part III
Foreign Accounts and Trusts

(See page B-2.)

If you had over $400 of interest or dividends **or** had a foreign account or were a grantor of, or a transferor to, a foreign trust, you must complete this part. | Yes | No

11a At any time during 1995, did you have an interest in or a signature or other authority over a financial account in a foreign country, such as a bank account, securities account, or other financial account? See page B-2 for exceptions and filing requirements for Form TD F 90-22.1 . . . .

b If "Yes," enter the name of the foreign country ▶

12 Were you the grantor of, or transferor to, a foreign trust that existed during 1995, whether or not you have any beneficial interest in it? If "Yes," you may have to file Form 3520, 3520-A, or 926 .

For Paperwork Reduction Act Notice, see Form 1040 instructions. — Printed on recycled paper — Schedule B (Form 1040) 1995

The Schedule B.

1099 Forms in All Shapes and Sizes

Interest income comes from your investments in banks, credit unions, and other financial institutions, in the form of savings accounts and other interest-bearing accounts, investments in bonds, and loans owed to you. Dividend income comes from your investment in corporations in the form of stock ownership. Interest income and dividend income are reported to you on forms called *1099-INT* and *1099-DIV*. (See the nearby sample 1099-INT form.) Although the IRS spent a lot of time and resources (and your tax dollars) designing nice little 1099 forms for payers of interest and dividends to fill out, many companies have decided to make their own 1099 forms. Therefore it's difficult to say what your 1099 will look like.

9292	☐ VOID	☐ CORRECTED		
PAYER'S name, street address, city, state, and ZIP code	Payer's RTN (optional)	OMB No. 1545-0112		
		1995 Form **1099-INT**		**Interest Income**
PAYER'S Federal identification number	RECIPIENT'S identification number	1 Interest income not included in box 3 $		**Copy A** **For**
RECIPIENT'S name		2 Early withdrawal penalty $	3 Interest on U.S. Savings Bonds and Treas. obligations $	**Internal Revenue Service Center** **File with Form 1096.**
Street address (including apt. no.)		4 Federal income tax withheld $		For Paperwork Reduction Act Notice and instructions for completing this form, see **Instructions for Forms 1099, 1098, 5498, and W-2G.**
City, state, and ZIP code		5 Foreign tax paid	6 Foreign country or U.S. possession	
Account number (optional)	2nd TIN Not. ☐	$		
Form **1099-INT**		Cat. No. 14410K		Department of the Treasury - Internal Revenue Service

The "official" 1099-INT form.

If you receive a statement in the mail that tells you about the earnings you or your investments received during 1995, look all around the form for the numbers **1099** followed by **INT** or **DIV**. Sometimes the form will look like a bank statement instead of a special IRS form. If you don't see 1099 anywhere on the form, there's probably yet another form on the way.

You should only receive one 1099 form for each of your investments or savings accounts.

Sometimes banks don't actually issue 1099 forms at the end of the year. Instead, on the December 31 statement, they include a phrase such as, "Total interest income for 1995." This is the amount you will transfer to Schedule B.

OOPS!

The IRS gets copies of your 1099 forms. Not only do they receive copies of the forms, they cross-reference the 1099 forms with your income tax return. If you fail to report some of your 1099 interest or dividend income, chances are good that the IRS will catch the discrepancy between their copies of forms and the amount you reported. Then you can look forward to exchanging friendly correspondence with the IRS while they encourage you to report all your income.

If you earned less than $10 in interest or dividend income from an investment, you may not get a 1099 form in the mail. The companies that paid the interest and dividends aren't required to send you a 1099 unless the amount you earned is at least $10. This doesn't mean you don't have to report the income from these low-paying investments. **It's your responsibility to know what you earned and report everything on your income tax return, whether or not you receive a statement in the mail.**

Your interest income gets reported on Schedule B, as shown in the figure on this page. Remember, if your total interest income is less than $400 (and your total dividend income, discussed below, is also less than $400), this form is optional.

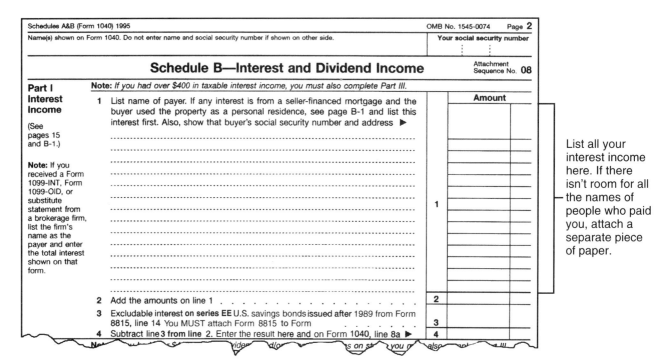

The Interest Income section of Schedule B.

If you receive interest on a personal loan, you probably won't receive a 1099 form. Suppose that you loaned your best friend, Jim, $1,000 and he agreed to pay you 10% interest. Jim repaid the loan by giving you $1,100. You must report the $100 interest income on your income tax return. List it with your other interest income on Schedule B, if you are filing that form, otherwise add it to the rest of your interest income and put it on line 8 of page one of your federal income tax return.

The 1099-DIV

Similar to the 1099-INT form, which shows you the interest your investments earned for you last year, the 1099-DIV form shows you the dividend income you earned during the past year from your ownership of stock.

9191	☐ VOID	☐ CORRECTED			
PAYER'S name, street address, city, state, and ZIP code		**1a** Gross dividends and other distributions on stock (Total of 1b, 1c, 1d, and 1e) $	OMB No. 1545-0110 19**95**	**Dividends and Distributions**	Several types of dividends are reported on this form.
		1b Ordinary dividends $	Form **1099-DIV**		
PAYER'S Federal identification number	RECIPIENT'S identification number	**1c** Capital gain distributions $	**2** Federal income tax withheld $	**Copy A**	
RECIPIENT'S name		**1d** Nontaxable distributions $	**3** Foreign tax paid $	**For Internal Revenue Service Center**	
Street address (including apt. no.)		**1e** Investment expenses $	**4** Foreign country or U.S. possession	**File with Form 1096.**	
City, state, and ZIP code		**Liquidation Distributions**		For Paperwork Reduction Act Notice and instructions for completing this form, see **Instructions for Forms 1099, 1098, 5498, and W-2G.**	
Account number (optional)	2nd TIN Not. ☐	**5** Cash $	**6** Noncash (Fair market value) $		
Form **1099-DIV**		Cat. No. 14415N	Department of the Treasury - Internal Revenue Service		

A sample 1099-DIV form.

Reading the Broker's Statement

Stock brokerage firms such as Merrill Lynch, Shearson, and others keep track of all your stock sales and purchases and the dividends earned on same. At the end of the year, instead of getting a separate 1099-DIV form in the mail from each company in which you own stock, the brokerage firm sends you one statement that summarizes all your transactions for the year. Expect to see all your stock dividends listed on this form as well as amounts earned by mutual funds, purchases of stock, sales of stock, purchases and sales of shares in mutual funds, and a summary of the investments you still own at the end of the year. This form is your 1099-DIV and the IRS received a copy of this form.

If you earn dividends from several companies and they are all reported on one statement from your broker, you only have to list the broker's name on your Schedule B with the total amount earned.

Unlike the 1099 form, the broker's statement doesn't usually have little boxes on it that easily identify which numbers are reported on your tax return. Instead, you are expected to actually *read* the broker's statement, and upon doing so you will find statements such as, "Total dividend income for 1995" or "Total interest income for 1995" or "Tax-exempt interest for 1995" (see the next section, "Tax-Exempt Interest" for more insight on what to do with this stuff). If you purchased or sold stocks or shares in mutual funds during the year you may have information about these transactions on your broker's statement. You will report sales of stocks on Schedule D instead of Schedule B (see Chapter 14, "Capital C, Capital G, Capital Gain (or Loss)," for more information).

> **OOOOH...**
>
> **By the Way**
> 1099-INT and 1099-DIV forms don't get attached to your tax return like W-2 forms do. These forms are for your records. Be sure to keep all your 1099 forms in a safe place along with other statements and receipts that you used as the basis for determining your taxable income. See "The Basement's Getting Full" in Chapter 6 for information on how long to save your tax return records.

Tax-Exempt Interest

Some interest income is exempt from federal income taxation. This favored status applies primarily to income from investments in state or local municipal bonds (accountants and other tax nerds call these *munis*, which rhymes with *gooneys*). Interest earned on municipal bonds is usually exempt from state income tax as well as federal income tax, if the bond was issued in your state.

OOPS!
Interest earned on investments in U.S. Treasury bonds, bills, notes, and zero coupon Treasury bonds is taxable on your federal income tax return but exempt from state and local income taxation.

If you earned interest that is exempt from federal income tax, why do you need to report it on your income tax return? This may seem kind of silly because you don't have to pay tax on it. Actually the IRS uses information about your tax-exempt interest for a couple of calculations:

➤ The amount of tax-exempt interest you earn from certain "private activity bonds" is used to determine your alternative minimum tax. See Chapter 25, "Other Kinds of Taxes (Including Taxes on Income You Didn't Know You Had)," for information about this strange tax.

➤ The amount of tax-exempt interest you earn is used to calculate how much of your Social Security income is taxable.

Tax-Deferred Interest Income

Tax-deferred interest income is not the same thing as tax-exempt interest income. Investments in tax-deferred annuities, IRAs, and some other forms of retirement funds can earn interest that is not subject to federal income tax...*this year*. At some point, down the road, when you retire and begin to withdraw the money from your retirement fund, you will pay income tax on the earnings of that fund as well as on any contributions you made which are currently excluded from your income.

Interest earned on tax-deferred retirement accounts is not included with tax-exempt interest income on page 1 of your federal income tax return. See Chapter 18, "Adjustments to Income," for more information on this topic.

Bizarre Dividends

The 1099-DIV you receive, or the broker's statement that tells you about the dividends you earned, may include a breakdown of exactly what type of dividends with which you are dealing. Usually, dividends represent a portion of a company's income that is being shared with all the people who own the company's stock (the shareholders). This income that has been passed on to you is added to the rest of your income and you pay tax on it. Sometimes, however, dividends receive special treatment. For that reason, there are a few special ways in which you can refer to dividend income: gross dividends, ordinary dividends, capital gain distributions, and nontaxable distributions. Here's the scoop on all of these strange bedfellows.

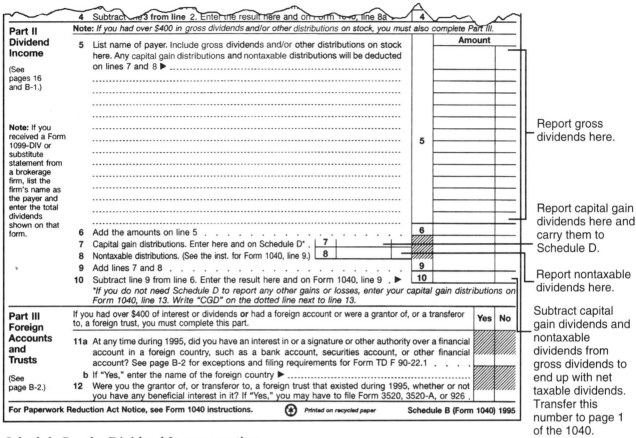

Schedule B—the Dividend Income section.

Gross Dividends

Any amount labeled "Gross Dividends" represents the total dividends you earned. Gross dividends on a 1099-DIV form represent the total earned from the company issuing the 1099-DIV. Gross dividends listed on a broker's statement may include dividends earned from several different companies. In either case, the gross dividend figure is the amount that you will put on Schedule B of your income tax return as shown in the preceding figure. This amount may be reduced before you have to pay tax on it, as noted in the next sections.

Ordinary Dividends

An amount labeled "Ordinary Dividends" is the amount that you eventually carry from Schedule B to page one of your federal income tax return. This is the part of your dividend that is subject to normal income tax and it doesn't receive any special treatment. If the ordinary dividend is equal to the gross dividend, then you really don't have to read the next two sections. If the two numbers don't agree, enter the ordinary dividend amount on Schedule B.

Capital Gain Distributions

Capital gain distributions represent income that is treated in a special way. It isn't included with your regular dividend income. Therefore, at the bottom of Schedule B (as shown in the preceding figure), you must list your capital gain distributions, then that amount will be deducted from your ordinary dividends before you carry your dividend total to the front page of your federal income tax return. The total of your capital gain distributions is carried over to Schedule D and included with long term capital gain income. You can read more about Schedule D in Chapter 14.

Nontaxable Distributions

Occasionally, companies pay dividends, not from their earnings, but as a return of your investment in the stock. These payments are called *nontaxable distributions*. It's important to remember that if you receive a nontaxable distribution, you must reduce your cost record of the stock by the amount of the distribution. This will affect your profit or loss when you sell the stock.

For example, suppose that you purchase some stock for $1,000. You receive a nontaxable distribution of $15. Now your cost basis in the stock is $985. If you sell the stock for $1,100, your profit is $115. The profit would have been $100, but for the nontaxable distribution.

> OOOOH...
>
> **By the Way**
>
> If you receive nontaxable distributions that add up to more than your original cost of the stock, the distribution should be reported as capital gain on Schedule D. Whether the gain is listed as short term gain or long term gain depends on the amount of time that passed from the time you purchased the stock to the time the dividend was paid. See Chapter 14 for additional information.

Federal Income Tax Withheld

Sometimes when you receive dividends, the company paying the dividends will withhold federal income tax for you. You'll see the federal income tax witholding reported on your 1099-DIV form. You may also see it listed on your broker's statement, if you receive such a statement.

If federal income tax has been withheld from your dividend income, you should add that to the rest of your tax withholding and put the combined amount on page 2 of your 1040 at line 55. In addition, you should check the little box on line 55 of your 1040 to indicate that some of your withholding is coming from a 1099 form.

Foreign Bank Accounts

If you have a bank account in a country other than the United States, or if you are the grantor of or transferor to a foreign trust, you must check "yes" in the appropriate box in Part III of Schedule B (see the next figure). Even if you don't otherwise have to prepare Schedule B, you must include it with your tax return if the answer to either of the foreign bank questions is *yes*.

Part III Foreign Accounts and Trusts (See page B-2.)	If you had over $400 of interest or dividends **or** had a foreign account or were a grantor of, or a transferor to, a foreign trust, you must complete this part.	Yes	No
	11a At any time during 1995, did you have an interest in or a signature or other authority over a financial account in a foreign country, such as a bank account, securities account, or other financial account? See page B-2 for exceptions and filing requirements for Form TD F 90-22.1		
	b If "Yes," enter the name of the foreign country ▶		
	12 Were you the grantor of, or transferor to, a foreign trust that existed during 1995, whether or not you have any beneficial interest in it? If "Yes," you may have to file Form 3520, 3520-A, or 926 .		

For Paperwork Reduction Act Notice, see Form 1040 instructions.	✪ *Printed on recycled paper*	Schedule B (Form 1040) 1995

The foreign bank and trust question on Schedule B. If you have to include Schedule B with your tax return, you must answer these questions.

In addition, if you checked "yes" to either of the foreign bank account questions, you are responsible for filing Form TD F 90-22.1, otherwise known as the *Report of Foreign Bank and Financial Accounts*. Do not attach this form to your federal income tax return; file it all by itself.

Call the IRS at 1-800-TAX-FORM and have them send you a copy of Form TD F 90-22.1 if you don't have one. Then file this foreign bank account form by June 30.

Income Tax Refunds

If you received a refund of state or local income tax during 1995, you may have to record it as income on line 10 of your federal income tax return. But don't just assume that you have to show the refund as income because it may not be taxable. Here's the rule: You report the state or local income tax refund as income on your federal income tax return if, in a previous year, you took a deduction for that tax *and* you received the benefit of that deduction.

In other words, suppose that you received a state income tax refund in 1994 of $55. Furthermore, in 1994, suppose that you were married and filed a joint 1994 income tax return with your spouse. On your 1994 income tax return (the one you filed in 1995), you included Schedule A to itemize your deductions, and you deducted state income tax of $850 which represented your state tax withholding at your job. If your itemized deductions were high enough to exceed the standard deduction of $6,350 for married people filing a joint 1994 tax return, then you were able to reduce your income by the total of your itemized deductions. You've met the first test of whether or not you have to add a state tax refund to your income: You itemized your deductions for the year in which you paid the tax.

If your itemized deductions exceeded $6,350 by at least $55, and if your taxable income was not less than $0, you've met the second test: The entire $55 was used as a deduction against your income for 1994. Therefore, you report the entire $55 as income on your federal tax return for 1995. It goes on line 10 on page one of your Form 1040. (Had your itemized deductions exceeded the standard deduction by only $40, then you would report only $40 of your tax refund as income on your 1995 income tax return. Alternatively, had your itemized deductions reduced your taxable income to –$10, then you would report only $45 of your tax refund as income on your 1995 income tax return.)

Alimony: Is it Income?

If you receive alimony, report it as income on line 11 of your 1040 and your former spouse takes a deduction for the payment(s). For alimony to be alimony, you must set it out in writing as part of a formal, enforceable divorce agreement.

Get Down to Brass Tax

If both you and your former spouse agree, you can forego reporting alimony as income and your former spouse can forego taking a deduction for the payment(s). You both have to agree to this in writing. The person receiving the alimony attaches a copy of the signed statement to his tax return each year the nonreporting agreement is in effect.

Alimony is alimony and child support is child support and never the twain shall meet. No deduction is allowed to the payor of child support and the recipient does not include the child support payments in income. No exceptions to this rule.

The Least You Need to Know

➤ Amounts on W-2 forms are combined and reported on your income tax return. Be sure to check your W-2 form for inaccuracies in your Social Security number.

➤ Income you earn on your investments is taxable—sooner or later. You should receive 1099 statements indicating how much you earned, from whom, and what type of income it is.

➤ Alimony is tax-deductible if you pay it and taxable if you receive it, unless you both agree in writing not to report the alimony.

➤ Child support is never taxable.

Chapter 13

Do It Yourself on Schedule C

In This Chapter

➤ Tax forms for the self-employed

➤ Reporting business income

➤ Offsetting business income with business expenses

➤ Taking depreciation expense on business assets

➤ Deducting vehicle expenses

➤ Home office expenses

Some people spend their entire adult lives working for someone else. Others strike out on their own. If you're one of those in whom an entrepreneurial fire burns, if you have to be your own boss, whether you work for yourself full time or you just operate a part-time do-it-in-your-free-time sort of business, you have to tell the IRS about it. That's where Schedule C comes in.

This chapter explains how to report business income and expenses on Schedule C.

The Schedule C

People who work for themselves, either full time or part time, report their income and related expenses on Schedule C, "Profit or Loss From Business." Farmers, however, report their income and related expenses on Schedule S, "Profit or Loss From Farming."

OOOOH...

By the Way

Legal fees and other costs relating to setting up a new business are called *start-up expenditures* and cannot be deducted all in one year as a business expense. Instead, summarize these expenses at the bottom of Form 4562 in the Amortization section. Divide the total amount of start-up expenses by 60 months and multiply the result by the number of months that your business operated in 1995. That amount gets transferred to Part V of your Schedule C as the 1995 portion of your start-up expense deduction. The balance of the expenses will be deducted on this form in future years, based on 12 months' worth of these expenses for each year.

Working for yourself means that you are not working as someone else's employee. You are considered to be an *independent contractor*. You may perform services for someone else and that someone else pays you for those services, but that someone else does not employ you. The IRS likes to look closely at relationships wherein you could be considered an employee, even if the person or company paying you doesn't withhold taxes from your income.

To be a true independent contractor you must have the right to control the means and methods of how you perform your work. If the person or company for whom you work controls not only *what you do* but *how you do it*, the IRS is likely to say you are an employee rather than an independent contractor. If that happens, then your employer is responsible for paying employment taxes such as Social Security and unemployment tax on your behalf.

To determine whether you are an employee or an independent contractor, the IRS plays a little game called "20 Questions." The more questions that generate a "yes" answer, the more likely it is that you are an employee:

1. Does your boss give you instructions that you have to obey?

2. Does the company you work for provide you with training?

3. Are your services integrated into the regular business operation of the place where you work?

4. Is it a requirement that you, personally, provide the services?

5. Are you prohibited from subcontracting the work?

6. Is the business relationship an ongoing one?

7. Does the person for whom you work set your hours?

8. Are you required to work full time for one organization?

9. Is your work performed at the premises of the person who pays you?

10. Does your boss tell you in what order to perform your tasks?

11. Must you submit reports (oral or written) summarizing your work progress?

12. Do you receive payment at regular intervals such as weekly or monthly?

13. Do you get reimbursed for business and travel expenses?

14. Does the person you work for provide your tools and supplies?

15. Do you not have a significant investment in the tools required to perform your job?

16. Is your work relationship such that you will never incur a loss from the services you provide?

17. Are you prohibited from working for more than one company or person at a time?

18. Are you prohibited from making your services available to the general public?

19. Is it the company's responsibility if you don't meet the specifications of your contract?

20. If you cause damages, is the company for which you work responsible?

The IRS has been looking closely at the employee/independent contractor issue in recent years. Those folks in Washington fear that companies are trying to reduce the amount of payroll taxes they have to pay by reclassifying employees as independent contractors. In order to prove to the IRS that you are an independent contractor, make sure that the following precautions are taken:

➤ The company paying you issues you a 1099-MISC form at the end of the year, reporting both to you and the IRS how much compensation they gave you during 1995.

➤ Anyone else who does work for that company in your capacity gets treated like an independent contractor, just like you.

➤ You have a good reason why you are an independent contractor instead of an employee.

The truth is that the IRS would prefer that everyone be an employee so that employers take the responsibility of paying payroll taxes. Therefore, you can bet the IRS is looking for reasons to reclassify you as an employee.

For example, suppose that you're in the lawn care business and you provide lawn service to various corporations in your town. If you set your own schedule, go to the companies when service is needed (either they call you or you decide when to follow up with services), you bill them for your services, and if you work for more than one company, chances are you will be considered an independent contractor. Alternatively, if you are expected to be on the grounds at a particular company at the same time every day and just be available for whatever lawn services the company decides to have you

> **OOOOH...**

> **By the Way**
> Reporting income and expenses from your own business can be tricky. The more complicated your business gets, the more you need to seek out a pro. When there are decisions to be made about things like how to value your inventory, how to depreciate your assets, or whether or not you're an independent contractor, it's time to talk to an accountant. Those accountants know what they're doing and can save you money (and the amount you pay them for their help is a deductible business expense!).

perform each day, if they pay you a fee that is unchanging from week to week, you start looking more like an employee to the IRS. The distinction between employee and independent contractor can be nebulous and the IRS has the right to decide for you.

The Schedule C questionnaire: Give the IRS pertinent information about your business here.

Income section: Report all income earned in your business in this section as well as the cost of items sold or produced by your business.

Expense section: Show all the costs of running your business here.

SCHEDULE C (Form 1040) Department of the Treasury Internal Revenue Service	**Profit or Loss From Business** (Sole Proprietorship) ➤ Partnerships, joint ventures, etc., must file Form 1065. ➤ Attach to Form 1040 or Form 1041. ➤ See Instructions for Schedule C (Form 1040).	OMB No. 1545-0074 **1995** Attachment Sequence No. 09

Name of proprietor | Social security number (SSN)

A Principal business or profession, including product or service (see page C-1) | B Enter principal business code (see page C-6) ➤

C Business name. If no separate business name, leave blank. | D Employer ID number (EIN), if any

E Business address (including suite or room no.) ➤ ....
   City, town or post office, state, and ZIP code

F Accounting method: (1) ☐ Cash (2) ☐ Accrual (3) ☐ Other (specify) ➤ ....

G Method(s) used to value closing inventory: (1) ☐ Cost (2) ☐ Lower of cost or market (3) ☐ Other (attach explanation) (4) ☐ Does not apply (if checked, skip line H) | Yes | No

H Was there any change in determining quantities, costs, or valuations between opening and closing inventory? If "Yes," attach explanation

I Did you "materially participate" in the operation of this business during 1995? If "No," see page C-2 for limit on losses.

J If you started or acquired this business during 1995, check here .... ➤ ☐

Part I Income

1 Gross receipts or sales. **Caution:** *If this income was reported to you on Form W-2 and the statutory employee" box on that form was checked, see page C-2 and check here* ➤ ☐	1	
2 Returns and allowances	2	
3 Subtract line 2 from line 1	3	
4 Cost of goods sold (from line 40 on page 2)	4	
5 **Gross profit.** Subtract line 4 from line 3	5	
6 Other income, including Federal and state gasoline or fuel tax credit or refund (see page C-2)	6	
7 **Gross income.** Add lines 5 and 6 ➤	7	

Part II Expenses. Enter expenses for business use of **your home only** on line 30.

8 Advertising	8		19 Pension and profit-sharing plans	19	
9 Bad debts from sales or services (see page C-3)	9		20 Rent or lease (see page C-4):		
10 Car and truck expenses (see page C-3)	10		a Vehicles, machinery, and equipment	20a	
11 Commissions and fees	11		b Other business property	20b	
12 Depletion	12		21 Repairs and maintenance	21	
13 Depreciation and section 179 expense deduction (not included in Part III) (see page C-3)	13		22 Supplies (not included in Part III)	22	
			23 Taxes and licenses	23	
			24 Travel, meals, and entertainment:		
14 Employee benefit programs (other than on line 19)	14		a Travel	24a	
15 Insurance (other than health)	15		b Meals and entertainment		
16 Interest:			c Enter 50% of line 24b subject to limitations (see page C-4)		
a Mortgage (paid to banks, etc.)	16a		d Subtract line 24c from line 24b	24d	
b Other	16b		25 Utilities	25	
17 Legal and professional services	17		26 Wages (less employment credits)	26	
18 Office expense	18		27 Other expenses (from line 46 on page 2)	27	

28 **Total expenses** before expenses for business use of home. Add lines 8 through 27 in columns ➤	28	
29 Tentative profit (loss). Subtract line 28 from line 7	29	
30 Expenses for business use of your home. Attach **Form 8829**	30	

31 **Net profit or (loss).** Subtract line 30 from line 29.
  ● If a profit, enter on **Form 1040, line 12,** and ALSO on **Schedule SE, line 2** (statutory employees, see page C-5). Estates and trusts, enter on Form 1041, line 3. | 31 |
  ● If a loss, you MUST go on to line 32.

32 If you have a loss, check the box that describes your investment in this activity (see page C-5).
  ● If you checked 32a, enter the loss on **Form 1040, line 12,** and ALSO on **Schedule SE, line 2** (statutory employees, see page C-5). Estates and trusts, enter on Form 1041, line 3. | 32a ☐ All investment is at risk.
  ● If you checked 32b, you MUST attach **Form 6198.** | 32b ☐ Some investment is not at risk.

For Paperwork Reduction Act Notice, see Form 1040 instructions. Cat. No. 11334P Schedule C (Form 1040) 1995

The first page of Schedule C summarizes your business income and expenses.

The Schedule C form represents an income statement for your business—a statement that displays a financial review of how your business did in 1995. You can use this form to help you analyze how your business is performing. You can use Schedule C as a basis for a 1996 budget. You can take your Schedule C to the bank when applying for a business loan.

The Schedule C-EZ

Some self-employed people can use Schedule C-EZ instead of Schedule C. Schedule C-EZ is a simpler schedule for businesses that don't have much activity. If you are self-employed, you can use Schedule C-EZ if the following conditions are met:

➤ Your *gross receipts* (income before any deductions) are not more than $25,000.

➤ Your business expenses are not more than $2,000.

➤ Your business didn't have any inventory all year.

➤ You only have one Schedule C–type business.

➤ You don't have any employees.

➤ You don't take a deduction for an office in your home.

➤ You don't take a deduction for depreciation expense.

➤ You don't have any suspended passive losses coming forward from last year's tax return, Form 8582 (relating to this business).

Answering All Those Questions

The top of your Schedule C contains questions and fill-in-the-blank sections about your business. Keep the IRS happy by answering all this stuff. Here's what to do with each item in the top part of the form:

Name of proprietor: This name should be either your name or possibly (if you are filing a joint return) your spouse's name. Put the proprietor's Social Security number on this line.

A Principal business or profession: A description of what your business does goes on this line.

B Enter principal business code: You can find this number in your IRS instructions for Schedule C. It is a four-digit number that describes your type of business. If none of the IRS business types describes your business, pick something that's close.

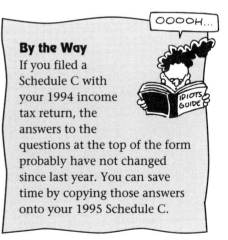

By the Way
If you filed a Schedule C with your 1994 income tax return, the answers to the questions at the top of the form probably have not changed since last year. You can save time by copying those answers onto your 1995 Schedule C.

C Business name: If your business uses a name different from your own (for example, Acme Lawn Service), enter that name here. Otherwise, leave this box blank.

D Employer ID number: The IRS might have issued you a separate business ID number. If you have an ID number, it goes here. Otherwise, leave this box blank.

E Business address: This will be the same as your home address if you run your business from home. If your business has a location away from your home, put that address here.

F Accounting method: If you are starting a new business, you may want to check with your friendly neighborhood accountant who can help you figure out which method is best for your type of business. You have three methods from which to choose:

Cash: Check the Cash box if you report your income in the year in which it was received, and your expenses in the year in which they were paid.

Accrual: Check the Accrual box if you report your income in the year in which it was earned, even if it is received in a different year, *and* you report your expenses in the year in which they were incurred, even if they are paid in a different year.

Other: Check the Other box if you use some combination of the Cash and Accrual methods. Write a brief description of your method in the line provided.

IRSpeak
The items you manufacture for sale, or the items you purchase for resale, are your *inventory*. The inventory is the stuff you have lying around that you hope someone will buy.

G Method(s) used to value closing inventory: When you sell your inventory you get to offset the sales income with the cost of the items you sold. The hard part is figuring out how much those items cost. That's where the methods for valuing your inventory come in to play. You value your closing inventory at the end of each year, add this year's purchases to last year's closing inventory, subtract the closing inventory from the end of this year, and the difference is how much inventory you sold during the year. Choose from one of these four methods and apply it to your entire inventory:

Cost: Check the Cost box if you value your inventory at the actual cost that you paid for it.

Lower of cost or market: Check the Lower of Cost or Market box if you keep track of the market value of your inventory and choose the lower of the two amounts (cost or market) for your method of valuing the inventory. If you use this method, you must apply market value to each type of item in your inventory, as opposed to using an overall market value applied to the entire inventory.

Other: If neither of the two preceding methods apply to you, check the Other box. Attach a statement to your tax return (just write out a paragraph and put it behind your Schedule C when you assemble your return) describing how you value your inventory. **Does not apply:** If your business doesn't have any inventory, check the Does Not Apply box.

H Was there any change in determining quantities, costs, or valuations between opening and closing inventory? Check the No box for this answer. The method by which you value your inventory doesn't change from one year to the next. (Leave this box blank if you checked "Does not apply" at item G.)

I Did you "materially participate" in the operation of this business? Check the No box if you are a business owner in name only; check the Yes box if you actually get your hands dirty. The IRS only cares if you materially participate when your business ends up with a net loss instead of that nice taxable income the IRS likes to see. If there's a loss and you just watched the business go by instead of working hard all year, you get to carry that loss forward until your business shows some income instead of deducting it currently. Better get back to work!

You materially participate in a business, according to the IRS, if you meet one of these tests:

1. You participate in the business for more than 500 hours during the year.

2. You are basically the only person who participates in this activity.

3. You participate in the business for more than 100 hours during the year and no one else participates more in the business than you do (someone else could, however, participate an equal amount of time as you).

4. You participate in several Schedule C–type businesses at a rate of more than 100 hours during the year and all together your time in these businesses adds up to more than 500 hours per year.

5. You met the material participation test for 5 of the past 10 tax years. If the business still exists, you are considered to be a material participant this year even if you don't meet any of the other tests. This rule is primarily for people who are retiring but still keeping marginally active in their business. But the IRS is more flexible about determining material participation if your business involves a service that you provide. See Rule 6, which discusses personal service businesses.

> **OOOOH...**
>
> **By the Way**
> When you choose an accounting method or a method for valuing your inventory, remember to use the same method consistently, year after year. You can't change accounting methods without written approval from the IRS.

> **OOOOH...**
>
> **By the Way**
> If you feel you have a good reason for adopting a new way in which to value your inventory this year, such as a drastic change in market conditions that significantly affects the pricing of your inventory items, you may request permission from the IRS and, upon approval, you may change methods. Get a professional involved if you think you have good reason to attempt to change your valuation method.

By the Way

Just to be on the safe side, keep a journal or calendar to document the time you spend in your business. You can save yourself headaches in an audit (there's that nasty word: *audit*— see Chapter 30, "Greetings, Taxpayer...," for the scoop on audits) if you can substantiate your material participation. Also, your spouse's time spent in a Schedule C business counts toward your total hours, as long as the spouse's time spent is the sort of time expected to be spent by a business owner.

OOPS!

If you have a check in your hand on December 31 that you earned in your business during 1995, you must claim it. Just because you don't deposit it in your bank account until January doesn't mean you didn't earn it in 1995. If you *could have* deposited the funds in 1995, you earned them in 1995. So, don't hold on to checks you receive at the end of the year to postpone the income.

6. If your business involves performing a personal service such as accounting, law, architecture, music, engineering, medicine, or consulting—something that requires your personal service in order to accomplish the job— you need only to have materially participated in the business for any three years in the past to continue material participation in the current year.

7. You participate in the business on a "regular, continuous, and substantial" basis. This last-chance test is subjective, and whether or not you meet this test is completely up to the IRS.

J If you started or acquired this business during 1995, check here. In other words, if this is your first Schedule C for this business, check this box.

Income Earned in Your Own Business

The income your business earned in 1995 gets reported in Part I of the Schedule C on line 1. If your business uses the cash basis of accounting (see "F" in the previous section) the amount your business earned will generally equate with the money deposited in your business bank account or all the cash you received during 1995. If you billed for some income and didn't receive it during 1995, it only gets included in 1995's income if you use the accrual basis of accounting (again, see "F" in the previous section).

Returns and Allowances

If your business had to issue a refund in 1995, or if you gave someone a discount after you already recorded the entire amount due as income, report these refund or discount (allowance) amounts on Schedule C, line 2, as "Returns and Allowances" and subtract them from your total income to arrive at line 3 on the Schedule C. (In other words, you don't have to record as income the money you returned to your customer.)

Cost of Goods Sold

If you purchase products and then sell them to someone else, your purchase price is referred to as the "Cost of Goods Sold"— the amount you paid for the items you sold. If you bought one doghouse, jacked up the price, and sold it to someone else, your cost of the doghouse is the Cost of

Goods Sold. The Cost of Goods Sold amount is pretty easy to figure out when you only sold one thing.

But what if you started the year with 100 doghouses, you purchased 5,000 more doghouses for a total of 5,100, and you sold 4,200? And what if the cost fluctuated so that all the doghouses you purchased didn't cost you the same thing? Now things start to get tricky.

First, remember that your Cost of Goods Sold is the cost of only the items that you sold, not all the purchases you made during the year. So, for the doghouse example, you must figure out the cost of the 4,200 doghouses that sold. The remaining 900 will hang around in your inventory into the next year.

Although you report the Cost of Goods Sold on line 4 of the Schedule C, you actually compute it in Part III, on the second page of the Schedule C. In Part III of Schedule C you start by filling in the value of your closing inventory from December 31, 1994. You can find this amount in the "Inventory at end of year" part of Schedule C on your 1994 tax return. If there was no ending inventory on last year's tax return, the beginning inventory for 1995 is zero. Next you enter the amount of all your inventory purchases in 1995. This will be the cost of all 5,000 doghouses in the example. Because you bought these doghouses rather than made them, skip the sections on cost of labor, materials and supplies, and other costs. (If you made the doghouses yourself, fill in the sections on labor, materials and supplies, and other costs.) Enter the value of your closing inventory as of the end of 1995. Finally, subtract the closing inventory amount from the total of the opening inventory plus your 1995 purchases. This will give you the Cost of Goods Sold amount that carries back to page 1, line 4 of the Schedule C.

Now, what do you do about those fluctuating prices? How do you figure out the costs of the inventory at the end of the year if the cost of the doghouses wasn't consistent during the year? You can choose from three methods for determining the value of your ending inventory:

> **Specific Identification:** If you have been able to track each doghouse in your inventory and know the cost of each one as you sell it, you can specifically identify the cost of the items remaining in your ending inventory. This is the most precise way of measuring your cost of sales.

> **FIFO:** Pronounced like *FieFoe* (as in Fee *Fie, Foe,* Fum) means First-In-First-Out. If you can't specifically identify the cost of each item in your inventory, or if there are just so many inventory items it would take you way too much time to figure out the individual costs of items in your inventory, you can value your inventory using this method. With FIFO, you assume that the first inventory items you purchased (First In) are the first ones you sold (First Out). Therefore, the 900 doghouses remaining in your inventory at the end of the year are the last 900 doghouses you bought, even if this isn't necessarily true.

This number comes from last year's tax return—it is the cost of the 100 doghouses you still had at the end of last year.

This is the cost of the 5,000 doghouses you bought this year.

This is the cost of the 900 doghouses remaining at the end of the year.

Schedule C (Form 1040) 1995   Page **2**

Part III   **Cost of Goods Sold** (see page C-5)

33	Inventory at beginning of year. If different from last year's closing inventory, attach explanation . .	33
34	Purchases less cost of items withdrawn for personal use	34
35	Cost of labor. Do not include salary paid to yourself	35
36	Materials and supplies	36
37	Other costs	37
38	Add lines 33 through 37	38
39	Inventory at end of year	39
40	**Cost of goods sold.** Subtract line 39 from line 38. Enter the result here and on page 1, line 4 . .	40

Part IV   **Information on Your Vehicle.** Complete this part **ONLY** if you are claiming car or truck expenses on line 10 and are not required to file Form 4562 **for this business.** See the instructions for line 13 on page C-3 to find out if you must file.

41   When did you place your vehicle in service for business purposes? (month, day, year) ▶ ....

42   Of the total number of miles you drove your vehicle during 1995 enter the number of miles you used your vehicle for:

   a   Business ....   **b** Commuting ....   **c** Other ....

43   Do you (or your spouse) have another vehicle available for personal use? . . . . ☐ **Yes**   ☐ **No**

44   Was your vehicle available for use during off-duty hours   . . . . ☐ **Yes**   ☐ **No**

45a   Do you have evidence to support your deduction?   . . . . ☐ **Yes**   ☐ **No**
   b   If "Yes," is the evidence written? . . . . ☐ **Yes**   ☐ **No**

Part V   **Other Expenses.** List below business expenses not included on lines 8–26 or line 30.

....		
....		
....		
....		
....		
....		
....		
....		
....		
46 **Total other expenses.** Enter here and on page 1, line 27	46	

✪ *Printed on recycled paper*

Compute the Cost of Goods Sold on page 2 of Schedule C.

LIFO: Pronounced like *Life-Oh*, it means Last-In-First-Out. If you use this method, you assume that the last items you purchased (Last In) are the first items you sold (First Out). Therefore the 900 doghouses remaining in your inventory are the first ones you purchased. Indeed, the cost of those first doghouses you purchased will remain in your inventory forever, or until you sell every item in your inventory.

After you figure out your Cost of Goods Sold and put it on line 4 of your Schedule C, subtract that cost from line 3 to arrive at *gross profit*. Gross profit is your primary business income (not counting miscellaneous things like the $500 bill you found under a box in the warehouse), minus the cost of your sales, before you start deducting all the expenses of running your business.

Miscellaneous Income

Some of the income you earn in your business might not be related to normal business operations. Types of miscellaneous income can include the following:

➤ Interest earned on invested funds or loans

➤ Rental income for building or equipment rent

➤ Gain from the sale of business assets

➤ Federal and state gasoline or fuel tax credits and refunds

> **IRSpeak**
>
> *FIFO* (First-In-First-Out) is a method of valuing inventory that assumes that you typically sell the oldest inventory items first. A grocery store is a good example: The oldest milk gets moved up to the front of the refrigerator case while the good, fresh stuff gets hidden in the back. The store owners hope you'll respect their desire to sell on a FIFO basis and take the old stuff off their hands before it expires.
>
> *LIFO* (Last-In-First-Out) is a method of valuing inventory that assumes that you typically sell the newest inventory items first. Grocery stores might think they're fooling you into a FIFO milk purchase, but if you poke around in the back of the shelf, you can generally find the newest milk and force them to sell on a LIFO basis.

Don't include income items of this sort with your gross receipts on line 1 of the Schedule C. Instead place them on line 6, "Other Income."

Add all this other income to your gross profit on line 5 and put the total on line 7 of Schedule C, "Gross Income."

Costs of Running a Business

They say you have to spend money to make money. This is a truth that every business owner understands. There are all kinds of costs involved in running a business beyond the costs of items sold, as discussed previously in this chapter. Costs such as payroll, rent, auto expense, supplies, and insurance all contribute to the operation of a business.

OOPS!

It's one thing to have business expenses that reduce your business income and, therefore, reduce your taxable income. It's another thing to have business expenses that wipe out your business income. If your Schedule C shows a loss in three of the past five years, the IRS is probably going to say your business is a hobby and not a real business. If that happens, your losses will be disallowed.

Expenses that relate to the operation of your business are listed on Schedule C and ultimately used to reduce your Schedule C income. These are the types of expenses you might have incurred in your business, and the lines in Part II of Schedule C where you report each type of expense:

➤ **8 Advertising:** The cost of promoting your business.

➤ **9 Bad debts:** The realization that an amount you formerly included in income (by using the accrual method of accounting) will never be collected (as in when a client of yours who owed you money goes out of business).

➤ **10 Car and truck expenses:** The business-related cost of operating a vehicle. See the next section for more details about calculating this expense.

➤ **11 Commissions and fees:** Amounts paid for memberships and licenses.

➤ **12 Depletion:** The wearing away and expensing over time of minerals or timber, including oil and gas.

➤ **13 Depreciation:** The wearing away and expensing over time of tangible, fixed assets such as office equipment, vehicles, buildings, and furniture. For example, if you buy a $50,000 piece of equipment for use in your business, the IRS frowns on your taking a deduction for that equipment all at once. Not only does it skew your net income, but it's also really not a realistic representation of your costs because you pay to use that equipment for many years. The IRS would like you to distribute the cost of that equipment over the years in which it will generate income for you. The "Depreciation" section later in this chapter explains how to calculate the depreciation amount to enter on this line.

➤ **14 Employee benefit programs:** The cost of health insurance paid on behalf of your employees. (Note: The cost of your own health insurance paid by your business is not deductible on Schedule C. Congress likes to futz with the deductibility of this expense. At the very least, you can deduct your health insurance cost on Schedule A as a medical expense. You may be able to deduct 30% of your health insurance expense as an *adjustment* at the bottom of page 1 of your 1040. Check the 1040 instructions to confirm this deduction.)

➤ **15 Insurance:** Liability insurance, workmen's compensation, and malpractice insurance.

➤ **16a Mortgage interest:** Interest paid on mortgage loans on business property.

➤ **16b Other interest:** Interest paid on business debts.

➤ **17 Legal and professional services:** Legal fees and tax return preparation fees (well, you may not need *those* anymore!).

➤ **18 Office expense:** Postage, secretarial supplies, computer supplies, business cards, and stationery.

➤ **19 Pension and profit-sharing plans:** Costs of retirement plans and profit-sharing plans paid on behalf of your employees.

➤ **20a Rent or lease of vehicles, machinery, and equipment:** Business rent expense of any items except office/building rent.

➤ **20b Rent expense of other business property:** Rent of real estate, including office, plant, warehouse, and factory rental.

➤ **21 Repairs and maintenance:** Expenses to repair and maintain equipment, rented property, and other assets.

➤ **22 Supplies:** Small tools, books, packaging material, and other incidental purchases necessary to the operation of the business.

➤ **23 Taxes and licenses:** Payroll taxes, property taxes, franchise taxes, and professional licenses and permits.

➤ **24a Travel:** Airplane, train, taxi, bus, limousine—any forms of transportation other than automobile expense (which has its own category). Also allowed as travel expenses are lodging and meals while traveling, cleaning and laundry expenses, telephone expenses (business calls only), and tips.

➤ **24b Meals and entertainment:** Meals and beverages relating to the operation of your business, tickets to athletic events and theaters, and hunting and fishing trips. Your deduction for expenses in this category is limited to 50% of the amount you spent. Enter the full amount of your expense on line 24b of Schedule C, then enter 50% of your expense on line 24c. Subtract 24c from 24b to arrive at your deductible meals and entertainment expense, which goes on line 24d.

Get Down to Brass Tax

The IRS has limited the types of things that constitute deductible entertainment expense. Dues to social and athletic clubs are not allowed as deductions. Rental of a skybox at an athletic event for a one-time-only event is deductible (subject to the 50% limit). Skybox rental for multiple events is limited to the cost of regular, nonluxury box seat tickets. Remember that in order to be deductible, any use of social and athletic clubs or attendance at athletic events must be for business purposes.

➤ **25 Utilities:** Gas, electric, water, and telephone related to your business.

➤ **26 Wages:** Payroll for your employees.

➤ **27 Other expenses:** Just about anything else you can think of in the way of expenses that relate to your business, such as copying, postage, and lab fees, can be listed in Part V of page 2 of Schedule C and summarized on lines 27 for "Other Expenses."

Add up all your expenses on lines 8 through 27 and put the total on line 28, "Total Expenses," of Schedule C.

Car and Truck Expenses

Drive a vehicle for your business and deduct the related expenses. There are two ways in which to deduct vehicle expenses and you can pick the method that gives you the best deduction—you can either deduct a per-mile amount for each of the miles you drove in conjunction with your business, or you can deduct the actual costs of operating the vehicle.

If you want to choose the mileage method for accounting for your vehicle expenses, you must do it in the first year you use the vehicle for business. You can change to the actual expense method in a later year if it gives you a better deduction. If you start out using the actual expense method, you must stick with that method for the life of that particular vehicle. (Note: If you drive more than one car in your business, you can't use the standard mileage method—you must deduct the actual expense of operating the vehicles.)

You report automobile expenses on line 10 of Schedule C, "Car and Truck Expenses." If you plan to take a depreciation expense for your car, you will report that amount on Form 4562 ("Depreciation and Amortization") with your other depreciable assets. The total expense from Form 4562 gets carried to line 13 of Schedule C. If you do not file a Form 4562 for this business, you must answer the automobile questions in Part IV of Schedule C. (These questions are duplicated on Form 4562.)

Mileage

No matter which method you use for accounting for automobile or other vehicle expenses, you must keep track of your mileage on the vehicle. If you are using the mileage method, you may deduct 30 cents per mile for each business mile driven. If you are using the actual expense method, you prorate the business and personal portions of your expenses by comparing business miles driven to total miles driven.

Commuting

Commuting from home to your job site is not considered business mileage and thus is not included in the computation in the previous section on mileage. Additionally, the cost of parking at your job (to which you have commuted) is considered a commuting expenses and is not deductible.

Parking and Tolls

No matter which method you use to report your automobile expenses, parking (except parking at your business site) and tolls are deductible. You should include them on line 2 in Part I of the Form 2106.

Vehicle Maintenance

If you are using the actual expense method of accounting for your vehicle expenses, you can deduct the cost of repairs and maintenance on the vehicle. This includes the following:

➤ Gasoline

➤ Oil

➤ Repairs

➤ Insurance

➤ Oil change

➤ Tires

➤ Lubrication

➤ Tune-up

Your deduction for these expenses is prorated between business and personal use based on the number of business versus personal (and commuting) miles driven.

Depreciation

Business property that is owned for the purpose of producing income is depreciable. Rather than deducting all at once the cost of an investment in an asset that you expect to use for several years, the IRS prefers that you spread the cost over the years during which you will use the asset in your business.

To provide some uniformity in determining how many years an asset will last, the IRS has set out guidelines for different types of assets. In general, these guidelines provide the following life expectancies for your depreciable assets:

➤ **3-year property**: breeding hobs, racehorses (at least 2 years old), and old horses (at least 12 years old)

➤ **5-year property**: automobiles and trucks, computer equipment, and office equipment such as typewriters (remember those?), calculators, and copiers

➤ **7-year property**: office furniture, tools, business equipment that doesn't fit in the 5-year class, and horses that don't fit in the 3-year class

➤ **10-year property**: trees and vines bearing fruit or nuts, and assets used in petroleum refining

➤ **15- and 20-year property**: sewers, treatment plants, telephone distribution plants, and communication equipment

➤ **27.5-year property**: residential rental property

➤ **31.5-year property**: commercial real estate property placed in service before May 12, 1993

➤ **39-year property**: commercial real estate placed in service after May 13, 1993

The depreciation deduction for assets is taken on Form 4562, "Depreciation and Amortization." You have two choices in the way in which you compute depreciation expense on these assets: MACRS and straight-line.

Choose straight-line if you want to save yourself a lot of headaches, but choose MACRS if you want some additional expenses up front—MACRS is a faster depreciation method, while straight-line spreads the deduction for cost of the asset evenly over the life of the asset. By using straight-line depreciation, in the first year you own the asset divide the cost by the number of years (based on the appropriate category above), divide that result by 2, and that's your first year depreciation. In the second and later years just divide the cost of the asset by the number of years for the appropriate category, until there isn't any more cost to deduct.

How you calculate depreciation also is affected by the convention (mid-year or mid-quarter) used. Your best bet for figuring out how to calculate depreciation is to call 1-800-TAX-FORM and ask for the IRS' depreciation guide.

Automobile Depreciation

If you are using the actual expense method of accounting for your vehicle expenses, you have the option of taking a deduction for depreciation on the vehicle. Depreciation expense is the deduction, over time, of the cost of an asset, such as a vehicle.

Get Down to Brass Tax

There is a downside to deducting depreciation on a business vehicle. A deduction for depreciation reduces the *basis* of the vehicle. You use the vehicle's basis in computing the gain or loss on the vehicle when you sell it, not the declining vehicle value. The more depreciation you take, the lower the basis of the vehicle; and the higher the potential gain when you sell the vehicle, the more tax you pay. You get a current deduction for depreciation, but you may end up recouping that deduction in the form of taxable gain in a future year when you sell the vehicle.

Compute your depreciation expense on Form 4562, "Depreciation and Amortization." You can put the expense for all the assets for one business on a single Form 4562, but you must file a separate Form 4562 for each business you report on your income tax return.

There are strict rules regarding how much depreciation you can deduct on an asset in a single year, and there are especially strict rules when a car is the asset being depreciated.

In general, you can spread the cost of a business vehicle over six years and deduct that cost on Form 4562 as a depreciation expense. You can deduct the cost over the five years by using *straight-line depreciation* and following this schedule:

> **By the Way**
> Depreciation calculations can get tricky. If you have questions, don't hesitate to call an authority. You might also want to call the IRS at 1-800-TAX-FORM and request a free copy of Publication 534, a booklet that contains everything you always hoped you'd never need to know about depreciation.

1st year	deduct 1/10th the cost of the vehicle
2nd year	deduct 1/5th the cost
3rd year	deduct 1/5th the cost
4th year	deduct 1/5th the cost
5th year	deduct 1/5th the cost
6th year	deduct 1/10th the cost

This has the effect of spreading the deduction over what the IRS has determined is the typical life of a car or truck. Alternatively, you can use the method called *MACRS*, which stands for something like Make Accountants Crazy with Rules and Slogans and is pronounced by those in the know as *Maykers* (rhymes with *shakers*). Using this method you will deduct the cost of your vehicle in the following manner:

1st year	deduct 1/5th of the cost of the vehicle
2nd year	deduct 32% of the cost
3rd year	deduct 19.2% of the cost
4th year	deduct 11.52% of the cost
5th year	deduct 11.52% of the cost
6th year	deduct 5.76% of the cost and you're finished (Whew!)

Form **4562** Department of the Treasury Internal Revenue Service (5)	**Depreciation and Amortization** **(Including Information on Listed Property)** ▶ See separate instructions. ▶ Attach this form to your return.	OMB No. 1545-0172 Attachment Sequence No. **67**

Name(s) shown on return   Identifying number

Business or activity to which this form relates

Part I   **Election To Expense Certain Tangible Property (Section 179)** (**Note:** *If you have any "Listed Property,"*
complete Part V before you complete Part I.)

1	Maximum dollar limitation (If an enterprise zone business, see instructions.)	**1**	$17,500
2	Total cost of section 179 property placed in service during the tax year (see instructions) . .	**2**	
3	Threshold cost of section 179 property before reduction in limitation	**3**	$200,000
4	Reduction in limitation. Subtract line 3 from line 2. If zero or less, enter -0-	**4**	
5	Dollar limitation for tax year. Subtract line 4 from line 1. If zero or less, enter -0-. (If married filing separately, see instructions.).	**5**	

(a) Description of property	(b) Cost	(c) Elected cost	
6			

7	Listed property. Enter amount from line 26.	**7**	
8	Total elected cost of section 179 property. Add amounts in column (c), lines 6 and 7 . . .	**8**	
9	Tentative deduction. Enter the smaller of line 5 or line 8	**9**	
10	Carryover of disallowed deduction from 1993 (see instructions)	**10**	
11	Taxable income limitation. Enter the smaller of taxable income (not less than zero) or line 5 (see instructions) . .	**11**	
12	Section 179 expense deduction. Add lines 9 and 10, but do not enter more than line 11 . .	**12**	
13	Carryover of disallowed deduction to 1995. Add lines 9 and 10, less line 12 ▶	**13**	

Note: *Do not use Part II or Part III below for listed property (automobiles, certain other vehicles, cellular telephones, certain computers, or property used for entertainment, recreation, or amusement). Instead, use Part V for listed property.*

Part II   **MACRS Depreciation For Assets Placed in Service ONLY During Your 1994 Tax Year (Do Not Include Listed Property)**

(a) Classification of property	(b) Month and year placed in service	(c) Basis for depreciation (business/investment use only—see instructions)	(d) Recovery period	(e) Convention	(f) Method	(g) Depreciation deduction
Section A—General Depreciation System (GDS) (see instructions)						
14a 3-year property						
b 5-year property						
c 7-year property						
d 10-year property						
e 15-year property						
f 20-year property						
g Residential rental property			27.5 yrs.	MM	S/L	
			27.5 yrs.	MM	S/L	
h Nonresidential real property			39 yrs.	MM	S/L	
				MM	S/L	
Section B—Alternative Depreciation System (ADS) (see instructions)						
15a Class life					S/L	
b 12-year			12 yrs.		S/L	
c 40-year			40 yrs.	MM	S/L	

Part III   **Other Depreciation (Do Not Include Listed Property)▶**

16	GDS and ADS deductions for assets placed in service in tax years beginning before 1994 (see instructions)	**16**	
17	Property subject to section 168(f)(1) election (see instructions)	**17**	
18	ACRS and other depreciation (see instructions)	**18**	

Part IV   **Summary**

19	Listed property. Enter amount from line 25.	**19**	
20	**Total.** Add deductions on line 12, lines 14 and 15 in column (g), and lines 16 through 19. Enter here and on the appropriate lines of your return. (Partnerships and S corporations—see instructions)	**20**	
21	For assets shown above and placed in service during the current year, enter the portion of the basis attributable to section 263A costs (see instructions)	**21**	

For Paperwork Reduction Act Notice, see page 1 of the separate instructions.   Cat. No. 12906N   Form **4562**

Depreciation expense on assets purchased in prior years gets summarized here.

Depreciable assets you acquired in 1995 get summarized here.

Form 4562—The Depreciation and Amortization form.

Form 4562   Page **2**

Part V — Listed Property—Automobiles, Certain Other Vehicles, Cellular Telephones, Certain Computers, and Property Used for Entertainment, Recreation, or Amusement

*For any vehicle for which you are using the standard mileage rate or deducting lease expense, complete **only** 22a, 22b, columns (a) through (c) of Section A, all of Section B, and Section C if applicable.*

Section A—Depreciation and Other Information (Caution: See instructions for limitations for automobiles.)

22a Do you have evidence to support the business/investment use claimed? ☐ Yes ☐ No   22b If "Yes," is the evidence written? ☐ Yes ☐ No

(a) Type of property (list vehicles first)	(b) Date placed in service	(c) Business/ investment use percentage	(d) Cost or other basis	(e) Basis for depreciation (business/investment use only)	(f) Recovery period	(g) Method/ Convention	(h) Depreciation deduction	(i) Elected section 179 cost
23 Property used more than 50% in a qualified business use (see instructions):							
		%						
		%						
		%						
24 Property used 50% or less in a qualified business use (see instructions):							
		%			S/L –			
		%			S/L –			
		%			S/L –			

25 Add amounts in column (h). Enter the total here and on line 19, page 1.   **25**

26 Add amounts in column (i). Enter the total here and on line 7, page 1   **26**

Section B—Information on Use of Vehicles—If you deduct expenses for vehicles:

- Always complete this section for vehicles used by a sole proprietor, partner, or other "more than 5% owner," or related person.
- If you provided vehicles to your employees, first answer the questions in Section C to see if you meet an exception to completing this section for those vehicles.

	(a) Vehicle 1	(b) Vehicle 2	(c) Vehicle 3	(d) Vehicle 4	(e) Vehicle 5	(f) Vehicle 6
27 Total business/investment miles driven during the year (DO NOT include commuting miles)						
28 Total commuting miles driven during the year						
29 Total other personal (noncommuting) miles driven						
30 Total miles driven during the year. Add lines 27 through 29.						

	Yes	No	Yes	No	Yes	No	Yes	No	Yes	No	Yes	No
31 Was the vehicle available for personal use during off-duty hours?												
32 Was the vehicle used primarily by a more than 5% owner or related person?												
33 Is another vehicle available for personal use?												

Section C—Questions for Employers Who Provide Vehicles for Use by Their Employees

Answer these questions to determine if you meet an exception to completing Section B. **Note:** Section B must always be completed for vehicles used by sole proprietors, partners, or other more than 5% owners or related persons.

	Yes	No
34 Do you maintain a written policy statement that prohibits all personal use of vehicles, including commuting, by your employees?		
35 Do you maintain a written policy statement that prohibits personal use of vehicles, except commuting, by your employees? (See instructions for vehicles used by corporate officers, directors, or 1% or more owners.)		
36 Do you treat all use of vehicles by employees as personal use?		
37 Do you provide more than five vehicles to your employees and retain the information received from your employees concerning the use of the vehicles?		
38 Do you meet the requirements concerning qualified automobile demonstration use (see instructions)?		

Note: If your answer to 34, 35, 36, 37, or 38 is "Yes," you need not complete Section B for the covered vehicles.

Part VI — Amortization

(a) Description of costs	(b) Date amortization begins	(c) Amortizable amount	(d) Code section	(e) Amortization period or percentage	(f) Amortization for this year
39 Amortization of costs that begins during your 1994 tax year:					

40 Amortization of costs that began before 1994   **40**

41 **Total.** Enter here and on "Other Deductions" or "Other Expenses" line of your return   **41**

Form 4562—Page 2. Information about your depreciable auto gets listed on this page.

If this is the first year for reporting depreciation on your vehicle, put the amount on line 14b of the Form 4562. If you started depreciating the vehicle in a year prior to 1995, put this year's deduction on line 16 of the Form 4562.

But wait! There's one more thing. Special limitations apply to cars and the amount of depreciation expense you can take in any one year. You can't take more than the amounts shown in Table 13.1 for depreciation expense on any one car.

Table 13.1 Maximum Depreciation Deduction

Year Placed in Service	1st Year	2nd year	3rd year	4th year*
1995	$3,060	$4,900	$2,950	$1775
1994	2,960	4,700	2,850	1,675
1993	2,860	4,600	2,750	1,675
1992	2,760	4,400	2,650	1,575
1991	2,660	4,300	2,550	1,575
1990	2,660	4,200	2,550	1,475
1989	2,660	4,200	2,550	1,475
Pre-1989	2,560	4,100	2,450	1,475

*And each year thereafter.

With the limitations presented by Table 13.1, you might end up depreciating your car over a period of more than five years. Just keep on going until the car is fully depreciated (or until you no longer own it).

But wait! There's still more! The amounts in Table 13.1 need to be proportionately reduced if you don't use your car 100% for business. If you only use your car 75% of the time for your business, your annual ceiling on depreciation is 75% of the amounts listed in the table.

Once you choose a depreciation method in the first year you owned your car, you must continue using that same method for each year you depreciate that car. When choosing between depreciation methods, consider the importance of having higher deductions in the current year versus years down the road. It may be that you expect your income to increase in future years; thus the straight-line method, which gives you a lower deduction right now, will provide you with greater benefits later on when you have more income against which to offset the deduction.

Whichever depreciation method you choose, you must stick with that method until the asset is fully depreciated. You can, however, choose different methods for different assets.

Turning Your Home into an Office

In addition to the benefit of being able to meet your children at the door with a plate of cookies when they come home from school, there are tax advantages to working from home.

Many of the amounts you spend on operating your home become deductible business expenses when your home is your office. And those expenses that would be deductible anyway—mortgage interest and property taxes—now are deductible on Schedule C instead of Schedule A (Itemized Deductions). So what? Well, for one thing, items that are deductible on Schedule C generally carry over to your state income tax return, so you get a reduction of state income taxes as a result of these deductions. Also, by pulling items out of your itemized deductions, you might reduce your itemized deductions to the level where the standard deduction is higher, thus giving you the benefit of the standard deduction and all your other deductions as well (because they are over on Schedule C). If that sounds Greek to you, check Chapter 19, "Itemized Deductions Most Taxpayers Can Take," for a more thorough explanation.

There are certain tests you must meet to take a deduction for business use of your home. To deduct part of your home on your Schedule C, you have to use the business part of your home exclusively and regularly as the principal location of your business, or as a place to meet or deal with patients, clients, or customers in the normal course of your business. *Exclusively* means that the part of your home used for your business cannot be used for anything else. An exception to this exclusivity rule is an in-your-home day care center. Also, an area used regularly to store inventory qualifies for a deduction.

If you meet the requirements for space in your home allocated to business use, you can deduct certain expenses relating to the cost and operation of your home. Use Form 8829 (see the next figure) for collecting and reporting your office in the home expenses and then send the result to Schedule C, line 30. These expenses are prorated based on the percentage of your home used for business.

➤ Types of expenses that qualify for the home office deduction:

➤ Mortgage interest

➤ Property tax

➤ Rent

➤ Utilities

➤ Repairs

➤ Insurance

➤ Depreciation

➤ Cleaning

Form **8829**	**Expenses for Business Use of Your Home**	OMB No. 1545-1266
	➤ **File only with Schedule C (Form 1040). Use a separate Form 8829 for each home you used for business during the year.**	
Department of the Treasury Internal Revenue Service (O)	➤ **See separate instructions.**	Attachment Sequence No. **66**

Name(s) of proprietor(s)	Your social security number

Part I — Part of Your Home Used for Business

1	Area used regularly and exclusively for business, regularly for day care, or for inventory storage. See instructions	1	
2	Total area of home	2	
3	Divide line 1 by line 2. Enter the result as a percentage	3	%

● **For day-care facilities not used exclusively for business, also complete lines 4–6.**

● **All others, skip lines 4–6 and enter the amount from line 3 on line 7.**

4	Multiply days used for day care during year by hours used per day	4	hr.
5	Total hours available for use during the year (365 days × 24 hours). See instructions	5	8,760 hr.
6	Divide line 4 by line 5. Enter the result as a decimal amount	6	.
7	Business percentage. For day-care facilities not used exclusively for business, multiply line 6 by line 3 (enter the result as a percentage). All others, enter the amount from line 3 ➤	7	%

Part II — Figure Your Allowable Deduction

| 8 | Enter the amount from Schedule C, line 29, **plus** any net gain or (loss) derived from the business use of your home and shown on Schedule D or Form 4797. If more than one place of business, see instructions | | 8 | |

See instructions for columns (a) and (b) before completing lines 9–20.

			(a) Direct expenses	(b) Indirect expenses			
9	Casualty losses. See instructions	9					
10	Deductible mortgage interest. See instructions	10					
11	Real estate taxes. See instructions	11					
12	Add lines 9, 10, and 11	12					
13	Multiply line 12, column (b) by line 7			13			
14	Add line 12, column (a) and line 13					14	
15	Subtract line 14 from line 8. If zero or less, enter -0-					15	
16	Excess mortgage interest. See instructions	16					
17	Insurance	17					
18	Repairs and maintenance	18					
19	Utilities	19					
20	Other expenses. See instructions	20					
21	Add lines 16 through 20	21					
22	Multiply line 21, column (b) by line 7			22			
23	Carryover of operating expenses from 1993 Form 8829, line 41			23			
24	Add line 21 in column (a), line 22, and line 23					24	
25	Allowable operating expenses. Enter the **smaller** of line 15 or line 24					25	
26	Limit on excess casualty losses and depreciation. Subtract line 25 from line 15					26	
27	Excess casualty losses. See instructions			27			
28	Depreciation of your home from Part III below			28			
29	Carryover of excess casualty losses and depreciation from 1993 Form 8829, line 42			29			
30	Add lines 27 through 29					30	
31	Allowable excess casualty losses and depreciation. Enter the **smaller** of line 26 or line 30					31	
32	Add lines 14, 25, and 31					32	
33	Casualty loss portion, if any, from lines 14 and 31. Carry amount to **Form 4684**, Section B					33	
34	Allowable expenses for business use of your home. Subtract line 33 from line 32. Enter here and on Schedule C, line 30. If your home was used for more than one business, see instructions ➤					34	

Part III — Depreciation of Your Home

35	Enter the **smaller** of your home's adjusted basis or its fair market value. See instructions	35	
36	Value of land included on line 35	36	
37	Basis of building. Subtract line 36 from line 35	37	
38	Business basis of building. Multiply line 37 by line 7	38	
39	Depreciation percentage. See instructions	39	%
40	Depreciation allowable. Multiply line 38 by line 39. Enter here and on line 28 above. See instructions	40	

Part IV — Carryover of Unallowed Expenses to 1995

| 41 | Operating expenses. Subtract line 25 from line 24. If less than zero, enter -0- | 41 | |
| 42 | Excess casualty losses and depreciation. Subtract line 31 from line 30. If less than zero, enter -0- | 42 | |

For Paperwork Reduction Act Notice, see page 1 of separate instructions. *Printed on recycled paper* Cat. No. 13232M Form **8829**

*U.S. Government Printing Office: 1994 — 375-468

Transfer the amount on this line to line 30, Schedule C.

Fill out Form 8829 when you deduct expenses for your home office.

128

Expenses for the use of your home as a business can only be deducted on your income tax return to the extent they do not exceed the net income of your business (this doesn't include mortgage interest and taxes that are deductible even if the business operates at a loss). So, if your business, after deducting all expenses except the business portion of your home, made $3,000, and the expenses for the use of your home totaled $4,000, you would be able to deduct only $3,000 of those expenses. The remaining $1,000 may be carried over and deducted in future years (subject to the same income limitations of your business).

OOPS!
Beware! Treating a portion of your home as a business expense separates that part of your home from the special rules that allow you to defer gain on the sale of a house. The business portion of your home gets treated like a business asset and is subject to the capital gain and loss rules that apply to any other business asset, as explained in Chapter 14.

Ten Business Expenses You Might Have Overlooked

Before you total your Schedule C and determine the final figure for your net business income, check over the following list and see if any of these deductions might apply to you:

1. A proportionate share of cleaning your home (if you are claiming a home office deduction) (include on Form 8829).

2. Tuition paid for training seminars relating to your business (list in Part V of Schedule C, then carry total from Part V to line 27 in Part II).

3. The cost of subscriptions to professional journals (again, Part V, Schedule C).

4. Gifts to customers and business associates, not exceeding $25 per person (Part V, Schedule C).

5. The cost of holiday parties for employees (Part V, Schedule C).

6. The purchase of benefit tickets to community events (can be considered as advertising expense on line 9 of Schedule C).

7. Computer and bundled software (prorate the business versus personal portion)—depreciate the computer on Form 4562 over five years just as you would a car (but without the dollar limitations mentioned previously). Software goes on Part V, Schedule C if you expect to upgrade within a year. Off-the-shelf software with a useful life of more than one year is depreciated over 36 months. Claim it in Part III of Form 4562.

8. Tractors, trailers, wagons, and other transporting equipment used exclusively (or partially) for your business (depreciate on Form 4562).

IRSpeak

At risk means that you're financially responsible for the "doings" of the business. If the business loses money, it's your money that gets lost (as opposed to having your father or an unsecured loan at the bank finance the operation). If your investment in this business is not at risk (to you, that is), and the business shows a loss, the loss that you may carry to page 1 of the 1040 is limited to the amount for which you are personally at risk.

9. Charitable contributions made by the business (note, however, that these items go on Schedule A, "Itemized Deductions," even though the business made the contribution).

10. Interest paid on a loan from a family member (line 16b of Schedule C).

Finish up Schedule C by adding up all your expenses and placing the total on line 28 at the bottom of the first page, "Total Expenses." Subtract the total expenses from the gross income (line 7), and place the difference on line 29. If line 29 is negative, put the negative number there; don't use zero. If you use Form 8829 for reporting the business use of your home, the amount from that form should appear on line 30. Subtract line 30 from line 29 and put the difference on line 31 (this can be a negative number, too).

Net income on line 31 (a positive number) goes right to Form 1040, line 12. Also put this amount on Schedule SE, line 2. If line 31 is a loss, make sure that the box at 32a is checked if your entire investment is *at risk*, then put the loss on line 12 of your 1040.

The Least You Need to Know

➤ If you work for yourself, your income gets reported on Schedule C.

➤ Self-employment income gets offset with business expenses.

➤ Purchases of furniture, equipment, and other items that you will use in your business for several years get depreciated. Report depreciation on Form 4562.

➤ You can take a deduction for use of your car in your business.

➤ If you use part of your home in your business, you might qualify for a tax deduction. In order to take a deduction, you must use the area in your home exclusively for business and you can't have an office at another location.

Chapter 14

Capital C, Capital G, Capital Gain (or Loss)

In This Chapter

➤ What makes a gain a capital gain

➤ Unraveling the hype about tax on capital gains

➤ Gains and losses on selling your home

➤ How to treat sales of business assets

➤ Gains and losses you didn't even know you had

When you sell something and make a profit, go ahead and pat yourself on the back and tell yourself what a savvy businessperson you are. But don't forget about your friends at the IRS. They want a piece of the action too.

There are capital gains and losses and there are noncapital gains and losses. All of these types of sales (listed here) get reported in the Income section of your 1040 form:

➤ Sales of items held for investment (capital assets) that produce capital gains and losses get reported on your Schedule D, appropriately named "Capital Gains and Losses." The gain or loss from Schedule D gets carried to line 13 of your 1040.

➤ Sales of inventory items (these are noncapital assets) get reported in the Gross Receipts or Sales line on Schedule C. Schedule C net income (or loss) gets carried to line 12 of the 1040.

IRSpeak

Assets are items that you own, and they fall into two categories: *capital assets* and *noncapital assets.* Capital assets are items that you own for pleasure or investment, such as your car or a stamp collection. Noncapital assets are items that you own for the purpose of resale or items that you use in your business. Examples of noncapital assets include inventory items that you sell in your business, copyrights, and depreciable property that you use in your business (depreciable property is discussed in Chapter 13).

IRSpeak

Gains represent profits on items that you sell. As you might suspect, *capital gains* are profits on sales of capital assets, *noncapital gains* are profits on sales of noncapital assets. *Losses* occur when you lose money on the sale of an asset. Guess what kind of asset you sell at a loss when the loss is a *capital loss?* You got it: a capital asset. And a *noncapital loss* occurs when you sell a noncapital asset at a loss.

➤ Sales of other business assets (these are not capital gains, although part of the gain might be treated as capital gain under Section 1231 rules and get reported on Schedule D; check with a CPA regarding Section 1231 rules) such as the business car, a computer, a piece of land, office furniture, or even company-owned tickets to the Indiana Pacers' playoff games, get reported on Form 4797, "Sales of Business Property." Gains and losses from form 4797 get carried to line 14 of the 1040.

➤ Sales of investment items such as stocks and bonds (capital gains/losses) get reported on Schedule D. It doesn't matter whether you sell these items for a profit or if you lose money in the deal. These Schedule D sales get carried to the 1040, line 13.

➤ The results of the sale of your home (capital gain/loss) get reported on Form 2119, even though there are times when you don't have to pay tax on the gain from this type of sale. If there is a loss on the sale of your home, the loss dies on the 2119. Gains from the sale of your home may get deferred to a later year (see "Selling Your Home" later in this chapter); otherwise the gains get dispatched to Schedule D and from there to the 1040, line 13.

➤ And sales of anything else you own, such as your car, your dining room furniture, your son's pet snake, if you sell at a profit (capital gain), get reported on your Schedule D and then flow through to the 1040, line 13.

Short-Term Versus Long-Term Gains and Losses

Different tax rules apply to items you sell depending on whether you owned the item(s) short term or long term. Short term, according to the IRS, is one year or less. Long term, therefore, is more than one year. When filling out the Form 4797 or the Schedule D, look at the section headings to find out which section is for short-term sales and which section is for long-term sales.

On the Schedule D, short-term sales get reported in Part I and long-term sales get reported in Part II. The form asks for the purchase date and the sale date of the item you sold. The IRS will check your computation and make sure that you put short-term items in the short-term section and long-term items in the long-term section.

SCHEDULE D (Form 1040) <small>Department of the Treasury Internal Revenue Service</small>	**Capital Gains and Losses** ▶ Attach to Form 1040. ▶ See Instructions for Schedule D (Form 1040). ▶ Use lines 20 and 22 for more space to list transactions for lines 1 and 9.	OMB No. 1545-0074 **1995** Attachment Sequence No. **12**

Name(s) shown on Form 1040   Your social security number

Part I   **Short-Term Capital Gains and Losses—Assets Held One Year or Less**

(a) Description of property (Example: 100 sh. XYZ Co.)	(b) Date acquired (Mo., day, yr.)	(c) Date sold (Mo., day, yr.)	(d) Sales price (see page D-3)	(e) Cost or other basis (see page D-3)	(f) LOSS If (e) is more than (d), subtract (d) from (e)	(g) GAIN If (d) is more than (e), subtract (e) from (d)
1						

2   Enter your short-term totals, if any, from line 21 . . . .   **2**

3   **Total short-term sales price amounts.** Add column (d) of lines 1 and 2 . . .   **3**

4   Short-term gain from Forms 2119 and 6252, and short-term gain or loss from Forms 4684, 6781, and 8824 . . . .   **4**

5   Net short-term gain or loss from partnerships, S corporations, estates, and trusts from Schedule(s) K-1 . . . .   **5**

6   Short-term capital loss carryover. Enter the amount, if any, from line 9 of your 1994 Capital Loss Carryover Worksheet **6**

7   Add lines 1 through 6 in columns (f) and (g) . . . .   **7** (   )

8   **Net short-term capital gain or (loss) Combine** columns (f) and (g) of line 7 . . . . . . ▶   **8**

Part II   **Long-Term Capital Gains and Losses—Assets Held More Than One Year**

9						

10   Enter your long-term totals, if any, from line 23 . . . .   **10**

11   **Total long-term sales price amounts.** Add column (d) of lines 9 and 10 . . .   **11**

12   Gain from Form 4797; long-term gain from Forms 2119, 2439, and 6252; and long-term gain or loss from Forms 4684, 6781, and 8824 . . . . .   **12**

13   Net long-term gain or loss from partnerships, S corporations, estates, and trusts from Schedule(s) K-1 . . . .   **13**

14   Capital gain distributions **14**

15   Long-term capital loss carryover. Enter the amount, if any, from line 14 of your 1994 Capital Loss Carryover Worksheet **15**

16   Add lines 9 through 15 in columns (f) and (g) . . . .   **16** (   )

17   **Net long-term capital gain or (loss).** Combine columns (f) and (g) of line 16 . . . . . . ▶   **17**

Part III   **Summary of Parts I and II**

18   Combine lines 8 and 17. If a loss, go to line 19. If a gain, enter the gain on Form 1040, line 13.
Note: *If both lines 17 and 18 are gains, see the* **Capital Gain Tax Worksheet** *on page 25* . .   **18**

19   If line 18 is a loss, enter here and as a (loss) on Form 1040, line 13, the **smaller** of these losses:
  a The loss on line 18; or
  b ($3,000) or, if married filing separately, ($1,500) . . . .   **19** (   )
     Note: *See the* **Capital Loss Carryover Worksheet** *on page D-3 if the loss on line 18 exceeds the loss on line 19* **or** *if Form 1040, line 35, is a loss.*

For Paperwork Reduction Act Notice, see Form 1040 instructions.   Cat. No. 11338H   **Schedule D (Form 1040) 1995**

— Show short-term sales in Part I.

— Show long-term sales in Part II.

The Schedule D.

Get Down to Brass Tax

You would think that the date you sell an item is the date you sell an item and that would be that. Not so in the land of IRS. When you sell stocks or bonds, there is a *trade date* and a *settlement date*. Both dates are listed on the sales confirmation form that your broker gives you. The trade date is the earlier of the two dates. If you sell the security at a loss, the date of sale that you report on your Schedule D is the trade date.

On the Form 4797, "Sales of Business Property," sales of assets used in the production of your income and held for more than one year get reported in Part I; sales of business assets held for one year or less go to Part II; and sales of business assets held more than one year and sold at a gain get reported in Part III. But see the section later in this chapter called "Gains and Losses on Sales of Items Used in Your Business" for more information about using this form.

Selling Items for a Profit

No matter what you sell, if you make a profit on the sale, you have to report the income. Sometimes it's not easy to tell if you've made any money on the transaction.

IRSpeak

The *cost basis* of an asset is generally the cost of the item, that is, the amount you paid for it. Additional amounts are added to the cost if they were paid in conjunction with the purchase: sales tax, freight, installation and testing charges, excise taxes, legal and accounting fees related to the purchase, revenue stamps, recording fees, and real estate taxes.

Start with the original cost of the item. The amount you paid for the item is the *cost basis*. Add the cost of any improvements, additions, extensions, or significant repairs you have made.

Deduct from this revised basis any depreciation expense you have taken on this item on tax returns over the years.

This computation gives you your *adjusted basis*. Compare the adjusted basis with the selling price. If the selling price is higher than the adjusted basis, you have a profit, or a gain. Report the gain on your income tax return and expect to pay tax on the gain. (Exception: The gain on the sale of your personal residence gets treated in a special way. See "Selling Your Home" later in this chapter.) If the selling price is lower than the adjusted basis, you have a loss.

What Happens When You Lose Your Shirt

The IRS wants to hear about any kind of gains you have. But what about losses? If you have to pay tax on your gains, shouldn't you be able to take a deduction on your income tax return for losses? The answer is "sometimes."

Losses on sales of *business assets* get reported on Form 4797, just as the gains. You get to take a deduction for the loss. Sometimes the deduction is limited to $3,000 per year. If your deduction gets limited, you get to carry the excess loss over to future years.

Losses on sales of investment items such as stocks and bonds get reported on Schedule D, just as the gains. Your deduction for this type of loss is offset against any other gains you might have. The net loss is limited to $3,000 per year. Losses in excess of $3,000 get carried over to future years.

Losses on the sale of your personal residence get reported on Form 2119. However, you do not get to take a deduction for this loss *unless part of your home was being treated as a business asset.* If you were depreciating your home on your most recent income tax return, either as a home office on Schedule C (see "Turning Your Home into an Office" in Chapter 13), or as rental property on Schedule E, and you sell your home at a loss, you can deduct the portion of the loss that represents the percentage of the home that you were depreciating on Schedule C or Schedule E. This business portion of the loss is carried from Form 4797 to Schedule D and is subject to the $3,000 per year deduction limitation.

Losses from the sales of personal assets, such as your family car or your college textbooks, are not deductible on your income tax return. Darn!

> **IRSpeak**
> To determine the adjusted basis of an asset, start with the cost basis. Increase the cost basis by the cost of improvements to the asset, assessments for improvements (such as sidewalks built by the city), and the cost of restoring the property if it was damaged. Decrease the amount by deductions taken for depreciation, casualty losses, and tax credits that apply to the asset.

Gains and Losses from Places You Didn't Expect

In addition to reporting all of your sales, there are other sources for gains and losses that get reported on your income tax return.

If you receive dividends from stock that you own, check the dividend statement (Form 1099-DIV) carefully. Sometimes part of the dividend you receive is designated as "Capital Gain Dividend." If you see something like this on your 1099 form, report the entire dividend you received from the company on Schedule B with the rest of your dividend income. At the bottom of Schedule B there is a line where you report the capital gain portion of your dividends and reduce the total dividends by this amount. The capital gain portion then gets carried over to line 14 of Schedule D and included with other gains and losses.

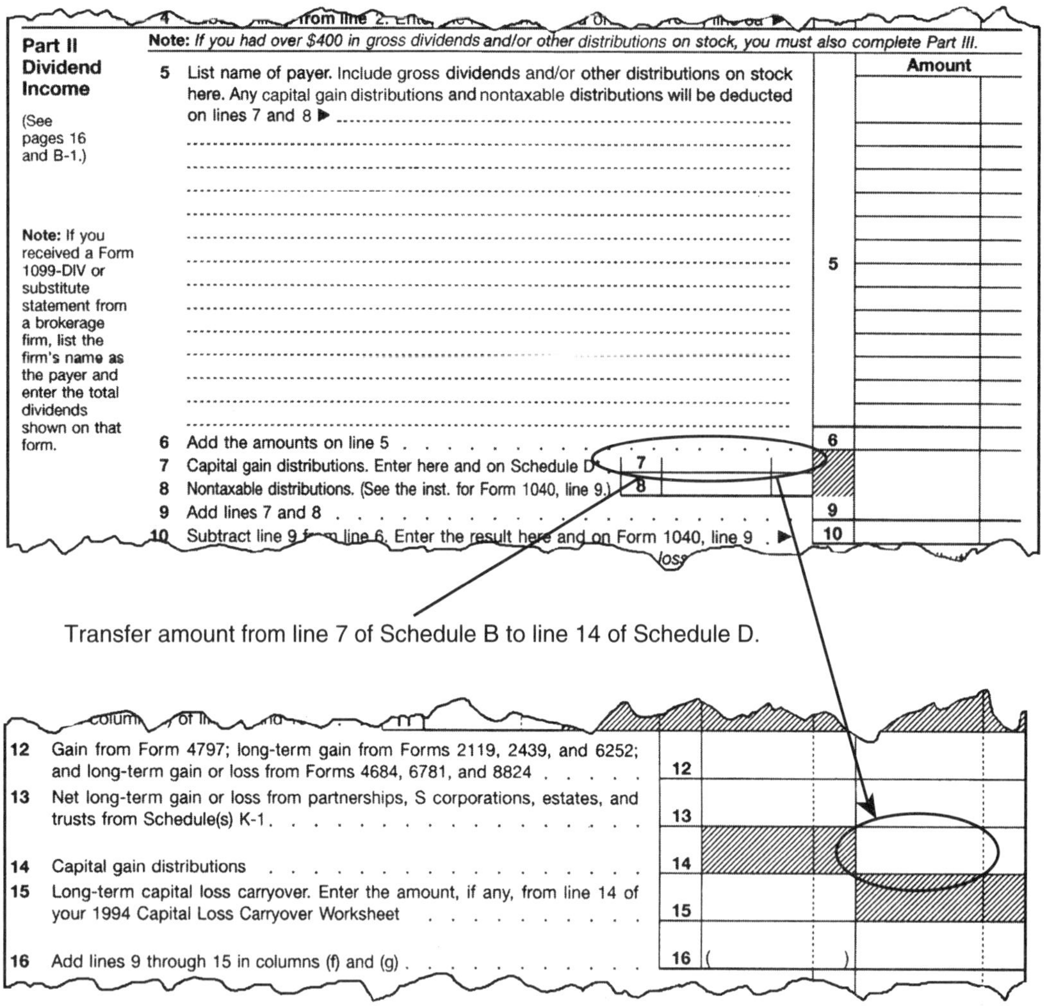

Transfer amount from line 7 of Schedule B to line 14 of Schedule D.

Reporting capital gain distributions.

If you own shares in an S corporation, if you are a partner in a partnership, or if you are the beneficiary of a trust, you receive a K-1 form each year reporting your income or loss from these entities. These K-1 forms sometimes include long-term or short-term capital gain or loss that you should report on your Schedule D. Every line on the K-1 form has a notation next to it showing you where to transfer the number on that line. For example, as the following figure illustrates, the long-term capital gain from this partnership gets placed on the taxpayer's Schedule D, line 13.

SCHEDULE K-1 (Form 1065) Department of the Treasury Internal Revenue Service	**Partner's Share of Income, Credits, Deductions, etc.** ▶ See separate instructions. For calendar year 1995 or tax year beginning , 1995, and ending , 19	OMB No. 1545-0099

Partner's identifying number ▶	Partnership's identifying number ▶
Partner's name, address, and ZIP code	Partnership's name, address, and ZIP code

A This partner is a ☐ general partner ☐ limited partner
☐ limited liability company member
B What type of entity is this partner? ▶ ....
C Is this partner a ☐ domestic or a ☐ foreign partner?
D Enter partner's percentage of: (I) Before change or termination (II) End of year
Profit sharing . . . . % .... %
Loss sharing . . . . % .... %
Ownership of capital . . . . % .... %
E IRS Center where partnership filed return:

F Partner's share of liabilities (see instructions):
Nonrecourse . . . . $ ....
Qualified nonrecourse financing . $ ....
Other . . . . $ ....
G Tax shelter registration number . ▶ ....
H Check here if this partnership is a publicly traded partnership as defined in section 469(k)(2) . . . . ☐
I Check applicable boxes: **(1)** ☐Final K-1 **(2)** ☐Amended K-1

J Analysis of partner's capital account:

(a) Capital account at beginning of year	(b) Capital contributed during year	(c) Partner's share of lines 3, 4, and 7, Form 1065, Schedule M-2	(d) Withdrawals and distributions	(e) Capital account at end of year (combine columns (a) through (d))
			)	

(a) Distributive share item		(b) Amount	(c) 1040 filers enter the amount in column (b) on:
1 Ordinary income (loss) from trade or business activities . . .	1		See pages 5 and 6 of Partner's Instructions for Schedule K-1 (Form 1065).
2 Net income (loss) from rental real estate activities	2		
3 Net income (loss) from other rental activities	3		
4 Portfolio income (loss):			
a Interest	4a		Sch. B, Part I, line 1
b Dividends	4b		Sch. B, Part II, line 5
c Royalties	4c		Sch. E, Part I, line 4
d Net short-term capital gain (loss)	4d		Sch. D, line 5, col. (f) or (g)
e Net long-term capital gain (loss)	4e		Sch. D, line 13, col. (f) or (g)
f Other portfolio income (loss) *(attach schedule)*	4f		Enter on applicable line of your return.

Your share of capital gains from a partnership, S corporation, or trust appear on the K-1 form and get transferred to Schedule D.

SCHEDULE D (Form 1040) Department of the Treasury Internal Revenue Service	**Capital Gains and Losses** ▶ Attach to Form 1040. ▶ See Instructions for Schedule D (Form 1040). ▶ Use lines 20 and 22 for more space to list transactions for lines 1 and 9.	OMB No. 1545-0074 19**95** Attachment Sequence No. **12**

Name(s) shown on Form 1040	Your social security number

Part I   **Short-Term Capital Gains and Losses—Assets Held One Year or Less**

(a) Description of property (Example: 100 sh. XYZ Co.)	(b) Date acquired (Mo., day, yr.)	(c) Date sold (Mo., day, yr.)	(d) Sales price (see page D-3)	(e) Cost or other basis (see page D-3)	(f) LOSS If (e) is more than (d), subtract (d) from (e)	(g) GAIN If (d) is more than (e), subtract (e) from (d)
1						

2 Enter your short-term totals, if any, from line 21	**2**					
3 Total short-term sales price amounts. Add column (d) of lines 1 and 2 . . .	**3**					
4 Short-term gain from Forms 2119 and 6252, and short-term gain or loss from Forms 4684, 6781, and 8824	**4**				
5 Net short-term gain or loss from partnerships, S corporations, estates, and trusts from Schedule(s) K-1	**5**				
6 Short-term capital loss carryover. Enter the amount, if any, from line 9 of your 1994 Capital Loss Carryover Worksheet	**6**				

11 Total long-term sales price amounts. Add column (d) of lines 9 and 10 . . .	**11**					
12 Gain from Form 4797; long-term gain from Forms 2119, 2439, and 6252; and long-term gain or loss from Forms 4684, 6781, and 8824	**12**				
13 Net long-term gain or loss from partnerships, S corporations, estates, and trusts from Schedule(s) K-1 . . .	**13**				
14 Capital gain distributions	**14**				
15 Long-term capital loss carryover. Enter the amount, if any, from line 14 of your 1994 Capital Loss Carryover Worksheet	**15**				

Reporting K-1 capital gains and losses.

Carryovers

You might have had a net capital loss on your Schedule D last year that exceeded $3,000. If you did, then you had to carry the excess over $3,000 to this year's Schedule D. Look at Part III of your Schedule D from 1994. If line 18 showed a loss and line 19 showed an amount less than the amount on line 18, the difference between the two should be carried to this year's Schedule D as either a short-term loss carryover or long-term loss carryover (depending on whether it was short-term or long-term last year). Short-term losses get used up before long-term losses.

> **HUH?**
>
> **IRSpeak**
>
> A capital loss *carryover* is the excess, nondeductible portion of a loss that was reported on a schedule D in a prior year. When your Schedule D results in a net capital loss of more than $3,000, you must carry over the excess to the next year.

You can figure out how much loss gets carried over and whether it is long-term or short-term by filling out the Capital Loss Carryover Worksheet that comes with your tax form instructions. Filling out this form is optional (because it doesn't get attached to your tax return) if you already know how much loss you have and whether it's long-term or short-term. Here's an example of how a loss carryover might work:

1994 net short-term loss	$2,000
1994 net long-term loss	$2,500
1994 total loss (short-term + long-term)	$4,500
1994 deduction (limited to $3,000)	$3,000
Carryover to 1995 (total loss – $3,000)	$1,500
Short-term portion of carryover	$0
Long-term portion of carryover	$1,500

All of the short-term loss in 1994 was absorbed by the $3,000 deduction, so all of the loss coming forward to 1995 is long-term in nature, as illustrated in the next figure.

Selling Your Home

If you sold your home during 1995 you need to file Form 2119, "Sale of Your Home," with your federal income tax return. You have to know the following pieces of information about your home in order to fill out Form 2119:

➤ Date of sale.

➤ Selling price of home.

➤ Selling expenses (real estate commission, inspection fees, title insurance, legal fees, other costs that appear on your closing statement, but don't include things that you can deduct as itemized deductions, such as interest expense and property taxes).

➤ Adjusted basis of home (original cost plus additions and improvements, less depreciation on business or rental portion of house).

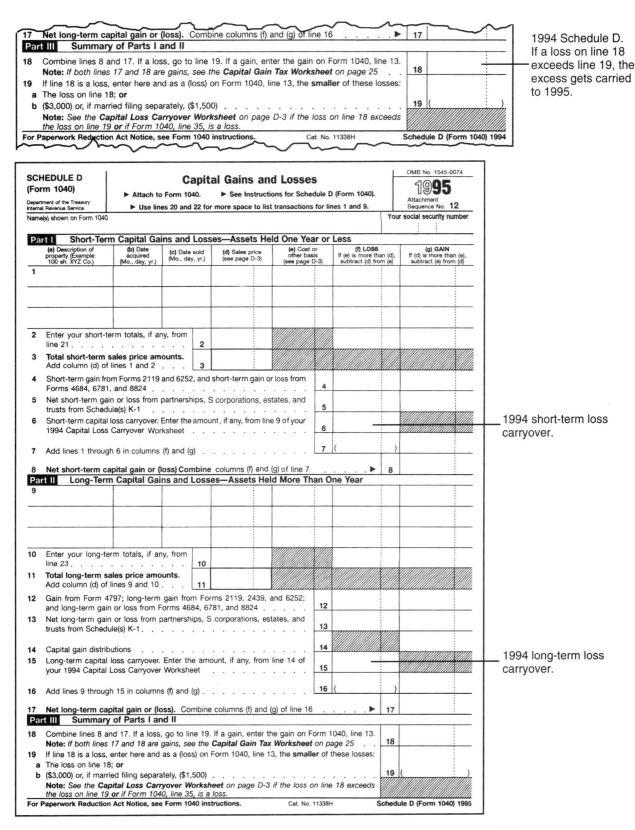

Carryover of capital loss: prior year Schedule D and Capital Loss Carryover worksheet.

The selling price of your home— you should receive a Form 1099 from your bank indicating this amount.

Form **2119**	**Sale of Your Home**	OMB No. 1545-0072

Department of the Treasury
Internal Revenue Service

➤ **Attach to Form 1040 for year of sale.**

➤ **See separate instructions.** ➤ **Please print or type.**

Attachment Sequence No. **20**

Your first name and initial. If a joint return, also give spouse's name and initial.   Last name

Your social security number

Fill in Your Address Only If You Are Filing This Form by Itself and Not With Your Tax Return

Present address (no., street, and apt. no., rural route, or P.O. box no. if mail is not delivered to street address)

Spouse's social security number

City, town or post office, state, and ZIP code

Part I   Gain on Sale

1	Date your former main home was sold (month, day, year) . . . . ▶	**1**	/ /
2	Have you bought or built a new main home?	☐ Yes ☐ No	
3	If any part of either main home was ever rented out or used for business, check here ▶ ☐ and see instructions.		
4	Selling price of home. Do not include personal property items you sold with your home . .	**4**	
5	Expense of sale (see instructions)	**5**	
6	Subtract line 5 from line 4	**6**	
7	Adjusted basis of home sold (see instructions)	**7**	
8	**Gain on sale.** Subtract line 7 from line 6	**8**	

Is line 8 more than zero?

Yes ➤ If line 2 is "Yes," you **must** go to Part II or Part III, whichever applies. If line 2 is "No," go to line 9.

No ➤ **Stop** and attach this form to your return.

9	If you haven't replaced your home, do you plan to do so within the **replacement period** (see instructions)? ☐ Yes ☐ No

* If line 9 is "Yes," stop here, attach this form to your return, and see **Additional Filing Requirements** in the instructions.
* If line 9 is "No," you **must** go to Part II or Part III, whichever applies.

Part II   One-Time Exclusion of Gain for People Age 55 or Older—By completing this part, you are electing to take the one-time exclusion (see instructions). If you are not electing to take the exclusion, go to Part III now.

10	Who was age 55 or older on the date of sale?	☐ You ☐ Your spouse ☐ Both of you	
11	Did the person who was age 55 or older own and use the property as his or her main home for a total of at least 3 years (except for short absences) of the 5-year period before the sale? If "No," go to Part III now . .	☐ Yes ☐ No	
12	At the time of sale, who owned the home?	☐ You ☐ Your spouse ☐ Both of you	
13	Social security number of spouse at the time of sale if you had a different spouse from the one above. If you were not married at the time of sale, enter "None" . . . . . . ▶	**13**	
14	**Exclusion.** Enter the **smaller** of line 8 or $125,000 ($62,500 if married filing separate return). Then, go to line 15	**14**	

Part III   Adjusted Sales Price, Taxable Gain, and Adjusted Basis of New Home

15	If line 14 is blank, enter the amount from line 8. Otherwise, subtract line 14 from line 8 . .	**15**	

* If line 15 is zero, stop and attach this form to your return.
* If line 15 is more than zero and line 2 is "Yes," go to line 16 now.
* If you are reporting this sale on the installment method, stop and see the instructions.
* All others, stop and **enter the amount from line 15 on Schedule D, col. (g), line 4 or line 12.**

16	Fixing-up expenses (see instructions for time limits)	**16**	
17	If line 14 is blank, enter amount from line 16. Otherwise, add lines 14 and 16	**17**	
18	**Adjusted sales price.** Subtract line 17 from line 6	**18**	
19a	Date you moved into new home ▶ / / **b** Cost of new home (see instructions)	**19b**	
20	Subtract line 19b from line 18. If zero or less, enter -0-	**20**	
21	**Taxable gain.** Enter the **smaller** of line 15 or line 20	**21**	

* If line 21 is zero, go to line 22 and attach this form to your return.
* If you are reporting this sale on the installment method, see the line 15 instructions and go to line 22.
* All others, **enter the amount from line 21 on Schedule D, col. (g), line 4 or line 12,** and go to line 22.

22	Postponed gain. Subtract line 21 from line 15	**22**	
23	**Adjusted basis of new home.** Subtract line 22 from line 19b	**23**	

Sign Here Only If You Are Filing This Form by Itself and Not With Your Tax Return

Under penalties of perjury, I declare that I have examined this form, including attachments, and to the best of my knowledge and belief, it is true, correct, and complete.

Your signature   Date   Spouse's signature   Date

If a joint return, both must sign.

For Paperwork Reduction Act Notice, see separate instructions.   Cat. No. 11710J   Form **2119**

☆ U.S. GPO:1994-375-330

✪ *Printed on recycled paper*

This is the gain that you may be able to roll over if you purchase a new house within the appropriate time period.

Reporting the sale of your house on Form 2119.

Get Down to Brass Tax

If you ever, in the course of living in your home, took a home office deduction for part of the home or treated part of the home as rental property, you were entitled to depreciate a portion of the home for those years. *Even if you chose not to take advantage of the depreciation deduction,* you have to add the depreciation you *could have deducted* back to the basis of your home. Bummer, huh? The exception to the "add-back of depreciation you didn't even deduct" rule is this: If you were unable to depreciate your home on Schedule C because the Schedule C showed a loss for your business, you don't have to add back *allowable* depreciation to your basis.

All of the information about the sale and basis of your home gets placed in Part I of Form 2119. If you used part of your home for business or rental property *in the year of the sale*, then you will report only the personal portion of the home on Form 2119. The sale of the business portion of the home gets reported on Form 4797.

Any gain on the sale of the home that is not rolling over to the next house (see next section, "Rolling Over") gets carried to Schedule D. Short-term gain (you owned the home less than one year) goes to line 4 on Schedule D, long-term gain goes to Schedule D, line 12.

Rolling Over

Most people usually think of dogs when they hear "roll over," but the IRS has a special meaning for the phrase. When you sell your personal residence at a gain, you can put off paying tax on that gain by "rolling over" the gain on the sale of the old house into the basis of the new house. When you get ready to sell the new house, the basis of the new house that you report on Form 2119 is reduced by the gain you deferred on the old house. Then if you sell the new house at a gain, you can roll that gain over into the *new* new house, and keep on going forever or until you turn 55, whichever comes first (see the next section, "The 55 or Over Get-It-While-You-Can Deduction").

As with everything the IRS touches, there are special rules to play by when you try to roll over a gain into the next house:

> ➤ The house you buy must cost more than the adjusted basis of the house you sell. If the cost of the new house exceeds the sales price of the old house, you can roll over the entire gain (assuming that the rest of the rules listed here are met). If the cost of the new house exceeds the adjusted basis of the old house but isn't as much as the sales price of the old house, you can roll over the lesser of the total gain

IRSpeak

When you sell your personal residence for a profit (gain), you have the right to defer paying income tax on that gain if the next house you buy is more expensive than the one you sold. This process of tax deferral is called *rollover* and it is used by homeowners who continuously move to pricier homes. You get stung when you buy a less expensive home—that's when you start paying income tax on the gain you previously deferred.

or the amount of gain that represents the difference between the amount you paid for the new house and the sales price of the old house. Confused? Try this:

a	Adjusted basis of house you sell	$65,000
b	Sales price	85,000
c	Gain on sale (b – a)	20,000
d	Purchase price of new house	80,000
e	Rolled over gain (lesser of [d – a] or c)	15,000
f	Adjusted basis of new house (d – e)	65,000

If the new house in the previous example was purchased for $110,000 instead of $80,000, the rolled over gain (e) would be $20,000 (the full amount of gain) and the adjusted basis of the new house (f) would be $90,000 ($110,000 – $20,000).

➤ Both the house you sell and the house you purchase must be your primary residence. You can't roll over a gain on the sale and purchase of a vacation home.

➤ The new house must be purchased and inhabited within the period commencing two years before the old house is sold and ending two years after the old house is sold. There can be no extension or exception to this time limit.

OOPS!
What happens if you sell a house at a gain, buy a new house, sell the new house at a gain, buy a third house, all within a two year time period? The gain on the first house gets rolled over into the *third* house. The gain on the second house gets taxed. Sorry.

If you sell your old house at a gain and buy a new house all within the same year, everything gets reported on the same Form 2119 in the same tax return. But what if this process takes more than one year or spans the December 31/January 1 cusp? No matter when the purchase of the new home happens, the sale of the old house goes on Form 2119 in the year of the sale.

If you think you are going to buy and inhabit a new house within two years from the date of sale of the old house, don't pay tax on the gain on the old house in the year of the sale. Show the gain on Form 2119, check the No box on line 2 where the form asks, "Have you bought or built a new main home?" and check the Yes box on line 9 of Part I on Form 2119 where it asks, "If you haven't replaced your home, do you plan to do so within the replacement period?" File the form with your tax return. When you buy or build the new house (next year or the year thereafter), fill out a new Form 2119, fill out Part IV showing the adjusted basis of the new house, and file that Form 2119 with the income tax return for the year of purchase.

If you planned on buying a new house within two years but didn't accomplish the purchase in time, or if you bought a new house but didn't pay enough to entitle you to postpone the entire gain on the sale of the first house, you will have to amend the tax return for the year of the sale (see Chapter 29, "Changing Your Tax Return") and pay tax on the portion of the gain you were unable to roll over.

The 55 or Over Get-It-While-You-Can Deduction

So, you sold your house and made a tidy profit. If you were still a 35-year-old kid you might be ready to purchase a more expensive house and roll the gain over into the basis of the new house. But you're not a kid. You're 55-years-old or over and you're ready to be finished with yard work and gutter repair. Or maybe you still want to own a home but your kids are grown and you're ready for a more modest, less expensive home.

Whether you decide you're ready to leave the headaches of home-ownership and head for an apartment, or you just want something smaller, you may find that you're all finished with rolling over gains into more and more expensive homes. You've had your last big house sale and your last big gain.

If you (or your spouse) are 55-years-old or over on the date of the sale of your house, you can exclude up to $125,000 of pent-up gains.

Get Down to Brass Tax

Keeping track of rolled over gains and home improvements requires good record-keeping. Period. Find an empty file folder and put a copy of every Form 2119 you ever prepared in the folder. Put a copy of every closing statement from each house you buy and sell in the folder too. Remember, you may be rolling over gains for the next 30 years. You need a trail to show where it all started and how you came up with your figures. You also need to keep a running list of all the additions and improvements you've made to your house. Start a sheet of paper for each house with the house address at the top. Begin with the purchase price and add the expenses of the sale. Reduce that sum by any rolled over gain from the prior house. Over the years, add the cost of home improvements to the list. Deduct the cost of repairing casualties (trees falling through the roof, for example. Don't laugh, it happened to me...), but add back any insurance reimbursements for your casualties. Keep this file in a safe place and add to it every time you do something that affects the basis of your house.

This 55 or over exclusion is computed on (what else?) Form 2119, in Part II. Here are the hoops you have to jump through in order to get the exclusion of gain on the house you sell:

➤ You (the person who is 55 or over on the date of sale) have to have lived in the house for three of the past five years. Those three years do not have to represent a block of consecutive time.

➤ You have to have owned the home. Owning it jointly is okay too, as long as you're one of the joints.

➤ You can't have taken the 55 or over exclusion at any other time in your life. It doesn't matter if you took it once before and only used part of the $125,000. You can only take this exclusion once.

Loss on the Sale of Your Home

If you sold your home for a loss instead of a profit you get no tax benefit. You still have to report the sale of the home on your Form 2119, but there is no deduction on your income tax return for the loss. Nothing gets carried to Schedule D or anyplace else.

The exception to this rule about no tax benefit for losses is if you were using the house for a business in the year just before you sold it. If you took a home office deduction on Schedule C or if part of the house was being used as rental property, the sale of the business portion of the house gets reported on Part III of Form 4797, "Sale of Business Property." Your income on your Form 1040 might get reduced for the business portion of the loss.

Gains and Losses on Sales of Items Used in Your Business

Businesses own things that contribute to the ability of the business to earn its income. These things are called assets and they can be tangible (you can see it), intangible (you know it's there, but you can't see it—such as a copyright or computer software), real (such as a building), or personal (such as furniture).

When a business sells an asset, the sale must be reported on Form 4797, "Sales of Business Property." This form is divided into three parts.

In Part I of Form 4797 you report long-term (that is, assets held for more than one year) sales of furniture, equipment, vehicles, land, and anything else that you use in your business to produce income. Short-term sales go in Part II. Business assets held for more than one year that result in a gain go in Part III. In Part III the gain is separated into true gain (capital gain based on an increase in value in the asset) and recapture gain (gain that is a result of a lowering of the asset's basis due to depreciation taken over the years). The tax treatment of the kind of gain differs.

If you get this far into Form 4797, look under some rocks until you find an accountant. This is complex stuff. Unless you're extremely comfortable reading IRS instructions, I recommend that you seek out someone who does tax preparation for a living.

Form **4797**	**Sales of Business Property**	OMB No. 1545-0184
	(Also Involuntary Conversions and Recapture Amounts Under Sections 179 and 280F(b)(2))	
Department of the Treasury Internal Revenue Service (O)	▶ Attach to your tax return. ▶ See separate instructions.	Attachment Sequence No. **27**

Name(s) shown on return | Identifying number

1 Enter here the gross proceeds from the sale or exchange of real estate reported to you for 1994 on Form(s) 1099-S (or a substitute statement) that you will be including on line 2, 11, or 22 . . . . | **1** |

Part I   Sales or Exchanges of Property Used in a Trade or Business and Involuntary Conversions From Other Than Casualty or Theft—Property Held More Than 1 Year

(a) Description of property	(b) Date acquired (mo., day, yr.)	(c) Date sold (mo., day, yr.)	(d) Gross sales price	(e) Depreciation allowed or allowable since acquisition	(f) Cost or other basis, plus improvements and expense of sale	(g) LOSS ((f) minus the sum of (d) and (e))	(h) GAIN ((d) plus (e) minus (f))
2							

> Show sales of items used to produce income in your business. Assets reported in this section must have been owned by you for at least one year.

3 Gain, if any, from Form 4684, line 39 . . . . | **3** |

4 Section 1231 gain from installment sales from Form 6252, line 26 or 37 . . . . . . | **4** |

5 Section 1231 gain or (loss) from like-kind exchanges from Form 8824 . . . . . . | **5** |

6 Gain, if any, from line 34, from other than casualty or theft . . . . | **6** |

7 Add lines 2 through 6 in columns (g) and (h) . . . . | **7** ( ) |

8 Combine columns (g) and (h) of line 7. Enter gain or (loss) here, and on the appropriate line as follows: . . . . | **8** |

Partnerships—Enter the gain or (loss) on Form 1065, Schedule K, line 6. Skip lines 9, 10, 12, and 13 below.

S corporations—Report the gain or (loss) following the instructions for Form 1120S, Schedule K, lines 5 and 6. Skip lines 9, 10, 12, and 13 below, unless line 8 is a gain and the S corporation is subject to the capital gains tax.

All others—If line 8 is zero or a loss, enter the amount on line 12 below and skip lines 9 and 10. If line 8 is a gain and you did not have any prior year section 1231 losses, or they were recaptured in an earlier year, enter the gain as a long-term capital gain on Schedule D and skip lines 9, 10, and 13 below.

9 Nonrecaptured net section 1231 losses from prior years (see instructions) . . . . | **9** |

10 Subtract line 9 from line 8. If zero or less, enter -0-. Also enter on the appropriate line as follows (see instructions): | **10** |

S corporations—Enter this amount (if more than zero) on Schedule D (Form 1120S), line 13, and skip lines 12 and 13 below.

All others—If line 10 is zero, enter the amount from line 8 on line 13 below. If line 10 is more than zero, enter the amount from line 9 on line 13 below, and enter the amount from line 10 as a long-term capital gain on Schedule D.

Part II   Ordinary Gains and Losses

11 Ordinary gains and losses not included on lines 12 through 18 (include property held 1 year or less):

12 Loss, if any, from line 8 . . . . | **12** |

13 Gain, if any, from line 8, or amount from line 9 if applicable . . . . | **13** |

14 Gain, if any, from line 33 . . . . | **14** |

15 Net gain or (loss) from Form 4684, lines 31 and 38a . . . . | **15** |

16 Ordinary gain from installment sales from Form 6252, line 25 or 36 . . . . | **16** |

17 Ordinary gain or (loss) from like-kind exchanges from Form 8824 . . . . | **17** |

18 Recapture of section 179 expense deduction for partners and S corporation shareholders from property dispositions by partnerships and S corporations (see instructions) . . . . . . | **18** |

19 Add lines 11 through 18 in columns (g) and (h) . . . . | **19** ( ) |

20 Combine columns (g) and (h) of line 19. Enter gain or (loss) here, and on the appropriate line as follows: . . . | **20** |

a For all except individual returns: Enter the gain or (loss) from line 20 on the return being filed.

b For individual returns:

(1) If the loss on line 12 includes a loss from Form 4684, line 35, column (b)(ii), enter that part of the loss here and on line 22 of Schedule A (Form 1040). Identify as from "Form 4797, line 20b(1)." See instructions . . . | **20b(1)** |

(2) Redetermine the gain or (loss) on line 20, excluding the loss, if any, on line 20b(1). Enter here and on Form 1040, line 14 . | **20b(2)** |

> Show sales of all business assets owned for less than one year in this section.

For Paperwork Reduction Act Notice, see page 1 of separate instructions. | Cat. No. 13086I | Form **4797**

Page 1 of Form 4797.

The Least You Need to Know

➤ The sales of personal assets, items you own yourself, get reported on Schedule D.

➤ The sale of your personal residence gets reported on Form 2119.

➤ The sales of business assets get reported on Form 4797.

Chapter 15

Retirement: IRAs and Social Security Benefits

In This Chapter

➤ Taxation of income from IRAs

➤ Reporting Social Security benefits

If you're planning on someday living on retirement income, you should have your financial house in order. Know from where your income is going to come and know how much of it is going to be taxed. Even if you aren't at a retirement age now, you should be knowledgeable about what tax surprises lie ahead.

If you receive income from a pension or an annuity, is it subject to income tax? Actually, that's a trick question because the answer is "sometimes." If your employer contributed all the money that you receive from a retirement fund and you didn't add to the fund yourself, the amounts you receive are taxable. On the other hand, if you made all the payments yourself to your retirement fund, or if you chipped in part of the payments, then when you get back the part you put into the fund, it might not be taxable to you. Here's how it works.

IRAs

Amounts withdrawn from IRAs (Individual Retirement Accounts) are generally taxable when you withdraw them. The way an IRA was meant to work is that you contribute up to a maximum of $2,000 per year to the account while you are earning money working in your job, and you get to deduct the amount you contribute on your income tax return, so you don't have to pay income tax on the amount you contribute. Then, when you retire, you start withdrawing money from the account. As you withdraw money from your IRA, you pay income tax on it, presumably at a tax rate lower than the rate at which you would have been taxed had you paid the income tax when you were earning the money.

The catch began in 1987 when Congress restricted the amount of tax-deductible contribution you could make to your IRA based on your income. The IRA deduction was disallowed for many taxpayers (see "Can We Still Deduct IRA Contributions?" in Chapter 18).

So, say you withdraw money from your IRA. If all the money you put in the IRA was tax deductible, then when you start withdrawing from the fund, everything you take out is taxable and gets reported on line 15a of your 1040 (or line 10a of Form 1040A). That seems easy enough.

But what if only part of what you put in the account was deducted from your income? How do you compute the taxable portion of the amount you withdraw? First of all, you have to know how much of the money in your IRA account was deducted from your income on your 1040. The easiest way to do this is to keep track as you go. Start a list of your contributions and add to it each year. In one column put the amount you contributed that you deducted from your income on your 1040. In the other column put the amount that you contributed to the IRA but were unable to deduct from your income. Keep this piece of paper in a safe place because you'll need it for a long time.

If you withdraw funds from your IRA before you reach age 59 1/2, the IRS expects you to add the amount you withdrew to your income, pay income tax on it, *and pay a 10% penalty on the early withdrawal.* That makes the cost of this money very high. If you need cash, a bank loan is a much more economical way to get it than an early IRA withdrawal.

IRSpeak

IRA stands for *Individual Retirement Account,* a type of savings account that is earmarked for retirement. This savings account is special because the IRS will sometimes let you take a deduction for amounts that you deposit in the account and you might not have to pay tax *currently* on the earnings of the account. Eventually, when you begin withdrawing amounts from your IRA, you pay tax on all the money you take out.

By the Way

You can take money out of your IRA temporarily without paying tax on it, either for purposes of transferring the money to a different account or even as a short-term loan. Once per year you can withdraw money from your IRA. You have 60 days from the date you withdraw the money to redeposit it and avoid being taxed on the withdrawal. Don't miss the 60-day date. There are no exceptions to this rule.

In any year you make a withdrawal from your IRA you must get a Form 8606, "Nondeductible IRAs (Contributions, Distributions, and Basis)." Fill out this form and attach it to your 1040 each year you withdraw any amount from your IRA. On this form fill in the nontaxable portion of your IRA—that is, the total amount of what is left in the fund that you contributed that was never deducted on your tax return. If you filed Form 8606 in a prior year, you can get this nontaxable portion (called the *basis*) from the prior year's form. If this is the first time you have had to prepare Form 8606, your basis will be the total amount in your IRA since the beginning of time that you have not deducted on an income tax return. Then you divide this basis by the total amount in the fund as of the end of 1995, giving you a percentage that you apply to your withdrawal of funds. The result of that computation is nontaxable to you. The balance is taxable and goes on line 15b of your 1040. Be sure to update your personal IRA worksheet (see the example worksheet on this page) each year for your records.

> **IRSpeak**
> The *basis* of your IRA is the amount you contributed and on which you already paid tax. In other words, if you made a contribution to your IRA and didn't get to take a deduction on your 1040 for your contribution, that amount gets added to your basis.

My IRA

Year	Deductible Contribution	Non-Deductible Contribution	Total Earnings	Balance	Percent of Balance that's deferred		
1988	$ 2,000.00	$ 0	$ 0	$2,000.00	0		
1989	2,000.00	0	160.00	4,160.00	0		
1990	2,000.00	0	312.00	6,472.00	0		
1991	0	2,000.00	420.68	8,892.68	67.47%		
1992	0	2,000.00	444.63	11,337.31	52.92%		
1993	0	2,000.00	510.18	13,847.49	43.33%		
1994	0	2,000.00	553.90	16,401.39	36.58%		
1995	0	2,000.00	656.06	19,057.45	31.48%		
total	6,000.00	10,000.00					

You can make a worksheet to keep track of your IRA contributions.

Get Down to Brass Tax

Here's a sample computation to find out if a withdrawal from an IRA is taxable.

a	Basis: Amount contributed that was not deducted in prior years:	15,000
b	Total amount in your IRA as of 12/31/95:	20,000
c	Amount withdrawn in 1995:	2,000
d	Nontaxable percentage (a ÷ b + c)	68%
e	Nontaxable part of amount withdrawn (c x d)	1,360
f	Taxable part of amount withdrawn (c – e)	640
g	Remaining basis in IRA account (a – e)	13,640
h	Basis for next year's Form 8606 (g):	13,640

(Note: Participants in SEP plans—Simplified Employee Pension Plans—are subject to the same rules as IRA participants for taxation of withdrawn amounts.)

Pensions and Annuities

Income from pension and annuity plans is usually taxable. Form 1099-R reports your retirement income, and it specifically lists the taxable portion.

Here's the amount you withdrew in 1995.

9898 ☐ VOID ☐ CORRECTED

PAYER'S name, street address, city, state, and ZIP code

1 Gross distribution $

2a Taxable amount $

OMB No. 1545-0119

1995

Form 1099-R

Distributions From Pensions, Annuities, Retirement or Profit-Sharing Plans, IRAs, Insurance Contracts, etc.

2b Taxable amount not determined ☐ Total distribution ☐

Copy A For Internal Revenue Service Center

PAYER'S Federal identification number

RECIPIENT'S identification number

3 Capital gain (included in box 2a) $

4 Federal income tax withheld $

File with Form 1096.

RECIPIENT'S name

5 Employee contributions or insurance premiums $

6 Net unrealized appreciation in employer's securities $

For Paperwork Reduction Act Notice and instructions for completing this form, see **Instructions for Forms 1099, 1098, 5498, and W-2G.**

Street address (including apt. no.)

7 Distribution code

IRA/ SEP ☐

8 Other $ %

City, state, and ZIP code

9a Your percentage of total distribution %

9b Total employee contributions $

Account number (optional)

10 State tax withheld $ $

11 State/Payer's state no.

12 State distribution $ $

13 Local tax withheld $ $

14 Name of locality

15 Local distribution $ $

Form 1099-R Cat. No. 14436Q Department of the Treasury - Internal Revenue Service

A sample Form 1099-R.

However, it may be that both you and your employer contributed to your retirement fund. If you put your own money into the plan in addition to amounts your employer contributed, then you need to know how much is yours and how much is your employer's. Usually the amount you contributed will be listed in box 5 of the Form 1099-R. The part that you contributed is not taxable as you withdraw money from the plan. The employer's contribution is taxable.

But, true to IRS form, there is a tricky method for figuring out how much of your retirement income is taxable and how much is tax-free due to your own investment. If you have withdrawn money from your retirement fund in prior years, then the method for reporting the taxable portion of retirement income is already in place. Use the same method this year. If this is the first year for withdrawing money from the retirement fund, here's the scoop on choosing a method for calculating the taxable portion.

If part of your retirement income is taxable and part is nontaxable, there are a couple of different ways in which you can compute the taxable portion. You can choose between the *General Rule* and the *Simplified General Rule*.

You can choose the Simplified General Rule if the following requirements are met:

➤ You didn't start receiving payments until after July 1, 1986.

➤ Your retirement plan continues to make periodic payments either until you die or until both you and your beneficiary die.

➤ The retirement plan is a qualified employee plan, a qualified employee annuity, or a tax-sheltered annuity (in other words the payments come from an official retirement plan organization, not your employer and not your rich uncle—check with your employer or the plan administrator if you're not sure whether the plan is qualified).

➤ Either you were younger than 75-years-old when the payments began or the payments are guaranteed for fewer than 5 years.

Follow this worksheet in order to figure out the tax-free portion of your payment using the Simplified General Rule.

a   Total pension payments received this year: _____

b   Total amount you contributed for all years: _____

c   Enter magic number (see the following table) _____

d   Divide amount on line b by magic number (c) _____

e   Line d times number of months in which
you received a payment this year _____

f   Tax-free amounts received in prior years _____

g   Line b minus line e _____

h   Enter smaller of line e or line g _____

i   Line a minus line h (don't enter less than zero) _____

Enter the magic number from this chart on line c in the preceding worksheet:

Your Age at Time You Started Receiving Retirement Payments	Magic Number
55 or under	300
56–60	260
61–65	240
66–70	170
71 and over	120

If you use the Simplified General Rule, you will recover your cost in the retirement plan, tax free over the "magic" number of months.

If you didn't meet the requirements for the Simplified General Rule, you must use the General Rule. If you use the General Rule, you will determine a fixed amount that represents the amount of your cost that is tax free each year. The amount doesn't change from year to year except that once your entire cost has been excluded from otherwise taxable retirement income, you stop reducing the taxable retirement payment by the tax-free amount.

In order to figure out how much you should count as your tax-free portion each year using the General Rule, you have to examine actuarial tables that the government uses to estimate how long you are going to live. If you have to figure this out yourself, call the IRS (1-800-TAX-FORM) and ask for a copy of Publication 939, "Pension General Rule (Nonsimplified Method)."

Social Security Benefits (Am I Missing Something?)

If you receive Social Security benefits, you will receive a Form SSA-1099, which summarizes how much in benefits you received during the year. A sample Form SSA-1099 is shown on the next page. Box 5 on the Form SSA-1099, "Net Benefits for 1995," contains the number you should report on your income tax return.

You might not understand the logic of the government giving Social Security benefits and then taking some back in the form of taxes. (Logic? Taxes? Can you really say those two words in the same sentence?) Most people tend to think of Social Security benefits as a return of their own money. After all, they earned that money, they paid tax on it when they earned it, now they're just taking it back when they need it, and, what's this? More tax?

Actually, the taxation of Social Security benefits is not such a bad deal if you consider the fact that employers match employee contributions. Furthermore, even after a person recoups everything that was put in the plan on his or her behalf, that person still gets to keep drawing out benefits.

List these net benefits from box 5 of the SSA-1099 on line 20a of your Form 1040. Putting this amount on your Form 1040 doesn't necessarily imply that you have to pay income tax on your Social Security benefits. Instead, you have to fill out a little worksheet that comes with your income tax return instructions to find out how much of your benefits are taxable.

FORM SSA-1099—SOCIAL SECURITY BENEFIT STATEMENT

• PART OF YOUR SOCIAL SECURITY BENEFITS SHOWN IN BOX 5 MAY BE TAXABLE INCOME.
• SEE THE REVERSE FOR MORE INFORMATION.

Box 1. Name	Box 2. Beneficiary's Social Security Number

Box 3. Benefits Paid in 1995	Box 4. Benefits Repaid to SSA in 1995	Box 5. Net Benefits for 1995 *(Box 3 minus Box 4)*

This is the amount that goes on line 20a of your Form 1040.

DESCRIPTION OF AMOUNT IN BOX 3	DESCRIPTION OF AMOUNT IN BOX 4

Box 6. Address

Box 7. Claim Number *(Use this number if you need to contact SSA.)*

Form SSA-1099-SM (1-96)   **DO NOT RETURN THIS FORM TO SSA OR IRS**

A sample Form SSA-1099.

Here's a sample Social Security benefits worksheet:

1. Start by adding up the total amount of box 5 on all Forms SSA-1099 you received during the year and put 1/2 that amount on this line: _____

2. List the total of all your income as shown on page 1 of your Form 1040. For retirement distributions (lines 14 and 15), just include the taxable portion; for interest income include both taxable and tax-exempt: _____

3. Add lines 1 and 2: _____

4. Enter the total adjustments from line 30 of your Form 1040 (I haven't even talked about adjustments yet—see Chapter 18, "Adjustments to Income," for information about figuring out your adjustments) _____

5. Subtract line 4 from line 2: _____

6. Enter one of the following amounts: _____

> **$25,000** if your filing status is Single, Head of Household, Qualifying Widow(er), or if your status is Married Filing Separately and you didn't live with your spouse at all during 1995.

> **$32,000** if your filing status is Married Filing Jointly.

> **$0** if your filing status is Married Filing Separately but you lived with your spouse at some time during 1995.

7. Subtract line 6 from line 5 (don't enter less than zero): _____

8. If line 7 is zero, none of your Social Security benefits are taxable and you should put a zero on line 20b of your Form 1040. If line 7 is not zero: _____

> **$12,000** goes on this line if you are Married Filing Jointly.

> **$0** goes on this line if you are Married Filing Separately and you didn't live with your spouse at all during 1995, otherwise…

> **$9,000** goes on this line.

9. Subtract line 8 from line 7 (don't enter less than zero) _____

10. Enter the smaller of line 7 or line 8 _____

11. Enter 1/2 of line 10 _____

12. Enter either line 11 or line 1, whichever is smaller _____

13. Multiply line 9 by 85% _____

14. Add lines 12 and 13 _____

15. Multiply your total Social Security benefits by 85% _____

16. Enter either line 14 or line 15, whichever is smaller _____

Whew! The amount on line 16 is the taxable portion of your Social Security benefits. This amount goes on line 20b of your income tax return.

The Least You Need to Know

➤ Retirement income is taxable in full to you if you haven't already paid tax on any of the money that went into the retirement fund.

➤ If you put your money into the retirement fund (or your employer withheld amounts from your wages and put that into the fund) and you haven't paid income tax on that money yet, everything you take out of your retirement fund is subject to income tax.

➤ If you or your employer put your money into the retirement fund and you already paid income tax on that money, you will have to figure out how much of your retirement proceeds represent already-taxed income. You don't want to pay income tax on that money twice!

➤ If you receive Social Security benefits, you need to fill out the worksheet to find out how much is taxable. Finish the rest of the front page of your federal income tax return before you make this calculation.

Chapter 16

Rents, Royalties, and Those Kooky K-1 Forms

In This Chapter

➤ Tax effects of renting your vacation home

➤ So you want to be a landlord?

➤ Reporting royalty income

➤ Income from partnerships and S corporations

➤ Beneficiaries of trusts

The Schedule E form that gets filed with some tax returns gives you a place to summarize all sorts of odd income—rents, royalties, and your share of amounts from partnerships and S corporations of which you may be a member. You may have none of these items (in which case you don't need to prepare a Schedule E and you can pass right over this chapter), or you may have many of these items that will all pile up on the same Schedule E.

You may be actively involved in the organizations whose income shows up on Schedule E (generating *nonpassive income)*, or you may be an onlooker, a ticket-holder in someone else's show, and you reap financial rewards with little or no expenditure of time and effort (resulting in *passive income*).

Get Down to Brass Tax

A *passive activity* is a business-related activity in which you do not materially participate (detailed rules for what constitutes "material participation" in a business are set out in Chapter 12, "W-2 and 1099 Forms"). For example, suppose that you invest in a local snowcone business; you put up the money, then hire someone else to actually run the day-to-day operations of the business while you plan to sit back and watch the money roll in. The business is a passive activity. If you're out there every day dishing up snowcones, the business is not a passive activity. Income from a passive activity is *passive income*. Loss from a passive activity is *passive loss* and can only be deducted to the extent that it is offset with passive income.

For rent and royalty income (or losses), Schedule E is a place to list the detailed information regarding these business interests. For pass-through items such as partnerships, S corporations, estates, and trusts, Schedule E represents a summary form, a place where you report your share of the activity of organizations that file their own tax returns with the IRS.

Vacation Homes

You've worked the better part of your life to be able to afford a second home, a place to get away from the rat race of your everyday life, a place to retreat to with your friends, a place to take the kids, a vacation spot that's all your own.

Suppose some friends of yours want to use the place for a week and insist on paying you a bit of cash for the right to do so. Is this taxable income? Does the IRS have to have a piece of this?

Well, amazing as it may seem, the answer is no. You have the right to rent out your vacation home for an extremely minimal amount of time each year and you don't even have to tell the IRS about it. Here's the way it works.

14-Day Rule

If you own a second home (a vacation cottage, a condo in the city, a houseboat, or whatever) and you rent it to someone else for *no more than 14 days* during the year, you don't have to report the rental income to the IRS. Likewise, any expenses you might incur on the property during those 14 days cannot be reported on your tax return as any kind of tax deduction. It's as if the whole experience never happened (and, of course, depending on the tenants you had, you may wish that were the case…).

Fourteen days is the magic number. Rent that home for 15 days and you've got yourself a tax-related transaction that you have to report on your income tax return (via Schedule E).

Something for Nothing

So, what's the catch, you ask? The IRS will let you have 14 days worth of good, old-fashioned income, and they don't even want to hear about it?

Actually, reporting that 14 or fewer days of rental income and related expenses is just too much trouble: too much trouble for you to prorate the expenses for just a few days to come up with the portion that would be deductible, and too much trouble for the IRS to check up on you and see whether you properly allocated the expenses on your house between personal and rental. For such a small number of days, chances are the income you get from the property would offset the expenses you could declare and that would result in no change in your taxable income. Watch out, though. This law may be repealed in the near future.

Serious Rental Property

Rent out your property for 15 days or more in a year and suddenly you find yourself a landlord with responsibilities not just to your tenants but also to the IRS.

Income from rents and any expenses related to generating rental income get reported in Part I of Schedule E, "Supplemental Income and Loss," which you attach to your 1040. In lines 1A, 1B, and 1C of this form, you give the address for each rental property you own.

Income from Rents

Tenants pay you rent and you record it as rental income in columns A, B, and C of line 3 on Schedule E. That's easy enough. There are a few confusing parts of collecting rent, however, and the IRS has made some convenient rules to alleviate the confusion.

➤ Security deposits are not rent. Do not report them with your rental income. Likewise, don't report them as an expense when you return them. Security deposits never show their faces on your income tax return.

➤ Security deposits that you intend to use as the last month's rent *are* rent and you should report them as rent income in the year in which you receive them.

➤ Payments you receive from tenants that represent reimbursement for repairs or costs of utilities should be added to your rental income. Deduct the offsetting expense with your other expenses, so the net effect is zero.

➤ Sometimes tenants make improvements to dwelling units in lieu of paying rent. For example, say your tenant paints his apartment and you let him skip a month's rent in return. You should record the missed rent as rent income, then deduct the same amount as the cost of painting the apartment.

SCHEDULE E (Form 1040) Department of the Treasury Internal Revenue Service (O)	**Supplemental Income and Loss** (From rental real estate, royalties, partnerships, S corporations, estates, trusts, REMICs, etc.) ▶ Attach to Form 1040 or Form 1041. ▶ See Instructions for Schedule E (Form 1040).	OMB No. 1545-0074 **1995** Attachment Sequence No. 13

Name(s) shown on return | Your social security number

Part I Income or Loss From Rental Real Estate and Royalties Note: *Report income and expenses from your business of renting personal property on Schedule C or C-EZ (see page E-1). Report farm rental income or loss from Form 4835 on page 2, line 39.*

Describe each rental property (use additional Schedules E if you have more than three properties).

1 Show the kind and location of each **rental real estate property:**

A ....

B ....

C ....

2 For each rental real estate property listed on line 1, did you or your family use it for personal purposes for more than the greater of 14 days or 10% of the total days rented at fair rental value during the tax year? (See page E-1.)

	Yes	No
A		
B		
C		

Income:

		Properties			Totals (Add columns A, B, and C.)
		A	B	C	
3 Rents received	3				3
4 Royalties received	4				4
Expenses:					
5 Advertising	5				
6 Auto and travel (see page E-2)	6				
7 Cleaning and maintenance	7				
8 Commissions	8				
9 Insurance	9				
10 Legal and other professional fees	10				
11 Management fees	11				
12 Mortgage interest paid to banks, etc. (see page E-2)	12				12
13 Other interest	13				
14 Repairs	14				
15 Supplies	15				
16 Taxes	16				
17 Utilities	17				
18 Other (list) ▶	18				
19 Add lines 5 through 18	19				19
20 Depreciation expense or depletion (see page E-2)	20				20
21 Total expenses. Add lines 19 and 20	21				
22 Income or (loss) from rental real estate or royalty properties. Subtract line 21 from line 3 (rents) or line 4 (royalties). If the result is a (loss), see page E-2 to find out if you must file **Form 6198**	22				
23 Deductible rental real estate loss. **Caution:** *Your rental real estate loss on line 22 may be limited. See page E-3 to find out if you must file **Form 8582**. Real estate professionals must complete line 42 on page 2*	23	(	)(	)(	)
24 **Income.** Add positive amounts shown on line 22. **Do not** include any losses					24
25 **Losses.** Add royalty losses from line 22 and rental real estate losses from line 23. Enter the total losses here					25 ( )
26 Total rental real estate and royalty income or (loss). Combine lines 24 and 25. Enter the result here. If Parts II, III, IV, and line 39 on page 2 do not apply to you, also enter this amount on Form 1040, line 17. Otherwise, include this amount in the total on line 40 on page 2					26

For Paperwork Reduction Act Notice, see Form 1040 instructions.   Cat. No. 11344L   Schedule E (Form 1040) 1995

Page 1 of Schedule E.

Rent is recorded as income when you receive it, not when it is applicable. If I pay you rent for January 1996, in December 1995, you should record it in December and report it on your 1995 income tax return.

Costs of Doing Business

As you probably already know, there are many expenses associated with owning property and making it available for rent. In addition to the cost of the property itself and improvements you make to it—items which get depreciated as discussed in the previous section—there are plenty of other items with which to fill up the "Expenses" section of Part I of Schedule E. Here's just a sampling of the types of expenses you might incur:

➤ Repairs

➤ Advertising

➤ Cleaning services

➤ Management fees

➤ Insurance

➤ Property taxes

➤ Mortgage interest

➤ Collection expenses

➤ Travel

➤ Wages paid to employees

➤ Lawn service

➤ Utilities

➤ Legal and accounting fees

➤ Office expenses

➤ Condominium association fees

OOPS!
The IRS is watching you. Sometimes your tenants report rent income to you on the informational Form 1099-MISC. The IRS gets a copy of this form as well. The rental income you report on your Schedule E should equal or exceed the amounts reported to you on Form 1099-MISC. If someone sends you an incorrect 1099-MISC, contact that person or organization and have a corrected form filed. It's your responsibility to make sure that the IRS has correct information.

Watch out! Don't try to deduct the following items, which aren't allowed as deductions for rental property on your income tax return:

➤ Points paid on the purchase of real estate. (You have to amortize the points over the loan period.)

161

OOPS!

If you use your property for at least 15 days or more than 10% of the total days the property was rented during the year (not counting the days you were there for cleaning, maintenance, and repairs, whichever was greater), the IRS considers the property to be a personal residence (as opposed to a rental residence). In this case, your deductions are limited to the income earned on the property minus interest and property taxes. Any of these deductions can be carried forward to next year. The same limitation rules will apply next year.

➤ Personal portion of repair and maintenance expenses. (You must prorate your expenses between rent time and personal time if you used the property personally for a portion of the year—personal time includes letting your Aunt Isabel stay there rent-free.)

If your rental expenses exceed your rental income, the IRS limits you to $25,000 per year as a loss on all your combined rental properties. This $25,000 limitation is based on the assumption that you "actively participate" in the management of the rental property. If you just collect the checks and a management company takes complete care of your property, including paying the bills and making decisions about the maintenance of the property, then the IRS is not likely to agree that you actively participate in the management. If you don't actively participate in the management of the property, your losses are restricted to the point where you can only deduct them if you have passive income against which to offset them. (See the "Passive (Yawn) Income" section later in this chapter.)

Note that this $25,000 allowance for rental losses is reduced by $1 for every $2 of adjusted gross income in excess of $100,000 ($30,000 if Married Filing Separately) that you show on your tax return.

Depreciation: Not the Bargain It Once Was

In the rental property good old days (pre-1984) you could buy a house, use it as rental property, and deduct the cost of the house (depreciate it) over as little as 15 years. The rental market hasn't been so attractive for a long time. Now the same house, acquired in 1995, gets depreciated over 27.5 years.

Depreciation expense is calculated on Form 4562 (shown in Chapter 13, "Do It Yourself on Schedule C"), and is carried to Schedule E, line 20. To depreciate your rental property, you must know the *adjusted basis* of the property. Generally speaking, the adjusted basis is the cost plus improvements.

Get Down to Brass Tax

Whenever you buy or convert a piece of property to use as rental property, start a worksheet on which you keep track of the adjusted basis of the property. Start with your cost, including nondeductible fees (legal fees, title search, and so on) that you paid in connection with the purchase of the property. As you continue to own the property over the years, add to your worksheet as you add permanent improvements such as a room addition, new furnace, and landscaping. All permanent improvements affect not just the basis for purposes of depreciating the property, but they also affect the basis when you sell the property. Therefore it's extremely important to keep all of this information together and in a safe place.

If you acquired rental property in a prior year, you must continue depreciating it the same way as in the past. Look to your records from your prior income tax return to see what has been done previously.

For rental property that you acquire in 1995, you must compute the depreciation expense and keep track each year of how much depreciation you have taken on your tax return.

The easiest way to keep track of your depreciable property is to create a worksheet. Then you can use the worksheet each year and update it. Here's one way of recording depreciation on your rental property:

OOPS!
If you purchase a house or other piece of property that includes a cost for land, the land portion of the cost is not depreciable and you must deduct it from the cost when you figure out your depreciation expense.

Item	Date Acq	Cost	Depr Method	Depr Period	1995 Depr	1996 Depr	1997 Depr
Condo	4/3/95	65,000	MACRS	27.5	1674		
Landscaping	6/18/95	2,000	MACRS	15	133		
Refrigerator	4/3/95	400	MACRS	7	57		

But what's this MACRS stuff, and how do you determine the depreciation period (the number of years over which you spread the deduction of property), and how do you figure out how much depreciation expense to take in a given year? Fortunately, you don't have to be a CPA to figure out these things.

MACRS (rhymes with *Quakers*) is the depreciation method most commonly used for writing off the value of business assets over time. If you care, it stands for Modified Accelerated Cost Recovery System, but those who use it in their daily lives just call it MACRS.

Business assets are items you buy for your business (renting property is a kind of a business) that you expect will last for several years. A house can be a business asset, so can a piece of furniture, a car, or a computer. A pencil isn't a business asset—it wears out pretty quickly. Same with a case of paper, batteries, glue, and stamps. Consider these items as supplies and deduct them as a business expense in the year in which you purchase them. Some assets last forever and therefore can't be depreciated, nor can you take a deduction for them like you can for paper clips. Land is an example of an asset that lasts forever. If you buy a house that you plan to use for rental property and the cost of the house includes the land on which the house sits, you have to separate the cost of the land before you can depreciate the house.

OOPS!
If, in calculating your depreciation, you discover you made a mistake in last year's depreciation calculation and didn't deduct as much as you were entitled to deduct, you can correct the error by filing an amended tax return for last year. (See Chapter 29.) If you took too much depreciation expense last year, you can reduce this year's depreciation expense by the amount of the coverage.

The IRS has determined guidelines for the life expectancy of your assets. These guidelines are based on averages and may not seem right for your situation. It doesn't matter. Use them anyway.

Type of Asset	Life in Years
Residential Rental Property, including furnaces, vents, water pipes, central air, roof, and room additions	27.5
Furniture and appliances	7.0
Carpeting	7.0
Computers and related equipment	5.0
Automobiles	5.0
Land improvements: shrubbery, sidewalks, roads, fences, and drainage ditches	15.0
Other stuff that doesn't seem to fit on this list	7.0

For everything except residential rental property, you can compute the depreciation as shown in Table 16.1.

Table 16.1 Depreciation Expense for 5-, 7-, and 15-Year Personal Property

Year	Expense Computation
1st Year	5- and 7-year property: Cost of asset divided by number of years in life (as determined by the preceding table)
	15-year property: Cost of asset multiplied by 5% (assuming the half-year convention applies)
2nd Year	Cost of asset less depreciation previously taken, divided by number of life years (from preceding table), multiplied by 2 for 5- and 7-year property, and multiplied by 1.5 for 15-year property
3rd Year	Same *computation* as 2nd year
4th Year	For 5-year property: 40% of remaining basis*
	For 7- and 15-year property: same *computation* as 2nd year
5th Year	For 5-year property: same *amount* as 4th year
	For 7-year property: 28.57% of remaining basis*
	For 15-year property: same *computation* as 2nd year
6th Year	For 5-year property: all of remaining basis*
	For 7-year property: same *amount* as 5th year
	For 15-year property: same *computation* as 2nd year

Year	Expense Computation
7th Year	For 7-year property: same *amount* as 5th year
	For 15-year property: 10% of remaining basis*
8th Year	For 7-year property: all of remaining basis*
	For 15-year property: same *amount* as 5th year
9th through 15th Years	For 15-year property: same *amount* as 5th year
16th Year	For 15-year property: all of remaining basis*

* original basis less depreciation taken in all prior years

For residential rental property, determine the depreciation in the first year using Table 16.2. After the first year, use 3.636% of the *original basis* (original basis = cost plus nondeductible costs of acquiring the property, such as title searches, inspection fees, and so on) each year for the next 27 years as your depreciation deduction. In the 28th year, your depreciation deduction is whatever amount is still undepreciated of the original basis.

Table 16.2   First Year Depreciation Expense for Residential Real Property

Month of Acquisition	1st Year Deduction
January	3.485%
February	3.182%
March	2.879%
April	2.576%
May	2.273%
June	1.970%
July	1.667%
August	1.364%
September	1.061%
October	0.758%
November	0.455%
December	0.152%

If you make a bunch of big purchases in the last quarter of the year—more than 40% of the cost of all depreciable items you purchased for your rental property during 1995 (not including the cost of the rental unit itself)—you qualify for the extra-special confusing depreciation calculation called *Mid-quarter Convention*. (This convention also applies to all property placed in service during the year if the 40% test is met without considering any residential rental property or non-residential real property.) By using this convention you can depreciate your items based on complex tables designed by little people with squinty eyes who wear green visors to deflect the light from bare lightbulbs dangling over their heads. Check out these tables (16.3 through 16.5) and see if they don't make your head spin.

If you must use these tables, multiply the applicable percentage times the *unadjusted* basis of the asset—in other words, the cost without a reduction for depreciation taken in prior years.

Table 16.3   Mid-quarter Convention for 5-year Property

Year	Quarter			
	1st Qtr	*2nd Qtr*	*3rd Qtr*	*4th Qtr*
1	35.00%	25.00%	15.00%	5.00%
2	26.00%	30.00%	34.00%	38.00%
3	15.60%	18.00%	20.40%	22.80%
4	11.01%	11.37%	12.24%	13.68%
5	11.01%	11.37%	11.30%	10.94%
6	1.38%	4.26%	7.06%	9.58%

Table 16.4   Mid-quarter Convention for 7-year Property

Year	Quarter			
	1st Qtr	*2nd Qtr*	*3rd Qtr*	*4th Qtr*
1	25.00%	17.85%	10.71%	3.57%
2	21.43%	23.47%	25.51%	27.55%
3	15.31%	16.76%	18.22%	19.68%

Year	Quarter			
	1st Qtr	*2nd Qtr*	*3rd Qtr*	*4th Qtr*
4	10.93%	11.97%	13.02%	14.06%
5	8.75%	8.87%	9.30%	10.04%
6	8.74%	8.87%	8.85%	8.73%
7	8.75%	8.87%	8.86%	8.73%
8	1.09%	3.33%	5.53%	7.64%

Table 16.5 Mid-quarter Convention for 15-year Property

Year	Quarter			
	1st Qtr	*2nd Qtr*	*3rd Qtr*	*4th Qtr*
1	8.75%	6.25%	3.75%	1.25%
2	9.13%	9.38%	9.63%	9.88%
3	8.21%	8.44%	8.66%	8.89%
4	7.39%	7.59%	7.80%	8.00%
5	6.65%	6.83%	7.02%	7.20%
6	5.99%	6.15%	6.31%	6.48%
7	5.90%	5.91%	5.90%	5.90%
8	5.91%	5.90%	5.90%	5.90%
9	5.90%	5.91%	5.91%	5.90%
10	5.91%	5.90%	5.90%	5.91%
11	5.90%	5.91%	5.91%	5.90%
12	5.91%	5.90%	5.90%	5.91%
13	5.90%	5.91%	5.91%	5.90%
14	5.91%	5.90%	5.90%	5.91%
15	5.90%	5.91%	5.91%	5.90%
16	0.74%	2.21%	3.69%	5.17%

Ten Rental Expenses You Might Not Have Thought of Deducting

Here they are! My top ten items most frequently overlooked as rental property deductions:

10. Postage costs to mail reminders to your tenants that their rent is overdue.

9. Extermination and pest control costs.

8. Tax return preparation fees to the extent that the fees represent help with your Schedule E.

7. Long distance telephone calls to check up on your property or to talk with prospective tenants and their references.

6. Bank fees, if you have a separate bank account for your rental property.

5. Maintenance expenses (such as cleaning, painting, and repairing) including miscellaneous items such as cleanser and sponges.

4. Cost of developing photos of the property for advertising purposes.

3. Property taxes and interest paid at closing. (You'll find these amounts on the actual closing statement.)

2. Subscription cost for related magazines and newspapers such as *Landlord Times*.

...and the number one most overlooked rental deduction is...

1. Casualty and theft losses on rental property—these are fully deductible on Form 4684 and Form 4797 (offset, of course, by any insurance reimbursement you might receive).

Royalty Income

The phrase, "rental income" makes sense: income from rentals. Likewise, "retirement income" means income from a retirement plan. But what about "royalty income"? Is the Queen of England going to give me some money? It seems like a good idea to me, but that's not quite where the IRS is going with this wordplay.

What's a Royalty?

You can earn royalties if you let someone remove oil from your well, timber from your forest, or coal from your mine. Royalties from sources such as these are usually reported to you on a K-1 form that comes from a partnership or an S corporation.

If you write the Great American Novel you can earn royalties, too. Royalties for artistic works are paid for the right for someone else to print and sell copies of your book, perform your song, or produce your play. Royalties for artistic works are typically reported to you on a 1099 form that comes from your publisher.

With royalties, you're not giving up your ownership interest, you're just letting someone else use your stuff. In this regard, royalties are much like rent: You don't sell your cottage, you let someone else use it. For this reason, you report income and expenses from royalties and rents to the IRS on the same form, Schedule E, "Supplemental Income and Loss."

Report your royalty income on Schedule E, line 4.

Expenses That Offset Royalty Income

The cost of generating royalty income is deductible on your Schedule E (or Schedule C if you're talking about artistic royalty income that's ongoing, not just a flash in the pan). Typical expenses you might incur include the following:

> **OOPS!**
> If you're in the regular and ongoing business of creating artistic works such as writing books, songs, or plays, report income and expenses from these ventures on Schedule C, not Schedule E. Use Schedule E for artistic-type royalties only when you write a song, book, or play for fun and not for a living. Check out Chapter 13 for more on filling out Schedule C.

➤ Interest expense

➤ Property taxes

➤ Depletion

This is like depreciation except it applies to minerals and standing timber, but it's more confusing. Time to find an accountant to help you if you need to compute your own depletion.

➤ Office expense

➤ Legal and accounting fees

➤ Auto, truck, and other travel

➤ Commissions

➤ Insurance

➤ Industry-related subscriptions

➤ Management fees

➤ Depreciation of buildings, equipment, and land improvements

➤ Repairs

Net losses on royalties are considered to be passive losses, which means that you can only deduct them as an offset to "passive income." All this passive stuff is discussed later in this chapter, in the "Passive (Yawn) Income" section.

Wrapping Up Schedule E (Page 1)

When you finish recording your rent and royalty income and expenses on page 1 of Schedule E, add up all your expenses and put the total on line 19. Add the amounts across and place the total in the Totals column. Compute the income or loss on each rental property by deducting the total expenses (line 19 plus depreciation expense on line 20, combined on line 21) from the income for the property (line 3). If the result is a loss, you may not be able to deduct the entire amount. Prepare Form 8582, "Passive Activity Loss Limitations" (reproduced in Appendix A), to see if you will be able to deduct your loss in 1995 or if you will have to carry some of it over to next year. Put the allowed loss (from Form 8582) on line 23. Net income from all your rental properties (just the positive numbers from each property on line 22) goes on line 24. Net losses shown on line 23 from all your rental properties get added together and placed on line 25. Subtract line 25 from line 24 and put the result on line 17 of your 1040.

Those Funky K-1 Forms

By the Way

If you have more than three rental properties, the IRS expects you to attach additional copies of Schedule E to accommodate those properties (one property goes in each column on the Schedule E). If you have more than three rental properties in your tax return and thus more than than one Schedule E, add the amounts for *all* the properties and put the totals on the top Schedule E. Only fill in the Totals column on the top Schedule E.

If you own a piece of a partnership, a share of an S corporation, or if you are the beneficiary of a trust or an estate, you should receive a funny form in the mail called a K-1 form. I can show you a standard IRS K-1 form, but this isn't always what you receive in the mail. Sometimes companies make up their own K-1 forms that don't look anything like this one. When that happens you just have to humor the company that sent you the form and look for the same information on their form that the IRS lists on its form.

The great thing about K-1 forms is that you don't have to understand a single thing on the form. Just follow the directions in the right margin of the form and put the numbers where they belong on your income tax return.

If you are preparing your income tax return using a computer software program (see Chapter 31, "Choosing a Software Program"), you will see a blank K-1 form on your computer screen. Then you just fill in the form on-screen, putting the numbers from your K-1 form on the corresponding lines of the computer K-1 form.

Do We Have a Tax Shelter Here?

Many years ago, in a more innocent taxpayer era, you could invest a relatively small amount of money in a type of partnership that would provide you with huge deductible losses for several years. On paper, the theory was that eventually the partnership would provide you with income so that you could recoup your investment and then some. But, in reality, the way it worked was that the partnership borrowed great amounts of money at its own risk (you weren't personally liable for the loans) and spent it all, generating great deductions for investors, and the recouping part came from the tax benefits of taking the deductions on your income tax return. Often the partnerships folded up without paying investors back for their up-front investment, but it didn't really matter because the IRS had graciously coughed up refunds of income taxes as a result of these big deductions.

SCHEDULE K-1 (Form 1065) Department of the Treasury Internal Revenue Service	**Partner's Share of Income, Credits, Deductions, etc.** ▶ See separate instructions. For calendar year 1995 or tax year beginning , and ending , 19	OMB No. 1545-0099 **1995**

Partner's identifying number ▶	Partnership's identifying number ▶
Partner's name, address, and ZIP code	Partnership's name, address, and ZIP code

A This partner is a ☐ general partner ☐ limited partner
☐ limited liability company member
B What type of entity is this partner? ▶ ....
C Is this partner a ☐ domestic or a ☐ foreign partner?
D Enter partner's percentage of: (I) Before change or termination (II) End of year
Profit sharing . . . . % .... %
Loss sharing . . . . % .... %
Ownership of capital . . . . % .... %
E IRS Center where partnership filed return:

F Partner's share of liabilities (see instructions):
Nonrecourse . . . . $ ....
Qualified nonrecourse financing . $ ....
Other . . . . $ ....
G Tax shelter registration number . ▶ ....
H Check here if this partnership is a publicly traded partnership as defined in section 469(k)(2) . . . . ☐
I Check applicable boxes: **(1)** ☐ Final K-1 **(2)** ☐ Amended K-1

J **Analysis of partner's capital account:**

(a) Capital account at beginning of year	(b) Capital contributed during year	(c) Partner's share of lines 3, 4, and 7, Form 1065, Schedule M-2	(d) Withdrawals and distributions	(e) Capital account at end of year (combine columns (a) through (d))

	(a) Distributive share item		(b) Amount	(c) 1040 filers enter the amount in column (b) on:
Income (Loss)	**1** Ordinary income (loss) from trade or business activities . . .	**1**		See pages 5 and 6 of Partner's Instructions for Schedule K-1 (Form 1065).
	2 Net income (loss) from rental real estate activities	**2**		
	3 Net income (loss) from other rental activities	**3**		
	4 Portfolio income (loss):			
	a Interest	**4a**		Sch. B, Part I, line 1
	b Dividends	**4b**		Sch. B, Part II, line 5
	c Royalties	**4c**		Sch. E, Part I, line 4
	d Net short-term capital gain (loss)	**4d**		Sch. D, line 5, col. (f) or (g)
	e Net long-term capital gain (loss)	**4e**		Sch. D, line 13, col. (f) or (g)
	f Other portfolio income (loss) *(attach schedule)*	**4f**		Enter on applicable line of your return.
	5 Guaranteed payments to partner	**5**		See page 6 of Partner's Instructions for Schedule K-1 (Form 1065).
	6 Net gain (loss) under section 1231 (other than due to casualty or theft)	**6**		
	7 Other income (loss) *(attach schedule)*	**7**		Enter on applicable line of your return.
Deduc-tions	**8** Charitable contributions (see instructions) *(attach schedule)* . .	**8**		Sch. A, line 15 or 16
	9 Section 179 expense deduction	**9**		See page 7 of Partner's Instructions for Schedule K-1 (Form 1065).
	10 Deductions related to portfolio income *(attach schedule)* . . .	**10**		
	11 Other deductions *(attach schedule)*	**11**		
Investment Interest	**12a** Interest expense on investment debts	**12a**		Form 4952, line 1
	b (1) Investment income included on lines 4a, 4b, 4c, and 4f above	**b(1)**		See page 7 of Partner's Instructions for Schedule K-1 (Form 1065).
	(2) Investment expenses included on line 10 above	**b(2)**		
Credits	**13a** Low-income housing credit:			
	(1) From section 42(j)(5) partnerships for property placed in service before 1990	**a(1)**		Form 8586, line 5
	(2) Other than on line 13a(1) for property placed in service before 1990	**a(2)**		
	(3) From section 42(j)(5) partnerships for property placed in service after 1989	**a(3)**		
	(4) Other than on line 13a(3) for property placed in service after 1989	**a(4)**		
	b Qualified rehabilitation expenditures related to rental real estate activities	**13b**		
	c Credits (other than credits shown on lines 13a and 13b) related to rental real estate activities.	**13c**		See page 8 of Partner's Instructions for Schedule K-1 (Form 1065).
	d Credits related to other rental activities	**13d**		
	14 Other credits	**14**		

For Paperwork Reduction Act Notice, see Instructions for Form 1065.   Cat. No. 11394R   Schedule K-1 (Form 1065)

The official (partnership) Schedule K-1.

Look in this column to see where each amount should go on your 1040.

Schedule K-1 (Form 1065) 1995   Page **2**

	(a) Distributive share item		(b) Amount	(c) 1040 filers enter the amount in column (b) on:
Self-employment	**15a** Net earnings (loss) from self-employment	15a		Sch. SE, Section A or B
	b Gross farming or fishing income	15b		See page 8 of Partner's Instructions for Schedule K-1 (Form 1065).
	c Gross nonfarm income	15c		
Adjustments and Tax Preference Items	**16a** Depreciation adjustment on property placed in service after 1986	16a		
	b Adjusted gain or loss	16b		See page 8 of Partner's Instructions for Schedule K-1 (Form 1065) and Instructions for Form 6251.
	c Depletion (other than oil and gas)	16c		
	d (1) Gross income from oil, gas, and geothermal properties	d(1)		
	(2) Deductions allocable to oil, gas, and geothermal properties	d(2)		
	e Other adjustments and tax preference items *(attach schedule)*	16e		
Foreign Taxes	**17a** Type of income ▶			Form 1116, check boxes
	b Name of foreign country or U.S. possession ▶			
	c Total gross income from sources outside the United States *(attach schedule)*	17c		Form 1116, Part I
	d Total applicable deductions and losses *(attach schedule)*	17d		
	e Total foreign taxes (check one): ▶ ☐ Paid ☐ Accrued	17e		Form 1116, Part II
	f Reduction in taxes available for credit *(attach schedule)*	17f		Form 1116, Part III
	g Other foreign tax information *(attach schedule)*	17g		See Instructions for Form 1116.
Other	**18** Section 59(e)(2) expenditures: a Type ▶			See page 9 of Partner's Instructions for Schedule K-1 (Form 1065).
	b Amount	18b		
	19 Tax-exempt interest income	19		Form 1040, line 8b
	20 Other tax-exempt income	20		
	21 Nondeductible expenses	21		See page 9 of Partner's Instructions for Schedule K-1 (Form 1065).
	22 Distributions of money (cash and marketable securities)	22		
	23 Distributions of property other than money	23		
	24 Recapture of low-income housing credit			
	a From section 42(j)(5) partnerships	24a		Form 8611, line 8
	b Other than on line 24a	24b		

25 Supplemental information required to be reported separately to each partner *(attach additional schedules if more space is needed)*:

....

....

....

....

....

....

....

....

....

....

....

....

....

....

....

....

....

....

....

    ✿ *Printed on recycled paper*

Form **8582**	**Passive Activity Loss Limitations**	OMB No. 1545-1008
Department of the Treasury Internal Revenue Service (O)	➤ See separate instructions. ➤ Attach to Form 1040 or Form 1041.	**1995** Attachment Sequence No. **88**
Name(s) shown on return		Identifying number

Part I   **1994 Passive Activity Loss**

Caution: *See the instructions for Worksheets 1 and 2 on pages 7 and 8 before completing Part I.*

Rental Real Estate Activities With Active Participation (For the definition of active participation see **Active Participation in a Rental Real Estate Activity** on page 3 of the instructions.)

1a Activities with net income (from Worksheet 1, column (a)) . . .   **1a**

  b Activities with net loss (from Worksheet 1, column (b)) . . . .   **1b** (   )

  c Prior year unallowed losses (from Worksheet 1, column (c)) . .   **1c** (   )

  d Combine lines 1a, 1b, and 1c **1d**

All Other Passive Activities

2a Activities with net income (from Worksheet 2, column (a)) . . .   **2a**

  b Activities with net loss (from Worksheet 2, column (b)) . . . .   **2b** (   )

  c Prior year unallowed losses (from Worksheet 2, column (c)) . .   **2c** (   )

  d Combine lines 2a, 2b, and 2c **2d**

3 Combine lines 1d and 2d. If the result is net income or zero, see the instructions for line 3. If this line and line 1d are losses, go to line 4. Otherwise, enter -0- on line 9 and go to line 10 .   **3**

Part II   **Special Allowance for Rental Real Estate With Active Participation**

Note: *Enter all numbers in Part II as positive amounts. (See instructions on page 8 for examples.)*

4 Enter the **smaller** of the loss on line 1d or the loss on line 3 . . . .   **4**

5 Enter $150,000. If married filing separately, see the instructions .   **5**

6 Enter modified adjusted gross income, but not less than zero (see instructions) **6**

Note: *If line 6 is equal to or greater than line 5, skip lines 7 and 8, enter -0- on line 9, and then go to line 10. Otherwise, go to line 7.*

7 Subtract line 6 from line 5 . . . .   **7**

8 Multiply line 7 by 50% (.5). **Do not** enter more than $25,000. If married filing separately, see instructions **8**

9 Enter the **smaller** of line 4 or line 8 . . . . **9**

Part III   **Total Losses Allowed**

10 Add the income, if any, on lines 1a and 2a and enter the total **10**

11 **Total losses allowed from all passive activities for 1995** Add lines 9 and 10. See the instructions to find out how to report the losses on your tax return **11**

For Paperwork Reduction Act Notice, see separate instructions.   Cat. No. 63704F   Form **8582**

Unused losses from last year appear here.

Here's how much passive loss you can deduct in 1995.

Use Form 8582 to determine if you can deduct your passive loss.

IRSpeak

A *tax shelter* is an investment that the IRS thinks might result in the investors getting to deduct a lot more expenses than they contributed in capital.

Well, wouldn't you know it, Congress eventually wised up and made its own rules about these partnerships. If a partnership tries to behave like the ones described here, tossing out deductions like confetti at a parade without making its partners liable for money borrowed, it has to register itself with the IRS as a *tax shelter*. Naturally, this act of registering sends up a red flag to IRS agents everywhere who immediately place themselves at lookout posts, trying to spot unwary partnership members looking for easy deductions.

If you belong to such a partnership, you will know it because at the top of your K-1 form, at item G, there appears a tax shelter registration number. You must file Form 8271, "Investor Reporting of Tax Shelter Registration Number," if a tax shelter number appears on your K-1 form. On this form you merely list the name of the partnership, the tax shelter registration number of the partnership, and the ID number of the partnership (found at the top right side of the K-1 form).

The other thing you need to know about tax shelters and, for that matter, any other type of partnership or S corporation, is that you can only deduct losses to the extent that you are "at risk" for those losses. In other words, if you have put money into the organization to offset those losses, you can deduct them. Furthermore, if you have made yourself liable on a loan that you used to finance the operations of the organization, you can add the amount of the loan for which you are personally liable to your investment in the organization when determining how much of your loss is deductible.

For example, suppose that you invested $5,000 in a partnership that produces Hollywood movies. In addition, you signed a note saying that you would personally guarantee up to $2,000 of the money the partnership borrowed from a lending source (fancy name for a bank). On your K-1 form you see your share of the partnership's loss for the year is $10,000. Your deduction is limited to $7,000 ($5,000 investment plus $2,000 loan guarantee). You can carry forward and deduct the remaining $3,000 when either of the following two things happen:

➤ You can offset the remaining loss against additional investments in the partnership, or

➤ You can offset the remaining loss against future income of the partnership.

If you never make another investment in the partnership or the partnership never reports income, only losses, you won't get the tax benefit of that additional $3,000 of loss.

Passive (Yawn) Income

Passive income is income for which you don't work. Sometimes you may feel like some of your coworkers must be earning passive income, but employee wages aren't passive. Rental income (from Schedule E) is usually passive unless being a landlord is your actual job. Income from investments in partnerships and S corporations (shown on page 2 of Schedule E) in which you don't really help with the business but just provide some money and someone else decides how to use it is passive income. If you receive money from a trust of which you are a beneficiary (also shown on page 2 of Schedule E), that is passive income too.

> **OOOOH...**
>
> **By the Way**
> You can carry passive losses forward indefinitely until you can use them. If you sell or otherwise dispose of your interest in the passive activity, your previously unclaimed losses may be used in the year of disposition.

Just as investments and trusts can provide you with passive income, they can also generate passive losses. The IRS has a serious interest in passive losses. If you have a loss from a passive investment, you can deduct that loss on your income tax return *provided you have income from a passive investment with which to offset the passive loss.* Figure out how much passive loss you can deduct by filling out Form 8582, "Passive Activity Loss Limitations." If passive income is not available to offset a passive loss, you can carry the loss forward to the next year's income tax return and the return for the year after that, with the hope that you will have passive income with which to offset the loss.

The Least You Need to Know

➤ Rent your house for 14 or fewer days during the year and don't worry about reporting the income (or the related expenses) to the IRS.

➤ Use your rental property personally for more than 14 days or 10% of the total days rented and your property qualifies as a personal residence instead of a rental residence. The amount of expenses you can deduct is subject to strict limits on a personal residence.

➤ Royalty income goes on page 1 of Schedule E unless you are an author, songwriter, or playwright; then it's off to Schedule C with you.

➤ Report income and losses from K-1 forms on page 2 of Schedule E. Remember that "passive losses" must be offset with "passive income" in order to deduct them.

Chapter 17

Strange and Unusual Forms of Income

In This Chapter

➤ Taxation of occasional earnings

➤ Tax treatment of unemployment compensation

➤ The wages of sin (that is, gambling)

Taxable, taxable, taxable. That's basically what the IRS has to say about miscellaneous forms of income, even little things that don't seem to fit anywhere in particular on your tax return. Just because there's not a specific line for a type of income, don't think you don't have to report the income to the IRS. You should know better than that!

For reporting some of your income to the IRS, you're on the honor system (actually, we're all on the honor system to even file our tax returns). Small bits of income, such as $100 won in the lottery, $25 from the neighbor whose cat you fed while she was on vacation (could have gotten a new cat for a lot less than that...), or miscellaneous cash fees for shoveling sidewalks in the neighborhood should be included on your tax return.

Unemployment Compensation

There was a time, years ago, when unemployment compensation—money you get from the federal or state government to hold you over while you're out of work and looking for a job—was not taxable. Tax laws have changed and you have to report your unemployment compensation now just like any other type of income. (Note: In prior years you could report unemployment compensation on Form 1040 and 1040A, but you couldn't use Form 1040EZ if you had this type of income. Beginning in 1995 you can use any of the three 1040 forms and still have a place to report your unemployment compensation.)

Unlike for some odds and ends of miscellaneous income, there is an actual line on your tax return on which you should report unemployment compensation. The total amount of your unemployment compensation goes on page 1 of your 1040, at line 19.

Put the total amount of your unemployment compensation here.

You should receive a Form 1099-G from the government telling you how much unemployment compensation you received during 1995. Write the amount from the 1099-G on line 19 of your 1040.

Prizes

Oh, now wait a minute! Do you mean to tell me that I'm supposed to pay income tax on the television set I won at the school raffle? And what about the $50 cash prize in the Beautiful Marigolds contest? What if I win the Publisher's Clearinghouse Sweepstakes (I'm told I'm one of the Super Select Special Grand Prize finalists)? Will I have to share that with the IRS, too? It hardly seems fair. I won the prize. The IRS didn't even help fill out my entry blank.

Whether it seems fair or not, you must report prize winnings on your income tax return and pay a bit of the prize over to the IRS in the form of income tax.

Report the amount of your prize winnings on line 21, "Other Income," on page 1 of your 1040. Cash prizes get reported at the actual amount of the cash you received. Report prizes of stuff (such as coffeemakers, cars, furs, and trips) at their fair market value. Fair market value means what the item is worth if you try to sell it or what you would pay for it if you tried to buy it at a store.

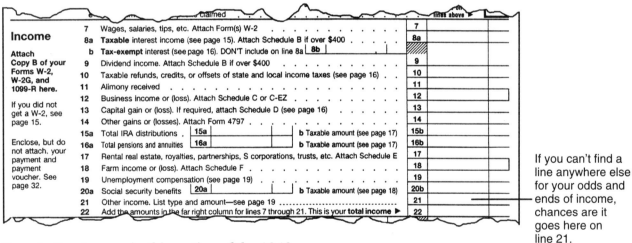

Report other income in this section of the 1040.

If you can't find a line anywhere else for your odds and ends of income, chances are it goes here on line 21.

Gambling Winnings

Just like prize winnings, you report gambling winnings on line 21, "Other Income," on page 1 of your 1040. Depending on how much you win and who is paying you, you might receive a Form W-2G reflecting your gambling winnings. If you win enough, you might even have income tax withheld from the winnings. That, too, will show up on the Form W-2G.

Income tax withheld from gambling winnings gets reported on page 2 of your 1040 on line 55 (the same place where you report your withholding from regular Forms W-2).

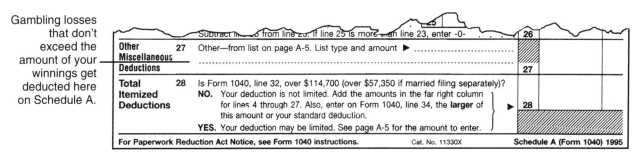

Total up all your federal income tax withholding and put it on line 55 of the 1040.

Gambling Losses

People usually don't spend much time talking about the money they lose at gambling. It's not exactly a braggable accomplishment. But here comes the IRS in what seems to be an act of unusual generosity, saying that you can take a deduction for money you lose while gambling.

The catch? There are two catches, actually. First, you can only deduct gambling losses up to the amount of money you win gambling. So at best you can wipe out the winnings and not have to pay tax on that amount, but you'll never come out ahead, deduction-wise, with the gambling loss deduction.

The other important part of taking a deduction for gambling losses is that you have to have a record of your losses. You can't just *think* you lost money gambling—you have to have a journal, a log, canceled checks, or some written evidence supporting your claim for a gambling loss deduction.

The deduction for gambling losses goes on Schedule A, "Itemized Deductions," at line 27. You have to be able to itemize your deductions in order to take advantage of the deduction for gambling losses. See Chapter 19, "Itemized Deductions Most Taxpayers Can Take," for more information.

Gambling losses that don't exceed the amount of your winnings get deducted here on Schedule A.

The Other Miscellaneous Deductions section of Schedule A.

Income That Doesn't Fit Anywhere Else (That Doesn't Mean You Don't Have to Report It)

Some forms of income don't seem to have a specific place on your tax return, but that doesn't relieve you of the responsibility to tell the IRS about them and pay tax on them. Here are some of the types of things you should report as other income on line 21 of the 1040:

➤ Jury duty payments

➤ Fees paid to you as a member of a board of directors of board of trustees

➤ Notary public fees

➤ Fair value of prizes won in raffles, lotteries, and contests

➤ Cash won in raffles, lotteries, and contests

➤ Profit on the sale of personal items

Some miscellaneous income items actually don't have to be reported as other income on your tax return: federal income tax refunds, and some scholarships and fellowships (if given strictly for academic pursuit and not as a stipend for teaching).

> **OOOOH…**
>
> **By the Way**
> What do you tell the IRS if your kind Aunt Gertrude gives you a gift of $50,000? If you answered, "I don't want to tell, please don't make me," you're absolutely right! Gifts aren't taxable to the recipient. Aunt Gertrude is going to have to contend with paying some *gift tax* (gift amounts over $10,000 per year to each individual are subject to gift tax), but you get your present free and clear. Of course, when you start earning interest and dividends on that money (because of course you're going to invest all of it right away), you'll have to pay income tax on the earnings.

Wrapping Up the Income Section

When you've finished entering all your income on page 1 of your 1040, add all the amounts on lines 7 through 21 and put the total on line 22. Wherever you see negative numbers (losses), deduct those amounts instead of adding them. You've now arrived at what the IRS calls Total Income. Time for you to take a Total Break!

The Least You Need to Know

➤ Unemployment compensation is taxed: It has its own line on page 1 of the 1040.

➤ You have to include prizes that you win on the "Other Income" line on your 1040 and pay tax on them.

➤ Gambling losses are deductible on Schedule A, but only to the extent that you report gambling winnings as income on page 1 of the 1040.

➤ A cash gift (or the value of an item given to you as a gift) is not taxable to you. You don't have to report the gift anywhere on your income tax return.

Part 4
Not So Gross: Reducing Gross Income

"…There is nothing sinister in so arranging one's affairs as to keep taxes as low as possible. Everybody does so, rich or poor; and all do right, for nobody owes any public duty to pay more than the law demands…"

Judge Learned Hand, Comm. V. Newman, 159 F. 2d 848 (CA-2, 1947)

Okay. You've done a lot so far. Let's recap: You've listed all your income on page 1 of your 1040, and you've added it up to produce an amount known as "Total Income" (shown on line 22 of the 1040). Now it's time to think about cutting down that total before you have to determine your income tax.

There are many (legal!) ways in which you can reduce your income before computing your tax. In this part of the book you'll learn about adjustments, itemized deductions, standard deduction, and exemptions—these various reductions to your income make the amount on which you pay tax a bit more palatable.

Chapter 18

Adjustments to Income

In This Chapter

➤ Deduction of contributions to IRAs

➤ Adjustments for the self-employment taxpayer

➤ Moving expenses

➤ Alimony payments

The first chance you have to chip away at your income comes on the bottom of page 1, in the section called "Adjustments." Adjustments are reductions you can apply to your income. Deducting adjustments from your total income (as reported on line 22 of your Form 1040) provides you with an amount called *adjusted gross income* (often called AGI). The AGI is a number that is referred to at other places in your tax return.

Adjustments to income are neater than itemized deductions (which are covered in Chapter 19, "Itemized Deductions Most Taxpayers Can Take") because you get to deduct these amounts from your income even if you don't have enough deductions to itemize.

Adjustments are also nice because they reduce your income for state income tax purposes whereas most states don't recognize itemized deductions.

Adjustments are taken "above the line"—that is, before the calculation for adjusted gross income.

IRSpeak
Add up all your income and deduct your adjustments on page 1 of your 1040 and you get *adjusted gross income (AGI)*. You use the AGI number as a basis for determining some of your limitations on itemized deductions (as discussed in Chapter 19).

HUH?

IDIOTS GUIDE

Individual Retirement Accounts

Retirement may seem a long way off and you may not have even started planning for it. Furthermore, some people find it difficult to think about ever retiring when they contemplate how long they are expected to live and how much money it might take to support them if they are no longer working.

Nevertheless, if you are planning for your retirement and are making monetary contributions to an Individual Retirement Account, otherwise known as an IRA, you may be entitled to a deduction for all or part of your contribution.

Get Down to Brass Tax

An *Individual Retirement Account (IRA)* is a retirement savings account. Special tax rules enable you to reduce your taxable income by part or all of your contributions to the IRA. An IRA is not just any savings account. You have to set up your IRA with a bank or stock brokerage firm—some organization that can make sure that the account meets the requirements set out by the IRS. You can withdraw money from an IRA when you reach age 59 1/2, but it is taxed at that time. If you withdraw money before that age, you may have to pay a penalty.

Can You Still Deduct IRA Contributions?

Way back in the early 1980s, baby boomers finished paying off school loans and began to experience some significant earning power, and they started thinking about their retirement. They came in droves—young executives in pin-striped suits, professional women with ties under the collars of their blouses, even stay-at-home spouses got into the act—all setting up their IRA accounts, making their yearly contributions, taking their deductions, reducing their income taxes.

The folks in Washington began to notice a bit of a shortfall in their resources due to all these IRA deductions and felt they had a responsibility to step in and limit the deductions. The result of their action became part of the Tax Reform Act of 1986.

Starting in 1987, certain limitations have come into play with regard to the deductibility of IRA contributions.

Who Qualifies?

The main stickler that gets in the way of deducting IRA contributions is participation in a retirement plan at work. If neither you or your spouse are participants in a retirement plan at your job, the IRA rules haven't changed. You can contribute up to $2,000 per year per working spouse. A nonworking spouse can contribute up to $250 per year.

Get Down to Brass Tax

The annual IRA contribution is actually limited to the lower end of a maximum of $2,000 per person or the person's earned income. Therefore, if you work at a job and only make $1,800 for the entire year, your IRA contribution is limited to $1,800 instead of $2,000.

Although no one can contribute more that $2,000 per year to an IRA, the limitations actually apply to a couple rather than an individual. Suppose that you work and your spouse does not. You can contribute up to $2,000 per year to an IRA and your spouse can contribute up to $250 per year. Actually that means that together you can contribute up to $2,250 to your IRAs. Neither of you can put more than $2,000 in your IRA, but aside from that limitation you can split the $2,250 any way you want between your IRAs—including $1,125 each.

Employees who participate in a pension plan at their place of employment face limitations on how much they can contribute to their IRA. Keep in mind that if you are married filing a joint return, it doesn't matter which spouse participates in a pension plan—if one of you participates, the limitations apply to both of you.

So how do these limitations work? If you're single and your Adjusted Gross Income is over $35,000, or if you're married, filing a joint return, and your AGI exceeds $50,000, you're out of luck when it comes to taking a deduction for an IRA contribution (but see the upcoming section "Nondeductible Contributions" for a discussion of how you can still make a contribution to an IRA even if you don't qualify for the deduction).

If you are single and your AGI is between $25,000 and $35,000, or if you are married, filing a joint return, and your AGI falls between $40,000 and $50,000, you deduct part of your contribution. See Table 18.1 for specific information on how much of your contribution you can deduct.

Table 18.1 Can I Deduct My IRA Contribution?

Filing Status	Maximum AGI Allowable for You to Take a Full IRA Deduction	Range of Acceptable AGI Values in Order for You to Take an IRA Deduction	No IRA Deductions Allowed if Your AGI Is Over This Amount
Single	$25,000	$25,000–$35,000	$35,000
Head of Household	$25,000	$25,000–$35,000	$35,000
Married Filing Jointly	$40,000	$40,000–$50,000	$50,000
Qualifying Widow(er)	$40,000	$40,000–$50,000	$50,000
Married Filing Separately	Not Applicable	$1–$10,000	$10,000

If your AGI falls in the Partial Deduction range, as set out in Table 18.1, your IRA deduction is reduced $.20 for every dollar your income exceeds the amount in the Maximum AGI for Full Deduction column. So, if you are married filing a joint return and the combined AGI for both you and your spouse is $46,000, the maximum deduction both of you can take for your IRA contribution is reduced by $6,000 ($46,000–$40,000, or your AGI minus the amount in the Maximum AGI for Full Deduction column) times $.20, or $1,200. Your contribution of $4,000 yields you and your spouse a $1,600 deduction.

Nondeductible Contributions

Just because you can't take a deduction for your IRA contribution or your deduction is limited by the calculation described in the previous section, doesn't mean you can't still contribute to the IRA. No matter what your tax status is or how much or how little AGI you have, you can still deposit up to $2,000 per year in your IRA. The difficulty in making nondeductible contributions to your IRA is the record-keeping involved. You have to keep track of how much you contribute each year, how much you deducted, how much the account earned, and how much of those earnings you report as taxable.

> **OOOOH...**
>
> **By the Way**
>
> You have the right to deposit up to $2,000 per year in your IRA, even if that $2,000 won't generate an adjustment to your income in the current year. Getting yourself in the habit of putting away a certain amount per year, whether or not you get a tax break, isn't such a bad idea.

The earnings on an IRA account generally are all nontaxable if your contributions are all tax-deductible. If all of your contributions are taxable, all the earnings on the account are also taxable. Chapter 15, "Retirement: IRAs and Social Security Benefits," discusses the tax treatment of income from IRA accounts.

But if you, like many people, contribute amounts to your IRA that are partially deductible due to the limitations set out in Table 18.1, or if you contributed deductible amounts back before you joined the company pension plan but now your contributions are not deductible, the fund is mixed with contributions that were deductible and contributions that were not deductible. You should keep a record similar to the My IRA worksheet shown in this chapter to keep track of the taxability of your deductions and earnings.

Amounts earned by your IRA (typically interest or dividends) are not taxable until they are withdrawn. It doesn't matter whether your contributions were deductible at the time you made them. All the earnings are treated the same way in an IRA account.

		My IRA					
Year	Deductible Contribution	Non-Deductible Contribution	Total Earnings	Balance	Percent of Balance that's deferred		
1988	$ 2,000.00	$ 0	$ 0	$2,000.00	0		
1989	2,000.00	0	160.00	4,160.00	0		
1990	2,000.00	0	312.00	6,472.00	0		
1991	0	2,000.00	420.68	8,892.68	67.47%		
1992	0	2,000.00	444.63	11,337.31	52.92%		
1993	0	2,000.00	510.18	13,847.49	43.33%		
1994	0	2,000.00	553.90	16,401.39	36.58%		
1995	0	2,000.00	656.06	19,057.45	31.48%		
total	6,000.00	10,000.00					

Use a worksheet like this one to keep track of the value of your IRA and what portions are taxable now and in the future.

On your worksheet (as shown in the preceding figure), enter the amount of contribution you make each year. Put the contribution in the Deductible column or the Nondeductible column, depending on whether you were able to take a tax deduction for the amount. Add the earnings of the fund to the contributions each year in order to arrive at a *balance* for the fund (the balance represents everything in the fund—all contributions plus all earnings).

IRAs for the Stay-At-Home Spouse

If you are married filing a joint return and either you or your spouse does not earn any income, an amount up to $250 toward your combined IRA contribution for the year (in addition to the working spouse's $2,000) may be deposited in an IRA. Together the spouses can contribute up to $2,250 for the year. Individually, they can split that amount any way they want to deposit in their IRA accounts as long as no more than $2,000 goes into one account.

Keogh ("Key Oh") Accounts

If you are self-employed, you can make tax-deductible contributions into a Keogh account. A Keogh is a lot like an IRA except you can contribute quite a bit more than $2,000 per year.

Your annual contribution to a Keogh account is generally limited to a percentage of your Schedule C income. Contributions are deducted on line 27 on page 1 of your Form 1040.

There are a few different ways in which you can set up your Keogh and compute contributions. This is an area

By the Way

OOOOH...

You can contribute to both a Keogh and an IRA. Participation in a Keogh based on your self-employment income doesn't negate your privilege to make tax-deductible contributions toward your IRA.

in which you should talk to a professional. You'll need to seek help from a financial advisor to get the plan set up in the first place. This person also can help you figure out the best way to calculate your contribution.

SEPs

An SEP is a retirement plan for self-employed individuals *and their employees.* Even if you are not self-employed, your employer may have set up an SEP in which you participate. An SEP is similar to a Keogh, but it has stringent reporting requirements and your employees generally must be able to participate in the plan, too.

You can contribute up to 15% of your net self-employment income (after subtracting your SEP contribution) to your SEP or up to the lesser of $30,000 or the plan contribution multiplied by the annual compensation limit (which is $150,000 for 1995), whichever is less. Contributions are deducted on line 27 on page 1 of your 1040—the same line you would use if you contributed to a Keogh plan.

So Which Plan Do I Pick?

Let's say that you're self-employed and all you can afford to contribute to a retirement plan is $2,000. How do you know which plan you should choose? You have to consider the nature of the plans and your retirement goals. One of your plans (if you have several retirement plans in place) may be earning more than the other plans. Or maybe you haven't decided which type of plan to set up. When you're contributing $2,000, any one of the plans will suffice. But what if, down the road, you plan to make a killing in your business? You may want to be able to contribute more than $2,000 per year so an IRA won't do. Before setting up any retirement plan, check with an investment counselor and get some advice that is based on an analysis of your personal financial condition and future plans.

One More (Slight) Advantage to Being Self-Employed

If you're self-employed, you know about self-employment tax. In a weak attempt to relieve some of the sting of the self-employment tax for our nation's hard-working entrepreneurs, the IRS graciously allows you to deduct one-half of your current-year self-employment tax on line 25 on page one of your 1040.

After you have computed all of your self-employment income, if you have to pay self-employment tax (if there is a tax owing on Schedule SE), record half of the tax as an adjustment to income on line 25. This doesn't reduce the amount of self-employment tax you have to pay, but it should cut your income tax a bit.

There's another little self-employment bonus as well. You can deduct a measly 30% of your health insurance on line 26 of page 1 of the 1040 if you are self-employed. Congress tried to let this deduction slip away in 1994, but it's back for 1995. See Chapter 4, "What Do You Know? They Changed the Law Again," for more information about this deduction.

Oh No! What Have They Done to the Moving Expense Deduction?

Moving expenses may well be the most changed deduction in the past decade. They once were adjustments, then they were itemized deductions, now they're hardly anything at all. To the extent that you can deduct any moving expenses, they are taken as an adjustment on line 24 on page 1 of the 1040.

You can take the adjustment for expenses of your move to a new home if you meet the following tests:

➤ **Your move has to be job-related.** If you are moving to a new house because you like the climate, your friends live nearby, the new house has a bigger backyard, you hate your former neighbors, or any other nonjob-related reason, that's okay, as long as you're changing jobs as well. The new job can be a job for a new company or it can be a transfer within the company for which you already work.

➤ **You can't just move across town and qualify for a deduction of your moving expenses.** Your new house has to be far away. How far is far? The new job must be at least 50 miles further from your old house than the old job was. So if you used to drive 20 miles from your old house to your old job, the new job must be at least 70 (50 plus 20) miles away from your old house. (Note: If the move is to your first job, the new house must be at least 50 miles from the old house.)

➤ **You can't just change jobs every six months and move from one house to the next, deducting your moving expenses as you go.** If you want to deduct your moving expenses, you have to stay put at your new job and work full time for at least 39 weeks during the first 12 months after you move to the new job location. You don't have to necessarily stay at the same job for all those 39 weeks, but you have to continue working in the same geographical area if you want the deduction. (Note: If you are self-employed, this test is a little different. You have to work full time for 39 weeks of the first 12 months at the new location **and** 78 weeks of the first 24 months.)

Why You Deduct Moving Expenses in the First Place

The premise behind allowing a deduction for moving expenses is pretty simple. The government feels that generally it's not your fault if you have to physically relocate for your job. The cost of moving is part of the cost of earning your living. Therefore you shouldn't have to pay income tax on the money you spend for that move.

Which Moving Expenses Can You Deduct?

There have always been some limitations on what you can deduct as a moving expense. But the laws changed in 1994 and gave new meaning to the term limitations. In years gone by, you could attempt to deduct all sorts of expenses only peripherally associated with your actual move, such as costs of selling your house, costs of hunting for a new place to live, meals and lodging in the new town before your house is ready, and more.

Now the law is very tight about what counts as a deductible moving expense. Moving expenses that you can deduct (that is, an adjustment taken on line 24 of page 1 of the 1040), provided you have met the tests previously listed that qualify you to deduct moving expenses, include:

➤ The cost of moving your household goods and personal belongings from the old house to the new house

➤ The cost of travel and necessary overnight lodging while moving your family members to the new house

➤ And that's it...

And that's not much.

Report your moving expenses on Form 3903. In the first section, report the number of miles from your old home to your new job and from your old home to your old job (remember, the difference between these two numbers has to be at least 50). On lines 4 and 5 of the Form 3903, show the amounts you spent on moving your household belongings and the amount it cost to move yourself and your family. Subtract from that total the amount your employer paid you for these expenses that were not included in your wages. The difference, the net amount that you spent beyond what you might have been reimbursed, is shown on line 8 of Form 3903, and then transferred to page 1 of the 1040.

Form **3903**		**Moving Expenses**	OMB No. 1545-0062
		➤ **Attach to Form 1040.**	
Department of the Treasury Internal Revenue Service		➤ **See separate Instructions.**	**62**
Name(s) shown on Form 1040			**Your Social Security Number**

Moving Expenses Incurred

Caution: *If you are a member of the armed forces, see the instructions before completing this part.*

1 Enter the number of miles from your **old home** to your **new workplace** .... | **1** | | miles

2 Enter the number of miles from your **old home** to your **old workplace** .... | **2** | | miles

3 Subtract line 2 from line 1. Enter the result but not less than zero .... | **3** | | miles

Is line 3 at least 50 miles?

Yes ➤ Go to line 4. Also, see **Time Test** in the instructions.

No ➤ You **cannot** deduct your moving expenses incurred in 1994. Do not complete the rest of this part. See the **Note** below if you also incurred moving expenses before 1994.

4 Transportation and storage of household goods and personal effects .... | **4** |

5 Travel and lodging expenses of moving from your old home to your new home. **Do not** include meals .... | **5** |

6 Add lines 4 and 5 .... | **6** |

7 Enter the total amount your employer paid for your move (including the value of services furnished in kind) that is **not** included in the wages box (box 1) of your W-2 form. This amount should be identified with code **P** in box 13 of your W-2 form .... | **7** |

Is line 6 more than line 7?

Yes ➤ Go to line 8.

No ➤ You **cannot** deduct your moving expenses incurred in 1994. If line 6 is less than line 7, subtract line 6 from line 7 and include the result in income on Form 1040, line 7.

8 Subtract line 7 from line 6. Enter the result here and on Form 1040, line 24. This is your **moving expense deduction for expenses incurred in 1994** .... | **8** |

Note: *If you incurred moving expenses before 1994 and you did not deduct those expenses on a prior year's tax return, complete Parts II and III on page 2 to figure the amount, if any, you may deduct on Schedule A, Itemized Deductions.*

For Paperwork Reduction Act Notice, see separate instructions. | Form **3903**

Moving expenses go on Form 3903.

Alimony Payments

Although alimony is becoming nothing more than a blurry memory in some states, there are places in the country where alimony is still paid. Alimony is money paid to a spouse or former spouse as a result of a court-ordered decree such as Separate Maintenance Agreement or Divorce Decree. If you pay alimony, you can reduce your income on page 1, line 29, of your 1040 by the amount of the alimony. If you take a deduction for alimony, the person receiving the payments must report the alimony as income and pay tax on the amount received.

To make sure that the amounts you pay count as deductible alimony, all the following requirements must be met:

➤ The payments must be required by a divorce or separation agreement

➤ The legal document requiring the alimony payment cannot designate the amount as something other than alimony (child support, for example)

➤ You cannot file a joint tax return with the recipient of the alimony, nor can the two of you live in the same household

➤ Payments must be made in cash (checks are okay) as opposed to property

➤ Payments will not continue if the recipient dies

Careful Planning

To benefit from a deduction for moving expenses, plan your move in conjunction with a job and plan to stay in the job long enough to qualify for the deduction. If you decide where you want to go before you actually have a job in that location, take job-hunting trips to the new location instead of moving there without a job. (There is a double tax benefit this way—you may also be able to deduct the costs of the job-hunting trips. See "Money Spent for the Job You Wish You Had" in Chapter 20.)

If you are contemplating retirement and think you might want to move to a new location, consider taking a job in the new location in order to qualify for a moving expense deduction. After you meet the 39-week time test on your new job, you can get back to the business of being retired.

Adjusted Gross Income (AGI)

Add up all the adjustments on page 1 of your 1040, putting the total on line 30, "Total Adjustments." Subtract line 30 from line 22, "Total Income," to arrive at *adjusted gross income* at line 31.

The AGI amount is used throughout your tax return in various computations.

The Least You Need to Know

➤ Contributions up to $2,000 per year to IRAs may be tax deductible, depending on your participation in a retirement fund at work and the level of your income.

➤ Moving expenses have "moved" to the "Adjustment to Income" section of the 1040.

➤ Self-employed individuals get a couple of tax breaks on page 1 of the 1040.

➤ You can deduct alimony if certain conditions are met.

Chapter 19

Itemized Deductions Most Taxpayers Can Take

In This Chapter

➤ What's an itemized deduction?

➤ Who gets to use itemized deductions?

➤ Deductions for medical expenses

➤ Deductions for tax expenses

➤ Deductions for interest expenses

Itemized deductions are deductions you can use to reduce your income before you figure your income tax. There's little logic behind what is allowed as an itemized deduction and what is not. Deduction naysayers claim that the Washington D.C. lobby groups with the most clout are behind what gets included as itemized deductions. I say it doesn't matter who's behind determining what you get to take as itemized deductions; the important thing is that you take this opportunity to recognize all the possible things you can deduct and take advantage of them. This is your chance to take a big chunk out of your income before you have to calculate the tax on it.

Taking the time to learn what expenses in your life are deductible accomplishes several things:

➤ The greater your awareness of the allowable deductions, the greater your opportunities will be to lower your income tax.

➤ If you know which expenses qualify as itemized deductions, you can save receipts and keep track of deductible expenses as you spend your money instead of trying to re-create your expenditures long after the time has past.

➤ You can make intelligent tax-saving expenditures during the year—or make decisions to defer expenses into a year in which you will have a higher income—if you know what types of expenses are deductible.

Who Gets to Itemize?

Not everybody benefits from using itemized deductions. Sound unfair? Well, it's really not. The way it works is that you get your choice of taking either the standard deduction or itemizing deductions—you can't do both. If you have itemized deductions that add up to more than the standard deduction (see Chapter 21, "The Standard Deduction," to see how much your standard deduction is), then you should itemize. But if your itemized deductions are less than the standard deduction, you don't need to itemize because you already get the standard deduction and that's a bigger deduction. Does that make sense now?

How Do Itemized Deductions Get Included in My Tax Return?

List all your itemized deductions on Schedule A, "Itemized Deductions." The total of all your deductions from the bottom of Schedule A goes to page 2, line 34 of your 1040 form. This is the same line on which you would report your standard deduction, so you can see that there isn't room for you to take both the standard deduction and itemized deductions. You have to pick the one that's best for you.

You should fill out Schedule A even if you think the standard deduction will be a better deal. First of all, who knows? You might get lucky and find out you had more itemized deductions than you thought—enough to leave the standard deduction in the dust. Furthermore, it's a nice way to organize your records. If it turns out that you don't use Schedule A with this year's return, it's a good starting point next year for keeping records and knowing where to look for itemized deductions. Finally, filling out the form gets you in itemized deduction mode—that is, it gets your mind on the track of looking for deductions—and that can help you for many tax years to come.

By the Way
To consider itemizing your deductions, you must file Form 1040—the 1040A and 1040EZ forms don't have a provision for itemized deductions.

The Schedule A (shown later in this chapter) has several sections representing different types of deductible expenses. Each section is totaled on a line in the far right column (for example, medical and dental expenses are totaled on line 4). All the sections may not apply to you—just fill out the ones that represent your expenses. When you finish filling out each section, add the totals in the far right column and put the grand total on line 29.

Get Down to Brass Tax

If your AGI (from Form 1040, line 32) exceeds $114,700 (or $57,350 if your filing status is Married Filing Separately), the amount of itemized deductions you can actually deduct may be limited. Fill out this worksheet to see whether you have to reduce your itemized deductions:

(a) Total deductions (line 28, Schedule A) _____

(b) Schedule A, lines 4, 13, 19, plus gambling losses included on line 27 _____

(c) Amount at (a) minus amount at (b) (if this amount is zero, stop here and you can deduct all your itemized deductions) _____

(d) Multiply (c) by 80% (.80) _____

(e) Enter your AGI from line 32 of your 1040 _____

(f) Enter 114,700 (57,350 if your filing status is Married Filing Separately) _____

(g) Subtract (f) from (e) _____

(h) Multiply (g) by 3% (.03) _____

(i) Enter the smaller of (d) or (h) _____

(j) Subtract (i) from (a). This is your **Total Itemized Deductions** _____

Medical Expenses

There was a time, during childhood, when getting sick meant staying home from school, sipping warm soup prepared by a loving family member, and having stories read to you while you snuggled under your cozy covers. These days, getting sick means making excuses to your boss, feeling miserable, and the high cost of getting well. Doctor visits, medicine, hospital rooms, more medicine—it all adds up to money out the door and little to show for it.

In comes the IRS and its medical deduction. "Reduce your adjusted gross income by the amount you spent for getting well." Sound good? Well, not so fast.

First, you must be able to itemize deductions before you can even think about including medical expenses (see the previous section, "Who Gets to Itemize?").

Next, your total medical expenses must add up to more than 7.5% of your adjusted gross income—the amount on line 32 of page 2 of your 1040 form. If you don't come close to passing this test, don't waste your time with this medical expense section of the book. If you think you're in the ballpark, read on.

Take Two Aspirin and Call Me in the Morning

A portion of your medical expenses counts for itemized deductions on Schedule A of your federal income tax return. You have to add up all your expenses before you will know how much of them you can deduct, so don't just save bills for the big amounts.

Keep track of all your medical expenses. This goes for yourself as well as for the members of your family. You need records to support your deduction, so save all those pesky receipts from the drugstore as well as your doctor and hospital bills.

In addition to doctors' visits, hospital care, and prescription drugs, these are the typical kinds of things you can treat as medical expense deductions. Remember, they all have to be for you or one of your dependents:

➤ Birth control pills (acquired with a prescription)

➤ Cosmetic surgery, if it is necessary to promote proper function of the body or prevent or treat illness

➤ Cost of removing structural barriers in your home to accommodate a physically challenged person

➤ Dental services, including orthodontics

➤ Eyeglasses and contact lenses

➤ Health, accident, contact lens, and dental insurance

➤ Hearing aids

➤ Inpatient treatment of alcoholism or drug addiction

➤ Insulin

➤ Legal abortion

➤ Lodging related to medical care

➤ Nurse wages and boarding costs for a live-in nurse

➤ Nursing home costs when medical care is provided

➤ Oxygen

➤ Physical therapy

➤ Prosthetic devices

➤ Psychiatric treatment

➤ Retirement community fees to the extent that they relate to medical care

➤ Special equipment used to mitigate effects of physical impairment

➤ Special schooling for physically or mentally challenged individuals

➤ Telephone equipment for a hearing-impaired person

➤ Vasectomy

➤ Weight reduction for the treatment of a specific disease

➤ Wheelchair

When is a Doctor a Doctor?

Exactly which doctor-provided services qualify as item- ized medical deductions? Medical doctors, psychiatrists and psychologists, optometrists, ophthalmologists, orthopedic surgeons, podiatrists, and chiropractors all provide services that qualify for a medical expense de- duction on Schedule A.

Basically, if you pay someone money to diagnose or improve your physical or mental well-being, the expense counts as a medical deduction and goes on your Schedule A.

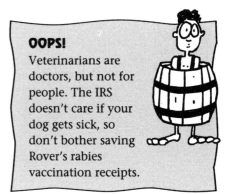

OOPS!
Veterinarians are doctors, but not for people. The IRS doesn't care if your dog gets sick, so don't bother saving Rover's rabies vaccination receipts.

The following types of doctors provide services that usually qualify as deductible medical expenses:

➤ Anesthesiologist

➤ Chiropractor (if licensed)

➤ Dentist

➤ Dermatologist

➤ Gynecologist

➤ Neurologist

➤ Obstetrician

➤ Ophthalmologist

➤ Optician

➤ Optometrist

➤ Orthodontist

➤ Orthopedist

➤ Osteopath (if licensed)

➤ Pediatrician

➤ Physiotherapist

➤ Plastic surgeon

➤ Podiatrist

➤ Psychiatrist

➤ Psychologist

Extra! Extra! Uncle Sam Pays for Drug Expenses!

Wouldn't it be nice if every time you bought a little bottle of aspirin, you could remind yourself that your taxes are going to be reduced by part of that expense? Dream on.

OOPS!
Your medicine must be obtained with a prescription or not be available over the counter in order for the IRS to accept the expense as a deduction.

To deduct the cost of medicine as an itemized deduction, the medicine must be prescribed by your doctor and must not be available over the counter. *Prescribed* doesn't mean, "My doctor told me I should swallow two spoonfuls of cough syrup before every meal, so I guess that means he prescribed this medicine." Uh-uh. A prescription is a little scrap of paper with some unintelligible scrawl on it that can only be read by someone in a white coat who works behind a drugstore counter that you have to be nine feet tall to see over.

Get Down to Brass Tax
You can include preventative medicine (as long as it is prescribed and not sold over the counter) as part of your deduction—this includes birth control medicine, appetite suppressants, dandruff shampoos, pimple creams.... Just be sure it comes on a prescription before you try to deduct it.

Drive, Don't Walk to the Doctor: The Mileage Deduction

In addition to letting you deduct the dollars you generously spend on the medical profession, the IRS recognizes that it may actually cost money to get to and from the doctor's office. Be it bus, taxi, train, plane, ocean liner, or covered wagon, if you paid to be transported to someplace or someone providing medical care, the cost is a medical deduction.

Furthermore, if you transport yourself, keep track of your miles, multiply the total by 9 cents (reduce that amount by the number of aspirin you consume trying to remember where to put the decimal point), and list the result as a medical mileage deduction.

Keep track of your mileage on paper, not in your head. Note on your calendar each time you drive for medical care, where you went, and how many miles you drove. Or fill out a workpaper, listing your medical travel information. File this paper with your other medical expenses. The most important thing is to keep this information current. You won't have to try to remember where you drove six months ago if your records are up-to-date, and if your tax return should happen to get examined by the IRS (and they choose to look at your medical expense deduction), you'll need to produce these mileage records.

It doesn't matter what kind of car you drive—9 cents is the going rate for the medical mileage deduction.

Get Down to Brass Tax

If you can prove you spent more than 9 cents per mile to get to your medical destination, by all means take the bigger deduction. This involves adding up (and often prorating) the costs of gas, oil, and repairs. If your car drinks oil and you need a new quart at every third gas station (hey, it can happen), or if you pierce your tire on some sort of impalement device on your way to see the doctor (for example, suppose that you decided to try that special shortcut that involves cutting through the drive-in theater by sneaking in the exit and driving over those giant spikes that point up toward incoming tires)—then those costs are specifically related to your drive to the doctor and count as medical transportation expenses. For most people, though, 9 cents per mile will do.

Be sure to figure in tolls and the cost of parking (and keep the receipts for these with your records, of course) when figuring your medical transportation expense. These count on top of the 9 cents per mile.

Medical Expenses You Can't Deduct

Some things might seem like qualified medical deductions, but they are not. Here are some things to look out for.

Helping an ailing relative (such as an uncle) with medical expenses doesn't help either one of you with the medical deduction on Schedule A. You can't deduct it if it is not for yourself or one of your dependents (see Chapter 11, "Dependents," if you need help determining who your dependents are). Your ailing uncle can't deduct it if he didn't pay for it. The medical expense has been paid. It meets all the requirements to qualify as an itemized deduction, but no one can claim it.

If you lend your ailing uncle the money and let him pay his own medical expenses, then he can take the deduction. Make sure that it is a bona fide loan and that you have reasonable expectations of getting repaid. Or, you can make a cash gift to your uncle. You can give cash gifts of up to $10,000 per person per year without running into a gift tax liability. Your uncle gets the money tax-free and can use it to pay for those medical expenses and take the deduction to boot. There's no way you can get that deduction yourself unless you make your uncle one of your dependents (see Chapter 11, "Dependents," for information on adding members to your tax family).

OOPS!
To take a deduction for medical expenses paid, the expenses must be for you or one of your dependents.

By the Way
If you have a medically deductible animal, such as a seeing-eye or hearing-ear dog, the cost of the animal's upkeep becomes a deductible medical expense.

OOOOH...

Get Down to Brass Tax

In order for you to deduct medical expenses paid for someone else, that person must have been your dependent either when the medical expenses were incurred or when they were paid. For example, suppose that your child, who is your dependent, is hospitalized for an injury. The next year, the child gets married and is no longer your dependent. You pay the hospital bill after the child is married. You get to take the medical deduction because the child was your dependent when the hospitalization occurred.

Health insurance *reimbursements* for medical expenses *reduce* the amount of the expense you can deduct. Maybe this doesn't seem fair, but think about it. You paid the doctor's fee. Your insurance paid you back for 80% of your cost. Your only cash outlay is the remaining 20%. This is the part you can claim as a medical expense. You've cashed in at the insurance company—you don't get to receive more money back as a reduction of your income tax for this expense you didn't even pay.

Beware of the end of the year. If you have filed an insurance claim for expenses paid in this year, but December comes and goes and you still haven't received your money from the insurance company, you are not supposed to take a deduction for the expense. If you know you will be paid by the insurance company, reduce your expenses by that amount. You can adjust your deduction next year to reflect the difference between what you thought you would get from your insurance company and what you actually received.

Oh No You Don't: The Floor on the Medical Deduction

Well, you've gotten this far; you've added up all your medical expenses for yourself and anyone else who counts as a dependent on this tax return; you've included the cost of transportation to and from doctors' offices, hospitals, and drugstores; you've reduced the expenses by the amount of insurance you got back or expect to get back; and you have put the amounts on line 1 of Schedule A of your tax return.

By the Way

If you file your tax return using the Married Filing Jointly status and one spouse incurs most of the medical expenses, it may behoove you to consider filing separate returns. This allows one spouse to offset the medical expenses with 7.5% of his or her income, rather than offsetting the expenses against the combined income of the two spouses.

Now here's the kicker. Add up all these medical expenses to arrive at the total that goes on line 1 of Schedule A. Go back to the bottom of page 1 of your 1040 form and get the adjusted gross income amount. Multiply the adjusted gross income by 7.5% (or .075) and place that amount under your total medical expenses. This is the medical deduction floor. If your total medical expenses are not higher than the floor, *you didn't spend enough to get the deduction.*

Hard as it is to believe, after all that figuring and uncrumbling of all the receipts, if your medical expenses do not exceed 7.5% of your adjusted gross income, you get *no deduction* for medical expenses.

On the other hand, if your medical expenses are higher than the medical deduction floor, you hit the medical deduction jackpot and get to take a deduction for the difference between your total medical expenses and 7.5% of your adjusted gross income.

Enter your adjusted gross income (Form 1040, line 32) here.

List all your medical expenses here in one lump sum.

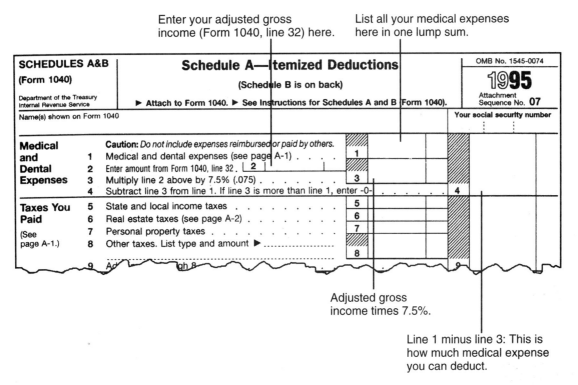

Adjusted gross income times 7.5%.

Line 1 minus line 3: This is how much medical expense you can deduct.

The Medical and Dental Expenses part of Schedule A.

Tax Expenses

I don't know about you, but sometimes I feel as if I've paid enough taxes to last me a lifetime: income tax, Social Security tax, sales tax, property tax. Everywhere I turn it seems as if I'm paying tax to somebody.

My children try to understand why, when something says it costs $5.00, they have to give the cashier $5.25. I've tried to explain that the extra quarter goes towards fixing the roads, feeding the hungry, and keeping us safe from crime, but then they just point out to me the holes in the road on the way home, the hungry people on street corners with their hands out, and the stories and pictures about crime in the newspaper every day. Already they recognize that taxpayers seem to be fighting a losing battle.

Nevertheless, taxpayers keep paying their taxes. Somewhere along the line the IRS decided that if you earn income and use that income to pay tax, you should get to deduct some of that tax from your income before you pay tax on it again. Thus the itemized deduction category for taxes.

State and Local Income Taxes

If you live in a state in which there are no state income taxes, and you don't have occasion to pay state income taxes to any other state, this section won't mean anything to you.

Most taxpayers, however, have to pay income tax at the state level, and sometimes even county and city taxes. County and city taxes are called *local income taxes* and they are treated exactly the same way in which the state income tax is treated on your Schedule A.

Any state or local income taxes that you paid during 1995 are deductible on your Schedule A on line 5 in the section called Taxes You Paid.

Deduct your state and local income taxes here.

SCHEDULES A&B (Form 1040) Department of the Treasury Internal Revenue Service	Schedule A—Itemized Deductions (Schedule B is on back) ▶ Attach to Form 1040. ▶ See Instructions for Schedules A and B (Form 1040).	OMB No. 1545-0074 1995 Attachment Sequence No. 07
Name(s) shown on Form 1040		Your social security number

Medical and Dental Expenses		**Caution:** *Do not include expenses reimbursed or paid by others.*	
	1	Medical and dental expenses (see page A-1)	1
	2	Enter amount from Form 1040, line 32 .	2	
	3	Multiply line 2 above by 7.5% (.075)	3
	4	Subtract line 3 from line 1. If line 3 is more than line 1, enter -0-	4
Taxes You Paid (See page A-1.)	5	State and local income taxes	5
	6	Real estate taxes (see page A-2)	6
	7	Personal property taxes	7
	8	Other taxes. List type and amount ▶	8
	9	Add lines 5 through 8	9
Interest	10	Home mortgage interest and points reported to you on Form 1098	10

Use the Taxes You Paid section of Schedule A to tell Uncle Sam about taxes you've already handed over.

There are several ways in which you might have paid state and local income taxes, and you want to be sure to check all of these places to find out how much you can deduct:

OOPS!

If you rent your home rather than own it, chances are part of your rent goes toward real estate taxes paid by the landlord. It's too bad, too, because he gets to take the deduction and you don't.

State and local withholding. If you are an employee, chances are you have state (and maybe local) taxes withheld from your pay. The amounts on your W-2 form for state taxes withheld and local taxes withheld count as taxes paid during 1995.

Payments made with last year's state and/or local income tax return. If you wrote a check for taxes and sent it in with your state and/or local income tax return during 1995, the amount on the check counts as an itemized deduction.

State and local estimated tax payments paid during 1995. Figuring this one out is a bit trickier. If you pay quarterly estimated taxes to your state or local government, the tax payments are deductible, but only in the year in which you pay them. So, chances are, you paid the 1994 fourth quarter estimate in January, 1995—that payment counts as a 1995 tax deduction. And if you pay the 1995 fourth quarter estimate in January, 1996, that amount won't count as a deduction until you fill out your 1996 tax return in 1997.

Here's an easy tax-planning tool you can use if you pay quarterly estimates to the state or local government. Suppose that it's December and your quarterly payment isn't due until January 15. You can make that state and/or local quarterly estimated tax payment in December and have it count as a 1995 deduction. If your income tax is likely to be higher in 1995 than in 1996, take the deduction in 1995 and get the advantage of the reduction in taxes a whole year early. On the other hand, if you can predict that in 1996 you're going to owe a lot of federal income tax, you may want to save that deduction and apply it to your 1996 tax return. It's your call.

Extra amounts paid to the state. If you file your state (or local) tax return, thinking everything is prepared correctly, and then, a few months later, you get a notice saying you made a mistake and you owe more tax, the additional tax you send in counts as a tax deduction in the year in which you make the payment. Watch out, though. If the notice from the state says you owe tax and interest and/or penalty, only the tax portion of your payment counts as a deduction.

> **OOPS!**
> Several states have begun soliciting taxpayers right on the tax form for contributions to various wildlife funds and other state-supported charitable organizations. If you write a check for taxes and it includes a contribution to a charity, that contribution amount doesn't count as a deduction for income tax payments. (See, however, the section in Chapter 20 called "Contribution Expenses.")

> OOOOH...
>
> **By the Way**
> If you pay your fourth quarter 1995 state tax estimate in January, 1996, you don't get to take a Schedule A tax deduction for this amount on your 1995 federal income tax return. The deduction comes on your 1996 tax return. The estimated payment still counts, however, as a 1995 payment toward the tax due on your state income tax return.

Real Property Taxes

You can take a deduction for the property taxes you pay on both real and personal property. Real property taxes include property tax paid on your personal residence, vacant lots you may own, and a vacation home. If you have a mortgage with a financial institution, the mortgage holder will often pay your real estate taxes for you (not out of the goodness of his or her heart, but with money from your mortgage payment that's been socked away for this purpose) and include the amount paid on your mortgage statement. You can transfer that

OOPS!
You can't just go around making big estimated state tax payments to give yourself a tax deduction. The IRS is on to this game. Make a big estimate in December and take a deduction for it, all the while knowing you're going to get the tax refunded when you file your state income tax return, and the IRS will disallow your deduction. Nice try, though.

amount to line 6 of Schedule A. If you own more than one property, total the tax amounts and enter the total on line 6.

If you bought or sold a house during the year, check your closing statement(s). There's a good chance you incurred additional real estate taxes that were paid at the closing. These taxes are deductible and should be added to other real estate taxes on Schedule A.

If you own a share in a cooperative housing corporation, part of your cooperative payment probably goes toward real estate taxes and is thereby deductible on your Schedule A. The co-op should provide you with a year-end statement telling you how much was paid in real estate taxes.

Remember, the deduction for real estate taxes isn't limited to taxes on your main home. Even if you own more than one home, you can take a deduction for all the real estate taxes you paid during the year.

Unreal Property Taxes

Personal property taxes are deductible, too, but sometimes they're a little difficult to find. You deduct these on line 7 of Schedule A.

The most common form of personal property tax is tax paid on your automobile (or other vehicle). Some states impose a vehicle personal property tax that is combined with the fee for a license plate renewal.

To figure out how much of your vehicle license fee is deductible as a property tax, you need to actually study the form that you get when you renew (or purchase a new) your license plate. Part of your fee will be the cost of the plate—a flat fee that has nothing to do with the value of your car and thus is not considered a property tax.

Be careful when figuring out the deduction for personal property tax on your automobile. First, many states don't assess property tax in this way, so the fee you pay for your license plate is just that, a fee for the plate and nothing more. Furthermore, the portion of your license fee that represents property tax is the part that is assessed based on the value of your vehicle. Closely examine the receipt to determine which part of the fee fluctuates based on vehicle value and which part is stable and charged to everyone purchasing a license plate. Only the portion based on the value of your automobile counts as a property tax deduction.

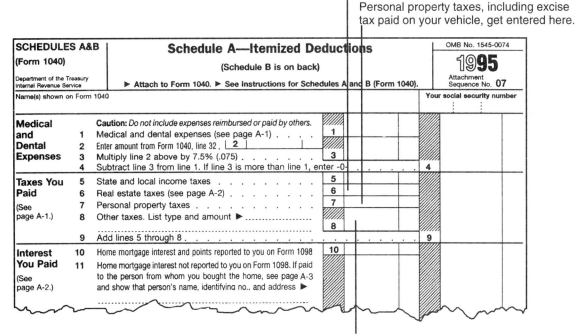

Real estate taxes get entered here.

Personal property taxes, including excise tax paid on your vehicle, get entered here.

Foreign taxes and unemployment taxes go here.

Property and other types of tax deductions.

Foreign Income Taxes

Receive income from a foreign source and open all sorts of tax questions. Foreign income is taxed by the IRS on your federal income tax return if you are a U.S. citizen. But the foreign country probably withheld tax too, before it sent the income on to you. To avoid paying income tax twice on the income, the IRS lets you recoup at least some of the foreign taxes on your 1040.

You can choose how you want to deal with your foreign income taxes. You can take a credit for the taxes paid (see Chapter 24, "Cutting Your Tax with Credits") or you can take a deduction here on line 8 in the tax deduction section of Schedule A. It's totally your choice and if you're talking about a large sum, you probably should work it out both ways and see which gives you the better result.

If you decide to take a deduction for the foreign income taxes that you paid, put the amount under Other Taxes on line 8 in the tax section of Schedule A.

Unemployment Taxes

Depending on state law, you may have unemployment taxes withheld from your pay. Alternatively, your employer may just pay these taxes for you and you may never be assessed for them. If you live in a state where unemployment taxes are paid by the employee rather than the employer and you have unemployment taxes withheld from your pay, you'll see the amount on your W-2 form, and you can include this amount in the Other Taxes entry on line 8 of Schedule A.

Taxes You Can't Deduct

Not all taxes qualify as deductible taxes. The ones that you get to pay without the benefit of deductibility include the following:

➤ Sales tax. (Taxpayers used to get to deduct this tax several years ago, but it was too difficult to figure out how much a person paid during the year in sales tax, so eventually this deduction was retired.)

➤ Taxes assessed by utility companies.

➤ City taxes for specific services such as trash pickup.

➤ Federal income taxes.

➤ Social Security and Medicare taxes.

➤ Estate and gift taxes.

➤ Parking and traffic tickets.

➤ Dog licenses.

➤ Specific assessments for street, sidewalk, and sewer repair.

➤ Cigarette and alcohol taxes.

Interest Expenses

There are people who pay cash all the way. They never borrow a dime and thus they have no interest expenses. Then there are people who take advantage of mortgages, loans, credit cards, and every kind of credit they can get their hands on. Most taxpayers fall somewhere in between, paying when they can, borrowing when they have to.

The cost of that borrowing is called *interest*, and some kinds of interest are deductible on Schedule A.

The High Cost of Borrowing

Interest rates seem to go up and down like a yo-yo. The percentage of interest you have to pay doesn't affect your ability to take a deduction for it. You don't have to prove to the IRS that you tried to get the best rate possible. To take a deduction for interest, you have to have paid the interest, you should have a statement supporting your claim for the deduction, and the interest has to be of a type the IRS will allow you to deduct.

> **HUH?**
>
> **IRSpeak**
>
> *Interest* is the amount you pay for the right to borrow money. When you pay back the money you borrow, you pay more than you originally borrowed. That additional amount is called interest.

The Home Mortgage

The most common form of interest that gets deducted these days is the home mortgage interest expense. List your mortgage interest on line 10 of Schedule A. If you borrowed money to purchase your home, you will get a statement (Form 1098) from the bank or financial institution telling you how much you paid in mortgage interest during 1995. It's always a little sobering, seeing how much of our mortgage payment goes to interest versus how much goes toward principal.

Mortgage interest is only deductible if it relates to your primary home or to a second, vacation-type home. If you own more than two homes, the interest on money borrowed to finance the other home(s) is not deductible. (However, if you own other homes and use them as rental properties, see Chapter 16, "Rents, Royalties, and Those Kooky K-1 Forms," for information on deduction of rental property expenses.)

Late mortgage payments sometimes generate an extra penalty-type fee—a bit of a bonus for the bank for waiting extra long for your payment. Go ahead and add this fee to your interest amount (if the bank didn't already do it for you on your mortgage statement). It represents extra interest—the cost of borrowing money from the bank. If you pay mortgage payments to an individual instead of a bank or other type of financial institution, put that person's name, address, and Social Security number on line 11 of Schedule A along with the amount of interest you paid. (Gee, I wonder why the IRS wants that information....)

Buying and Selling Your House

Tricky interest deductions come into play if you buy or sell a house. Check the closing statement from the purchase or sale of your house. There will most likely be interest payments recorded on this statement. Some of the interest will have been paid by the borrower, some by the seller of the home. Take the portion that applies to you and add it to your mortgage interest expense on line 11 of Schedule A.

Did you buy a house this year and pay points to your lending institution? Points are an extra fee paid for the privilege of borrowing money. Points get included with your mortgage interest for purposes of Schedule A deductions. Just add the points to the amount you report on line 10 of Schedule A.

If you own two or more houses, only points on your primary residence can be deducted on Schedule A in the year paid. Beyond your first home, the IRS wants very little to do with your points. Buy a second or third (fourth, fifth, and so on) home and your points get prorated over the life of the mortgage. Borrow money for 15 years on that second home and you can only deduct 1/15th of your points each year.

SCHEDULES A&B		Schedule A—Itemized Deductions		OMB No. 1545-0074
(Form 1040)		(Schedule B is on back)		**19**95
Department of the Treasury Internal Revenue Service		➤ Attach to Form 1040. ➤ See Instructions for Schedules A and B (Form 1040).		Attachment Sequence No. 07

Name(s) shown on Form 1040 — Your social security number

Medical and Dental Expenses		Caution: *Do not include expenses reimbursed or paid by others.*	
	1	Medical and dental expenses (see page A-1)	1
	2	Enter amount from Form 1040, line 32 . ⌊2⌋	
	3	Multiply line 2 above by 7.5% (.075)	3
	4	Subtract line 3 from line 1. If line 3 is more than line 1, enter -0-	4
Taxes You Paid (See page A-1.)	5	State and local income taxes	5
	6	Real estate taxes (see page A-2)	6
	7	Personal property taxes	7
	8	Other taxes. List type and amount ▶	8
	9	Add lines 5 through 8	9
Interest You Paid (See page A-2.)	10	Home mortgage interest and points reported to you on Form 1098	10
	11	Home mortgage interest not reported to you on Form 1098. If paid to the person from whom you bought the home, see page A-3 and show that person's name, identifying no., and address ▶	
Note: Personal interest is not deductible.		....	11
	12	Points not reported to you on Form 1098 See page A-3 for special rules . . . . See . . .	12
	13	Investment interest. If required, attach Form 4952. (See page A-3.)	13
	14	Add lines 10 through 13 . . . . , . . .	14
Gifts to Charity	15	Gifts by cash or check If you made any gift of $250 or more, see page A-3	15
If you made a	16	Other than by cash or check If any gift of $250 or more,	

All of your deductible interest expenses get listed here.

Deductions for interest expense.

Borrow, Borrow, Borrow (Against Your House, That Is)

The IRS allows you to take an interest expense deduction if you borrow money by using your house as collateral (otherwise known as a *home equity* loan). It doesn't matter whether you use the money for home improvement, education, or any personal purposes. As long as the house is behind the loan, the interest is deductible. The only catch is that the loan cannot exceed the fair market value of the house. If it does, then the house no longer collateralizes the full amount of the loan, and the deductible status of the loan is lost. Deduct the interest on your home equity loan along with other mortgage interest on line 10 of Schedule A. Home equity debt has to be $100,000 or less ($50,000 if Married Filing Separately).

Interest Expense on Investment Property

Borrow money to invest and you can deduct the related interest. For example, suppose that you have a margin account with your stockbroker. The interest on that account is deductible as investment interest. If you borrow money to invest in a business or to buy securities, the interest on that money is deductible. Investment interest gets reported on line 13 of Schedule A.

Watch out, though. Borrow money for an investment that is tax free, such as tax-exempt bonds or your IRA account, and you lose the right to deduct the related interest. The investment has to generate taxable income in order for the interest on the money borrowed to be tax deductible.

Form **4952**	**Investment Interest Expense Deduction**	OMB No. 1545-0191
Department of the Treasury Internal Revenue Service (R)	➤ **Attach to your tax return.**	Attachment Sequence No. **12A**
Name(s) shown on return		Identifying number

Part I   Total Investment Interest Expense

1	Investment interest expense paid or accrued in 1994. See instructions	**1**
2	Disallowed investment interest expense from 1993 Form 4952, line 7	**2**
3	**Total investment interest expense.** Add lines 1 and 2	**3**

Part II   Net Investment Income

4a	Gross income from property held for investment (excluding any net gain from the disposition of property held for investment)	**4a**
b	Net gain from the disposition of property held for investment . . . **4b**	
c	Net capital gain from the disposition of property held for investment **4c**	
d	Subtract line 4c from line 4b. If zero or less, enter -0-	**4d**
e	Enter all or part of the amount on line 4c that you elect to include in investment income. Do not enter more than the amount on line 4b. See instructions . . . . ▶	**4e**
f	Investment income. Add lines 4a, 4d, and 4e. See instructions	**4f**
5	Investment expenses. See instructions	**5**
6	**Net investment income.** Subtract line 5 from line 4f. If zero or less, enter -0-	**6**

Part III   Investment Interest Expense Deduction

7	Disallowed investment interest expense to be carried forward to 1995. Subtract line 6 from line 3. If zero or less, enter -0-	**7**
8	**Investment interest expense deduction.** Enter the smaller of line 3 or 6. See instructions . .	**8**

Paperwork Reduction Act Notice

We ask for the information on this form to carry out the Internal Revenue laws of the United States. You are required to give us the information. We need it to ensure that you are complying with these laws and to allow us to figure and collect the right amount of tax.

The time needed to complete and file this form will vary depending on individual circumstances. The estimated average time is:

Recordkeeping	13 min.
Learning about the law or the form	15 min.
Preparing the form	21 min.
Copying, assembling, and sending the form to the IRS . .	10 min.

If you have comments concerning the accuracy of these time estimates or suggestions for making this form simpler, we would be happy to hear from you. You can write to both the IRS and the Office of Management and Budget at the addresses listed in the instructions for the tax return with which this form is filed.

General Instructions

Section references are to the Internal Revenue Code unless otherwise noted.

Purpose of Form

Interest expense paid by an individual, estate, or a trust on a loan that is allocable to property held for investment may not be fully deductible in the current year. Form 4952 is used to figure the amount of investment interest expense deductible for the current year and the amount, if any, to carry forward to future years

For more details, get **Pub. 550,** Investment Income and Expenses.

Who Must File

If you are an individual, estate, or a trust, and you claim a deduction for investment interest expense, you must complete and attach Form 4952 to your tax return, unless **all** of the following apply:

• Your only investment income was from interest or dividends,

• You have no other deductible expenses connected with the production of interest or dividends,

• Your investment interest expense is not more than your investment income, and

• You have no disallowed investment interest expense from 1993.

Cat. No. 13177Y   Form **4952**

Determine your investment interest expense limitation on Form 4952.

The amount of investment-related interest you can deduct is limited to the net amount of investment income on your tax return. Investment income includes interest, dividends, and capital gains. If you can't deduct all your investment interest due to the investment income limitation, you can carry forward the portion of investment interest that didn't get deducted this year and try again next year (subject to the same investment income limitations). You can keep carrying forward unused investment interest expenses forever, trying again and again to take the deduction.

The Good Old Days of Interest Deductions

If you've been paying taxes for a long time, you may remember some other interest deductions that have gone by the wayside. No longer can you deduct the interest paid on credit card debt, car loans, personal loans, college loans, or any other kind of personal loan. These payments were once fully deductible, then they went through a phase-out period where for several years you were able to deduct a smaller and smaller percentage of the interest on personal indebtedness.

More recently, the IRS attempted to regulate the use of money borrowed against your house. If you refinanced your home to borrow against your equity, you could only deduct the interest if you used it for medical expenses not covered by insurance or for costs of tuition and related education expenses.

Everyone quickly found out what a nightmare of accounting it was to try to keep track of just how the proceeds from a home equity loan were used. This rule was quickly repealed and replaced with today's rule: You can take out a home equity loan and use the proceeds for any darn thing you please and still deduct the interest as long as the debt doesn't exceed $100,000 (or $50,000 if Married Filing Separately). Whew!

Interest Expenses You Can't Deduct

Here is a recap of the types of interest expenses you can't deduct on Schedule A:

➤ Mortgage interest on a home other than your primary residence or your secondary residence.

➤ Points paid on any residence but your primary residence (although points on your second home may be stretched out over the term of the mortgage and partially deducted each year).

➤ Interest on commercial credit (such as bank loans and credit cards).

➤ Interest on loans paid to individuals (unless the individual holds the mortgage to your home).

➤ Investment interest that exceeds your net investment income (the undeducted balance is calculated on Form 4952 and can be carried forward to future years).

➤ Investment interest if the income from the related investment is tax-exempt.

➤ Interest paid to the IRS or state or local taxing authorities for late tax payments.

Wrapping Up Your Schedule A

At this point, you may have no more deductions to claim on Schedule A. If you think you may be able to deduct amounts for charitable contributions, casualties, thefts, employee business expenses, gambling losses, or other miscellaneous deductions, see Chapter 20, "Counting Up a Few More Deductions," before completing Schedule A.

If you are finished reporting all of your itemized deductions, total each section and put the total in the far-right column of Schedule A. Add all the numbers in this column and put the total on line 28 of Schedule A. Compare that total to the standard deduction amount for your filing status to determine whether you have enough itemized deductions to use Schedule A. (If you need to look up your standard deduction, see Chapter 21, "The Standard Deduction.")

The standard deduction is the amount you get to deduct even if you don't have any itemized deductions. To make Schedule A worthwhile, your itemized deductions on line 28 should exceed the standard deduction for your filing status.

The Least You Need to Know

➤ Medical expenses are deductible, but only if they exceed 7.5% of your adjusted gross income.

➤ State and local income taxes, real estate taxes, personal property taxes, and foreign income taxes are all deductible as itemized deductions.

➤ Home mortgage interest and investment are the only types of interest you can deduct on Schedule A these days.

Chapter 20

Counting a Few More Deductions

In This Chapter

➤ Deductions for charitable contributions

➤ Deductions for casualties and thefts

➤ Deductions for miscellaneous expenses

This is the second chapter about itemized deductions. In this chapter I cover the sections of Schedule A that include charitable contributions as well as some of the more obscure deductions such as casualties and thefts, employee business expenses, education, and other miscellaneous deductions.

Chapter 19 covers itemized deductions for medical expenses, taxes, and interest, so this chapter picks up where that one leaves off, right in the middle of the Schedule A.

On your Schedule A each section gets totaled, then the totals are totaled for a grand total at the bottom of the schedule. Watch out! If your AGI on line 32 of the 1040 is over $114,700 (or $57,350 if your filing status is married filing separately), your itemized deductions may be limited. There's a worksheet in Chapter 19 (in the section called, "How Do Itemized Deductions Get Included on My Tax Return?") that can help you figure out the limitation on itemized deductions.

Charitable Contributions

One of the nicest things you'll find as you plow through your tax return is the right to take a deduction for charitable giving. It's sometimes hard to believe that the IRS doesn't have an ulterior motive other than encouraging you to support organizations that do good things. It makes sense though. If enough taxpayers support charitable organizations, the government can stick to the big ticket items of fighting terrorist attacks, and keeping the playgrounds safe for children.

Give Unto Others What You Would Have the IRS Return Unto You

Use the charitable contribution deduction as a means of sharing your contribution with the IRS. Suppose that you want to donate $1,000 to your favorite charity. You can look at this donation in two ways.

If you give $1,000 to charity and take a deduction for the $1,000, you reduce your taxable income by $1,000. If your highest tax rate is 28%, you get a tax benefit of $280 ($1,000 × 28%). Therefore it only cost you $720 to make a $1,000 contribution ($1,000 – $280).

Alternatively, suppose that you really want to have $1,000 less in your bank account when you're finished with your contribution. A bit of algebra tells me that you can afford to give $1,389 to your charity. A $1,389 contribution generates a tax saving (in the 28% bracket) of $389, thus making your out-of-pocket expense exactly $1,000 ($1,389 – $389 = $1,000).

No matter which way you look at it, charitable contributions result in tax deductions for people who itemize their deductions. You can give a lot, too. Your limitation for charitable giving is, for the most part, 50% of your adjusted gross income (or AGI). Any unused contributions can be carried forward for up to five years and applied to your AGI each year as you attempt to use them.

What Do You Mean, My Brother is Not a Charity?

To qualify as charitable, your contribution must be to a tax-exempt organization recognized by the IRS as a charity. If you have any doubts about the tax-exempt status of the organization to which you are donating, just ask them. They know whether they qualify. You can also call the IRS and they'll tell you whether an organization qualifies.

Tax-exempt status is granted by the IRS to private and public charities that are nonprofit organizations that perform certain types of services deemed appropriate by the IRS. Qualified charitable organizations include churches, schools, medical facilities, government units, museums, service organizations such as the Red Cross, the Salvation Army, Boy and Girl Scouts, humane societies, film preservation groups, public television, and symphony orchestras.

Charitable contributions to any of these types of groups and many others count as deductible contributions. Donations to individuals, no matter how needy they may be, do not qualify.

Keeping Track of What You Give

It's up to you to keep track of what you give and to whom. Keep canceled checks and receipts from the organizations receiving your contribution.

You must have a receipt for contributions over $250. When receipts are not practical, keep written records. If you put a handful of coins in the bell-ringer's bucket on the street corner, or give cash when the basket is passed in church, write down how much you gave and when.

The better your records, the more likely it is that the IRS is going to accept them should your tax return get examined.

If you purchase items from a charitable organization, chances are a part of the cost of the items goes back to the organization. For example, if school children come to your door selling candy or gift wrap or plants to benefit their school, the school gets part of the price of the items, thus a portion of what you pay can be considered a charitable contribution. But how do you find out what percentage represents a deductible contribution?

The children selling these items probably don't know what part is deductible, nor do their parents. That shouldn't stop you from pursuing a charitable contribution deduction. When you make your purchase, take a few minutes to call the school or church and ask to speak to someone knowledgeable about the fund-raising program. Ask what portion of your purchase price will be funneled back into the organization for their use. Be sure to keep your canceled check and a receipt for your purchase. If the amount you spend is substantial, ask the person you speak to at the organization to send you written confirmation of the portion of your cost that is tax-deductible.

It may take some digging, but you can get a tax deduction for your efforts. If you spend $20 and half of that amount gets returned to the school, you get a $10 charitable contribution deduction. In the 28% tax bracket, that's a $3 savings in income tax. That may not sound like much, but it adds up if you make several purchases like this during a year. Furthermore, you've already made the contribution—why not get a tax benefit too, even if it's a small one?

Be careful about taking deductions for events. You may purchase tickets to a church social or a school carnival or a symphony concert—events that are considered fund-raising events by the organization sponsoring them. But if you benefit from your contribution by receiving a meal or some entertainment, then the amount you paid represents the cost of the food or the entertainment and is therefore not deductible to you. You've made a purchase rather than a contribution. On the other hand, if you purchase tickets to a program and are unable to use them, you may be able to turn the tickets back in for a receipt stating that you made a tax-deductible contribution to the organization.

It makes sense to keep a folder, envelope, or shoebox for your charitable receipts so that they'll all be in one place when it's time to prepare your tax return. Keep a worksheet in the folder and add to it every time you make a contribution, cash or otherwise. If you stay on top of this all year, you'll save yourself a lot of time and aggravation at tax time, not just in assembling the information, but in trying to re-create every place you donated money during the year. Furthermore, the more organized your records, the more likely they are to pass IRS inspection in the case of an audit. At the end of the year, add up all your cash contributions and report the total on line 15 of Schedule A.

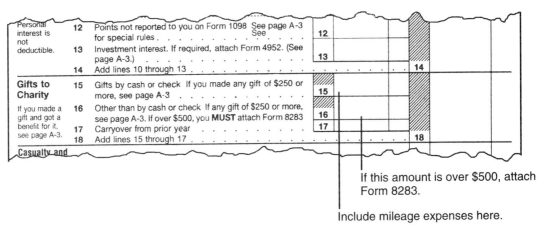

Deduct your charitable contributions on Schedule A.

Old Clothes and Furniture

Probably the most common form of property contribution is not appreciated property. Just the opposite—they are things that are worn out, outgrown, or that have outlasted their usefulness to you. There are plenty of churches and service organizations that will take unneeded clothing and household goods off your hands and put them into the hands of others who can use them.

You are entitled to a charitable contribution for these noncash contributions. If the value of your noncash charitable contributions exceeds $500 you must attach Form 8283, "Noncash Charitable Contributions," to your tax return and list the particulars of what you donated and to whom on this form.

When making noncash charitable contributions, you must keep detailed records of what you contributed, to whom the contribution was made, and when it was made. If a contribution is at least $250 in value, you must obtain a signed receipt from the recipient.

As with everything, the better your records, the happier the IRS will be. Although you don't have to attach to your tax return a detailed list of the items you donate, you should keep one for your records. You can make a copy of the Property Donation Record worksheet in this chapter, and it can not only help you organize your items so that you can make a donation, but it also can be signed by the organization receiving the donation and kept for your records.

Property Donation Record

Donated to (organization):_____

Donation date:_____

Description	Quantity	Estimated Total Value	Description	Quantity	Estimated Total Value
Men's shirts			Children's skirts		
Men's pants			Children's dresses		
Men's suits 2pc			Children's sweaters		
Men's suits 3pc			Children's sweats		
Men's T-shirts			Children's pajamas		
Men's shoes			Children's bathrobes		
Men's belts			Children's jackets/coats		
Men's sweaters			Children's boots		
Men's sweats			Roller skates		
Men's pajamas			Ice skates		
Men's bathrobes			Children's gloves/mittens		
Men's jackets			Tables		
Men's coats			Chairs		
Women's blouses			Couches		
Women's pants			Lamps		
Women's skirts			Bookcases		
Women's dresses			Desks		
Women's suits			Computer tables		
Women' s T-shirts			Computers		
Women's shoes			Radios		
Women's belts			Televisions		
Women's sweaters			VCRs		
Women's sweats			Stereo Equipment		
Women's pajamas			Books		
Women's nightgowns			Records		
Women's bathrobes			Dishes		
Women's jackets			Mattresses		
Women's coats			Sofas		
Adult boots			Fabric		
Adult gloves			Lumber		
Children's shirts			Other:		
Children's pants					
Children's suits					
Children's T-shirts					
Children's shoes					
Children's belts			**Total:**		

Make copies of this checklist and use it whenever you make a noncash contribution.

Most organizations that receive clothing and household goods for charity rely on you to place a value on the items. The best way to value your donations is to do some comparative shopping. If you're new to shopping at garage sales, flea markets, and resale shops, you may be in for a shock regarding the value of your precious possessions. Some service organizations publish a list itemizing their pricing procedures. A trip to the local Goodwill store with a pencil and paper will probably give you most of the price information you need for coming up with your own valuation. In general, you should value your clothing and other items for purposes of your tax deduction at the amount that you would expect the items to sell for at a resale shop or a garage sale.

Enter the value of your noncash donations on line 16 of the Schedule A. If the total of your noncash donations exceeds $500, you must also attach Form 8283, "Noncash Charitable Contributions." Fill out Part I of Form 8283, which asks for the following items:

➤ The organization(s) to whom you donated goods

➤ The address of the organization receiving goods

➤ The date of the donation

➤ The value you assigned to the donation

➤ How you valued the property

Your method of valuing property goes in column (h): Method used to determine the fair market value. In this column the IRS wants to see a phrase like "Thrift Shop Value," "Appraisal," "Comparable Sales," or "Catalog" (for items such as stamp or coin collections).

Use a separate line for each organization to which you donated and for the separate dates on which you donated. You can attach more than one copy of Form 8283 to your tax return if you must.

Form **8283**	**Noncash Charitable Contributions**	OMB No. 1545-0908
(Rev. November 1992)	▶ Attach to your tax return if the total deduction claimed for all property contributed exceeds $500.	Expires 11-30-95
Department of the Treasury Internal Revenue Service	▶ See separate instructions.	Attachment Sequence No. **55**

Name(s) shown on your income tax return | Identifying number

Note: Figure the amount of your contribution deduction before completing this form. See your tax return instructions.

Section A—Include in this section **only** items (or groups of similar items) for which you claimed a deduction of $5,000 or less per item or group, and certain publicly traded securities (see instructions).

Part I Information on Donated Property—If you need more space, attach a statement.

1	(a) Name and address of the donee organization	(b) Description of donated property
A		
B		
C		
D		
E		

Note: If the amount you claimed as a deduction for an item is $500 or less, you do not have to complete columns (d), (e), and (f).

	(c) Date of the contribution	(d) Date acquired by donor (mo., yr.)	(e) How acquired by donor	(f) Donor's cost or adjusted basis	(g) Fair market value	(h) Method used to determine the fair market value
A						
B						
C						
D						
E						

Part II Other Information—If you gave less than an entire interest in property listed in Part I, complete lines 2a–2e. If restrictions were attached to a contribution listed in Part I, complete lines 3a–3c.

2 If less than the entire interest in the property is contributed during the year, complete the following:

a Enter letter from Part I that identifies the property _____. If Part II applies to more than one property, attach a separate statement.

b Total amount claimed as a deduction for the property listed in Part I: (1) For this tax year _____ (2) For any prior tax years _____.

c Name and address of each organization to which any such contribution was made in a prior year (complete only if different than the donee organization above).

Name of charitable organization (donee)

Address (number, street, and room or suite no.)

City or town, state, and ZIP code

d For tangible property, enter the place where the property is located or kept _____

e Name of any person, other than the donee organization, having actual possession of the property _____

3 If conditions were attached to any contribution listed in Part I, answer the following questions and attach the required statement (see instructions): **Yes | No**

a Is there a restriction, either temporary or permanent, on the donee's right to use or dispose of the donated property?

b Did you give to anyone (other than the donee organization or another organization participating with the donee organization in cooperative fundraising) the right to the income from the donated property or to the possession of the property, including the right to vote donated securities, to acquire the property by purchase or otherwise, or to designate the person having such income, possession, or right to acquire?

c Is there a restriction limiting the donated property for a particular use?

For Paperwork Reduction Act Notice, see separate instructions. Cat. No. 62299J Form **8283** (Rev. 11-92)

The total of amounts in this column goes to Schedule A.

			11	
Note: Personal interest is not deductible.	12	Points not reported to you on Form 1098 See page A-3 for special rules . See	12	
	13	Investment interest. If required, attach Form 4952. (See page A-3.)	13	
	14	Add lines 10 through 13		14
Gifts to Charity	15	Gifts by cash or check If you made any gift of $250 or more, see page A-3	15	
If you made a gift and got a benefit for it, see page A-3.	16	Other than by cash or check If any gift of $250 or more, see page A-3. If over $500, you **MUST** attach Form 8283	16	
	17	Carryover from prior year	17	
	18	Add lines 15 through 17		18

Use Form 8283 to report noncash contributions.

Donating Uncle Jed's "Oil on Bark" Masterpiece

In addition to donations of cash, you can take a contribution deduction for the value of art work, stock certificates, antiques, and other types of property that appreciate (you hope) over the years. Take deductions for donations of property on line 16 of Schedule A.

OOPS!

If you give tangible property such as paintings or antiques (as opposed to stocks), find out what the organization is going to do with the property before you donate it. If they keep the item and use it in a museum-type display setting, your deduction for the appreciated value is safe. If they sell it for cash, however, you lose. Your deduction is limited to your cost of the item, no matter how much it is sold for.

To take a donation for the appreciated (increased) value of property, you have to have owned the property for at least one year and it has to be property that would generate a taxable gain for you if you sold it.

When you donate property that has increased in value, you get to take a contribution deduction for the fair market value of the property as opposed to what you paid for it. If you bought a painting from an unknown artist for $100 and ten years later the artist is the talk of the town and her paintings are selling for $10,000, your donation of the art work is worth $10,000 and that is the amount of your charitable contribution. What's more, you don't have to pay tax on the gain as you would if you sold the painting.

Donated property gets reported on Form 8283 and then carried to line 16 of Schedule A. If the property is valued at more than $5,000, you'll need to fill out the back page of Form 8283—Section B—and have an appraiser sign the form attesting to the value of the property.

Get Down to Brass Tax

There's one hitch to consider when donating appreciated property. Tax preferences are like tax shelters—deductions and losses that are specifically designed to help people avoid paying income tax. The IRS hates to see people avoid paying tax, thus they devised the Alternative Minimum Tax as a tax on preferences. If you have high enough income and enough preferences, you may be subject to tax on things like the $9,900 ($10,000 minus your cost of $100) appreciated value in your painting.

Form 8283 (Rev. 11-92)
Page **2**

Name(s) shown on your income tax return

Identifying number

Section B—Appraisal Summary—Include in this section only items (or groups of similar items) for which you claimed a deduction of more than $5,000 per item or group. Report contributions of certain publicly traded securities only in Section A.

If you donated art, you may have to attach the complete appraisal. See the **Note** in Part I below.

Part I | **Information on Donated Property**—To be completed by the taxpayer and/or appraiser.

4   Check type of property:

☐ Art* (contribution of $20,000 or more)   ☐ Real Estate   ☐ Gems/Jewelry   ☐ Stamp Collections
☐ Art* (contribution of less than $20,000)   ☐ Coin Collections ☐ Books   ☐ Other

*Art includes paintings, sculptures, watercolors, prints, drawings, ceramics, antique furniture, decorative arts, textiles, carpets, silver, rare manuscripts, historical memorabilia, and other similar objects.

Note: *If your total art contribution deduction was $20,000 or more, you must attach a complete copy of the signed appraisal. See instructions.*

5	(a) Description of donated property (if you need more space, attach a separate statement)	(b) If tangible property was donated, give a brief summary of the overall physical condition at the time of the gift	(c) Appraised fair market value
A			
B			
C			
D			

➤ Describe the property here.

	(d) Date acquired by donor (mo., yr.)	(e) How acquired by donor	(f) Donor's cost or adjusted basis	(g) For bargain sales, enter amount received	See instructions	
					(h) Amount claimed as a deduction	(i) Average trading price of securities
A						
B						
C						
D						

Part II | **Taxpayer (Donor) Statement**—List each item included in Part I above that is separately identified in the appraisal as having a value of $500 or less. See instructions.

I declare that the following item(s) included in Part I above has to the best of my knowledge and belief an appraised value of not more than $500 (per item). Enter identifying letter from Part I and describe the specific item: _____

Signature of taxpayer (donor) ▶ _____   Date ▶ _____

Part III | **Certification of Appraiser**

I declare that I am not the donor, the donee, a party to the transaction in which the donor acquired the property, employed by, married to, or related to any of the foregoing persons, or an appraiser regularly used by any of the foregoing persons and who does not perform a majority of appraisals during the taxable year for other persons.

Also, I declare that I hold myself out to the public as an appraiser or perform appraisals on a regular basis; and that because of my qualifications as described in the appraisal, I am qualified to make appraisals of the type of property being valued. I certify that the appraisal fees were not based upon a percentage of the appraised property value. Furthermore, I understand that a false or fraudulent overstatement of the property value as described in the qualified appraisal or this appraisal summary may subject me to the civil penalty under section 6701(a) (aiding and abetting the understatement of tax liability). I affirm that I have not been barred from presenting evidence or testimony by the Director of Practice.

Sign Here | Signature ▶ _____   Title ▶ _____   Date of appraisal ▶ _____

Business address (including room or suite no.)

Identifying number

➤ The appraiser signs here.

City or town, state, and ZIP code

Part IV | **Donee Acknowledgment**—To be completed by the charitable organization.

This charitable organization acknowledges that it is a qualified organization under section 170(c) and that it received the donated property as described in Section B, Part I, above on _____
(Date)

Furthermore, this organization affirms that in the event it sells, exchanges, or otherwise disposes of the property (or any portion thereof) within 2 years after the date of receipt, it will file an information return (**Form 8282**, Donee Information Return) with the IRS and furnish the donor a copy of that return. This acknowledgment does not represent concurrence in the claimed fair market value.

Name of charitable organization (donee)	Employer identification number	
Address (number, street, and room or suite no.)	City or town, state, and ZIP code	
Authorized signature	Title	Date

Section B of Form 8283 is used for donations of property valued at more than $5,000.

How to Enjoy That Girl Scout Camping Trip

If you donate your time to charitable organizations, you do it out of the goodness of your heart and, although the IRS may admire your efforts, there is no tax deduction waiting for you when you come home.

If you incur out-of-pocket expenses related to your benevolent behavior, such as mileage (12 cents per mile), parking, postage, or supplies, you can take a charitable contribution for the amounts you spent, but not for your time.

Driving for Fun and Profit: The Mileage Deduction

If you drive your vehicle for charitable purposes such as delivering meals to shut-ins, hauling school groups to and from field trips, transporting supplies for your church, or taking that Girl Scout troop on a camping expedition, keep track of the number of miles you drive. You can take a deduction of 12 cents per mile for all your charitable mileage. You can also deduct the costs of related parking and tolls. Include your mileage, parking, and toll contributions with other cash contributions on line 15 of Schedule A.

Keep track of your charitable mileage by keeping a record of your miles. Use your calendar or keep a separate worksheet listing all the places you drove for charity, the dates you drove, and how many miles you drove. Keep this information with your tax records for this 1995 tax return.

Contributions You Can't Deduct

There are limits to what kinds of contributions generate tax relief from the IRS. You can't donate amounts to needy individuals and get a tax deduction. And donations to the following types of organizations and events won't qualify you for the charitable contribution deduction:

➤ Chambers of Commerce

➤ Lobbying groups

➤ Political candidates and their organizations

➤ Raffles

➤ Lottery tickets

➤ Dues to fraternal organizations

➤ Dues to alumni associations

➤ Blood donations

Casualty and Theft Losses

If you lose something due to theft or if you suffer damage due to some unforeseen event, you can qualify for a deduction on line 19 of Schedule A. You have to jump through a lot of hoops to please the IRS regarding the nature of your loss and the value of the items that were stolen or damaged. Furthermore, the IRS sets strict rules as to how much can be deducted in this area. Not only do you have to reduce the amount of each loss by $100 (suppose that you have a really bad year and suffer storm damage twice and have your wallet stolen), each occurrence is reduced by $100 right from the start, so that's $300 you can't deduct.

In addition to the $100 per occurrence, you have to reduce your deduction for any casualty or theft loss (of personal property) by 10% of your adjusted gross income. And insurance reimbursements come off as well, of course, so the chances of getting to benefit from this deduction are small. Yet, for those of you who may be able to eke out a deduction, here's how it works.

Earthquake! Hurricane! Flood! Stop, Thief!

A casualty loss is defined by the IRS as one of the following:

A sudden event—one that is swift, not gradual or progressive.

An unexpected event—one that is ordinarily unanticipated and unintended.

An unusual event—one that is not a day-to-day occurrence and that is not typical of the activity in which you were engaged.

Disasters such as earthquakes, storms, tornadoes, fires, cyclones, plane crashes in your back yard, volcanic eruptions, ice storms, and hail are what casualties are made of. Disasters that take time to occur, such as droughts, bug infestations, and erosion don't count as casualties as far as the IRS is concerned.

A casualty can also include a government-ordered condemnation and demolition of property.

A theft is the unlawful taking and removing of your belongings with the intent to deprive you of those items. If a friend comes to visit and accidentally puts on your coat instead of his own when he leaves, that doesn't count as theft. But if the same "friend" slips your CD player under his arm on the way out the door, you're in business, theft-wise.

IRSpeak

A *casualty* is a sudden, unexpected, or unusual event, by IRS standards. An event that doesn't fit into one of these descriptions doesn't garner you a casualty loss deduction on your Schedule A.

The amount of your casualty or theft loss is the lesser of your adjusted basis in the property (your cost plus the cost of improvements less any depreciation expense) or the fair market value of the property (the amount you would expect to pay to purchase the property you lost).

Proving the Loss Occurred

It's not bad enough that you've suffered. If you want to try for the casualty and theft loss deduction on your tax return, you have to convince the IRS that you've suffered.

Proving that you have incurred a casualty means identifying the type of casualty and when it occurred, showing that your loss was a result of the casualty, and being able to show that you owned the property that was damaged. Gather everything you can—it's always better to have too much than not enough evidence. Prove the casualty occurred with newspaper reports and photographs. Insurance reports are useful too. Before and after pictures are terrific. And dig up the proof that you owned whatever was damaged—a bill of sale for your car that got smashed under a falling tree, your deed if the roof blew off your house, a receipt for your mink coat that got burned in a fire, and so on.

If you suffered a theft, you probably have a police report. That's the place to start in proving a theft occurred. Also, you have to show that you owned the property that was stolen, and you need to identify when you discovered the loss.

What About My Insurance?

Insurance coverage for your loss kind of negates the need for a tax deduction. The theory is that tax deductions are for unreimbursed losses. Make an insurance claim and receive a payment for your loss, and you in effect haven't lost anything; at least that's the way the IRS sees it.

If insurance doesn't cover the loss, or if it only covers part of the loss, then you have a deduction to claim on your tax return.

Insurance proceeds that are expected but that haven't come in by the time you file your tax return, should still be considered on your tax return. If you anticipate an insurance reimbursement, then you can't take a deduction for the part of the loss that will be covered by the reimbursement.

Gain resulting from an insurance reimbursement for a casualty loss is taxable income. This can happen if you have something insured for its replacement value. Your loss, as far as the IRS is concerned, is your cost of the item, not its fair market value. So if I have a 1966 Mustang convertible in pristine condition and insured for $20,000, even though it only cost me $2,600 back in 1966, and a tree falls on the car and flattens it, my insurance company is going to pay me $20,000. The IRS will expect me to report $17,400 as capital gain income on Schedule D and pay tax on that. Bummer!

The Casualty Loss Floor

Report the casualties and thefts on Form 4684. On this form you will reduce each casualty and theft loss by $100 and then deduct 10% of your AGI from the total. If anything is left when you get to the bottom line, race over to line 19 of the Schedule A with the amount of your casualty and/or theft loss before the IRS figures out another way to chip away at it.

Form **4684**

Department of the Treasury
Internal Revenue Service

Casualties and Thefts

► See separate instructions.
► Attach to your tax return.
► Use a separate Form 4684 for each different casualty or theft.

OMB No. 1545-0177

Attachment
Sequence No. **26**

Name(s) shown on tax return

Identifying number

SECTION A—Personal Use Property (Use this section to report casualties and thefts of property **not** used in a trade or business or for income-producing purposes.)

1 Description of properties (show type, location, and date acquired for each):

Property **A** ....

Property **B** ....

Property **C** ....

Property **D** ....

Properties (Use a separate column for each property lost or damaged from one casualty or theft.)

		A	B	C	D
2	Cost or other basis of each property				
3	Insurance or other reimbursement (whether or not you filed a claim). See instructions				
	Note: *If line 2 is **more than** line 3, skip line 4.*				
4	Gain from casualty or theft. If line 3 is **more than** line 2, enter the difference here and skip lines 5 through 9 for that column. See instructions if line 3 includes insurance or other reimbursement you did not claim, or you received payment for your loss in a later tax year				
5	Fair market value **before** casualty or theft . . .				
6	Fair market value **after** casualty or theft				
7	Subtract line 6 from line 5				
8	Enter the **smaller** of line 2 or line 7				
9	Subtract line 3 from line 8. If zero or less, enter -0-				

10	Casualty or theft loss. Add the amounts on line 9. Enter the total	**10**	
11	Enter the amount from line 10 or $100, whichever is **smaller**	**11**	
12	Subtract line 11 from line 10	**12**	
	Caution: *Use only one Form 4684 for lines 13 through 18.*		
13	Add the amounts on line 12 of all Forms 4684	**13**	
14	Combine the amounts from line 4 of all Forms 4684	**14**	
15	• If line 14 is **more than** line 13, enter the difference here and on Schedule D. Do not complete the rest of this section (see instructions).	**15**	
	• If line 14 is **less than** line 13, enter -0- here and continue with the form.		
	• If line 14 is **equal to** line 13, enter -0- here. Do not complete the rest of this section.		
16	If line 14 is **less than** line 13, enter the difference	**16**	
17	Enter 10% of your adjusted gro~~ss~~ ~~and~~ trusts, see instructions	**17**	
18	Subtract line 17 from line 16. ~~Sche~~dule A (Form 1040), line 19. Estates and trusts, enter on t~~~~	**18**	

For Paperwork Reduction Act N~~otice~~

Cat. No. 12997O

Form **4684**

If you made a gift and got a benefit for it, see page A-3.	16	Other ~~gift~~ see p~~~~	~~~~fe, ~~2~~283	16		
	17	Carr~~~~		17		
	18	Add~~~~				18
Casualty and Theft Losses	19	C~~~~	~~s~~ee page A-4.)			19
Job Expenses and Most	20	~~~~	~~~~el, union ~~mu~~ST attach			
~~Other~~		~~Fo~~rm 210~~6~~				

Carry this number over to Schedule A.

Use Form 4684 to report casualties and thefts.

Miscellaneous Expenses

The Miscellaneous Expense catch-all on your Schedule A is a place for deductions that don't seem to fit anywhere else. Job-related expenses go here, as well as tax preparation expenses, education, and investment expenses.

As with medical and casualty/theft expenses, there is a threshold you have to overcome before you can take the deduction for miscellaneous expenses. The miscellaneous expense floor is only 2% of your AGI—not nearly as hefty as the floor on medical and casualty/theft expenses—but nevertheless, you can't just take your deduction and be done with it. That would be too easy.

Money Spent for Your Job

Employee Business Expenses is the all-encompassing category that takes into account automobile and travel expenses, entertainment, business gifts, professional dues, subscriptions, continuing education, union dues, uniforms, and just about anything else you can think of that constitutes money you spent on behalf of your job.

If you were reimbursed for your employee business expenses and your reimbursement equals your expenses, you don't have to report any of your expenses or your reimbursement on your income tax return. Job-related expenses get listed first on Form 2106, "Employee Business Expenses," and then carried in total over to line 20 of the Schedule A.

Any job-related use you made of your car during 1995 can be deducted in this section of Schedule A. Enter your car expenses on page 2, Part II of Form 2106. You have the option of using the Standard Mileage Rate, computed at 30 cents per mile for your business miles, not including commuting, or deducting your actual automobile expenses including gas, oil, repairs, and so on, prorated for the business portion of your automobile usage. If you decide to use the actual expenses and have questions about what expenses qualify, see the "Car and Truck Expense" section of Chapter 13.

All other job-related expenses beyond your automobile expenses get reported on page 1 of Form 2106. This section includes all the following types of expenses:

➤ Parking and tolls (no matter which method you use of computing automobile expense)

➤ Overnight travel expenses

➤ Business gifts (limited to $25 per person per year)

➤ Uniforms

➤ Union dues

➤ Dues to professional organizations

➤ Subscriptions to business publications

➤ Cost of small tools used in your work

➤ Professional license costs

➤ Continuing education costs for maintaining license

➤ Job-related insurance

Form 2106				Page **2**

Part II — **Vehicle Expenses** (See instructions to find out which sections to complete.)

Section A.—General Information

			(a) Vehicle 1	(b) Vehicle 2
11	Enter the date vehicle was placed in service	11	/ /	/ /
12	Total miles vehicle was driven during	12	miles	miles
13	Business miles included on line 12	13	miles	miles
14	Percent of business use. Divide line 13 by line 12	14	%	%
15	Average daily round trip commuting distance	15	miles	miles
16	Commuting miles included on line 12	16	miles	miles
17	Other personal miles. Add lines 13 and 16 and subtract the total from line 12	17	miles	miles
18	Do you (or your spouse) have another vehicle available for personal purposes?	☐ Yes ☐ No		
19	If your employer provided you with a vehicle, is personal use during off duty hours permitted? ☐ Yes ☐ No ☐ Not applicable			
20	Do you have evidence to support your deduction?	☐ Yes ☐ No		
21	If "Yes," is the evidence written?	☐ Yes ☐ No		

Section B.—Standard Mileage Rate (Use this section only if you own the vehicle.)

22	Multiply line 13 by 29¢ (.29). Enter the result here and on line 1. (Rural mail carriers, see instructions.)	22		

— Standard mileage rate is computed here.

Section C.—Actual Expenses

			(a) Vehicle 1		(b) Vehicle 2	
23	Gasoline, oil, repairs, vehicle insurance, etc.	23				
24a	Vehicle rentals	24a				
b	Inclusion amount (see instructions)	24b				
c	Subtract line 24b from line 24a	24c				
25	Value of employer-provided vehicle (applies only if 100% of annual lease value was included on Form W-2—see instructions)	25				
26	Add lines 23, 24c, and 25 . .	26				
27	Multiply line 26 by the percentage on line 14 . . .	27				
28	Depreciation. Enter amount from line 38 below	28				
29	Add lines 27 and 28. Enter total here and on line 1	29				

— If you use actual expenses, list them here.

Section D.—Depreciation of Vehicles (Use this section only if you own the vehicle.)

			(a) Vehicle 1		(b) Vehicle 2	
30	Enter cost or other basis (see instructions)	30				
31	Enter amount of section 179 deduction (see instructions) .	31				
32	Multiply line 30 by line 14 (see instructions if you elected the section 179 deduction) . . .	32				
33	Enter depreciation method and percentage (see instructions) .	33				
34	Multiply line 32 by the percentage on line 33 (see instructions) . .	34				
35	Add lines 31 and 34	35				
36	Enter the limitation amount from the table in the line 36 instructions	36				
37	Multiply line 36 by the percentage on line 14 . . .	37				
38	Enter the **smaller** of line 35 or line 37. Also, enter this amount on line 28 above	38				

✿ *Printed on recycled paper*

Report your job-related automobile expenses on page 2 of Form 2106.

Money Spent for the Job You Wish You Had

The cost of looking for a job is deductible on line 22 in the miscellaneous deduction section of Schedule A, even if you don't get a new job. The job search must be for a job in the same profession in which you are currently working. That nixes a deduction for job search expenses for a first job.

The types of expenses you can deduct relating to your job search include employment agency fees, the cost of preparing and printing a résumé, mileage and other travel expenses to go to interviews, parking, postage, purchase of publications that list job offerings in your profession, and long-distance telephone calls.

If you buy a new suit of clothes so you'll look sharp at your interview, you're not going to get away with a deduction for it. The costs have to be specifically and exclusively related to searching for a new job.

Home Sweet Home, with an Office

Do you work out of your home? If you have an office away from home, you can't take a deduction for a home office as well. But if you work exclusively from home, you can take a deduction for the cost of the space you use for your office. A portion of your living expenses, such as utilities, home repairs, insurance, and cleaning, can qualify for home office expenses. In addition, you can depreciate the part of your home that is used for your office. For more information on the deductibility of home office expenses, see the section on "Turning Your Home into an Office" in Chapter 13.

Go Back to School (Do Not Collect $200)

If you pay for the cost of going back to school for additional education, after you are employed, that cost can be a deductible expense in the miscellaneous deductions section of Schedule A. There are certain strict requirements you must meet to qualify for an education deduction.

First, to take a deduction for education expense, the education must be required by your employer in order for you to keep your job or the education must help maintain your skills at your current job level. If your employer wants you to take a computer class to keep current on the latest version of the program you use in your job, that's a deductible expense. You can also take time off from your job to attend classes that maintain your current job skills. The cost of these classes is deductible.

Education that trains you for a new job doesn't qualify for the miscellaneous expense deduction. A person who is a salesperson by day but who is enrolled in law school at night is studying for a new profession. The cost of the law school classes are not deductible.

Education that meets the minimum requirements of your job is not deductible education. For example, if you are a law school graduate and are hired by a law firm to work as a lawyer, it is expected that you will pass the bar exam. The cost of a bar review course is not deductible—passing the bar exam is a minimum requirement of keeping your job.

If you meet the requirements to deduct education expenses, the types of education expenses you can deduct include the following:

➤ Tuition

➤ Books

➤ Supplies

➤ Laboratory fees

➤ Travel costs to get to and from the education site

Education expenses get included on Form 2106, line 4. The expenses then get carried over to Schedule A, line 20.

Costs of Nurturing Your Investments

Expenses related to maintaining your investments that you can deduct in the Miscellaneous Expense section on Schedule A include the following:

➤ Fees for brokers (commissions on the purchase and sale of stock, however, are added to the cost of the stock or are considered an expense of the sale)

➤ Safe-deposit box rental

➤ Subscriptions to investment publications and newsletters

➤ Books and magazines you purchase for investment advice

➤ Computer software to track your investments

➤ Travel expenses to visit your broker or to buy and sell investments

Interest on investment indebtedness is allowed as a deduction in the Interest Expense section of Schedule A.

The Cost of This Book

Take a miscellaneous deduction on line 21 of Schedule A for the cost of preparing your tax return. This deduction would include tax preparer fees, copying and postage, computer software used to prepare your tax return, and the cost of this book if you bought it in 1995!

Get Down to Brass Tax

If you have a Schedule C business or rental property reported on Schedule E and can claim that the costs of getting professional tax advice relate directly to those businesses, you can deduct the cost on those schedules. That gives you a double advantage: first, your cost is not limited by the 2% AGI floor that affects miscellaneous deductions on Schedule A; and second, your deduction occurs "above the line"—up on page 1 of the 1040, where it will flow through to your state income tax computation as well.

A computer used for investment tracking and accumulation of tax records can be partially deductible as a miscellaneous deduction if you can break out the investment and tax related portions of the usage from any personal usage. The IRS wants to see a log of time spent on the machine if you attempt to do this. Note that depreciation rules apply for computers.

Not So Fast! The Miscellaneous Deduction Floor

You've finished summarizing all your miscellaneous deductions on Schedule A; your unreimbursed business expenses have been carried over from Form 2106; now it's time to slash these deductions with the 2% AGI reduction.

Multiply your AGI by 2% and put that amount on line 25 on Schedule A. Deduct this from your miscellaneous deductions. If you have anything left, you can celebrate and grab yourself a miscellaneous deduction. If the 2% amount is higher than your combined miscellaneous deductions, you just have to chalk all this hard work up to experience and try again next year.

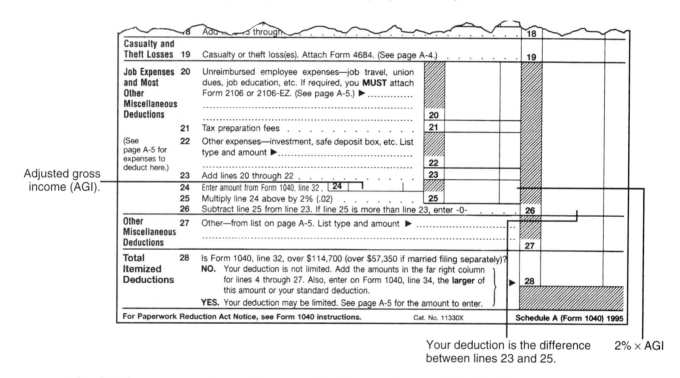

Adjusted gross income (AGI).

Your deduction is the difference between lines 23 and 25.

2% × AGI

Job-related expenses and miscellaneous deductions go here on Schedule A.

Wrapping Up Your Schedule A

See the section with this same title at the end of Chapter 19 for a lesson on how to complete your Schedule A and carry the amounts to your Form 1040.

The Least You Need to Know

➤ Contributions to recognized charities are deductible. Noncash contributions of clothing, household goods, and appreciated property are allowed as deductions and must be listed on Form 8283 if they exceed $500.

➤ Strict record-keeping requirements apply to noncash charitable contributions including detailed records of what you contributed, to whom, when, and, if a contribution exceeds $250 in value, signed receipts from the recipient.

➤ Casualty and theft losses get reported on Form 4684 and slashed by the IRS limitations. Then, if there's anything left, the losses get carried to Schedule A.

➤ All sorts of job-related expenses can be deducted as miscellaneous deductions on Schedule A—the catch is that they have to exceed 2% of your adjusted gross income.

The Standard Deduction

In This Chapter

➤ What's this standard deduction?

➤ The standard deduction vs. itemized deductions

➤ Strange and unusual variations on the standard deduction

The *standard deduction* is an amount that taxpayers can use to reduce taxable income. You take the standard deduction off of your adjusted gross income, or AGI, (all your income less your adjustments, as discussed in Chapter 18, "Adjustments to Income"). Basically, everyone does not have to pay tax on income up to the amount of the standard deduction. If you still have income left, after subtracting the standard deduction from AGI, you proceed with the tax calculation. If you don't have any income left, then the IRS figures you've suffered enough, and you can stop computing—your income tax is zero and you may be finished with your tax return at this point.

The theory behind the standard deduction is that the IRS has better things to do than attempt to verify all sorts of little itemized deductions for all the taxpayers in the country. Instead, some clever folks at the IRS decided to come up with the standard deduction, figuring that if everybody gets to take a few thousand bucks off their income, only the big spenders will have enough deductions to itemize, and the IRS won't have to hire so many people to check tax returns in the spring.

So, How Much Is This Standard Deduction, Anyway?

The amount that you get to count as your standard deduction depends on your filing status. (Remember filing status? See Chapter 10, "Your Filing Status," for a refresher.) The standard deduction changes a bit each year to reflect current economic times. Here are the amounts for 1995 income tax returns:

Table 21.1 Allowable 1995 Standard Deduction Amounts

Filing Status	Standard Deduction
Single	$3,900
Married Filing Jointly	$6,550
Married Filing Separately	$3,275
Surviving Spouse	$6,550
Head of Household	$5,750

If you are Married Filing Separately and your spouse itemizes deductions, you cannot claim the standard deduction. You report your standard deduction on line 34 on page 2 of the 1040 (or line 19 on page 2 of the 1040A).

Use the standard deduction that fits your filing status.

Form 1040 (1995)			Page **2**
Tax Compu-tation (See page 23.)	32	Amount from line 31 (adjusted gross income)	32
	33a	Check If: ☐ **You** were 65 or older, ☐ Blind; ☐ **Spouse** was 65 or older, ☐ Blind. Add the number of boxes checked above and enter the total here . . . . . ▶ **33a**	
	b	If your parent (or someone else) can claim you as a dependent, check here . ▶ **33b** ☐	
	c	If you are married filing separately and your spouse itemizes deductions or you are a dual-status alien, see page 23 and check here . . . . ▶ **33c** ☐	
	34	Enter the larger of your: { **Itemized deductions** from Schedule A, line 28, **OR** **Standard deduction** shown below for your filing status. **But if you checked any box on line 33a or b,** go to page 23 to find your standard deduction. If you checked **box 33c,** your standard deduction is zero. ● Single—$3,900 ● Married filing jointly or Qualifying widow(er)—$6,550 ● Head of household—$5,750 ● Married filing separately—$3,275 }	34
	35	Subtract line 34 from line 32	35
	36	If line 32 is $86,025 or less, multiply $2,500 by the total number of exemptions claimed on line 6e. If line 32 is over $86,025, see the worksheet on page 24 for the amount to enter .	36
If you want the IRS to figure your tax, see page 24.	37	**Taxable income.** Subtract line 36 from line 35. If line 36 is more than line 35, enter -0-	37
	38	Tax. Check if from a ☐ Tax Table, b ☐ Tax Rate Schedules, c ☐ Capital Gain Tax Worksheet, or d ☐ Form 8615 (see page 24). Amount from Form(s) 8814 ▶ e ____	38
	39	Additional taxes. Check if from a ☐ Form 4970 b ☐ Form 4972	39
	40	Add lines 38 and 39 . . . . ▶	40
Credits (See page 24.)	41	Credit for child and dependent care expenses. Attach Form 2441	41	
	42	Credit for the elderly or the disabled. Attach Schedule R . .	42	
	43	Foreign tax credit. Attach Form 1116	43	
	44	Other credits (see page 25). Check if from a ☐ Form 3800 b ☐ Form 8396 c ☐ Form 8801 d ☐ Form (specify)____	44	
	45	Add lines 41 through 44	45
	46	Subtract line 45 from line 40. If line 45 is more than line 40, enter 0 . . . . . . ▶	46
Other	47	Self-employment tax. Attach Schedule SE	47

Report your standard deduction on line 34 on page 2 of the 1040.

Does Everybody Use the Standard Deduction?

You can't take both the standard deduction and itemized deductions; you must choose the one that works best for you. If you itemize your deductions (as described in Chapters 19, "Itemized Deductions Most Taxpayers Can Take," and 20, "Counting a Few More Deductions"), you may not use the standard deduction. If you take the standard deduction, then you can't itemize. The idea is that you only itemize if your deductions are more than the standard deduction, otherwise there would be no reason to itemize because you get the standard deduction anyway.

If you think your itemized deductions come close to the allowable standard deduction, you ought to go ahead and try to itemize. If it turns out you don't have enough deductions to make itemizing worthwhile, there's no harm done except for the time that you perhaps could have spent in a more interesting pursuit.

Mildly Unusual Standard Deductions

If you are preparing a tax return for your child whom you are claiming as a dependent on your income tax return, the child is entitled to a standard deduction on his tax return, but the deduction amount will probably be smaller than the amounts set out on Table 21.1. The standard deduction for children who are claimed as dependents on their parents' tax return is a minimum of $650 and a maximum of the child's *earned* income (that is, income from a job as opposed to interest or dividends earned on investments), but limited to the appropriate amount on Table 21.1.

Taxpayers who qualify as blind and/or elderly are entitled to a standard deduction bonus.

You can add a bonus to your regular standard deduction for each occurrence of blindness and elderliness in either you or your spouse. The bonus amount is $950 if the taxpayer is single or files a tax return by using the Head of Household status; the bonus is $750 if the taxpayer is married filing jointly, married filing separately, or a qualifying widow or widower. So, for example, suppose that Tom and Laurie Lowry are married and file a joint tax return. If both Tom and Laurie are blind and elderly, they can add $3,000 ($750 x 4) to their standard deduction.

OOOOH...

By the Way
You really don't need to worry about the standard deduction if you use Form 1040A or Form 1040EZ for your federal tax return. You can't itemize deductions and file these forms (you have to use the "long form," Form 1040 if you itemize), so it's understood that you have to use the standard deduction if you file on these shorter forms. The standard deduction is already worked into the 1040A and 1040EZ form for you.

OOOOH...

By the Way
Itemized deductions can be claimed on the tax returns of dependent children in lieu of the standard deduction if the itemized deductions exceed the $650 standard deduction limit.

HUH?

IRSpeak
According to the IRS, you are *blind* if your doctor says your vision is no better than 20/200 in your best eye, with glasses. You have to attach a letter to your tax return the first year you claim the deduction for blindness.

There is no blind or elderly bonus, however, for taxpayers who itemize their deductions. The itemized deductions are the itemized deductions, and no extra amounts get added to the itemized deductions if you or your spouse are blind or elderly. Itemizers, in fact, need to have more deductions to justify itemizing over the standard deduction bonus.

Tax Planning Relating to the Standard Deduction

It's difficult to plan on being blind, but you all know when you're going to turn 65. The standard deduction increases for taxpayers over age 65, so if you are a year or two away from turning into an official elderly person, consider paying some itemized-type deductions early, while you're still 64, and taking advantage of itemizing while your standard deduction is lower. When you turn 65 your standard deduction increases and it's harder to get the benefit of itemized deductions. For more information on what kinds of things qualify as itemized deductions and how you can control into what year the deductions fall, see Chapter 19, "Itemized Deductions Most Taxpayers Can Take."

IRSpeak

According to the IRS, you are *elderly* for the 1995 income tax return if your 65th birthday falls on or before January 1, 1996.

The Least You Need to Know

➤ Every taxpayer is entitled to a standard deduction.

➤ The amount of your standard deduction varies depending on your filing status.

➤ You can't itemize deductions and take the standard deduction too: You have to choose one or the other.

➤ There is a bonus added to the standard deduction if you and/or your spouse are blind and/or elderly.

Chapter 22

Exemptions: Counting the Players

In This Chapter

➤ How to claim your exemptions

➤ Dependents finally pay off

➤ Exemption limitations

After doing the hard work of figuring out your income and adjustments, choosing whether to itemize deductions, comparing itemized deductions to the standard deduction and taking the best deal, it's about time for an easy step.

An *exemption* is an amount you can take as a deduction on your tax return, like an allowance, for each taxpayer being supported by the income on the tax return. You don't have to fill out any special forms or get on your knees at the IRS office to get your exemptions—they just come with the tax return territory, a little present from the IRS.

There are two kinds of exemptions: personal exemptions and dependency exemptions. *Personal exemptions* are for the people whose names go at the top of the tax return—yourself and, if there is one, your spouse. There's one exemption for each of you. *Dependency exemptions* are for the people you claimed as dependents on page 1 of the 1040. Again, you get one exemption per dependent.

Over on page 1 of the 1040, in the dependent section, you checked little boxes: one for yourself, and one for your spouse if you're filing a joint tax return. In addition, you listed all your dependents. The total number of boxes checked and dependents listed is the total number of exemptions you can take on this tax return.

So How Much Do I Get and How Do I Get It?

The amount you get to claim as a deduction for your exemptions varies from year to year. Congress keeps changing the exemption amounts as the cost of living changes. For 1995, you can deduct from your income $2,500 for each exemption.

Exemptions get claimed on page 2 of the 1040 on line 36.

Sometimes Exemptions Aren't All They're Cracked Up to Be

There's one catch to reporting exemptions on your income tax return. If you earn a lot of money during the year, the IRS doesn't think you deserve to get all your exemptions, too. So, at a certain point, as you earn more, your allowable exemptions decrease. Here's how it works.

Your exemptions get reduced by 2% for every $2,500 (or fraction thereof) that your adjusted gross income (AGI) exceeds the threshold amount in Table 22.1. For example, suppose that you are married, filing a joint return, and have four exemptions. Four × $2,500 = $10,000 and that is what your exemptions will total if your income is under $172,050. But suppose that your AGI is $200,000. Your AGI exceeds $172,050 by $29,750. The $2,500 goes into $29,750 more than 11 times (so it gets rounded up to 12), and you reduce your exemptions by 2% × 12 or 24%, which equals $2,400. Your $10,000 exemption deduction just turned into $7,600 ($10,000 – $2,400).

Table 22.1 If Your AGI Is Over This Amount You Have to Reduce Your Exemptions

Filing Status	AGI Threshold
Single	114,700
Married Filing Jointly	172,050
Head of Household	143,350
Qualifying Widow(er)	172,050
Married Filing Separately	86,025

Form **1040**	Department of the Treasury—Internal Revenue Service **U.S. Individual Income Tax Return** 19**95**		IRS Use Only—Do not write or staple in this space.

For the year Jan. 1–Dec. 31, 1995, or other tax year beginning , 1995, ending , 19 | OMB No. 1545-0074

Label
(See instructions on page 12.)

Use the IRS label. Otherwise, please print or type.

Your first name and initial | Last name | Your social security number

If a joint return, spouse's first name and initial | Last name | Spouse's social security number

Home address (number and street). If you have a P.O. box, see page 12. | Apt. no.

City, town or post office, state, and ZIP code. If you have a foreign address, see page 12.

For Privacy Act and Paperwork Reduction Act Notice, see page 7.

Presidential Election Campaign
(See page 12.)

Do you want $3 to go to this fund? . . . .
If a joint return, does your spouse want $3 to go to this fund? . . . .

Yes | No | Note: Checking "Yes" will not change your tax or reduce your refund.

Filing Status
(See page 12.)

Check only one box.

1 Single
2 Married filing joint return (even if only one had income)
3 Married filing separate return. Enter spouse's social security no. above and full name here. ▶ _____
4 Head of household (with qualifying person). (See page 12.) If the qualifying person is a child but not your dependent, enter this child's name here. ▶
5 Qualifying widow(er) with dependent child (year spouse died ▶ 19). (See page 13.)

Exemptions
(See page 13.)

6a ☐ **Yourself.** If your parent (or someone else) can claim you as a dependent on his or her tax return, **do not** check box 6a. But be sure to check the box on line 33b on page 2
b ☐ **Spouse** . . . .
c **Dependents:**

(1) First name Last name	(2) Dependent's social security number If born in 1995 see page 14	(3) Dependent's relationship to you	(4) No. of months lived in your home in 1995

No. of boxes checked on 6a and 6b

No. of your children on 6c who:
• lived with you _____
• didn't live with you due to divorce or separation (see page 14) _____
Dependents on 6c not entered above _____

If more than six dependents, see page 14.

d If your child didn't live with you but is claimed as your dependent under a pre-1985 agreement, check here ▶ ☐
e Total number of exemptions claimed . . . .

Add numbers entered on lines above ▶ | **5**

Income

7 Wages, salaries, tips, etc. Attach Form(s) W-2 . . . . . | **7**
8a ~~Taxable interest income (see page 15).~~ ~~Attach Sch~~ ~~if over $400.~~ | **8a**

Form 1040 (1995) | Page **2**

Tax Computation
(See page 23.)

32 Amount from line 31 (adjusted gross income) . . . . | **32**
33a Check if: ☐ **You** were 65 or older, ☐ Blind; ☐ **Spouse** was 65 or older, ☐ Blind.
Add the number of boxes checked above and enter the total here . . . . ▶ **33a**
b If your parent (or someone else) can claim you as a dependent, check here . . ▶ **33b** ☐
c If you are married filing separately and your spouse itemizes deductions or you are a dual-status alien, see page 23 and check here . . . . ▶ **33c** ☐

34 Enter the larger of your:
{ **Itemized deductions** from Schedule A, line 28, **OR**
Standard deduction shown below for your filing status. **But if you checked any box on line 33a or b,** go to page 23 to find your standard deduction. If you checked **box 33c,** your standard deduction is zero.
• Single—$3,900 • Married filing jointly or Qualifying widow(er)—$6,550
• Head of household—$5,750 • Married filing separately—$3,275 } | **34**

35 Subtract line 34 from line 32 . . . . | **35**
36 If line 32 is $86,025 or less, multiply $2,500 by the total number of exemptions claimed on line 6e. If line 32 is over $86,025, see the worksheet on page 24 for the amount to enter . | **36** | 12,500
37 **Taxable income.** Subtract line 36 from line 35. If line 36 is more than line 35, enter -0- . | **37**

If you want the IRS to figure your tax, see page 24.

38 Tax. Check if from a ☐ Tax Table, b ☐ Tax Rate Schedules, c ☐ Capital Gain Tax Worksheet, or d ☐ Form 8615 (see page 24). Amount from Form(s) 8814 ▶ e _____ | **38**
39 Additional taxes. Check if from a ☐ Form 4970 b ☐ Form 4972 . . . . | **39**
40 Add lines 38 and 39 . . . . ▶ | **40**

Credits

41 Credit for child and dependent care expenses. Attach Form 2441 | **41**
42 Credit for the elderly or the disabled. Attach Schedule R . . | **42**

$2,500 × 5 = $12,500.

Enter $2,500 times each of your exemptions on line 36.

241

For taxpayers filing using the Married Filing Separately status, the 2% reduction in exemptions occurs at every $1,250 (or fraction thereof) of the amount exceeding the threshold amount of $86,025.

Computing Your Taxable Income

To compute taxable income on line 37 of your 1040, subtract your total amount for exemptions on line 36 from the amount of income minus deductions that appears on line 35. The result, taxable income, is used in later computations in your tax return, including your calculation of 1996 estimated income taxes.

The Least You Need to Know

➤ Each of your dependents on page 1 of your 1040 qualifies you for an exemption deduction.

➤ The IRS changes the value of exemptions from year to year. For 1995, tax returns exemptions are worth $2,500 each.

➤ If your adjusted gross income gets too high (by IRS standards), your exemptions may be reduced.

Part 5
Taxes and Credits (and More Taxes)

"Sound principles will not justify our taxing the industry of our fellow citizens to accumulate treasure for wars to happen we know not when, and which might not perhaps happen but from the temptations offered by that treasure."

Thomas Jefferson, First annual message to Congress, 1801

Now that the hard part is done—determining what qualifies as income and what you can deduct in order to bring that income down to a manageable size—it's time to start figuring out your tax. Dust off your calculator, hold your nose, and get ready to figure out either how much you owe or (keeping figures crossed) how much you will get back in a refund.

Beyond the income tax there is self-employment tax, alternative minimum tax, capital gains tax, and more. But wait! There are also credits! You can reduce your tax bite with dependent care credit, earned income credit, elderly credit, foreign tax credit, and others.

All sorts of taxes and credits combine to create "the bottom line"—the most important number on your income tax return—that is, the amount that either needs to be paid to the IRS or the amount you get back in a refund.

Chapter 23

Figuring the Base Income Tax: Tables and Rates

In This Chapter

➤ How to read the tax tables

➤ Tax tables vs. tax rates

➤ Calculating tax on capital gains

➤ The Kiddie Tax

➤ Tax on certain distributions from retirement funds

You'd think there would just be income tax and that would be it. But the IRS can't seem to resist adding to the system and tweaking things here and there. The result is a big, ugly pile of different types of taxes and different ways in which these taxes can be computed.

This chapter focuses on taxes on income; it covers these taxes in order, just as they appear on your tax return. You can follow along, figuring the tax bite as you go. In the next chapter, you can figure out how to reduce that tax with various tax credits.

In this chapter you learn how to figure out what amounts go on lines 38 through 40 of your 1040 (line 10 of the 1040EZ, or line 23 of the 1040A)—the income tax calculation.

> OOOOH...

By the Way
Filers of 1040EZ may only compute their income tax using the Tax Tables, so the parts of the chapter that cover taxes other than the Tax Tables are not applicable to the 1040EZ filer. Form 1040A filers may only compute their income tax using the Tax Tables or Form 8615 (the "Kiddie Tax"). Parts of the chapter dealing with taxes other than these two methods are not applicable to the 1040A filer.

Reading the Tables

Most income tax is computed by using the Tax Tables, cumbersome lists you find in the middle of your Federal Income Tax booklet, with endless columns of tiny numbers guaranteed to hurry the best eyesight in the direction of the special exemption for the blind. The tables are also reproduced in Appendix C of this book.

Find your filing status here.

Your taxable income will fall between two numbers in these columns.

The number at the intersection of your taxable income and your filing status is your income tax.

1995 Tax Table—Continued

If line 37 (taxable income) is—		And you are—				If line 37 (taxable income) is—		And you are—				If line 37 (taxable income) is—		And you are—			
At least	But less than	Single	Married filing jointly *	Married filing separately *	Head of a household	At least	But less than	Single	Married filing jointly *	Married filing separately *	Head of a household	At least	But less than	Single	Married filing jointly *	Married filing separately *	Head of a household
		Your tax is—						Your tax is—						Your tax is—			
50,000						**53,000**						**56,000**					
50,000	50,050	10,972	8,937	11,559	9,945	53,000	53,050	11,812	9,777	12,489	10,785	56,000	56,050	12,652	10,617	13,419	11,625
50,050	50,100	10,986	8,951	11,575	9,959	53,050	53,100	11,826	9,791	12,505	10,799	56,050	56,100	12,666	10,631	13,435	11,639
50,100	50,150	11,000	8,965	11,590	9,973	53,100	53,150	11,840	9,805	12,520	10,813	56,100	56,150	12,680	10,645	13,450	11,653
50,150	50,200	11,014	8,979	11,606	9,987	53,150	53,200	11,854	9,819	12,536	10,827	56,150	56,200	12,694	10,659	13,466	11,667
50,200	50,250	11,028	8,993	11,621	10,001	53,200	53,250	11,868	9,833	12,551	10,841	56,200	56,250	12,708	10,673	13,481	11,681
50,250	50,300	11,042	9,007	11,637	10,015	53,250	53,300	11,882	9,847	12,567	10,855	56,250	56,300	12,722	10,687	13,497	11,695
50,300	50,350	11,056	9,021	11,652	10,029	53,300	53,350	11,896	9,861	12,582	10,869	56,300	56,350	12,736	10,701	13,512	11,709
50,350	50,400	11,070	9,035	11,668	10,043	53,350	53,400	11,910	9,875	12,598	10,883	56,350	56,400	12,750	10,715	13,528	11,723
50,400	50,450	11,084	9,049	11,683	10,057	53,400	53,450	11,924	9,889	12,613	10,897	56,400	56,450	12,764	10,729	13,543	11,737
50,450	50,500	11,098	9,063	11,699	10,071	53,450	53,500	11,938	9,903	12,629	10,911	56,450	56,500	12,778	10,743	13,559	11,751
50,500	50,550	11,112	9,077	11,714	10,085	53,500	53,550	11,952	9,917	12,644	10,925	56,500	56,550	12,792	10,757	13,574	11,765
50,550	50,600	11,126	9,091	11,730	10,099	53,550	53,600	11,966	9,931	12,660	10,939	56,550	56,600	12,806	10,771	13,590	11,779
50,600	50,650	11,140	9,105	11,745	10,113	53,600	53,650	11,980	9,945	12,675	10,953	56,600	56,650	12,822	10,785	13,605	11,793
50,650	50,700	11,154	9,119	11,761	10,127	53,650	53,700	11,994	9,959	12,691	10,967	56,650	56,700	12,837	10,799	13,621	11,807
50,700	50,750	11,168	9,133	11,776	10,141	53,700	53,750	12,008	9,973	12,706	10,981	56,700	56,750	12,853	10,813	13,636	11,821
50,750	50,800	11,182	9,147	11,792	10,155	53,750	53,800	12,022	9,987	12,722	10,995	56,750	56,800	12,868	10,827	13,652	11,835
50,800	50,850	11,196	9,161	11,807	10,169	53,800	53,850	12,036	10,001	12,737	11,009	56,800	56,850	12,884	10,841	13,667	11,849
50,850	50,900	11,210	9,175	11,823	10,183	53,850	53,900	12,050	10,015	12,753	11,023	56,850	56,900	12,899	10,855	13,683	11,863
50,900	50,950	11,224	9,189	11,838	10,197	53,900	53,950	12,064	10,029	12,768	11,037	56,900	56,950	12,915	10,869	13,698	11,877
50,950	51,000	11,238	9,203	11,854	10,211	53,950	54,000	12,078	10,043	12,784	11,051	56,950	57,000	12,930	10,883	13,714	11,891
51,000						**54,000**						**57,000**					
51,000	51,050	11,252	9,217	11,869	10,225	54,000	54,050	12,092	10,057	12,799	11,065	57,000	57,050	12,946	10,897	13,729	11,905
51,050	51,100	11,266	9,231	11,885	10,239	54,050	54,100	12,106	10,071	12,815	11,079	57,050	57,100	12,961	10,911	13,745	11,919
51,100	51,150	11,280	9,245	11,900	10,253	54,100	54,150	12,120	10,085	12,830	11,093	57,100	57,150	12,977	10,925	13,760	11,933
51,150	51,200	11,294	9,259	11,916	10,267	54,150	54,200	12,134	10,099	12,846	11,107	57,150	57,200	12,992	10,939	13,776	11,947
51,200	51,250	11,308	9,273	11,931	10,281	54,200	54,250	12,148	10,113	12,861	11,121	57,200	57,250	13,008	10,953	13,791	11,961
51,250	51,300	11,322	9,287	11,947	10,295	54,250	54,300	12,162	10,127	12,877	11,135	57,250	57,300	13,023	10,967	13,807	11,975
51,300	51,350	11,336	9,301	11,962	10,309	54,300	54,350	12,176	10,141	12,892	11,149	57,300	57,350	13,039	10,981	13,822	11,989
51,350	51,400	11,350	9,315	11,978	10,323	54,350	54,400	12,190	10,155	12,908	11,163	57,350	57,400	13,054	10,995	13,838	12,003
51,400	51,450	11,364	9,329	11,993	10,337	54,400	54,450	12,204	10,169	12,923	11,177	57,400	57,450	13,070	11,009	13,853	12,017
51,450	51,500	11,378	9,343	12,009	10,351	54,450	54,500	12,218	10,183	12,939	11,191	57,450	57,500	13,085	11,023	13,869	12,031
51,500	51,550	11,392	9,357	12,024	10,365	54,500	54,550	12,232	10,197	12,954	11,205	57,500	57,550	13,101	11,037	13,884	12,045
51,550	51,600	11,406	9,371	12,040	10,379	54,550	54,600	12,246	10,211	12,970	11,219	57,550	57,600	13,116	11,051	13,900	12,059
51,600	51,650	11,420	9,385	12,055	10,393	54,600	54,650	12,260	10,225	12,985	11,233	57,600	57,650	13,132	11,065	13,915	12,073
51,650	51,700	11,434	9,399	12,071	10,407	54,650	54,700	12,274	10,239	13,001	11,247	57,650	57,700	13,147	11,079	13,931	12,087
51,700	51,750	11,448	9,413	12,086	10,421	54,700	54,750	12,288	10,253	13,016	11,261	57,700	57,750	13,163	11,093	13,946	12,101
51,750	51,800	11,462	9,427	12,102	10,435	54,750	54,800	12,302	10,267	13,032	11,275	57,750	57,800	13,178	11,107	13,962	12,115
51,800	51,850	11,476	9,441	12,117	10,449	54,800	54,850	12,316	10,281	13,047	11,289	57,800	57,850	13,194	11,121	13,977	12,129
51,850	51,900	11,490	9,455	12,133	10,463	54,850	54,900	12,330	10,295	13,063	11,303	57,850	57,900	13,209	11,135	13,993	12,143
51,900	51,950	11,504	9,469	12,148	10,477	54,900	54,950	12,344	10,309	13,078	11,317	57,900	57,950	13,225	11,149	14,008	12,157
51,950	52,000	11,518	9,483	12,164	10,491	54,950	55,000	12,358	10,323	13,094	11,331	57,950	58,000	13,240	11,163	14,024	12,171
52,000						**55,000**						**58,000**					
52,000	52,050	11,532	9,497	12,179	10,505	55,000	55,050	12,372	10,337	13,109	11,345	58,000	58,050	13,256	11,177	14,039	12,185
52,050	52,100	11,546	9,511	12,195	10,519	55,050	55,100	12,386	10,351	13,125	11,359	58,050	58,100	13,271	11,191	14,055	12,199
52,100	52,150	11,560	9,525	12,210	10,533	55,100	55,150	12,400	10,365	13,140	11,373	58,100	58,150	13,287	11,205	14,070	12,213
52,150	52,200	11,574	9,539	12,226	10,547	55,150	55,200	12,414	10,379	13,156	11,387	58,150	58,200	13,302	11,219	14,086	12,227
52,200		11,588	9,553	12,241	10,561	55,200	55,250	12,428	10,393	13,171	11,401	58,200	58,250	13,318	11,233	14,101	12,241

The Tax Tables.

To compute your income tax using the Tax Tables, get the taxable income number from line 37 of your 1040 (line 6 of the 1040EZ, or line 22 of the 1040A). Find the number nearest to your taxable income in the columns containing bold numbers in the Tax Tables. Your taxable income should fall between two numbers in the bold columns of the Tables. Put your finger on the place in the Tax Tables, or draw a line under the amount, so you won't lose your place.

Get Down to Brass Tax

You may not be able to use the Tax Tables to compute your income tax. If your taxable income is $100,000 or higher you need to use the Tax Rate Schedules (see the next section in this book). If the tax return is for a child under the age of 14 and that child has investment income exceeding $1,300, you need to prepare Form 8814, "Tax for Children Under Age 14 Who Have Investment Income of More Than $1,300." This form is discussed later in the "Kiddie Tax" section of this chapter.

Now look up at the top of the page where it says, "And you are —." This isn't an attempt by the IRS to call you a name ("And you are —" [fill in the blank]). Instead, it's an attempt to match you with your filing status (check back on page 1 of the 1040 if you forget what you marked).

Find the filing status that agrees with what you selected on your tax return, and follow down that column with an available finger until you reach the line you marked. The number you see at the place where the line on which your income falls and the column coming down from your filing status is your income tax; put that number on line 38 of your 1040 (line 23 of the 1040A or line 10 of the 1040EZ).

Using the Rate Schedules

If your taxable income is $100,000 or higher you must use the Tax Rate Schedules to compute your tax because the Tax Tables don't go that high.

The Tax Rate Schedules are found in your tax forms booklet that the IRS sent to you. These schedules are also reproduced in Appendix C of this book.

Be sure to select the correct Tax Rate Schedule for your filing status, as listed in Table 23.1.

By the Way
If your income is under $100,000 you can still use the Rate Schedules. Your income tax should work out to be very close to (if not precisely) what it is with the Tax Tables.

OOOOH...

Table 23.1 Choose the Correct Tax Rate Schedule

Filing Status	Tax Rate Schedule
Single	Schedule X
Married Filing Jointly	Schedule Y-1
Married Filing Separately	Schedule Y-2
Head of Household	Schedule Z
Qualifying Widow(er)	Schedule Y-1

Once you're looking at the proper schedule, compute your tax in this way:

1. Find the range in which your taxable income falls in the columns on the left.

2. Subtract the amount in the last column from your taxable income.

3. Take the answer you get in step 2 and multiply that number by the percentage in the third column.

4. Take the answer you get in step 3 and add that to the number in the second column: the answer you get is your income tax.

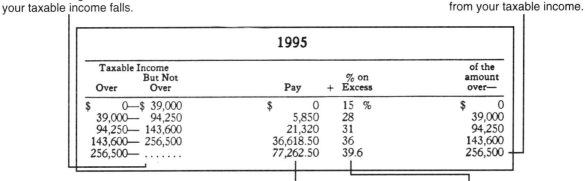

1. Find the range in which your taxable income falls.

2. Subtract this amount from your taxable income.

4. Add the answer you got in step 3 to this amount to get your income tax.

3. Multiply the answer you got in step 2 by this percentage.

A sample Tax Rate Schedule.

For example, using the Tax Rate Schedule illustrated in this chapter, say your filing status is Married Filing Jointly and your taxable income is $112,000. You figure your tax by using Tax Rate Schedule Y-1, as shown in the illustration of Rate Schedule Y-1. Table 23.2 explains how you would compute your tax.

Table 23.2 Computing Your Income Tax with the Y-1 Rate Schedule

Steps to Follow	Calculation
1. Find the range in which your income falls.	94,250 – 143,600
2. Subtract the amount in the last column from your taxable income.	112,000 – 94,250 = 17,750
3. Multiply the answer from step 2 by the percentage in the third column. (Note: You can round this answer to 5,503.)	17,750 × 31% = 5,502.50
4. Add the answer from step 3 to the amount in the second column.	5,503 + 21,320 = 26,823

Tax Calculation on Capital Gains

If you file a Schedule D with your tax return or if you receive Capital Gain Distributions from companies in which you have invested (these would be reported to you on Form 1099-DIV, the same forms on which you receive reports of dividend income), you may qualify for a lower tax rate. This lower rate is called the *Maximum Tax on Capital Gains*.

First, check to see if there is any amount on line 13 of page 1 of your 1040. If there is no amount here, then this special tax rate doesn't apply to you and you're finished with this section of the book. If the amount on line 13 is a loss, again you're finished. No capital gain tax rate for you.

If the amount on line 13 on page 1 of your 1040 is a gain, you may be able to use this capital gain tax rate. Okay class, turn to your Schedule D. On Schedule D, check to see if there is a gain on line 17, "Net long-term capital gain or (loss)." If it's a loss, you're out-a-here (as the ump would say); if it's a gain, you're in business. You should figure your income tax right here in Part IV of Schedule D.

> **IRSpeak**
>
> The *Maximum Tax on Capital Gains* applies if Schedule D shows a gain on line 18 and part of that gain includes long-term capital gain that would appear on line 17 of Schedule D. This method of computing your tax gives you a lower tax rate on the part of your income that comes from sales of capital assets.

> **Get Down to Brass Tax**
>
> But wait! If the percentage of income tax you pay on your income doesn't exceed 28%, the capital gains tax won't save you anything. You can tell the highest percentage of tax you are paying on your income by looking up your tax on the rate schedules. If you come in under 28% on those schedules, the capital gains tax won't help you. It doesn't hurt, however, to use Schedule D to compute your tax. If you're uncertain whether the capital gains tax will be useful to you, go ahead and figure your tax using the worksheet in the instructions.

Tax Planning for the Capital Gains Tax

If you can control the timing of capital gains, by choosing what year in which you sell stock, for example, you can (1) wait until you've held your capital assets for more than a year so that the gain will be long-term rather than short-term, and (2) force capital gains into a year in which your income is going to be high enough to be taxed at a rate higher than the capital gains tax, thus making the capital gains tax a worthwhile alternative.

The Kiddie Tax

A form of income tax that is a fairly new addition to the tax laws of recent years is the "Tax for Children Under Age 14 Who Have Investment Income of More Than $1,300," commonly known as the *Kiddie Tax*. The Kiddie Tax was created to prevent families from shifting income to their children by putting investments in the names of their children and thus getting the income on those investments taxed at the child's lower rates. The Kiddie Tax forces children with investment income of over $1,300 to pay tax on that income at their parents' tax rate.

> **HUH?**
>
> **IRSpeak**
>
> Remember that the Kiddie Tax taxes investment income. *Investment income* is income from interest, dividends, rents, and royalties. If the child had a paying job, the income from the job is *earned income*—income for which the child worked.

A complaint about this tax is that, although it does discourage parents from shifting income to their children solely for the purpose of avoiding higher income tax, it penalizes the children who actually have their own investments, whether those investments came about through serious allowance-saving, inheritances, distributions from trusts, hard work, or even finding buried treasure.

To qualify for the Kiddie Tax, your child must

➤ Be under 14 years of age

➤ Have net investment income in excess of $1,300 for the year

A child who doesn't meet these requirements can file a tax return and not worry about the tax rate of his parents.

Children who meet these requirements file Form 8615 with their 1040, "Tax for Children Under Age 14 Who Have Investment Income of More Than $1,300." The child's income tax is computed on this form. Form 8615 cannot be filled out until the parents' tax return is completed because some of the numbers from the parents' 1040 must be brought onto Form 8615.

Form **8615**	Tax for Children Under Age 14 Who Have Investment Income of More Than $1,200	OMB No. 1545-0998
Department of the Treasury Internal Revenue Service	▶ See instructions below and on back. ▶ Attach ONLY to the child's Form 1040, Form 1040A, or Form 1040NR.	Attachment Sequence No. **33**

Child's name shown on return		Child's social security number

A   Parent's name (first, initial, and last). **Caution:** *See instructions on back before completing.*   **B**   Parent's social security number

C   Parent's filing status (check one):

☐ Single   ☐ Married filing jointly   ☐ Married filing separately   ☐ Head of household   ☐ Qualifying widow(er)

Step 1   **Figure child's net investment income**

1	Enter child's investment income, such as taxable interest and dividend income. See instructions. If this amount is $1,200 or less, **stop here**; do not file this form	1	
2	If the child DID NOT itemize deductions on Schedule A (Form 1040 or Form 1040NR), enter $1,200. If the child ITEMIZED deductions, see instructions	2	
3	Subtract line 2 from line 1. If the result is zero or less, **stop here**; do not complete the rest of this form but ATTACH it to the child's return	3	
4	Enter child's **taxable** income from Form 1040, line 37; Form 1040A, line 22; or Form 1040NR, line 36	4	
5	Enter the **smaller** of line 3 or line 4 . . . . ▶	5	

Step 2   **Figure tentative tax based on the tax rate of the parent listed on line A**

6	Enter parent's **taxable** income from Form 1040, line 37; Form 1040A, line 22; Form 1040EZ, line 5; or Form 1040NR, line 36. If the parent transferred property to a trust, see instructions . .	6	
7	Enter the total net investment income, if any, from Forms 8615, line 5, of ALL OTHER children of the parent identified above. **Do not** include the amount from line 5 above	7	
8	Add lines 5, 6, and 7	8	
9	Tax on line 8 based on the **parent's** filing status. See instructions. If from Capital Gain Tax Worksheet, enter amount from line 4 of that worksheet here ▶ _____	9	
10	Enter parent's tax from Form 1040, line 38; Form 1040A, line 23; Form 1040EZ, line 9; or Form 1040NR, line 37. If from **Capital Gain Tax Worksheet**, enter amount from line 4 of that worksheet here ▶ _____	10	
11	Subtract line 10 from line 9. If line 7 is blank, enter on line 13 the amount from line 11; skip lines 12a and 12b	11	
12a	Add lines 5 and 7	12a		
b	Divide line 5 by line 12a. Enter the result as a decimal (rounded to two places)	12b	× .
13	Multiply line 11 by line 12b . . . . ▶	13	

Step 3   **Figure child's tax**—If lines 4 and 5 above are the same, enter -0- on line 15 and go to line 16.

14	Subtract line 5 from line 4	14		
15	Tax on line 14 based on the **child's** filing status. See instructions. If from Capital Gain Tax Worksheet, enter amount from line 4 of that worksheet here ▶ _____	15	
16	Add lines 13 and 15	16	
17	Tax on line 4 based on the **child's** filing status. See instructions. If from Capital Gain Tax Worksheet, check here . . . . ▶ ☐	17	
18	Enter the **larger** of line 16 or line 17 here and on Form 1040, line 38; Form 1040A, line 23; or Form 1040NR, line 37. Be sure to check the box for "Form 8615" even if line 17 is more than line 16 . ▶	18	

Investment income of the child goes here.

Taxable income from the parents' tax return goes here.

Enter the parents' income tax here.

Figure the child's tax here as if there were no Kiddie Tax.

General Instructions

Purpose of Form.—For children under age 14, investment income over $1,200 is taxed at the parent's rate if the parent's rate is higher than the child's rate. If the child's investment income is more than $1,200, use this form to figure the child's tax.

Investment Income.—As used on this form, "investment income" includes all taxable income other than earned income as defined on page 2. It includes income such as taxable interest, dividends, capital gains, rents, royalties, etc. It also includes pension and annuity

income and income (other than earned income) received as the beneficiary of a trust.

Who Must File.—Generally, Form 8615 must be filed for any child who was under age 14 on January 1, 1995, had more than $1,200 of investment income, and is required to file a tax return. If neither parent was alive on December 31, 1994, do not use Form 8615. Instead, figure the child's tax in the normal manner.

Note: *The parent may be able to elect to report the child's interest and dividends on his or her return. If the parent makes this election, the child will not have to*

file a return or Form 8615. For more details, see the instructions for Form 1040 or Form 1040A, or get **Form 8814**, *Parents' Election To Report Child's Interest and Dividends.*

Additional Information.—For more details, get **Pub. 929**, Tax Rules for Children and Dependents.

Incomplete Information for Parent.—If the parent's taxable income or filing status or the net investment income of the parent's other children is not known by the due date of the child's return, reasonable estimates may be used. Write "Estimated" on the appropriate line(s) of Form 8615. For more details, see Pub. 929.

For Paperwork Reduction Act Notice, see back of form.	Cat. No. 64113U	Form **8615**

Form 8615, "The Kiddie Tax."

OOOOH...

By the Way
Instead of preparing Form 8615 for each qualifying child, you can add your child's income to your own and pay everybody's tax on the same tax return. This generally isn't a good idea, even though it can save you some postage. Adding the child's income to your income raises your AGI, potentially limiting itemized deductions, and generally wreaking havoc in unexpected places.

To complete Form 8615, transfer taxable income from line 37 of the parents' 1040 to line 6 of Form 8615. The parents' income tax from line 38 of the 1040 goes on line 10 of Form 8615. The child's income tax is calculated in step 3 of Form 8615. This form has the effect of taxing the child's investment income (interest and/or dividends) at the top tax rate of the parents and the rest of the child's income at the lower, single-taxpayer rate. The two taxes are added together on line 16 of Form 8615. This tax on line 16 is compared to what the tax would be if Form 8615 weren't necessary. The higher of the two taxes gets transferred to the child's Form 1040, line 38 (or Form 1040A, line 23).

A couple of additional taxes appear on line 39 of the 1040. Tax from Form 4970 is tax on accumulated distributions of a trust. Tax from Form 4972 is tax on a lump-sum distribution from a retirement plan. You should consult with a tax professional if you anticipate owing either of these taxes.

Taxes from lines 38 and 39 get added together and placed on line 40 of the 1040. The income tax from line 40 gets reduced by any credits you may have on line 45 (see Chapter 24, "Cutting Your Tax with Credits," for more information on tax credits). The balance of the tax after credits have been applied gets increased by any taxes that appear on lines 47 through 53 of the 1040. The total tax, which eventually appears on line 54, is the tax you must pay. If you've already paid too much, you will be entitled to a refund of the difference between the total tax and the amount you paid.

The Least You Need to Know

➤ Income tax is most frequently computed by matching your taxable income and your filing status with the amounts on the Tax Tables.

➤ If your taxable income is $100,000 or more, use the Tax Rate Schedules to figure your income tax.

➤ Capital gains shouldn't be taxed at a rate higher than 28%.

➤ Children under age of 14 with investment income exceeding $1,300 figure their tax on Form 8615 and pay at their parents' highest tax rate.

Chapter 24

Cutting Your Tax with Credits

In This Chapter

➤ The credit for child and dependent care expenses

➤ The credit for the elderly or disabled

➤ The credit for taxes paid to other countries

➤ The investment tax credit

➤ The earned income credit

➤ The gas tax credit

➤ The credit for excess withholding of Social Security tax

Just like Henny Penny in the children's story, you may think the sky is falling when you see how much of your income goes to pay your income tax. But before you run for cover, look over the credits in this chapter. Credits are direct, dollar-for-dollar reductions of your income tax—much better than deductions.

This chapter covers the Credits section of page 2 of the Form 1040 which includes lines 41 to 46.

Child and Dependent Care

With so many families sporting dual-working spouses these days, the child and dependent care credit has become a common item on many tax returns. The credit is prepared on Form 2441, "Credit for Child and Dependent Care Expenses," and it entitles taxpayers to a small break in their tax for amounts that were paid to care for dependents while they were out earning taxable income. This credit follows the same theory that supports the deductions for employee business expenses (see Chapter 19, "Itemized Deductions Most of Us Can Take")—if you have to spend money to earn a living, that's an offsetting cost of the job and shouldn't be taxed.

> **OOOOH...**
>
> **By the Way**
>
> Tax credits are way cooler than itemized deductions. Suppose that you have $40,000 of income, you pay income tax at the 28% rate, and you can choose a $2,000 deduction or a $2,000 credit. $40,000 less the $2,000 deduction equals $38,000 taxed at 28%, or $10,640 in tax. $40,000 taxed at 28% is $11,200 in tax, less a $2,000 credit, resulting in $9,200 in tax. The credit is a much better deal.

Rather than allow a deduction for dependent care, the IRS lets you take a credit against your income tax. If you have no income tax, you get no credit; if your credit is higher than the income tax, you only get as much credit as you have income tax—there is no refund for unused dependent care credits.

Here's how this credit works. First, figure out if you qualify to try for the credit. To get the dependent and child care credit, you need to pay a third party for the care of one of your dependents. The people who qualify as dependents for purposes of this credit include:

➤ Your dependent children (but only up to 12 years old)

➤ Other dependents of yours who can't take care of themselves

➤ Your spouse, if that person needs care

The types of third-party expenses that count as dependent care include:

➤ Cost of an in-home care provider; this cost can include incidental housekeeping expenses if that is part of the care; the in-home care provider can be your own child if that child is at least 19 years of age.

➤ Cost of day care or other care outside the home if the dependent spends at least eight hours a day in your home (in other words, the costs of constant away-from-home care, such as a hospital or institution, do not qualify for this credit).

➤ Nursery school or kindergarten costs if the school is considered to be providing care in addition to education and the education cost cannot be separated from the child care. (If the two costs are stated separately, then only the child care portion qualifies as a dependent care cost.)

➤ Cost of summer day camp (overnight camp doesn't count).

To qualify for this credit both you and your spouse (if you are married and filing a joint return) must work while the care is being provided. One exception to this work rule is that one spouse can be a full-time student and not negate the opportunity for the couple to claim the dependent care credit.

The credit is based on a percentage of the costs you pay for child care. The child care costs can't exceed the earned income of the lesser-earning spouse.

Computing Your Earned Income

Form 2441, "Credit for Child and Dependent Care," asks for your (and your spouse's, if applicable) earned income. If the taxpayer has no earned income, there can be no dependent care credit. If your filing status is Married Filing Jointly but only one spouse had earned income, there is no credit allowed.

So what's earned income? Earned income is income you worked for as opposed to income you get as a result of investments. Income from your job is earned, interest on your savings account is not.

Most income is easily categorized between earned and unearned. One notable exception occurs if the filing status of the taxpayers is Married Filing Jointly and one spouse is a full-time student. Because both spouses have to have earned income to qualify for the credit, the IRS allows the taxpayers to say that the student spouse earned $200 per month for each month during which he or she is a full-time student. This deemed $200 per month income is increased to $400 per month if there are two or more qualifying dependents. (Note: Saying that you earned $200 per month to get this dependent care credit in no way increases your actual income by $200 per month—the number never goes anywhere beyond Form 2441.)

Figuring the Credit

Enter the names, addresses, and Social Security numbers (or federal ID numbers) of your dependent/child care providers at the top of Form 2441 in Part I (see the nearby figure).

Fill out the Form 2441 and attach it to your Form 1040 in order to claim the child and dependent care credit.

Part II **Credit for Child and Dependent Care Expenses**

4 Enter the amount of **qualified expenses** you incurred and paid in 1994. DO NOT enter more than $2,400 for one qualifying person or $4,800 for two or more persons. If you completed Part III, enter the amount from line 25 4

5 Enter YOUR **earned income** 5

6 If married filing a joint return, enter YOUR SPOUSE'S earned income (if student or disabled, see the instructions); **all others**, enter the amount from line 5 6

7 Enter the **smallest** of line 4, 5, or 6 7

8 Enter the amount from Form 1040, line 32 8

9 Enter on line 9 the decimal amount shown below that applies to the amount on line 8

If line 8 is—		Decimal amount is	If line 8 is—		Decimal amount is
Over	But not over		Over	But not over	
$0—10,000		.30	$20,000—22,000		.24
10,000—12,000		.29	22,000—24,000		.23
12,000—14,000		.28	24,000—26,000		.22
14,000—16,000		.27	26,000—28,000		.21
16,000—18,000		.26	28,000—No limit		.20
18,000—20,000		.25			

9 × .

10 Multiply **line 7** by the decimal amount on line 9. Enter the result. Then, see the instructions for the amount of credit to enter on Form 1040, line 41 10

Caution: *If you paid $50 or more in a calendar quarter to a person who worked in your home, you must file an employment tax return. Get Form 942 for details.*

For Paperwork Reduction Act Notice, see separate instructions. Cat. No. 11862M Form **2441**

Form 1040 (1995) Page **2**

Tax Computation

(See page 23.)

32 Amount from line 31 (adjusted gross income) 32

33a Check if: ☐ **You** were 65 or older, ☐ Blind; ☐ **Spouse** was 65 or older, ☐ Blind. Add the number of boxes checked above and enter the total here . . . ▶ 33a

b If your parent (or someone else) can claim you as a dependent, check here . ▶ 33b ☐

c If you are married filing separately and your spouse itemizes deductions or you are a dual-status alien, see page 23 and check here . . . . . . ▶ 33c ☐

34 Enter the larger of your:
Itemized deductions from Schedule A, line 28, **OR**
Standard deduction shown below for your filing status. **But if you checked any box on line 33a or b,** go to page 23 to find your standard deduction. If you checked box **33c,** your standard deduction is zero.
• Single—$3,900 • Married filing jointly or Qualifying widow(er)—$6,550
• Head of household—$5,750 • Married filing separately—$3,275
34

35 Subtract line 34 from line 32 35

36 If line 32 is $86,025 or less, multiply $2,500 by the total number of exemptions claimed on line 6e. If line 32 is over $86,025, see the worksheet on page 24 for the amount to enter . 36

37 **Taxable income.** Subtract line 36 from line 35. If line 36 is more than line 35, enter -0- 37

If you want the IRS to figure your tax, see page 24.

38 Tax. Check if from **a** ☐ Tax Table, **b** ☐ Tax Rate Schedules, **c** ☐ Capital Gain Tax Worksheet, or **d** ☐ Form 8615 (see page 24). Amount from Form(s) 8814 ▶ **e** _____ 38

39 Additional taxes. Check if from **a** ☐ Form 4970 **b** ☐ Form 4972 39

40 Add lines 38 and 39 . . . . ▶ 40

Credits

(See page 24.)

41 Credit for child and dependent care expenses. Attach Form 2441 — 41

42 Credit for the elderly or the disabled. Attach Schedule R . . 42

43 Foreign tax credit. Attach Form 1116 43

44 Other credits (see page 25). Check if from **a** ☐ Form 3800 **b** ☐ Form 8396 **c** ☐ Form 8801 **d** ☐ Form (specify) _____ 44

45 Add lines 41 through 44 45

46 Subtract line 45 from line 40. If line 45 is more than line 40, enter 0 . . . . . . ▶ 46

Other Taxes

47 Self-employment tax. Attach Schedule SE 47

48 Alternative minimum tax. Attach Form 6251 48

49 Recapture taxes. Check if from **a** ☐ Form 4255 **b** ☐ Form 8611 **c** ☐ Form 8828 49

Take this credit to Form 1040, line 41.

The credit from Form 2441 gets transferred to line 41 of your Form 1040.

Enter your total dependent and child care expenses on line 4 in Part II of Form 2441, but don't enter more than $2,400 (or $4,800 if you pay for care for two or more dependents). Follow this with the total earned income of the first taxpayer listed on the tax return. Next, if you are married and filing a joint return, enter the earned income of the spouse. Of these numbers—the care expenses and the earned income of the taxpayer(s)—enter the smallest on line 7. This number is used in the computation of the credit.

Your adjusted gross income goes on line 8 and this number gets compared to the chart on Form 2441. Find the percentage from the chart and multiply the amount on line 7 by this percentage. (The highest percentage is 30%. The percentage goes down as your income goes up, eventually fading to 20%, the lowest percentage available.) This is the credit you can take for 1995. Your credit from Form 2441 goes on line 41 of your 1040 (as shown in the preceding figure).

What Happened? My Credit Disappeared!

Later on, in Chapter 25, "Other Kinds of Taxes (Including Taxes on Income You Didn't Know You Had,") you learn about the Alternative Minimum Tax. If you have to pay Alternative Minimum Tax you may lose your dependent care credit.

Credit for the Elderly or Disabled

The credit for the elderly or disabled, filed on Schedule R, is available to taxpayers who meet one of these two tests:

➤ You are age 65 or older.

➤ You are retired on permanent and total disability.

Meeting one of these tests doesn't guarantee that you *will* get the credit, but not meeting one of them guarantees that you *won't* get the credit. There are also income levels that limit your access to this credit. To stay in the running for the credit for the elderly or disabled, you must have income lower than the income limits set out in the following table and you must not have Social Security payments equal to or greater than the Social Security limit. If you meet one of the first two tests, check Table 24.1 to see if you are still in the ballpark.

OOPS!
Don't leave off the Social Security numbers of your dependent/child care providers. The IRS has the right to deny your credit if this information is omitted.

OOPS!
Don't put more than $4,800 on line 4 of Form 2441. Even if you have more than two dependents for whom you provide care while you work, the maximum credit is based on $4,800 of expenses.

OOPS!
If you receive tax free reimbursements from an employer to pay child care expenses, then you cannot claim a credit for these expenses—that would be double-dipping.

Table 24.1   Income Limits for the Credit for the Elderly or the Disabled

Filing Status Limit	Adjusted Gross Income Limit	Social Security
Single	17,500	5,000
Married, Joint, just one spouse	20,000	5,000
Head of Household	17,500	5,000
Married, Joint, both spouses	25,000	7,500
Qualifying Widow(er)	17,500	5,000
Married, Separate all year	12,500	3,750

Still with me? If you pass the tests and qualify for this credit, you need to fill out Schedule R. The first two parts of Schedule R help you tell the IRS about your filing status, your age, and your disability (if you have one). In Part III, you actually figure the credit.

To calculate the credit for the elderly or the disabled, follow these steps beginning on page 2 of Schedule R:

Line 10: Start by entering the Social Security limit on line 10. The Social Security limit is shown in Table 24.1.

Line 11: Enter any taxable disability income you may have received.

Line 12: Enter the smaller of lines 10 and 11 (unless line 11 is blank, then enter the amount from line 10).

Line 13: On these lines, 13a and 13b, enter the amounts you received from Social Security and other retirement plans that are not subject to income tax; add them up and put the total on 13c.

Line 14: Adjusted gross income goes here.

Line 15: Enter the amount designated on line 15.

Lines 16–21 work you through the mathematical calculation of figuring out your credit. If there is an amount on line 21, carry it to your 1040, line 42 (as shown in the nearby figure). This is your credit.

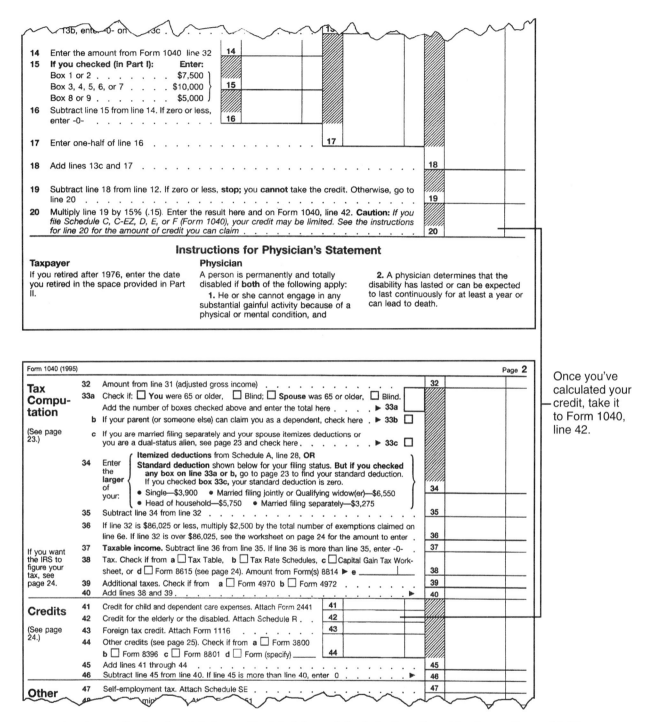

14 Enter the amount from Form 1040 line 32 . . . . **14**

15 **If you checked (in Part I):**   **Enter:**
    Box 1 or 2 . . . . $7,500 ⎫
    Box 3, 4, 5, 6, or 7 . . . . $10,000 ⎬ **15**
    Box 8 or 9 . . . . $5,000 ⎭

16 Subtract line 15 from line 14. If zero or less, enter -0- **16**

17 Enter one-half of line 16 . . . . **17**

18 Add lines 13c and 17 . . . . **18**

19 Subtract line 18 from line 12. If zero or less, **stop;** you **cannot** take the credit. Otherwise, go to line 20 . . . . **19**

20 Multiply line 19 by 15% (.15). Enter the result here and on Form 1040, line 42. **Caution:** *If you file Schedule C, C-EZ, D, E, or F (Form 1040), your credit may be limited. See the instructions for line 20 for the amount of credit you can claim* **20**

Instructions for Physician's Statement

Taxpayer

If you retired after 1976, enter the date you retired in the space provided in Part II.

Physician

A person is permanently and totally disabled if **both** of the following apply:

1. He or she cannot engage in any substantial gainful activity because of a physical or mental condition, and

2. A physician determines that the disability has lasted or can be expected to last continuously for at least a year or can lead to death.

Form 1040 (1995)   Page **2**

Tax Computation

(See page 23.)

32 Amount from line 31 (adjusted gross income) **32**

33a Check if: ☐ **You** were 65 or older, ☐ Blind; ☐ **Spouse** was 65 or older, ☐ Blind.
     Add the number of boxes checked above and enter the total here . . . . ▶ **33a**

  b If your parent (or someone else) can claim you as a dependent, check here . ▶ **33b** ☐

  c If you are married filing separately and your spouse itemizes deductions or you are a dual-status alien, see page 23 and check here . . . . ▶ **33c** ☐

34 Enter the larger of your: ⎰ Itemized deductions from Schedule A, line 28, **OR**
     Standard deduction shown below for your filing status. **But if you checked any box on line 33a or b**, go to page 23 to find your standard deduction. If you checked **box 33c,** your standard deduction is zero.
     ● Single—$3,900   ● Married filing jointly or Qualifying widow(er)—$6,550
     ● Head of household—$5,750   ● Married filing separately—$3,275 ⎱ **34**

35 Subtract line 34 from line 32 . . . . **35**

36 If line 32 is $86,025 or less, multiply $2,500 by the total number of exemptions claimed on line 6e. If line 32 is over $86,025, see the worksheet on page 24 for the amount to enter . **36**

37 **Taxable income.** Subtract line 36 from line 35. If line 36 is more than line 35, enter -0- . **37**

(If you want the IRS to figure your tax, see page 24.)

38 Tax. Check if from **a** ☐ Tax Table, **b** ☐ Tax Rate Schedules, **c** ☐ Capital Gain Tax Worksheet, or **d** ☐ Form 8615 (see page 24). Amount from Form(s) 8814 ▶ **e** _____ **38**

39 Additional taxes. Check if from **a** ☐ Form 4970 **b** ☐ Form 4972 . . . . . . **39**

40 Add lines 38 and 39 . . . . ▶ **40**

Credits

(See page 24.)

41 Credit for child and dependent care expenses. Attach Form 2441 **41**

42 Credit for the elderly or the disabled. Attach Schedule R . . **42**

43 Foreign tax credit. Attach Form 1116 . . . . **43**

44 Other credits (see page 25). Check if from **a** ☐ Form 3800 **b** ☐ Form 8396 **c** ☐ Form 8801 **d** ☐ Form (specify) _____ **44**

45 Add lines 41 through 44 . . . . **45**

46 Subtract line 45 from line 40. If line 45 is more than line 40, enter 0 . . . . . ▶ **46**

Other

47 Self-employment tax. Attach Schedule SE **47**

Once you've calculated your credit, take it to Form 1040, line 42.

Transfer the credit for the elderly or disabled from Schedule R to line 42 of your Form 1040.

Foreign Tax Credits

Do you have investments in countries besides the U.S.? Perhaps you own stock in a German company, or maybe you have a savings account in Australia. Whatever the situation may be, if you pay income tax to another country as a U.S. citizen and resident of this country you can take a credit for that tax. It seems only fair when you think about it—the income is subject to U.S. income tax; to not give you a credit would be to tax the income twice.

OOOOH...

By the Way...
You have the right to take a deduction for foreign taxes paid as itemized deductions on Schedule A. It's your choice—deduction or credit—but you can't do both.

File Form 1116, "Foreign Tax Credit," with your tax return. On this form you designate the name of the country from which you earned the taxable income, the amount you earned from that country, any expenses you may have incurred related to earning the money in that country, and the amount of tax you paid. The foreign tax credit gets carried from Form 1116 to your Form 1040, line 43 (as shown in the nearby figure).

Investment Tax Credit (Is That Thing Still Around?)

Years ago, prior to 1986, a credit existed called the investment tax credit. It was a credit that gave, primarily businesses, incentive to invest in capital assets, depreciable items such as office furniture and cars. The credit was issued during the year in which you bought the item, and you were expected to own the item for several years in order to make the credit good. If you sold the item prior to the expected holding period (usually 3, 5, or 7 years), you had to *recapture* some of your credit—that is, give it back to the government. The accounting for these assets was a bit of a nightmare.

Now the investment tax credit is still available but only in limited doses. The credit is only available for rehabilitation of real property, and there are very strict rules about what type of property qualifies. If you think you may qualify for this credit, carefully read the instructions that accompany Form 3468 to learn the rules for taking the credit and how much credit you are entitled to. If you do qualify for the investment tax credit, fill out Form 3468 and carry the amount of the credit to your Form 1040, line 44. Check box d on line 44 of the 1040 and write the form number, **3468**, in the blank after the check box.

For most of us, the investment credit is a thing of the past.

Refundable Tax Credits

You've learned about several tax credits that get reported in the Credits section of your federal income tax return. These are credits that apply against your tax, as long as you have tax. If your tax is zero when you get to the credit section, you're out of luck. But a few special credits are called *refundable credits*, so-called because you get them even if you don't owe any tax. It's as if you paid an extra amount of withholding and get a refund. In fact, these credits get reported down in the Payments section of your income tax return, as surely as if you had written a check to the IRS for too much tax.

20 Multiply line 19 by line 18 (maximum amount of credit) . . . . | 20 |

21 Enter the amount from line 13 or line 20, whichever is smaller. (If this is the only Form 1116 you are completing, skip lines 22 through 29 and enter this amount on line 30. Otherwise, complete the appropriate lines in Part IV.) . . . . ▶ | 21 |

| **Part IV** | **Summary of Credits From Separate Parts III** (See instructions.) |

22	Credit for taxes on passive income	22	
23	Credit for taxes on high withholding tax interest	23	
24	Credit for taxes on financial services income	24	
25	Credit for taxes on shipping income	25	
26	Credit for taxes on dividends from a DISC or former DISC	26	
27	Credit for taxes on certain distributions from a FSC or former FSC	27	
28	Credit for taxes on lump-sum distributions	28	
29	Credit for taxes on general limitation income (all other income from sources outside the United States)	29	

30 Add lines 22 through 29. . . . . | 30 |

31 Reduction of credit for international boycott operations. See instructions for line 12. . . . . . | 31 |

32 Subtract line 31 from line 30. This is your foreign tax credit. Enter here and on Form 1040, line 43; Form 1040NR, line 41; Form 1041, Schedule G, line 2a; or Form 990-T, line 38a. . . . . . ▶ | 32 |

The foreign tax credit gets transferred to line 43 of your Form 1040.

page 24.

| 39 | Additional taxes. Check if from a ☐ Form 4970 b ☐ Form 4972 . . . . . . | 39 | |
| 40 | Add lines 38 and 39 . . . . ▶ | 40 | |

Credits

(See page 24.)

41	Credit for child and dependent care expenses. Attach Form 2441	41	
42	Credit for the elderly or the disabled. Attach Schedule R . .	42	
43	Foreign tax credit. Attach Form 1116	43	
44	Other credits (see page 25). Check if from a ☐ Form 3800 b ☐ Form 8396 c ☐ Form 8801 d ☐ Form (specify)_____	44	
45	Add lines 41 through 44	45	
46	Subtract line 45 from line 40. If line 45 is more than line 40, enter 0 . . . . ▶	46	

Other

| 47 | Self-employment tax. Attach Schedule SE . . . . | 47 | |

Totaling Your Credits

So, you've calculated all the tax credits you can take and placed the resulting amounts in the Credits section of page 2 of your Form 1040. Now it's time to add up the credits on lines 41–44 of the Form 1040 and place the total on line 45. The amount on line 45 gets deducted from your tax on line 40. In other words, every dollar of credit reduces your income tax by a dollar. The new amount of tentative income tax (line 40 less line 45) goes on line 46 of your 1040.

The Earned Income Credit

The earned income credit is a credit against tax that was devised to help offset income taxes for certain people who don't make very much money. To qualify for the credit, you must meet all of these rules:

➤ You have to have a dependent child living with you for more than half of the year (referred to hereafter as the *qualifying child*) **OR** you must be at least age 25, under age 65, and cannot be claimed as a dependent on someone else's tax return.

➤ You must have earned some income—that is, you have to have a job that pays you for the work you do.

➤ Your earned income and your adjusted gross income must both be less than $24,396 if you have only one qualifying child, $26,673 if you have more than one qualifying child, or $9,230 if you have no qualifying children.

➤ You can't use the Married Filing Separately filing status.

➤ You can't be a qualifying child for someone else who is claiming the earned income credit.

➤ Your qualifying child can't be the qualifying child of someone else whose adjusted gross income is higher than yours.

➤ If your qualifying child is married, that child has to be claimed as your dependent.

➤ You do not file Form 2555, "Foreign Earned Income."

If you meet all these requirements, fill out Schedule EIC, "Earned Income Credit." On this form you simply list information about your qualifying child(ren). This is the form that gets attached to your tax return. The IRS will figure your credit for you. Be sure to write the letters EIC next to line 57 on your Form 1040. Or, figure the credit using the worksheet in the instructions.

SCHEDULE EIC	Earned Income Credit	OMB No. 1545-0074
(Form 1040A or 1040)	(Qualifying Child Information)	**1995**
Department of the Treasury Internal Revenue Service	➤ Attach to Form 1040A or 1040. ➤ See instructions on back.	Attachment Sequence No. **43**
Name(s) shown on return		Your social security number

Before You Begin . . .

- Answer the questions on page 47 of the Form 1040A instructions or page 27 of the Form 1040 instructions to see if you can take this credit.
- If you can take the credit, fill in the worksheet on page 48 (1040A) or page 28 (1040) to figure your credit. **But if you want the IRS to figure it for you, see page 42 (1040A) or page 24 (1040).**

Then, you **must** complete and attach Schedule EIC only if you have a qualifying child (see boxes on back).

Information About Your Qualifying Child or Children

If you have more than two qualifying children, you only have to list two to get the maximum credit.

Caution: If you don't attach Schedule EIC and fill in all the lines that apply, it will take us longer to process your return and issue your refund.	**(a) Child 1**	**(b) Child 2**
	First name Last name	First name Last name
1 Child's name		
2 Child's year of birth	19___	19___
3 If the child was born **before 1977** AND—		
a was **under age 24** at the end of 1995 **and** a student, check the "Yes" box, **OR**	☐ Yes	☐ Yes
b was permanently and totally disabled (see back), check the "Yes" box	☐ Yes	☐ Yes
4 Enter the child's social security number. If born in 1995, see instructions on back		
5 Child's relationship to you (for example, son, grandchild, etc.) .		
6 Number of months child lived with you in the United States in 1995	months	months

TIP: Do you want the earned income credit added to your take-home pay in 1996? To see if you qualify, get **Form W-5** from your employer or by calling the IRS at 1-800-TAX-FORM (1-800-829-3676).

For Paperwork Reduction Act Notice, see Form 1040A or 1040 instructions.   Cat. No. 13339M   **Schedule EIC (Form 1040A or 1040) 1995**

Attach this filled-out form to your tax return and the IRS will figure your earned income credit.

Write EIC here to have the IRS figure your credit.

		Form 1040 (1995)		Page **2**
Tax Compu-tation (See page 23.) If you want the IRS to figure your tax, see page 24.	32	Amount from line 31 (adjusted gross income)	**32**	
	33a	Check if: ☐ You were 65 or older, ☐ Blind; ☐ **Spouse** was 65 or older, ☐ Blind. Add the number of boxes checked above and enter the total here . . . . ▶ **33a**		
	b	If your parent (or someone else) can claim you as a dependent, check here . ▶ **33b** ☐		
	c	If you are married filing separately and your spouse itemizes deductions or you are a dual-status alien, see page 23 and check here . . . . ▶ **33c** ☐		
	34	Enter the larger of your: { **Itemized deductions** from Schedule A, line 28, **OR** **Standard deduction** shown below for your filing status. **But if you checked any box on line 33a or b,** go to page 23 to find your standard deduction. If you checked **box 33c,** your standard deduction is zero. ● Single—$3,900 ● Married filing jointly or Qualifying widow(er)—$6,550 ● Head of household—$5,750 ● Married filing separately—$3,275 }	**34**	
	35	Subtract line 34 from line 32	**35**	
	36	If line 32 is $86,025 or less, multiply $2,500 by the total number of exemptions claimed on line 6e. If line 32 is over $86,025, see the worksheet on page 24 for the amount to enter .	**36**	
	37	**Taxable income.** Subtract line 36 from line 35. If line 36 is more than line 35, enter -0-	**37**	
	38	Tax. Check if from **a** ☐ Tax Table, **b** ☐ Tax Rate Schedules, **c** ☐ Capital Gain Tax Work-sheet, or **d** ☐ Form 8615 (see page 24). Amount from Form(s) 8814 ▶ **e** _____	**38**	
	39	Additional taxes. Check if from **a** ☐ Form 4970 **b** ☐ Form 4972	**39**	
	40	Add lines 38 and 39 . . . . ▶	**40**	
Credits (See page 24.)	41	Credit for child and dependent care expenses. Attach Form 2441	**41**	
	42	Credit for the elderly or the disabled. Attach Schedule R . .	**42**	
	43	Foreign tax credit. Attach Form 1116	**43**	
	44	Other credits (see page 25). Check if from **a** ☐ Form 3800 **b** ☐ Form 8396 **c** ☐ Form 8801 **d** ☐ Form (specify) _____	**44**	
	45	Add lines 41 through 44	**45**	
	46	Subtract line 45 from line 40. If line 45 is more than line 40, enter 0 . . . . . . ▶	**46**	
Other Taxes (See page 25.)	47	Self-employment tax. Attach Schedule SE	**47**	
	48	Alternative minimum tax. Attach Form 6251	**48**	
	49	Recapture taxes. Check if from **a** ☐ Form 4255 **b** ☐ Form 8611 **c** ☐ Form 8828 .	**49**	
	50	Social security and Medicare tax on tip income not reported to employer. Attach Form 4137	**50**	
	51	Tax on qualified retirement plans including IRAs. If required, attach Form 5329 . . .	**51**	
	52	Advance earned income credit payments from Form W-2	**52**	
	53	Household employment taxes. Attach Schedule H	**53**	
	54	Add lines 46 through 53 This is your **total tax** . . . . ▶	**54**	
Payments Attach Forms W-2, W-2G, and 1099-R on the front.	55	Federal income tax withheld. If any is from Form(s) 1099, check ▶ ☐	**55**	
	56	1995 estimated tax payments and amount applied from 1994 return .	**56**	
	57	**Earned income credit.** Attach Schedule EIC if you have a qualifying child. Nontaxable earned income: amount ▶ _____ and type ▶ ..EIC.......................	**57**	
	58	Amount paid with Form 4868 (extension request)	**58**	
	59	Excess social security and RRTA tax withheld (see page 32) .	**59**	
	60	Other payments. Check if from **a** ☐ Form 2439 **b** ☐ Form 4136	**60**	
	61	Add lines 55 through 60. These are your **total payments** . . . . ▶	**61**	
Refund or Amount You Owe	62	If line 61 is more than line 54, subtract line 54 from line 61. This is the amount you **OVERPAID** . ▶	**62**	
	63	Amount of line 62 you want **REFUNDED TO YOU** . . . . ▶	**63**	
	64	Amount of line 62 you want **APPLIED TO YOUR 1996 ESTIMATED TAX** ▶	**64**	
	65	If line 54 is more than line 61, subtract line 61 from line 54. This is the **AMOUNT YOU OWE** For details on how to pay including using **Form 1040-V,** Payment Voucher, see page 32	**65**	
	66	Estimated tax penalty (see page 33). Also include on line 65	**66**	
Sign Here Keep a copy of this return for your records.	Under penalties of perjury, I declare that I have examined this return and accompanying schedules and statements, and to the best of my knowledge and belief, they are true, correct, and complete. Declaration of preparer (other than taxpayer) is based on all information of which preparer has any knowledge.			
	Your signature ▶	Date	Your occupation	
	Spouse's signature. If a joint return, BOTH must sign. ▶	Date	Spouse's occupation	
Paid Preparer's Use Only	Preparer's signature ▶	Date	Check if self-employed ☐	Preparer's social security no.
	Firm's name (or yours if self-employed) and address ▶		E.I. No.	
			ZIP code	
		✿ *Printed on recycled paper*		

The IRS can help with the earned income credit.

What Do You Mean, My Employer Withheld Too Much?

Depending on how much you earn, some of your income may not be subject to Social Security tax. Your employer knows how much Social Security tax to withhold from your regular pay and he or she stops withholding when you reach the limit ($61,200 in wages for 1995).

But what happens if you change jobs in the middle of the year and earn, say, $40,000 at one job and $30,000 at the other job? Both employers withhold Social Security tax on your income, as well they should because your income doesn't exceed the limit at either job; however, combined, your income is over the $61,200 limit and your Social Security tax withholding should have stopped when your income reached that amount.

If you worked more than one job and had too much Social Security tax withheld as a result of your wages exceeding $61,200, figure out the excess Social Security tax (6.2%) on the income over $61,200.

In this example, if your income is $70,000 from two different jobs, and your Social Security tax withholding should have stopped at $61,200, multiply the excess income ($70,000 − $61,200 = $8,800) by 6.2% ($8,800 × 6.2% = $545.60). Place the excess Social Security withholding (in this example, $545.60) (and you can round to the nearest dollar) on your 1040 at line 58. This amount counts as a payment toward your income tax.

Yee Hah! Grab That Gas Tax Credit!

If you use a nonhighway vehicle, such as a boat, a piece of farm equipment, or some other vehicle that you don't use on normal roads, you can take a credit for the federal tax on gasoline you bought for the vehicle. Likewise, if you purchased a diesel-powered vehicle for highway use and you are the first owner of the vehicle, you can take a one-time credit on the purchase.

The catch is, in order to qualify for this credit, the vehicle has to be used for a business purpose. Gasoline bought for a pleasure boat doesn't qualify for this credit, but gasoline bought for a commercial fishing boat does.

The gas and diesel-powered vehicle credits are claimed on Form 4136, "Credit for Federal Tax Paid on Fuels." The results of Form 4136 go on page 2 of your 1040 at line 60.

To file Form 4136, you have to know the number of gallons of gasoline you purchased for nonhighway vehicles. Fill in the number of gallons on the appropriate line, based on the type of vehicle involved, and multiply across to figure the tax.

> **OOPS!**
> If you took a credit in 1994 on Form 4136 for a vehicle that no longer qualifies for the credit, that credit gets added into your income for 1995. Place last year's credit on line 21, "Other Income," on page 1 of your 1040. Alternatively, if you took the credit for gas bought for farm equipment, report the credit as income on Schedule F, line 10.

Form **4136**	**Credit for Federal Tax Paid on Fuels**	OMB No. 1545-0162
Department of the Treasury Internal Revenue Service (R)	(And Credit for Purchase of Diesel-Powered Highway Vehicles) ➤ **Attach this form to your income tax return.**	Attachment Sequence No. **23**
Name (as shown on your income tax return)		Social security or employer identification number

Part I Diesel-Powered Highway Vehicle Credit

			(a) Number of vehicles	(b) Credit per vehicle	(c) Credit (col. (a) × col. (b))	CRN
1	Diesel-powered cars	1		$102.00	$	
2	Diesel-powered light trucks and vans	2		198.00		
3	Total diesel-powered highway vehicle credit. Add lines 1 and 2, column (c) ➤	3			$	318

Part II Fuel Tax Credit

Caution: *If you claimed any fuel tax refunds on* **Form 8849,** *Claim for Refund of Excise Taxes,* **Form 843,** *Claim for Refund and Request for Abatement, or* **Schedule C (Form 720),** *Adjustments and Claims, you cannot claim those amounts as credits on Form 4136.*

4 **Nontaxable Use of Gasoline** (See instructions.)

		Rate	Gallons	Amount of credit	CRN
a	Off-highway business use	$.184			
b	Use on a farm for farming purposes	.184			301
c	Other nontaxable use (specify) ➤	.184			

Compute your credit here.

5 **Nontaxable Use of Gasohol** (See instructions.)

		Rate	Gallons	Amount of credit	CRN

Other Taxes (See page 25.)	47	Self-employment tax. Attach Schedule SE	47	
	48	Alternative minimum tax. Attach Form 6251	48	
	49	Recapture taxes. Check if from a ☐ Form 4255 b ☐ Form 8611 c ☐ Form 8828	49	
	50	Social security and Medicare tax on tip income not reported to employer. Attach Form 4137	50	
	51	Tax on qualified retirement plans including IRAs. If required, attach Form 5329	51	
	52	Advance earned income credit payments from Form W-2	52	
	53	Household employment taxes. Attach Schedule H	53	
	54	Add lines 46 through 53 This is your **total tax** ➤	54	
Payments Attach Forms W-2, W-2G, and 1099-R on the front.	55	Federal income tax withheld. If any is from Form(s) 1099, check ➤ ☐	55	
	56	1995 estimated tax payments and amount applied from 1994 return	56	
	57	**Earned income credit.** Attach Schedule EIC if you have a qualifying child. Nontaxable earned income: amount ➤ _____ and type ➤ _____	57	
	58	Amount paid with Form 4868 (extension request)	58	
	59	Excess social security and RRTA tax withheld (see page 32)	59	
	60	Other payments. Check if from a ☐ Form 2439 b ☒ Form 4136	60	
	61	Add lines 55 through 60. These are your **total payments** ➤	61	
Refund or Amount You Owe	62	If line 61 is more than line 54, subtract line 54 from line 61. This is the amount you **OVERPAID** ➤	62	
	63	Amount of line 62 you want **REFUNDED TO YOU** ➤	63	
	64	Amount of line 62 you want **APPLIED TO YOUR 1996 ESTIMATED TAX** ➤	64	
	65	If line 54 is more than line 61, subtract line 61 from line 54. This is the **AMOUNT YOU OWE** For details on how to pay including using **Form 1040-V,** Payment Voucher, see page 32	65	
	66	Estimated tax penalty (see page __). Also include on line 65	66	

Carry your gas tax credit to Form 1040 and check the Form 4136 box.

The gas tax credit.

The Least You Need to Know

➤ Taxpayers who pay for child or dependent care while they are at work are entitled to a credit against their income tax for a portion of that payment.

➤ Taxpayers over age 65 or taxpayers who are totally disabled and who have low incomes may be entitled to a credit against their income tax.

➤ Taxpayers who pay income tax to another country on their income can take a credit for those payments.

➤ Taxpayers with low income and who support at least one child may be entitled to a credit.

➤ Taxpayers who buy gasoline for nonhighway vehicles and use those vehicles in a business can take a credit for the federal gas tax paid.

➤ Taxpayers who work at more than one job and have Social Security tax withheld on wages in excess of $61,200 can take a credit for the extra Social Security tax withheld.

Chapter 25

Other Kinds of Taxes (Including Taxes on Income You Didn't Know You Had)

In This Chapter

➤ Swallowing the self-employment tax

➤ Understanding (not!) the alternative minimum tax

➤ Paying tax on your tips

➤ Getting yourself into penalty trouble with your IRA

"Enough is enough!" some people may be heard to say after they've computed their income tax. But try telling that to the IRS. Just in case you thought you were finished, here are a few more types of taxes that, if nothing else, tax your patience as you wade through them, trying to figure out if they apply to you.

16 Tons and What Do You Get? Self-Employment Tax and Deeper in Debt

Self-employment tax may be the single most difficult tax to swallow for many Americans. And the funny thing is, we all pay this tax, but only the self-employed taxpayers actually see it happen.

Self-employment tax is Social Security tax with a different name. All employed workers have Social Security tax withheld directly from their paychecks—they never have to write a check to Uncle Sam for this amount. What's more, employees only see *half* of their Social Security tax as it gets reported on their

By the Way
Schedule C taxpayers aren't the only ones subject to self-employment tax. Farmers filing Schedule F have the same responsibility. Also, people who own interests in partnerships and S corporations may find self-employment income reported on their K-1 forms. Self-employment income from all sources gets carted over to Schedule SE.

pay stub. Their employers are paying the same amount—the other half, if you will—without the employees ever seeing it. It's a little trick the Social Security Administration uses to collect its revenue with the American public being only vaguely aware of the act.

For the self-employed taxpayer, however, there is no employer to play along with the game, blithely sending in a matching Social Security contribution without our knowing it. So self-employed people have to do it themselves—they pay both their share and the employer's share of Social Security and Medicare—a whopping 15.3% of their income as compared to the 7.65% the rest of working America thinks it pays.

Whether this makes sense or whether it's all shadow play doesn't really matter. What matters is that self-employed taxpayers *really hurt* come April 15. And if this is the first year you've been self-employed, you might be in for a shock when you compute your tax on your Schedule C income.

To compute self-employment tax, the Schedule C taxpayer takes his or her net self-employment income (line 31 from Schedule C or line 3 from Schedule C-EZ) and carries the amount over to Schedule SE, "Self-Employment Tax."

If you have income from a W-2 form and the sum of your self-employment income plus your W-2 wages exceeds $61,200, you have to prepare page 2 of Schedule SE, otherwise known as "The Long Form." If your self-employment income plus your W-2 income is under the $61,200 threshold, or if you don't have any W-2 income, fill out Schedule SE on the front page only—"The Short Form."

If you use the Schedule SE short form, put your income from farms on line 1 and all your other self-employment income on line 2. Add the two together and put the sum on line 3. Multiply the amount on line 3 by 92.35% (.9235) and put the answer on line 4. If line 4 is under $400, you're finished with the form—you don't owe any self-employment tax. If line 4 is $400 or more, but less than $61,200, multiply the amount on line 4 by 15.3% (.153) (Social Security tax plus Medicare tax) and put the answer on line 5. If line 4 is over $61,200, multiply line 4 by 2.9% (.029) (Medicare tax), add $7,588.80 to the answer, and put the sum on line 5.

Carry the amount on line 5 to the self-employment tax line on your 1040, page 2, line 47.

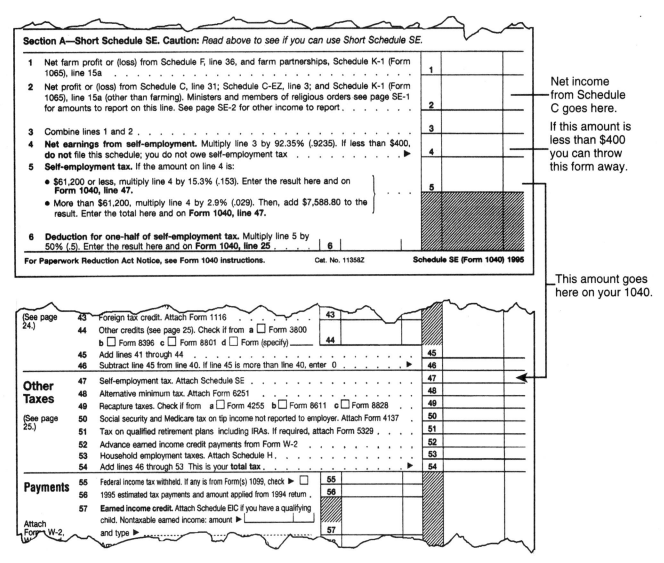

Carry the self-employment tax over to your Form 1040.

The Schedule SE long form is just a little more complex because it takes into account people who have a combination of W-2 wages and self-employment income that exceeds $61,200.

Alternative Minimum Tax (Isn't There a Contradiction in Terms Here?)

Here it is, one of the most befuddling aspects of income taxation: the alternative minimum tax. This tax is targeted at people with high incomes who have opportunities to shelter some of their income from tax. The alternative minimum tax (AMT) is designed to force wealthy taxpayers to pay a higher tax than they may otherwise have calculated.

> **OOOOH...**
>
> **By the Way**
>
> If you hire an accountant to help with the AMT, that doesn't necessarily mean you have to hire someone to do your entire tax return. You can do everything up to this point and just hire someone to help with the sticky issues.

The AMT requires special handling. If you participate in tax shelters, take accelerated depreciation on business assets, if you purchase stocks at reduced rates through employee incentive plans, or if any of the tax documents you receive from your various income sources refer to amounts that are for alternative minimum tax purposes, you might have a responsibility to prepare Form 6251, "Alternative Minimum Tax." This is hire-an-accountant stuff. I wouldn't suggest messing with it on your own because the AMT is very complex.

Taxes on Tips (Shame on You if You Thought You Could Slip Them By Old Uncle Sam)

If you receive tips on your job, it's your responsibility to report those tips to your employer and pay taxes on them. When you report tips to your employer, he or she withholds tax on your regular wages to be applied to the tip income. If your employer is unable to withhold enough Social Security and Medicare tax from your wages to cover the required withholding for your tips, you must report this tax on your income tax return.

Social Security and Medicare tax, which should have been withheld but was not, will show up on your W-2 form in box 13—the amount will be coded with an **A** or a **B**. Put this tax from your W-2 form on line 54 of your 1040.

a Control number	22222	Void ☐	For Official Use Only ▶ OMB No. 1545-0008		
b Employer's identification number				1 Wages, tips, other compensation	2 Federal income tax withheld
c Employer's name, address, and ZIP code				3 Social security wages	4 Social security tax withheld
				5 Medicare wages and tips	6 Medicare tax withheld
				7 Social security tips	8 Allocated tips
d Employee's social security number				9 Advance EIC payment	10 Dependent care benefits
e Employee's name (first, middle initial, last)				11 Nonqualified plans	12 Benefits included in box 1
				13 See Instrs. for box 13	14 Other
f Employee's address and ZIP code				15 Statutory employee ☐ Deceased ☐ Pension plan ☐ Legal rep. ☐ Hshld. emp. ☐ Subtotal ☐ Deferred compensation ☐	
16 State Employer's state I.D. No.	17 State wages, tips, etc.	18 State income tax	19 Locality name	20 Local wages, tips, etc.	21 Local income tax

Cat. No. 10134D

Department of the Treasury—Internal Revenue Service

Form W-2 **Wage and Tax Statement** **1995**

For Paperwork Reduction Act Notice, see separate instructions.

Copy A For Social Security Administration

> Social Security and Medicare tax that didn't get withheld.

> Include this amount on line 54 of your 1040 and print UNCOLLECTED TAX to the left of the number.

	45	Add lines 41 through 44	45
	46	Subtract line 45 from line 40. If line 45 is more than line 40, enter 0 ▶	46
Other Taxes (See page 25.)	47	Self-employment tax. Attach Schedule SE	47
	48	Alternative minimum tax. Attach Form 6251	48
	49	Recapture taxes. Check if from a ☐ Form 4255 b ☐ Form 8611 c ☐ Form 8828	49
	50	Social security and Medicare tax on tip income not reported to employer. Attach Form 4137	50
	51	Tax on qualified retirement plans including IRAs. If required, attach Form 5329	51
	52	Advance earned income credit payments from Form W-2	52
	53	Household employment taxes. Attach Schedule H	53
	54	Add lines 46 through 53 This is your **total tax** . . . . . UNCOLLECTED TAX. ▶	54
Payments Attach Forms W-2, W-2G, and 1099-R on the front.	55	Federal income tax withheld. If any is from Form(s) 1099, check ▶ ☐	55
	56	1995 estimated tax payments and amount applied from 1994 return	56
	57	**Earned income credit.** Attach Schedule EIC if you have a qualifying child. Nontaxable earned income: amount ▶ ___ and type ▶ ___	57
	58	Amount paid with Form 4868 (extension request)	58
	59	Excess social security and RRTA tax withheld (see page 32)	59
	60	Other Check if a ☐ Form 2439 b ☐ Form 4	60

Take this tax to your 1040.

I Had to Do It! That IRA Was So Juicy!

These days it's hard for many people to save money. IRA accounts (see Chapter 18, "Adjustments to Income," for a more complete discussion of IRAs) provide some saving security because its difficult to take money out of such an account before age 59 1/2, unless you're disabled or taking it out under an annuity exception.

OOOOH...

By the Way

You can temporarily withdraw funds from your IRA in the form of a short-term loan without subjecting yourself to the 10% early withdrawal penalty. If you take money from your IRA and redeposit it (either back in the same IRA or in a new IRA account) within 60 days the withdrawal is considered a *rollover* and is not subject to the penalty. You can only do this once in a calendar year.

Difficult, but not impossible. You can take money out of your IRA—after all, it's *your* money—but you pay a price when you do this. The amount you withdraw from your IRA account gets added to your income as an IRA distribution on page 1 of your 1040. The amount also gets subjected to a 10% penalty. You must compute the penalty on Form 5329 and add it in with other taxes on line 51 of page 2 of the 1040. (Note: If you have a penalty on an early withdrawal from an IRA, you cannot file Form 1040A or 1040EZ—you must use Form 1040.) Don't think you can just forget to report the IRA distribution and hope the IRS won't notice. The IRS gets a statement from your IRA banker or broker telling it when you pull some money out of that account. If you don't report the withdrawal, you *will* hear from the IRS.

The Least You Need to Know

➤ Self-employed people pay their own Social Security and Medicare taxes in the form of the self-employment tax on Schedule SE.

➤ The alternative minimum tax (AMT) places a minimum tax on people who may otherwise not pay their fair share (according to the IRS).

➤ Tip income is subject to Social Security and Medicare tax. If your employer did not withhold these taxes and pay them for you, you have to do it yourself.

➤ Taking money out of your IRA may be tempting, but consider the consequences: income tax on the amount withdrawn and a flat 10% penalty if under 59 1/2 for sticking your fingers into the pie.

Chapter 26

Pay Now, Play Later (Estimated Taxes)

In This Chapter

➤ What's an estimated tax payment?

➤ Who pays estimated taxes?

➤ When do I make estimated tax payments?

➤ How do I figure estimated tax payments?

➤ What should I do if I miss an estimated tax payment?

The most common way taxes get paid to the government is through withholding. You know how it works: You have a job, your employer withholds tax from your salary, he or she sends the tax to the government, and you try to live on what's left.

But what if your withholding isn't enough? Suppose that you have a lot of investments earning money on top of your salary—there isn't any tax withholding on your dividends and interest. Or what if you're self-employed and nobody does the withholding for you? If your income tax withholding comes up more than $500 short when you prepare your tax return, it's time to think about paying estimated taxes.

By the Way

If you are Married Filing Jointly, remember, it takes two to pay taxes. One self-employed spouse may have taxable income that requires the payment of quarterly estimates. The other spouse may be employed. Instead of paying quarterly estimated taxes, consider increasing the amount of taxes withheld from the employed spouse's salary. File Form W-4 with your employer to adjust the amount of your tax withholding.

Estimated taxes are a way of paying extra income tax during the year so that you don't get caught short in April. Estimated taxes are paid more or less quarterly (April, June, September, and January).

Paying estimated taxes isn't just an option or a choice you make if you feel like being generous with the IRS. It's a requirement if you have to write a check for more than $500 with your income tax return. If you don't pay the estimates during the year, you're hit with a penalty.

If you have to pay quarterly estimates, it's up to you to get yourself some estimated tax forms, 1040-ES (unless you were lucky enough to have some sent to you by the IRS), and remember when the payments are due.

Form **1040-ES**
Department of the Treasury
Internal Revenue Service

1995 Payment Voucher **1**

OMB No. 1545-0087

File only if you are making a payment of estimated tax. Return this voucher with check or money order payable to the **"Internal Revenue Service."** Please write your social security number and "1995 Form 1040-ES" on your check or money order. Do not send cash. Enclose, but do not staple or attach, your payment with this voucher.

Calendar year—Due April 17, 1995

Amount of payment

Put the amount of your estimated tax payment here.

$..................

Please type or print

Your first name and initial	Your last name	Your social security number
If joint payment, complete for spouse		
Spouse's first name and initial	Spouse's last name	Spouse's social security number
Address (number, street, and apt. no.)		
City, state, and ZIP code. (If a foreign address, enter city, province or state, postal code, and country.)		

For Paperwork Reduction Act Notice, see instructions on page 1.

Page 7

The estimated tax voucher: Form 1040-ES.

Due Dates for Estimated Taxes

Estimated taxes are often called *quarterly estimates* because the due dates for the payments sort of fall during each *quarter* of the year. It's not quite quarterly, but it's close. The payment due dates for 1996 estimated tax payments are as follows:

1st quarter	April 15, 1996
2nd quarter	June 17, 1996
3rd quarter	September 16, 1996
4th quarter	January 15, 1997

Normally the due date is the 15th of the month, but if the 15th falls on a Saturday or Sunday, as it does in June and September of 1996, the payment due date is bumped back to the next Monday.

For a payment to count as having been mailed on the due date it must be postmarked by that date. Just taking the envelope out to your mailbox at the end of the driveway before midnight on the 15th doesn't count. Either mail the payment a day or two early to ensure the postmark, or, if you're a procrastinator, find a post office that stays open at night and deliver the envelope before midnight.

By the Way

Quarterly *state* estimated payments are generally due on the same dates as the federal estimated payments. Check your state's requirements if you find yourself paying federal estimated taxes.

Wait a Minute! Where Do These Get Mailed?

Probably just to confuse all of us, the IRS doesn't want you to mail your estimated payments to the same place you mail your tax return. This is particularly frustrating if it's nearing midnight on April 15 and you have your tax return all addressed and ready for the late-night run to the post office. Wouldn't it be nice if you could just slip your estimated payment in the same envelope? No such luck.

Estimated payments are processed at different IRS offices than the income tax returns are. I expect the working environment is much calmer at the estimated tax branches than it is at the income tax branches. No addition to check, no W-2s to cross-reference—just open the envelope, enter the taxpayer's Social Security number and the amount paid into a computer screen, and deposit the check. Simple!

The addresses of these placid, estimated tax processing centers are located way back in Chapter 2, "But Do I Have to File a Tax Return?" under the section, "Where to Send the Return." You will find two sets of addresses there—the tax return address and the estimated payment address. Make sure that you use the correct one for mailing your estimated payments.

Computing Your Estimated Taxes

The estimated payments are supposed to be a reflection of what you think you're going to owe on your 1040 in the year ahead. If you happen to have a functioning crystal ball, you can just look inside, read what it says you're going to owe, divide it by four, and pay 1/4 the total with each quarterly payment.

If your income fluctuates during the year, you may not have to make equal quarterly estimates. In fact, there may be a quarter when you don't have to make an estimated payment at all. Because it's sometimes difficult to see clearly into your crystal ball, the IRS has devised methods by which you can rough out an estimate of your future taxes. The official IRS methods for determining your quarterly estimated payments are discussed on the next page.

Have handy your 1995 federal and state income tax returns (most states require estimated payments too, if your withholding isn't enough to cover your tax liability) as well as a couple sheets of paper and a sharpened pencil for calculating your income for 1996.

If you have to pay quarterly estimates, the IRS generally wants you to split the quarterly amount and pay the same amount each quarter. Leaving the total amount until the fourth quarter and paying it all at once can negate the effect of the estimated payments and still result in an underpayment penalty. The exception to this equal payment rule is Method 3 for computing estimated payments.

Method 1: Last Year's Tax

One of the safest ways to estimate your 1996 taxes for the purpose of making quarterly payments is to look at your 1995 income tax return (which you've presumably been preparing as you've been working your way through this book). Check line 65 of your 1995 Form 1040 and see what you had to pay above and beyond your withholding. If your total tax was $12,000 and your withholding was $10,000 and you paid $2,000 with your tax return when you filed it, the $2,000 may well have triggered an underpayment penalty. If you owe more than $500 with your income return you frequently end up owing a penalty for underpayment of your tax. Therefore, the $2,000 that you had to pay with your 1995 income tax return is a good place to start for figuring how much your quarterly payments will be for 1996.

> **IRSpeak**
>
> The *total tax* for a tax year is the sum of all taxes owed for that year offset by the sum of all credits. So, for example, if on your 1995 tax return you compute income tax of $15,000, a child care credit of $480, self-employment tax of $2,500, and a foreign tax credit of $20, your total tax is $17,000 ($15,000 + $2,500 – $480 – $20). The total tax appears on line 54 of your 1040 (line 28 of the 1040A).

The rule is that you won't have to pay any penalty for underpayment of your 1996 income taxes if the tax payments you've made for 1996, through withholding and estimated payments, equal or exceed 100% of the 1995 total tax. This rule assumes that your quarterly estimated payments are made on a timely basis.

If your adjusted gross income for 1995 was higher than $150,000 and you want to use Method 1 for figuring out your estimated payments, the quarterly payments you make for 1996 have to be 110% of the 1995 tax instead of 100%.

Method 2: This Year's Tax

As an alternative to paying 100% of your prior (1995) year's tax in withholding and estimated payments, you can choose to pay 90% of the current (1996) year's tax.

By using this method, you estimate what your 1996 income is going to be, then go to the tax tables (or the tax rate schedules, if your taxable income is $100,000 or more), and compute your 1996 tax. Multiply that number by 90%. Estimate what your withholding will be based on the income tax that is being withheld from your paychecks. The difference between 90% of your estimated tax and your withholding is what you need to pay in estimated payments—1/4 with each payment.

For example, suppose you estimate that your 1996 tax will be $18,000 and you expect your withholding in 1996 to total $13,000. Ninety percent of $18,000 is $16,200. Subtract your estimated withholding from this number: $16,200 – $13,000 = $3,200. Each estimated payment should be $800 ($3,200 ÷ 4).

You need a fairly well-polished crystal ball to use this method. If you aren't changing jobs, you know what your salary is going to be, your investments aren't expected to change, and you can probably do a pretty good job of guessing what your 1996 income and therefore your 1996 tax is going to be. If you expect your financial life to change in 1996, you may be better off using Method 1 or Method 3 to compute your estimates.

Be sure to update your calculations each quarter and make sure that you're still on track. If your income has changed since the first part of the year, adjust your remaining quarterly payments accordingly. Your quarterly payments don't have to equal each other. In fact, see Method 3 for a way of computing a different estimated payment each quarter.

Method 3: Annualizing Income

The third method of figuring payments for estimated tax is called *annualizing your income*. By using this method you monitor your income during the year basing your estimated payments on actual income rather than estimates. This method is particularly useful for people whose income fluctuates during the year—seasonal workers, for example—who can then pay more tax at the times when they are earning more money, less tax when their receipts are down.

To annualize your income for the first quarter estimated payment, the one due April 15, 1996, follow these steps:

1. Figure out your actual income and deductions for the first three months of the year: January through March 1996.

2. Multiply your income and deductions by 4. In effect, you are saying that you earned exactly one fourth of your income during the first quarter of the year, so four times that income will give you the amount you expect to earn for the whole year.

3. If your annualized itemized deductions from step 2 don't exceed the standard deduction for your filing status (see Chapter 21, "The Standard Deduction," for information about the standard deduction), use the standard deduction in place of itemized deductions for this method. Reduce your total estimated income for the year by either the estimated itemized deductions or the standard deduction to result in a net income amount.

4. Deduct your exemption(s) from the net income determined in step 3 to determine your annualized taxable income for 1996. Each exemption is expected to be worth $2,550 for 1996; check Form 1040-ES for 1996.

By the Way
You can choose the best method for computing your estimated taxes on a quarter-by-quarter basis. If one method gives you a lower tax in one quarter and another method is better in the next quarter, you can switch methods.

5. Figure the income tax on the taxable income as computed in step 4. If you expect to owe other taxes such as self-employment tax, or if you expect to have credits against your tax, be sure to estimate these items for the entire year.

6. Multiply the tax that you computed in step 5 by 90% and divide it by 4. This is the amount you should pay for your first quarter estimated payment.

For the second quarter payment, due June 17, 1996, determine the first five months of your income and deductions through May 1996, and multiply by 2.4 to annualize it. Then continue with steps 3 through 6. The third quarter payment, due in September, will cover your income through August. Multiply your income through August by 1.5 to annualize it. The fourth quarter payment, due in January, will encompass your income and deductions for the entire year of 1996.

What Happens if I Forget to Make a Payment?

There's no changing the calendar as far as the IRS is concerned. Payments due on the 15th of the month are due on the 15th of the month, and if they are postmarked on the 16th of the month, they are considered late and penalties can be assessed. Just how penalties are assessed is discussed in Chapter 27, "The Underpayment Penalty."

First, remember that penalties are assessed based on how late the payment is made. If you remember on the 16th that you missed your payment due the 15th, just send it in. The payment will be considered only one day late.

Another way to avoid penalties for late payments is to adjust your withholding at work rather than send in the late estimated payment. Ask your boss to have more tax withheld from your next paycheck (or the next several paychecks, if you want to spread it out). Withholding is considered by the IRS to be evenly spaced over the entire calendar year, no matter when it actually occurs.

The Least You Need to Know

➤ Estimated taxes are tax payments you make on a quarterly basis when your withholding isn't enough to cover your tax liability.

➤ Quarterly tax payments are due on the 15th of April, June, September, and the following January—if the 15th falls on Saturday or Sunday the payment is due the following Monday.

➤ Don't send your estimated tax payment to the same address as your income tax return—there are separate IRS offices for estimates to be mailed.

➤ Late quarterly payments are subject to underpayment penalties.

Chapter 27

The Underpayment Penalty

In This Chapter

➤ What is an underpayment penalty?

➤ Who has to pay the penalty?

➤ How to figure out the penalty

➤ Getting the best possible deal

When you finish preparing your tax return, computing your income tax, and figuring out what you owe, check to see if you owe more than $500. If you owe more than $500 and the amount you owe is more than 10% of the total tax you owe, chances are you are liable for an underpayment penalty.

In other words, suppose that the total of all your tax is $7,500, your withholding comes to $6,900, so you owe an additional $600 with your tax return. You owe more than $500, which will first get the attention of the IRS, but the amount you owe, $600, is less than 10% of the total amount of tax, $750 ($7,500 × 10%), so there should be no penalty.

Even if you owe more than $500 and more than 10% of your total tax, the penalty may not apply. But if you do owe that much, even if the penalty doesn't apply, the IRS will probably look at your return, raise its collective eyebrows, and mail you a notice saying you owe a penalty. Then it's time for you to respond with a penalty computation of your own, as explained in this chapter.

You Can Let the IRS Figure This Out

Perhaps the wisest thing to do, if it looks like you may owe a penalty, is just file your tax return, pay your tax, don't fill anything in on the penalty line (line 66 on the 1040, line 34 of the 1040A), and let the IRS tell you about any penalty they think you owe. They will gladly compute your penalty for you and mail you a notice of the amount due. (Note: If you file on Form 1040EZ and it looks like you may owe a penalty, you can let the IRS figure out your penalty and send you a notice. If, however, you want to compute your penalty yourself, you cannot file Form 1040EZ; you must use Form 1040A.)

Leave this blank and the IRS will graciously figure your penalty for you.

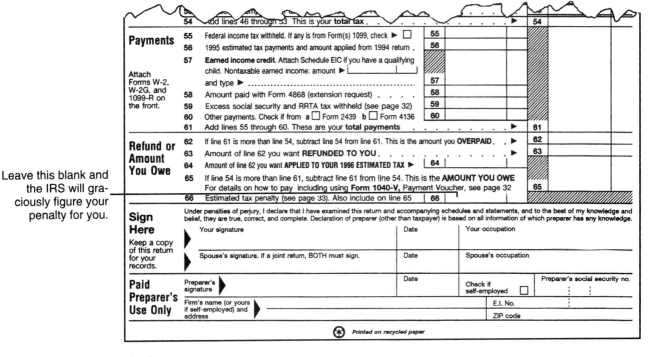

The penalty box.

Having the IRS compute the penalty for you accomplishes two tasks: First, it gives you a starting point for figuring out your penalty yourself—the penalty computation can be difficult and the IRS will do all the math for you (if you're convinced the IRS is wrong in their computation—and they often are—you can contest it; see "There are Underpayment Penalties and There are Underpayment Penalties," later in this chapter); second, it postpones the date on which you have to pay your penalty. If you compute your penalty on your tax return and send in the payment, the IRS will think you're wonderful and they'll deposit your money right away. If you wait and let the IRS compute your penalty for you, you won't owe any more than you would if you had paid it on the day you filed your tax return, and you will have bought yourself several weeks of not having to pay the penalty.

If your tax return shows an amount due exceeding $500 or 10% of your total tax liability, eventually you can expect to see a penalty notice from the IRS in the mailbox.

Calculating Your Penalty

If you decide to tackle the penalty calculation yourself, and you can do this either when you file your tax return or in response to a notice from the IRS, you need to get Form 2210 and be prepared for some fairly complicated computations. If you calculate the penalty, add the amount on line 66 of Form 1040 (or line 34 of Form 1040A) and add the penalty to the total tax calculated on line 65 of the 1040 (line 33 of the 1040A). You cannot file Form 1040EZ if you are adding in a penalty.

First, remember your goals: Your first goal is to pay no penalty at all, and your second goal, if the first goal doesn't work, is to pay as little penalty as possible. If you stay focused on these goals this section will be a little easier to follow.

When the IRS figures out your underpayment penalty, it takes your tax for the year and divides it by four to figure out how much you owed for each quarter. Then it considers your payments for the year, withholding, and estimated payments. Withholding is divided in four and spread evenly across the year. Estimated payments are recorded by the IRS when they were paid (date postmarked or the due date, whichever is later). The sum of your withholding and estimated payment for each quarter is compared to your tax due for that quarter. If the tax is higher than the amounts paid for any quarter, a penalty is applied to that quarter. If the payments are higher than the tax for any quarter, the excess payments are applied, first, to prior quarters in which there may have been a shortfall, and then to the current quarter.

So, for example, suppose that your total income tax for the year is $16,000. The IRS divides that by four to come up with $4,000 that you owe each quarter. Furthermore, suppose that your withholding (taxes your employer withheld from your paycheck) was $10,000 (which the IRS declares paid evenly, $2,500 per quarter) and you paid estimated tax as follows:

1st quarter	April 15	$1,500
2nd quarter	June 15	Forgot to send the payment
3rd quarter	September 15	$3,000
4th quarter	January 15	$ 500

In the first quarter the IRS assumes that your withholding was $2,500 (1/4 of the total $10,000). Add this to your estimated payment of $1,500 for a total of $4,000. Your first quarter results in no penalty. In the second quarter your withholding is $2,500, but you have no estimated payment, so there is a shortfall of $1,500 on which the IRS will figure a penalty. In the third quarter your withholding is $2,500 and your estimated payment is $3,000. Of the total

$5,500 paid for the third quarter, the first $1,500 is applied to the shortfall in the second quarter, thus stopping the penalty that has been increasing each month since the second quarter ended, and the remaining $4,000 is applied to the third quarter. (The penalty is figured at a rate of 9%—except for the second quarter, for which the rate is 10%—so from June 15 to September 15 an underpayment penalty will be assessed on the second quarter underpayment: $1,500 × 9% calculated for 3 months, or $33.75.)

There are Underpayment Penalties and Then There Are Underpayment Penalties

If the tax you owe is more than $500 or 10% of your income, there are three ways in which you can avoid liability for the underpayment penalty.

Method One. If the amount of tax you paid during the year for 1995 was paid evenly throughout the year and equals at least 100% of the amount of tax you owed on your 1994 income tax return, you are not liable for the penalty.

OOPS!
By using Method One, if the adjusted gross income on your 1994 tax return exceeds $150,000, your 1995 tax payments must exceed *110% of your 1994 tax,* instead of 100%, in order for you to use this method.

If all your tax payments are from withholding, fill out all of Part II on Form 2210, placing the 1994 tax on line 12. If part of your tax payments come from estimated taxes, go on and fill out all of Part III of Form 2210 and fill in your estimated tax payments on line 15.

Method Two. If the amount of tax you paid during the year for 1995 was paid evenly throughout the year and is equal to at least 90% of your 1995 tax, you are not liable for the penalty.

If all your tax payments are from withholding, fill out all of Part II on Form 2210, placing the 1994 tax on line 12. If part of your tax payments comes from estimated taxes, go on and fill out all of Part III of Form 2210 and fill in your estimated tax payments on line 15.

Method Three. The third method for avoiding a penalty situation is more complex. Use this method only if method one or two doesn't help you and if your income was not earned evenly during 1995. With Method Three you *annualize* your income, demonstrating to the IRS that it was earned sporadically during the year and therefore substantiating your tax payments as being appropriate to the income you had earned in each quarter.

When you *annualize* your income you figure out your actual income for each quarter, as opposed to just dividing your total income for the year by four. In any given quarter you figure out what your income would be for the entire year if you continued to earn at the rate you've earned at thus far. So, if your total income for the first quarter of 1995 is $10,000, when you annualize your income you are saying that as of the end of the first quarter you expect to earn $40,000 for the entire year. Your first quarter estimated tax is then based on the assumption that your income for the entire year is $40,000; the tax on $40,000 is divided by four to arrive at the required estimate.

Form **2210**	**Underpayment of**	OMB No. 1545-0140

Form 2210

Department of the Treasury
Internal Revenue Service

**Underpayment of
Estimated Tax by Individuals, Estates, and Trusts**
▶ See separate instructions.
▶ Attach to Form 1040, Form 1040A, Form 1040NR, or Form 1041.

OMB No. 1545-0140

Attachment
Sequence No. **06**

Name(s) shown on tax return

Identifying number

Note: *In most cases, you do not need to file Form 2210. The IRS will figure any penalty you owe and send you a bill. File Form 2210 only if one or more boxes in Part I apply to you. If you do not need to file Form 2210, you still may use it to figure your penalty. Enter the amount from line 20 or line 36 on the penalty line of your return, but do not attach Form 2210.*

Part I **Reasons For Filing**—If 1a, b, or c below applies to you, you may be able to lower or eliminate your penalty. But you **MUST** check the boxes that apply and file Form 2210 with your tax return. If 1d below applies to you, check that box and file Form 2210 with your tax return.

1 Check whichever boxes apply (if none apply, see the **Note** above):

a ☐ You request a **waiver.** In certain circumstances, the IRS will waive all or part of the penalty. See **Waiver of Penalty** on page 1 of the instructions.

b ☐ You use the **annualized income installment method.** If your income varied during the year, this method may reduce the amount of one or more required installments. See page 4 of the instructions.

c ☐ You had Federal income tax withheld from wages and you treat it as paid for estimated tax purposes when it was **actually** withheld instead of in equal amounts on the payment due dates. See the instructions for line 22.

d ☐ Your required annual payment (line 13 below) is based on your 1993 tax and you filed or are filing a joint return for either 1993 or 1994 but not for both years.

Part II **Required Annual Payment**

2	Enter your 1994 tax after credits (see instructions)	**2**	
3	Other taxes (see instructions)	**3**	
4	Add lines 2 and 3	**4**	
5	Earned income credit	**5**	
6	Credit for Federal tax paid on fuels	**6**	
7	Add lines 5 and 6	**7**	
8	Current year tax. Subtract line 7 from line 4	**8**	
9	Multiply line 8 by 90% (.90)	**9**	
10	Withholding taxes. **Do not** include any estimated tax payments on this line (see instructions)	**10**	
11	Subtract line 10 from line 8. If less than $500, stop here; **do not** complete or file this form. You do not owe the penalty	**11**	
12	Enter the tax shown on your 1993 tax return (110% of that amount if the adjusted gross income shown on that return is more than $150,000, or if married filing separately for 1994, more than $75,000). **Caution:** *See instrucions*	**12**	
13	**Required annual payment.** Enter the **smaller** of line 9 or line 12	**13**	

Note: *If line 10 is equal to or more than line 13, stop here; you do not owe the penalty. Do not file Form 2210 unless you checked box 1d above.*

Part III **Short Method** (Caution: *Read the instructions to see if you can use the short method. If you checked box* **1b** *or* **c** *in Part I, skip this part and go to Part IV.*)

14	Enter the amount, if any, from line 10 above	**14**	
15	Enter the total amount, if any, of estimated tax payments you made	**15**	
16	Add lines 14 and 15	**16**	
17	**Total underpayment for year.** Subtract line 16 from line 13. If zero or less, stop here; you do not file Form 2210 unless you checked box 1d above	**17**	
18	Multiply line 17 by .05725	**18**	
19	● If the amount on line 17 was paid **on or after** 4/15/95, enter -0-. ● If the amount on line 17 was paid **before** 4/15/95, make the following computation to find the amount to enter on line 19. Amount on line 17 × Number of days paid before 4/15/95 × .00025	**19**	
20	**PENALTY.** Subtract line 19 from line 18. Enter the result here and on Form 1040, line 65; Form 1040A, line 33; Form 1040NR, line 66; or Form 1041, line 26 ▶	**20**	

For Paperwork Reduction Act Notice, see page 1 of separate instructions.   Cat. No. 11744P   Form **2210**

Enter 1995 federal income tax withholding here.

Enter 1994 total tax here.

1995 estimated payments go here.

Filling out Form 2210.

For example, suppose that you are a house builder who works in a cold climate. You work when the weather lets you work. If you didn't have income in January and February of 1995 and only started earning some income in March, your first quarter would have a small amount of income compared to your earnings for the rest of the year. Your estimated tax payment for that first quarter can also reflect this downtime by being low. When the IRS looks at your return and considers 1/4 of your income to be earned in the first quarter of the year, naturally they are going to think you should have paid in 1/4 of your tax in the first quarter. But the IRS will be wrong.

Use Schedule AI of Form 2210, "Annualized Income Installment Method," to annualize your income, spreading it appropriately across the year in the quarters in which it was earned. Also on this schedule, compute the required estimated payments that match your income and carry those payments to Form 2210. Be sure to attach Form 2210 to your tax return.

On Schedule AI you show how much you estimated for your income for each quarter. Watch out, however, quarters aren't exactly quarters according to the IRS. The first "quarter" is January, February, and March. So far, so good. The second "quarter" is April and May, just two months. The third "quarter" is June, July, and August, and the fourth "quarter" is four months—September through December. These are the groupings of months the IRS wants to hear about when you designate your income and compute your estimated tax by quarter.

For each quarter, determine your adjusted gross income for that particular quarter, including all income items such as interest, dividends, state tax refunds, rents, wages, miscellaneous income, and self-employment income. Schedule AI shows you how to multiply the amount by the correct number in order to annualize the income (spread it over the entire year). You then do the same thing with itemized deductions—enter the actual amount for a particular quarter, then multiply by the correct number to get the annual amount. Deduct the full amount for your exemptions, then compute your tax just as it tells you to on Schedule AI. If the tax you compute for the quarter exceeds the amount of tax you paid in for the quarter, whether your payment is in withholding, estimated payments, or both, this method won't help you. It looks as if you're stuck with paying the penalty for the quarter. If, on the other hand, your tax equals or is less than the amount you paid, your payment covers your tax and you're not subject to a penalty for this quarter!

Remember, the point of this exercise is to prove to the IRS that your estimated payments were appropriate to the income you earned in each quarter.

Form 2210 — Page **3**

Schedule AI—Annualized Income Installment Method (see instructions)

Estates and trusts, **do not** use the period ending dates shown to the right.
Instead, use the following: 2/28/94, 4/30/94, 7/31/94, and 11/30/94.

		(a) 1/1/94–3/31/94	(b) 1/1/94–5/31/94	(c) 1/1/94–8/31/94	(d) 1/1/94–12/31/94

Part I Annualized Income Installments Caution: *Complete lines 20–26 of one column before going to the next column.*

		(a)	(b)	(c)	(d)
1	Enter your adjusted gross income for each period (see instructions). (Estates and trusts, enter your taxable income without your exemption for each period.)				
2	Annualization amounts. (Estates and trusts, see instructions.)	4	2.4	1.5	1
3	Annualized income. Multiply line 1 by line 2				
4	Enter your itemized deductions for the period shown in each column. If you do not itemize, enter -0- and skip to line 7. (Estates and trusts, enter -0-, skip to line 9, and enter the amount from line 3 on line 9.)				
5	Annualization amounts	4	2.4	1.5	1
6	Multiply line 4 by line 5 (see instructions if line 3 is more than $55,900)				
7	In each column, enter the full amount of your standard deduction from Form 1040, line 34; or Form 1040A, line 19 (Form 1040NR filers, enter -0-. **Exception:** Indian students and business apprentices, enter standard deduction from Form 1040NR, line 33.)				
8	Enter line 6 or line 7, whichever is **larger**				
9	Subtract line 8 from line 3				
10	In each column, multiply $2,450 by the total number of exemptions claimed (see instructions if line 3 is more than $83,850). (Estates and trusts and Form 1040NR filers, enter the exemption amount shown on your tax return.)				
11	Subtract line 10 from line 9				
12	Figure your tax on the amount on line 11 (see instructions)				
13	Form 1040 filers only, enter your self-employment tax from line 35 below				
14	Enter other taxes for each payment period (see instructions)				
15	Total tax. Add lines 12, 13, and 14				
16	For each period, enter the same type of credits as allowed on Form 2210, lines 2, 5, and 6 (see instructions)				
17	Subtract line 16 from line 15. If zero or less, enter -0-				
18	Applicable percentage	22.5%	45%	67.5%	90%
19	Multiply line 17 by line 18				
20	Add the amounts in all preceding columns of line 26	▨			
21	Subtract line 20 from line 19. If zero or less, enter -0-				
22	Enter ¼ of line 13, Form 2210, in each column				
23	Enter amount from line 25 of the preceding column of this schedule	▨			
24	Add lines 22 and 23 and enter the total				
25	Subtract line 21 from line 24. If zero or less, enter -0-				▨
26	Enter the **smaller** of line 21 or line 24 here and on Form 2210, line 21 ▶				

Part II Annualized Self-Employment Tax

Form 2210 — Page **2**

Part IV Regular Method (See the instructions if you are filing Form 1040NR.)

		Payment Due Dates			
Section A—Figure Your Underpayment		(a) 4/15/94	(b) 6/15/94	(c) 9/15/94	(d) 1/15/95
21	**Required installments.** If box 1b applies, enter the amounts from Schedule AI, line 26. Otherwise, enter ¼ of line 13, Form 2210, in each column				
22	Estimated tax paid and tax withheld (see instructions). For column (a) only, also enter the amount from line 22 on line 26. If line 22 is equal to or more than line				

Enter your actual income from each quarter on line 1 of Form 2210 Schedule AI.

Transfer this amount to Form 2210 line 21.

Annualizing your income to calculate an underpayment penalty.

The Least You Need to Know

➤ Anyone is a potential candidate for an underpayment as far as the IRS is concerned *if* the amount of tax due on the Form 1040 is more than $500 and more than 10% of the tax you owe.

➤ The IRS will compute your penalty for you if you let them.

➤ Use Form 2210 to compute your underpayment penalty yourself.

➤ To avoid the underpayment penalty, use Form 2210 to show that you: paid in as much tax in 1995, prior to filing your tax return, to equal or exceed the tax on your 1994 tax return; paid in as much tax in 1995, prior to filing your tax return, to equal or exceed 90% of your 1995 total tax; or annualized your income and match your estimated payments to the quarters in which you earned your income.

Chapter 28

The Final Hour

In This Chapter

➤ Checking over your tax return for the last time

➤ FICA over-withholding

➤ Finalizing the tax payment/refund

➤ Putting together the pieces of your tax return

➤ Mailing your tax return

It's almost time to put this puppy to bed. You've worked hard and no doubt are ready to say a final sayonara to your tax return and send it on its way. You've come this far—wait just a few more minutes, read through this chapter, and see if there's anything you might have missed.

From A to Z: Last Chance Deductions You Might Have Overlooked

When you read through your tax return for the last time, checking to see if you've done everything you can to lower your tax bite, look for opportunities to save. Here's a hot handful of deductions that may apply to you that you may not have been aware of:

➤ Artificial limbs and teeth qualify as medical expenses on Schedule A.

➤ Baby-sitting while both spouses work counts toward the child and dependent care credit on Form 2441.

➤ Clothing and the cleaning thereof is a deductible miscellaneous expense on Schedule A if the clothing is a uniform required for your job and not suitable for everyday use.

➤ Dental expenses count as medical deductions on Schedule A.

➤ Employment agency fees can be considered deductible job-hunting expenses under miscellaneous deductions on Schedule A.

➤ Flowers sent to the funeral of a client can count as a business expense on Schedule C.

➤ Gambling losses, to the extent that there are offsetting gambling winnings, count as a miscellaneous deduction (not subject to the 2% adjusted gross income limit) on Schedule A.

➤ Hearing-Ear dogs, just like Seeing-Eye dogs, are allowed as medication deductions on Schedule A.

➤ Ice storms can generate casualty losses on Schedule A.

➤ Jury duty pay is included in other income on line 21 of your 1040. If you have to give the money to your employer because he or she is keeping you on salary, you can deduct the amount you give your employer as an adjustment to income. Just add the jury duty pay to the total adjustments on line 30 of the 1040, noting to the left of the amount that jury duty pay has been included.

➤ Keogh plan contributions of self-employed individuals are allowed as adjustments to income on page 1 of the 1040.

➤ Legal fees that are associated with earning your living or keeping your job are deductible as an employee business expense on Schedule A (or as a business deduction on Schedule C).

➤ Medicare premiums (Part B type) are deductible as medical expenses. The amount of allowable deduction will be noted on your Social Security form, SSA-1099.

➤ Newsletters that keep you abreast of investing trends are deductible as miscellaneous deductions on Schedule A—make sure that you have some investments producing income before you take this deduction.

➤ Overalls required to work on the job can qualify as a uniform expense under miscellaneous deductions on Schedule A.

➤ Parking fees can be deducted as an employee business expense on Schedule A or as a business expense on Schedule C if use of your car is required for your work.

➤ Qualified electric vehicles are eligible for a credit against your tax: purchase a primarily electric 4-wheel highway vehicle as a first-time owner and qualify for a tax credit of 10% of the cost up to $4,000; fill out Form 8834 and write in the amount of the credit on line 44 of your 1040.

➤ Repairs of business property are deductible as business expenses on Schedule C (rental property repairs go on Schedule E).

➤ Seminars that maintain or improve job skills are deductible as employee business expenses on Schedule A or can be included with other expenses on Schedule C.

➤ Taxi cab fares when incurred as part of your job are deductible as employee business expenses on Schedule A or can be included with other expenses on Schedule C.

➤ Union dues are deductible as employee business expenses on Schedule A.

➤ Vacation homes and the costs of maintaining the homes qualify as rental property expenses on Schedule E if the home is rented out for 15 days or more during the year.

➤ Water counts as a utility expense for the Office in the Home deduction on Schedule C.

➤ X-ray fees count as a medical expense on Schedule A.

➤ Year-end tax planning advice from an accountant or investment counselor counts as a miscellaneous deduction on Schedule A.

➤ Zero coupon bonds come in a tax-exempt variety—actually an income item rather than a deduction, zero coupon bonds represent an investment that earns interest that is either tax-deferred until the time at which the bond matures or, in some cases, tax exempt.

Your Personal FICA Kickback

If you work for more than one employer, don't overlook the little Social Security bonanza that may be waiting for you. Your employer is only supposed to withhold Social Security tax on the first $61,200 of your income. You should notice on your W-2 form the box called Social Security Wages. This number won't be higher than $61,200. However, if you work for more than one employer, *each employer has the right to withhold Social Security on wages up to $61,200.*

If the total of box 4 from all your W-2 forms is more than $3,794.40, you can treat the excess as a tax payment.

a Control number		Void	For Official Use Only ▶		
	22222	☐	OMB No. 1545-0008		

b Employer's identification number		1 Wages, tips, other compensation	2 Federal income tax withheld
c Employer's name, address, and ZIP code		3 Social security wages	4 Social security tax withheld
		5 Medicare wages and tips	6 Medicare tax withheld
		7 Social security tips	8 Allocated tips
d Employee's social security number		9 Advance EIC payment	10 Dependent care benefits
e Employee's name (first, middle initial, last)		11 Nonqualified plans	12 Benefits included in box 1
		13 See Instrs. for box 13	14 Other

15 Statutory employee ☐	Deceased ☐	Pension plan ☐	Legal rep. ☐	Hshld. emp. ☐	Subtotal ☐	Deferred compensation ☐

f Employee's address and ZIP code

16 State	Employer's state I.D. No.	17 State wages, tips, etc.	18 State income tax	19 Locality name	20 Local wages, tips, etc.	21 Local income tax

Cat. No. 10134D   Department of the Treasury—Internal Revenue Service

Form **W-2** **Wage and Tax Statement** **1995**

For Paperwork Reduction Act Notice, see separate instructions.

Copy A For Social Security Administration

Too much Social Security tax.

To see if too much Social Security tax has been withheld, add together the amounts in the boxes labeled Social Security Tax Withheld on all your W-2 forms. If this number exceeds $3,794.40, you have a refund coming.

To get a refund of your over-withheld Social Security tax, add up the Social Security withholding amounts from box 4 of each of your W-2 forms. Subtract $3,794.40 from the total. The difference is the amount of excess withholding. Enter this difference on line 59 of page 2 of the 1040. This excess withholding counts as one of your tax payments and gets applied against any tax you owe. If your withholding and estimated payments already cover the tax you owe, the IRS will refund the excess Social Security.

Computing the Bottom Line

Drumroll, please! It's time to add it all together and see how you come out. If your payments exceed your taxes—if line 61 of your 1040 is higher than line 54—you're in Refund Land. Subtract the payments from the taxes, enter the amount on line 62 of the 1040, and celebrate!

If you are entitled to a refund, you have another decision to make before finishing off this tax return. You can ask to have the refund mailed to you by repeating the full amount from line 62 on line 63, "Amount of line 62 you want **REFUNDED TO YOU**." Or you can request to have all or part of your refund credited to next year's tax by placing an amount on line 64.

If the taxes on line 54 exceed the payments on line 61, get out your checkbook. The difference goes on line 65, "**AMOUNT YOU OWE**" and you get the pleasure of writing a check payable to Internal Revenue Service for the amount due.

Assembling the Tax Return

You might think all you have to do at this point is gather up all your forms, shove them into an envelope addressed to the proper Internal Revenue Service Center (see "Where to Send the Return" in Chapter 2, "But Do I Have to File a Tax Return?"), and get down to the business of cleaning up the tax return preparation mess you left in your living room.

Not so fast! As with everything the government touches, there is an easy way and there is a government way to do things. In the case of mailing your tax return, you have to use the government way.

There is an order in which your tax forms are supposed to be stacked before they get mailed, and that order might surprise you. The 1040, page 1 and 2, goes on top of the stack. That's easy. From there on, you'd think you would just follow the schedule letters and form numbers to get the pages of your tax return lined up right. Wrong!

OOPS!

Not so fast! Before you write a check for the amount of tax on line 65, check line 66 to see if you computed an underpayment penalty (underpayment penalties are discussed in Chapter 27). The penalty on line 66 gets added to the amount on line 65 and your check should be written for the combined amount.

In the upper-right corner of each form (not including the 1040), right under the 1995, which may well be some secret number of its own but which bears a striking resemblance to the year for this tax return, there is a little secret number. You have to look closely to see this secret number.

For example on Form 2106, "Employee Business Expenses," the secret number is 54. On Form 6251, "Alternative Minimum Tax," the secret number, which you would think would come in somewhat higher than the number on Form 2106, is 32. And on Form 3903, "Moving Expenses," the secret number is 62. So if you use all three of these forms with your tax return, you have to use the secret numbers to know how to stack them behind your 1040:

Logical Order	IRS Order: Little Secret Number
Form 2106	Form 6251:32
Form 3903	Form 2106:54
Form 6251	Form 3903:62

You're supposed to know that this secret number represents the order in which you should put together the forms in your tax return. But how many tax returns have you mailed to the IRS in the past without ever noticing this secret number? Chances are the number is higher than any of the secret numbers lurking on these tax forms.

By the Way
Once you've assembled your income tax return and have managed to get a staple through it, don't forget to gather up your W-2 forms and staple them to the front page of the 1040. And that's not all. If you are sending a check to your favorite Uncle Sam, be sure to staple that onto the front of the 1040 too.

This is really a highly secret test being run by the revenue agents at the IRS. These are the same people who have the right to bring you into their office under the guise of conducting a tax audit and ask you personal questions about how often you do your laundry (if you had the nerve to take uniform expenses as a miscellaneous deduction on Schedule A) and when was the last time you mowed your lawn (if you tried to claim you see clients at your office in your home) while you sweat bullets. These IRS agents are conducting this test to see what kind of people actually read those little secret numbers and take the time to find out what they mean and then care enough to put their tax forms in the completely illogical secret number order.

The results of this secret test are being assembled even now, and we'll probably see some expensive government reports come out in the next five years, analyzing the personal eating and hygiene habits of people who can't figure out the order in which their tax forms go.

Free Pizza and Ice Cream! Getting Everything Mailed on Time

All right, you've figured out the order in which your tax forms go and you more or less put them that way. Now it's about 11:00 p.m. on April 15 and you start thinking about how you're going to get this tax return mailed before midnight and whether anyone would notice if you just draw your own April 15 postmark on the envelope and mail it tomorrow.

As in so many aspects of our lives, government agencies once again come to the rescue! Recent years have seen a new development in government services: the April 15 midnight post office party. At cities all across the country, people gather at the post office at midnight with hopes of getting free food and letting their friends see them on television because all the better television news stations send reporters and camerapeople, who would otherwise have to report on boring stuff such as murders and robberies and government corruption, to the post office to take pictures of all the people who couldn't get their tax returns mailed any earlier. The post offices encourage local restaurants to bring samples of their food to pass out to the hungry taxpayers who are bleary-eyed from trying to read the secret numbers on their tax returns. It's like a Taste of _____ (fill in the blank with your city name) right in the post office parking lot. People actually go to the post office at midnight on April 15 just to watch other people mail their tax returns (and to get some free food).

Don't Go Yet! Final Preparations Before Mailing Your Tax Return

Here it is, my top ten list of things you need to do before you put that tax return in the mail:

Top Ten Things People Usually Forget to Do Before Mailing Tax Returns:

10. Sign the tax return (bottom of page 2 of the 1040).

9. Sign forms other than the 1040. (Don't just flip through the pages signing your name on available blank lines. Look through the forms—a few of them require signatures at the bottom.)

8. Sign your state tax return. (Just because the feds have the April 15 limelight, don't forget to give attention to your state return.)

7. Check the order of the forms (those little secret numbers, remember?).

6. Include Social Security numbers and tax ID numbers on your child and dependent care expenses form (Form 2441).

5. Save your appetite if you're going to the post office around midnight on April 15.

4. Take a few minutes to look over each form and see if you missed anything.

3. Staple your tax forms together so they don't get separated.

2. Attach W-2 forms to the front of page 1 of the 1040.

And the number one thing to remember to do before you unleash your tax return on the IRS:

1. Attach your check, if you owe the IRS, to the front of your 1040.

The Least You Need to Know

➤ It's worth your time to take a few relaxing minutes to go over your tax return after it's finished, looking for things that didn't get filled in or potential deductions you might have missed.

➤ If you have two employers and earned over $61,200, you probably had too much Social Security tax withheld—the excess Social Security tax can be treated as a tax payment on your 1040.

➤ The IRS gives you a clue in the form of secret numbers to help you organize your forms.

➤ Check out the party at your local post office on April 15—even if your tax return was filed months ago!

Chapter 29

Changing Your Tax Return

In This Chapter

➤ Oops! I made a mistake on my tax return!

➤ I filed my tax return two years ago and now I want to change it!

➤ Amending state income tax returns

Into this world of complex income tax returns comes the realization that sometimes, hard as it is to believe, people make mistakes and omissions. Hang on, though. You don't have to wallow in regret about that missed deduction for little Jimmy's orthodontic implant and you no longer have to hide your head in shame because you forgot to report the interest on your old savings account from the grade school banking program.

Leave it to your pals at the IRS to find a way for you to fix tax returns that might not have started out correctly.

Amending Your 1040: The 1040X

Use Form 1040X, "Amended U.S. Individual Income Tax Return," to change or remove amounts that appeared erroneously in your original 1040 or to add to that original form. A copy of Form 1040X appears in Appendix B of this book.

Fill in the top portion of the 1040X, identifying your name and address (use your current address if your address has changed since your original 1040 was prepared). There's a line for entering the original address (and name too, if applicable) if it has changed since you filed the original tax return.

By the Way

You can prepare a Form 1040X to change your filing status. You can't, however, change from Married Filing Jointly to Married Filing Separately after the due date for your original tax return has passed.

Enter the location of the Internal Revenue Service Center where you originally filed your 1040. If you have moved since you filed the original 1040, the address to which you mailed the original 1040 is not necessarily the same location to which you will file this amended return. Send the 1040X to the Internal Revenue Service Center address based on where you live now. The Service Center addresses are in Chapter 2, "But Do I Have to File a Tax Return?".

There are a few questions to answer at the top of the 1040X about your contact with the IRS and this tax return—the IRS wants to know if you are amending this return as a result of some communication with the IRS.

If your filing status is changing on this tax return, you can check the appropriate box for the new status. Note, however, that you cannot change from Married Filing Jointly to Married Filing Separately. That change has to be made before the original due date of the tax return.

By the Way

References in this book are to amending your original income tax return. You can also amend an amended return. Fill in numbers in the left column of the 1040X from the *last version of the tax return that was filed*, whether that is the original 1040 or the most recent 1040X.

The 1040X can also be used to change your dependents and exemptions. Changes in these items get made on the top of page 2 of the 1040X.

In the body of the Form 1040X there are three columns. Fill in the left column with numbers right off your original Form 1040.

In the column all the way to the right, fill in the corrected numbers. The middle column represents the difference between column A and column C. Just subtract A from C to get the amount for column B.

Down at the bottom of page 1 of the 1040X you can compute the tax based on the new, revised numbers.

Whenever you file a 1040X, you not only have to fill out the front of the return, you also have to explain yourself on the back. Use Part II to describe, line by line, the changes you've made to your original 1040.

Time Limits for Amending Your Income Tax Return

You can't just send in a 1040X whenever you please for any tax year from your gnarly past. There are rules about these things.

You can't file a 1040X until you have filed the 1040. That just makes sense. Until you file the 1040 you have nothing to amend.

You can't file a 1040X more than three years after the date the *original* 1040 was filed. You can stretch this a bit, however. Suppose that you filed your original 1040 on February 26, 1993. You would think you would have until February 26, 1996, to amend the original 1040. Not so! When considering the deadline for filing Form 1040X, the IRS treats your original 1040 as having been filed on April 15 (the due date) of the year in which it was due. So the 1040 filed February 26, 1993, can be amended all the way up until April 15, 1996.

Don't Forget Your State!

When amending your federal income tax return, remember that changes to numbers "above the line"—that is, changes that affect your adjusted gross income—will probably flow through into your state income tax return.

Contact the revenue department in your state and ask them to send you a form for amending a state income tax return.

Read the rules for your state amended tax return to see if there are any specific requirements regarding attachments of forms. You probably will have to attach a copy of your federal 1040X to the state return.

The Least You Need to Know

➤ If you want to change a number on your 1040 after it's been filed, use Form 1040X.

➤ Form 1040X has to be filed within three years of the due date of your original 1040 (or three years from the date you actually filed it, if that date is later than the due date).

➤ Don't forget to consider amending your state income tax return if the federal 1040 is changing.

"Greetings, Taxpayer..."

It's one of those perfect days—the sun is shining, the weather is warm, the birds are singing in the trees, children are playing in the yard, you're happy in your work, all is right with the world. And then, you open the mailbox. Nestled in amongst the bills and ads and magazines is a brown envelope that suddenly looks larger than life itself. Glaring back at you from the return address corner are the words, "Internal Revenue Service."

Suddenly dark clouds swirl overhead, a chill cuts through the air, children run for cover, and your once serene world is filled with uncertainty as you stand there, staring at the envelope, feeling your self-confidence and your faith in the federal government crumbling around you.

It is the tax audit, the IRS examination, the bane of our existence. Your mind conjures up all the stories you've heard of people who go into audits and never come back, or at least never come back the same. House, livelihood, car, children—all are seized by the ruthless thugs who call themselves tax collectors. It's the stuff of late-night B movies and novels that never got published. Scary stuff, these tax audits.

So what is an audit and why do taxpayers have to have them? The tax system is a voluntary system. The government sends out millions of tax forms each December and then crosses its fingers and hopes millions of taxpayers will send the forms back. The main way the IRS has of ensuring that taxpayers comply with filing tax returns is to check up on them from time to time. So checking on compliance is one reason that there are audits.

Another reason the IRS audits tax returns is to find out what to expect. Every few years the IRS chooses a handful of professions and goes looking for tax returns filed by members of those professions. Audits of those tax returns provide the IRS with information about the earnings and deductions of the typical doctor, lawyer, teacher, shoe salesperson, and so on. The information garnered from these audits is used to set standards for analyzing other tax returns for members of the same professions. Once the IRS knows what the typical ice cream vendor earns and deducts, it can look at the tax returns of other ice cream vendors to see if their tax returns are similar to the norm. Ice cream costs too high? Audit time.

First, let me explain who gets selected; then I'll try to put some of your fears to rest as I describe the audit process as an experience that perhaps you won't relish, but at least you don't need to dread.

Why Me?

There are many reasons why tax returns get selected for audit. Remember that it is the *tax return* that is getting selected, not the *taxpayer*. You're not under fire, just the pieces of paper that you mailed last April. The first rule to surviving a tax audit is: Don't take it personally.

Here are some of the reasons why your tax return might have gotten selected for audit:

➤ **Just lucky, I guess.** Some returns each year get selected purely by chance.

➤ **Right place at the wrong time.** Every couple of years the IRS chooses a particular kind of taxpayer to go after—doctors, lawyers, hairdressers, firefighters—it doesn't matter what the category is. The interesting thing to remember is that the real reason the IRS has chosen a particular category of taxpayer to examine is not because they have anything personal against that type of taxpayer, but because they are trying to gather statistics about what kinds of income and deductions those types of taxpayers have.

➤ **You've been here before.** If you've been audited in the past and the IRS has found errors in your tax return, you are a more likely candidate for a repeat audit—the IRS's way of checking to see if you've cleaned up your act.

➤ **Someone doesn't like you.** The IRS is not above listening to tattle-tales. In fact, they pay a bounty for tips that lead them to people who may be filing returns that aren't quite on the up and up.

➤ **You amended your tax return from a prior year.** Amending your return can call attention to yourself. It's like turning in a paper late at school. People notice.

What to Do if You Get Audited

It may seem like a good time to plan that extended out-of-the-country excursion when the audit notice arrives. Don't bother. You can't escape. You can't cajole your way out of it either. You may be able to reschedule your examination appointment if there is a time that would be better for you, but for the most part, you might as well grin and bear it.

As an alternative to a traditional audit where you have to walk down the IRS corridors, shamefaced, and present yourself as the sacrificial lamb to the tax examiner, the IRS sometimes prefers to participate in the quick and dirty audit. The quick and dirty audit comes to you as a statement in the mail labeled, "Statement of Changes to Your Account." The Statement of Changes simply states that the IRS has taken it upon itself to alter some of the numbers on your tax return.

Remember that whether you find yourself under the bare, dangling light bulb in the basement of the IRS building undergoing an audit, or you receive a notice in the mail saying they've already made the changes, YOU ARE NOT AT THE MERCY OF THE IRS! There are proper ways to contest the changes that the IRS wants to make to your tax return. See "When and How to Appeal" later in this chapter.

Stay Calm

One of the most important things to remember if the IRS invites you in for an examination, is to not get nuts about it. All the IRS wants to do is ask you some specific questions about the numbers on your tax return. Pretend you are explaining to your spouse or your tax accountant where the numbers come from. The IRS agent is just another person. (I can say that with a straight face on paper—it's a good thing you can't see me!)

Assuming that you did your best job of gathering information for your tax return and you believe that the numbers you presented represent the actual financial activity in your household for the year under audit, you have nothing to fear.

If you fudged on some of the documentation for your tax return, if you guessed at numbers, if you stretched the truth, forgot to report income, fabricated deductions—basically, if you cheated—then you might not be quite so comfortable going to an audit.

What Do I Bring with Me to an Audit?

Bring exactly the items for which the IRS asks. Along with your audit notice you will receive a list of items they want to see. If the IRS has requested specific documents or forms, you must bring those with you to your audit if you possibly can. If you've been asked to bring canceled checks to support the deductions on your Schedule C, bring the canceled checks. Can't find the canceled checks? Then try to find something that will provide the same information, such as receipts showing amounts you spent or your check register. You may be able to request copies of canceled checks from your bank.

If you can't find the specifically requested support that you need for your deductions, don't give up. Look for other evidence that will back up the numbers. Remember, when you spend money there are two parties involved in the transaction. Try checking with the person or organization to whom you paid the money in order to get evidence to support your deductions.

Don't bring items for which the IRS hasn't asked. If you give the IRS something "extra" (such as receipts or statements that go beyond the items the IRS requested), then they have the right to question you on those items as well. Don't complicate the audit by introducing new information. For example, if you are supposed to bring the canceled checks to support your postage and freight expenses, don't bring *all* of your canceled checks—just bring the checks relating to postage and freight.

If it turns out the evidence you bring with you to the IRS audit is not sufficient to support the amounts on your tax return, you can ask for additional time to gather information.

Face to Face (Sort of) with the IRS

You have the right to not present yourself alone in front of the IRS. You may bring a tax accountant or a lawyer or even a friend or a family member to your audit and you may authorize that person to answer questions on your behalf.

You also have the right to send a tax accountant or a lawyer in your place to the audit. You don't even have to go! To be represented by someone at the audit, the person you choose must be approved to practice before the IRS and you must sign a Power of Attorney form designating that person as the person who may answer tax-related questions on your behalf. Most practicing CPAs and lawyers and many non-CPA accountants are approved to practice before the IRS, and all of them will have Power of Attorney forms that you can sign. No matter how much the IRS agent may want to talk to someone else, without the signed Power of Attorney form, he or she cannot discuss your tax situation with anyone but you.

If you go to your audit yourself, remember the rules your mother taught you: Dress nicely and be polite. Don't interrupt, don't cough without covering your mouth, don't use slang, don't pick your nose—you know, the basic "act like a grown-up" stuff.

The Most Important Rule

Here it is, the most important rule to remember when facing down an IRS agent. KNOW WHAT THE AGENT HAS A RIGHT TO ASK AND DON'T GIVE HIM OR HER ANY ADDITIONAL INFORMATION.

As nice as we want to believe the IRS agents are, and some of them actually are real people, just like you and me, just trying to do a job, remember that they are also machines. They are trained to delve and probe and ask leading questions and find out everything they can about you.

When you get your notice in the mail telling you that you are about to be blessed with an audit, there will be a list with that letter telling you exactly what the tax examiner is concerned with. It may be that there is some question about your miscellaneous deductions on Schedule A, maybe your interest income is the issue, perhaps you have a Schedule C and a hefty business meal deduction has caught the ever-watchful eye of the IRS.

Look this list over carefully. No matter what things are being examined, the items on that list are the ONLY things the IRS agent has a right to ask questions about, and the receipts that support those items are the only things the agent has a right to see.

Throughout the audit, remember the things on the list. If your Schedule C is being examined and the IRS agent asks if you have support for the contribution deduction you took on Schedule A, your answer is not, "Uh, I think so," nor is it, "Well, of course I do!" (even if that is the true answer). Your answer is, "I'm sorry. That wasn't on the list you sent me and I didn't come prepared to answer questions about contributions." Then stop. Don't say any more. Don't try to fill empty space with conversation. Answer every question the auditor asks completely and succinctly but don't offer more than the question asks and don't answer questions about things that aren't on the list.

If the auditor feels he or she has reason to ask you questions that go beyond the list, he or she needs to prepare a new list that you can take home with you and to set a new appointment, and you need to plan on coming back with support for the additional things the auditor wants. If you think there's no connection between the new things the auditor is asking for and the original list, check with a tax professional in the interim period between audit visits.

When and How to Appeal

Okay, you've been to the audit (whew!), the auditor has made suggested changes to your original return, and you are asked to pay more money to the IRS.

If you agree with the changes, pay your tax and put the entire experience behind you. If, however, you want to object to the changes, you have that right as well.

Your first step is to call the auditor with whom you originally had your meeting. Discuss the areas of disagreement over the phone or arrange for another meeting. Ask if there is more information that you can bring in that would help establish your case. Maybe there was some misunderstanding. The auditor wants this situation cleared up as much as you do (honest!), so talk it out and see if you can reach an agreement.

If the auditor won't budge, ask for either a telephone or a personal audience with a manager. The manager has the right to override the auditor's decision. Maybe you just didn't explain things well enough to the auditor, or maybe there was a personality conflict and you'll get along better with the manager. Know that the manager will want to back the auditor, but that doesn't mean the manager won't listen to your story and give you a chance to explain your disagreement with the auditor.

If you can't settle up between the auditor and the auditor's manager, your next stop is the appeal process.

There's little reason not to file an appeal with the IRS, unless you have something on this tax return you want to hide. If you truly believe the IRS is wrong and can support your theory, go for it. An appeal is free and chances are (even if you don't get the IRS to go along with you on appeal) you will be able to reach a settlement that will lower the tax bill. At the very least the appeal process postpones the time when you have to pay the IRS the amount that was determined you owe at the audit.

You can appeal on your own or you can hire a tax professional to help you (then, of course, the appeal is no longer free...).

If you get a notice from the auditor setting out the findings of the audit and the additional amount the IRS thinks you owe, and you want to appeal this notice, don't sign it and don't mail it in. The IRS will send you another notice called a "30-Day Letter," which sets out your appeal rights and to which you have 30 days to respond. It is important that you respond within the 30 days.

To respond to a 30-Day Letter, prepare a letter of your own—a personal letter—setting out precisely what you disagree with on the audit and your reasons for disagreement. Attach the 30-Day Letter to your letter and mail them both to the IRS address designated on the 30-Day Letter.

An appeals conference will be scheduled for you, much like the audit conference, but with a different, higher-up person. This person has the right to negotiate and settle cases. When you attend the conference, bring all your documentation supporting your side of the story, present your case clearly and succinctly (again, you can bring someone with you if you like), and listen to see with the appeals officer has to say.

If the officer agrees with you, pat yourself on the back and tell yourself the system works after all. The appeals officer won't disagree with you without explaining the law behind his decision. Make sure that you understand the law as the officer explains it. There might be more things that you can bring the officer that will support your claim. Once the two of you understand each other, if the IRS still thinks you owe more tax, you can suggest a settlement. You might be able to work out a payment amount and arrangement that is mutually acceptable.

Your avenues of protest don't stop with the appeals officer. If you feel you have a strong case, you can go to tax court and even to the U.S. Supreme Court to argue your case. The higher up in the court system, the more likely you will need professional assistance. You'll have to weigh both the cost of the tax at issue and the value of arguing for your principles with the cost of hiring professional help in order to take you through the court system.

The Least You Need to Know

➤ Anybody can get audited—even you!

➤ Don't be afraid of auditors; they're (more or less) people just like you and me.

➤ Mom's rules apply: Remember to be polite when meeting the IRS agent.

➤ You have the right to appeal any decision by the IRS.

Part 6
Automating Tax Preparation with Your (Deductible) Computer

"Unquestionably, there is progress. The average American now pays out almost as much in taxes alone as he formerly got in wages."

H. L. Mencken, 1949

When I took my first computer class in college, there was one computer on campus and it filled an entire room of a building. I wrote my computer programs out long-hand, then diligently keypunched the hundreds of cards necessary for inputting the programs into the machine. It took approximately 24 hours from the time I submitted a program to the time when I would get the results. One little comma out of place would send me back to the keypunch machines, punching more cards, waiting another 24 hours for my results.

To think of that experience in comparison with the ease of turning on an income tax software program on my home computer, viewing tax forms on the screen, typing in numbers to fill in the blanks—it takes my breath away.

Chapter 31

Deciding to Join the Electronic Age

In This Chapter

➤ What is tax preparation software?

➤ Advantages to using tax preparation software

➤ Disadvantages to using tax preparation software

➤ How does the IRS feel about tax preparation software?

Some things evolve slowly, taking thousands of years to change. Continents shift, weather patterns alter, glaciers melt. Then there's the burgeoning computer industry in which glacier-like changes take place in a time period of months, changes in weather patterns not only happen instantaneously, you can track them on-screen and predict them for any point in the world, and continents no longer need to shift—they're all linked electronically through massive network systems.

The computer may actually be the key to saving the world. For the first time in recorded history, all the people of the world are joined in a common cause—communication. Foreign lands seem much less foreboding when you can communicate with their residents right from your desktop. Even as you read this, governments of the world continue to do battle while their constituents chat over telephone wires late into the night. Someday, I predict that computers will help people understand each other to the point that they can overcome the differences that drive them to war. Who knows, Bill Gates may win the Nobel Peace Prize yet...

What Will a Computer Program Do for Me?

More and more people have computers in their homes. In an effort to provide a service that is useful to many Americans, several companies have produced their version of tax preparation software—computer programs designed to accept all the pieces of information that go into your income tax return and spit out the forms you need, all filled out and ready for you to sign.

Generally speaking, computer tax preparation programs all do the same thing. They provide you with the ability to type on the computer keyboard the numbers and pieces of information that are required for the preparation of your tax return and they print a tax return that is acceptable to the IRS.

So what's the advantage of a computer program over filling out the forms yourself? Here is a list of several advantages:

➤ **You don't have to scrounge around for tax forms.** The computer program prints them out for you.

➤ **You can change your mind.** Alter one little number on one form of your computer-prepared tax return and the computer program will look at every other form in your tax return and make appropriate changes.

➤ **You can save time.** Save the amount of time spent figuring out what forms you need and then attempting to get them to your house. Also, save the amount of time it takes to enter information on one form and then make sure that information gets carried to all other appropriate forms.

➤ **You don't have to be good with numbers.** The program performs a calculation of your income tax instantaneously.

➤ **You don't have to try to figure out difficult, confusing forms.** Just try reading the instructions to Form 6251, "Alternative Minimum Tax," for example, and you'll understand the benefit of a computer tax preparation program.

➤ **You can prepare a return suitable for electronic filing right in the comfort of your home.** The future trend in tax return filing is electronic, if the IRS has anything to say about it. Be on the cutting edge by preparing your return in the style appropriate to electronic filing, then dispatch it to an electronic filing center via modem from your home, or take it to such a center in your town.

➤ **You really don't have to understand how the tax forms link together.** The computer program will tie all the forms together and carry information from one to the next as appropriate.

➤ **Carryovers are a snap!** If you used a tax preparation program last year, all carryover amounts as well as boring stuff such as your name, address, and Social Security number are carried forward to the current year's return.

Okay, so there are advantages to using a computer program. What about disadvantages to automating your tax preparation process? Here is a list of several disadvantages:

➤ **You have to buy a computer.** Sorry, but a computer tax preparation program doesn't work by osmosis.

➤ **You have to know a little bit about computers, like how to turn one on and how to install a tax program (beyond that, it's amazing how little you need to know).**

➤ **You also have to know a little bit about taxes.** The computer tax programs can hold your hand and pull you along through the tax preparation process, but it helps immensely if you understand what the program is asking for when it poses a question like, "Did you contribute to a tax-sheltered annuity in 1995?" or "Did you incur any intangible drilling costs during 1995?"

By the Way
They say nothing in life is free, and electronic tax filing is not nothing. Expect to pay a fee to file your tax return electronically. Because you have to pay a fee to file your income tax return electronically, it's usually not cost effective to file your tax return electronically if you owe taxes with the return.

➤ **You have to figure out which computer tax program to buy, and then listen to your neighbor talk about his or her program which will always sound better than the one you picked.**

Computer tax programs aren't human; they do some confusing things and sometimes they just stop working for no apparent reason at all. You may find yourself in computer tax program panic mode on the eve of April 15 if you're new to computers and you wait until the last minute to try out the program.

Will I Ever Be the Same Again?

Do you stay awake nights wondering about this computer revolution and what it's doing to our lifestyles? Well, no, most people don't. But the fact is that having a computer can and probably will change your lifestyle, and having a computer tax preparation program will probably give you a level of tax preparation confidence that you may otherwise lack.

There's something about seeing professional-looking tax forms shooting out of your printer, all filled out and all adding up properly, that gives the observer a little rush, a sense of awe at where we are today compared to where we were back in 1913.

I expect that if you have a computer and try one of the many tax preparation programs on the market today, you will probably not go back to preparing your tax return by hand.

Will the IRS Like My Computer-Generated Tax Return?

Not only will the IRS like your computer-generated tax return, you can expect a quicker turn-around in processing time with a return prepared on a computer, simply because it's easier to read than one written by hand.

And, because the IRS is attempting to move into an era of electronic tax preparation alternatives, you will find yourself positioned to participate in the electronic trend if you prepare your tax return on a computer.

In the extremely near future, you will be able to take your tax return information to terminals situated in banks and other prominent locations and electronically transmit your tax return to the IRS. This system is under experimentation in 1995. Phone-in tax return filing has been tested for the past two years. The IRS is determined to reduce paperwork and improve accuracy of tax returns and it is convinced that computers provide the answer to those problems.

Picking and Choosing a Tax Software Program

Chapter 32, "Choosing a Software Program," and Chapter 33, "Taking a Look at the Competition," discuss the methods for choosing a tax software program. Refer to these chapters before contemplating the purchase of either a new computer or a tax program to run on it.

The Least You Need to Know

➤ Do-it-yourself computer software programs seem to be the rage.

➤ Electronic tax return filing is for those who have no penalty associated with their tax return.

EEMY, MEENY, MINY, MOE...

Choosing a Software Program

In This Chapter

➤ What things to look for in a tax preparation software program

➤ How to make a decision

➤ Installing the program

➤ Troubleshooting software programs

You're going to find, as you survey the market of available tax software programs, that each one does essentially the same thing: it enables you to prepare your income tax return on a computer. That, of course, is what you want it to do. Beyond that, the choice is personal. What do you like about certain programs? If everyone liked exactly the same thing, there would only be a need for one program on the market.

How Do I Start?

Before there were computer programs, there were computers. Start with the hardware. If you already have a computer, you're in business. If you're not yet a member of the byte-set, your first step is to acquire a computer.

If you want a computer only for your tax preparation and you'll never use it again for the rest of your life, you probably don't want to make a big investment. Instead, consider renting a machine for a month, or check with a friend. You'd be surprised how many computer people have "out-of-date, but-still-perfectly-good" machines sitting around the dark recesses of their house. (I have four computers at my house due to my constant motivation to upgrade.) Check with people you know who use computers regularly, see if they have last year's model sitting idle, and, while you're at it, recruit the friend to help you with your software selection and installation.

Computers come in all different sizes and shapes. Before purchasing a computer software program, make sure that it will run on the computer you have. Find out the vital statistics about your computer—chip size, RAM size, and hard disk capacity (if you don't know these things, ask your children or enlist the aid of the nearest 11-year-old). Take this information with you when you go to the store to purchase your tax software. Compare your numbers with those listed on the box as the minimum hardware requirements. Your numbers need to be greater than or equal to the numbers on the box.

What Should I Expect from a Tax Program?

Okay, you know you want your tax return program to produce a tax return for you. (Wouldn't it be nice if you could just wave your hand over the box and presto! A tax return is born!) But what else makes up a good tax return program? There are lots of criteria to consider when making a purchase.

OOPS!
Don't judge a book by its cover—and the same goes for computer programs. With so many sources of information available, as mentioned in this chapter, no one should ever have to make an uninformed computer purchase again.

How do you determine what a program is going to do? Look at the box and look at the manual inside the box. Most software shops will let you open a box—some will even let you play with the program on one of their machines. If you're lucky, you may find someone behind the counter who will demonstrate the program for you.

Check magazine articles, especially in computer magazines. Each spring articles appear about the latest tax software programs, showing representative screens and output. Many bookstores and libraries offer computer-oriented magazines.

Ask your friends with computers. More and more people are using tax programs and have opinions about the ones they use and others they have seen. Ask around. You'll be surprised at how much insight you can get this way.

Call your local computer users group. You'll probably find such a group in the phone book. They can provide advice and suggestions about buying software. They may even have a demonstration planned for a spring meeting, showing the various tax software programs.

No matter which program you pick, they're all going to do the same things:

➤ **Appearance.** Tax programs produce forms that are eye-appealing and professional looking.

➤ **Ease of use.** All the major tax programs have features that walk you through the preparation of your tax return, asking questions on-screen to guide you in entering all the proper information.

➤ **Help and assistance.** An important factor of any tax program is its ability to provide on-screen help. Pop-up help screens, reproductions of IRS instructions, interpretations of those instructions—these are the sorts of features you want to find in your tax program. Some programs provide more on-screen help than others. Manuals come with the programs, some better than others. Independently published books have been written to help users with some of the programs. All the programs provide telephone support as well, but getting through to telephone support desks in the spring is like trying to climb a wall of ice wearing roller skates. You're better off finding a friend who has used the program if the on-screen help and the manuals aren't enough.

➤ **Forms.** You want a program that can produce all the forms you need. Typically the programs will list all their forms on the box. If not, ask to open the box and look at the manual. If a program doesn't produce a form you need in your tax return, the usefulness of the program declines rapidly.

➤ **State taxes.** You might want to use your program to produce state income tax returns as well as federal returns. Some of the programs do states, some do not. Some that do states don't do *all* states. Check out the state situation carefully if it is important to you. Also find out if the state tax program is a separate program from the federal program or if they are combined in one box. If the state is a separate program, that will also mean an extra cost.

➤ **Price.** Do a little price shopping. Not only is there some disparity in price among the different programs, you can find the same program priced drastically differently at different stores. Save yourself some window-shopping time by calling around and asking for prices. Unlike a word-processing program that you might purchase once and use for years, the tax program is a throw-away after the tax year ends. When considering the price of a program, remember that you will need to purchase a new program each year.

➤ **Timing.** Several tax programs come out with early bird versions before the end of the tax year, to get a jump on the market and to let people like you experiment a bit with the program before the April crunch. You'll start seeing these programs around November. If you purchase a tax program before the end of 1995, you will have to get a final version of the program before you can actually produce your tax return. Check the information that came with the early version. There will be a form to send in or a number to call if you are to receive the final version in the mail. Alternatively, there might be a coupon to take back to the store where you bought the program and trade it in for a copy of the final version. Typically there is no additional charge for the final version of a tax program if you purchased the early version.

Performance

Computer tax preparation programs with a track record are your best bets. If a new program comes out onto the market this spring, wait until it has grown some legs before trying it out. The last thing you want is to be stuck with an unfinished tax return as April 15 nears.

There are several tax programs that have been around for years (some of them are mentioned in Chapter 33, "Taking a Look at the Competition"). I feel safer choosing a program that has proven itself than experimenting with something completely new—especially if you are new yourself to the whole process of computer tax returns.

A little research in the public library's periodical section can give you insight as to how a particular program has performed in the past, as can friends who have used the program.

Speed

Again, you're going to have to do some experimentation to find out about the speed of a program, and word of mouth is often one of the best ways to discover information like this.

The speed of a program is in part dependent on the equipment you use. Slower computer equipment and slower printers make a program run slowly.

If you get a chance to sample some programs, run a test. Produce the same form containing the same information on more than one program and time the programs as they work.

Automatic Transmission

You want a program that is going to install easily onto your computer and will then be easy to access when you want to use it. Ask the clerk at the computer shop or a friend who uses the program, *"How do I start this program once it's on my machine?"* A simple enough sounding question, but an important one, especially if you are relatively new to computers and don't want to have to rely on your own expertise to poke around the computer and find the program.

AM/FM Stereo Sound

You may not find stereo sound on your program (actually, it's available if you have the right equipment), but almost all computer tax programs have some forms of "bells and whistles." Many of the programs run in the Windows environment and have attractive screens. Particularly nice are programs that show you the actual tax form on-screen as you are filling it in. Some programs use a mouse; others use menus you have to access from your keyboard.

Don't be too concerned about the looks and gimmicks of a tax program. If it does what you want it to do in terms of producing a tax return and if the price is right, those should be your main concerns.

Demos and Other Freebies

Call the companies that produce tax programs (see Chapter 33 for some names and phone numbers). Often they will send out demos of their programs with which you can experiment. They might also have descriptive brochures that they can send that will help you analyze what the program can do and if you think you will like it.

Check with friends or computer clubs who might have copies of last year's version of the programs around gathering dust. You may be able to experiment with a copy of last year's program before you decide whether you want to make a purchase yourself.

What if I Can't Get This Thing to Work?

So, you've taken the plunge, you've purchased a computer tax preparation program, you managed to install it on your computer, and...nothing!

If your program doesn't seem to work, try reinstalling it and make sure that you follow all the installation instructions to the letter.

Still no luck? Check the manual or whatever paperwork accompanied the program. There may be some step you need to take before the program can be used.

If the program is still not working the way you think it should, call the technical support number that comes with the software. You may have to hold for a while to get someone on the phone, but eventually the company that made the program can provide you with someone who can walk you through the beginning stages of getting the program running.

The Least You Need to Know

➤ Look for a tax program that will work on your computer.

➤ Determine your needs before you shop.

➤ Try to get demos or copies of last year's program to see how a program works and to help determine whether you'll like it.

➤ Check around to various stores and compare prices.

➤ The software company won't let you down. If you have problems with the program, call them and they can help.

317

Hmmmmn...

Chapter 33

Taking a Look at the Competition

In This Chapter

➤ A summary of key features analyzed in the tax programs

➤ TurboTax for DOS/Windows

➤ Parson's Personal Tax Edge for DOS/Windows

➤ Kiplinger's Tax Cut

This analysis of various individual income tax preparation packages is not meant to be exhaustive, rather it is meant to give you a sense of what is available in the marketplace and what you can expect to pay to acquire a tax program.

In considering the following programs, I looked at the following factors:

➤ Overall appearance

➤ Ease of installation

➤ Hardware requirements

➤ Available platforms (Windows, DOS, Macintosh, and so on)

➤ Variety of tax forms supported

➤ Quality of printed forms

➤ Available on-screen help

➤ Availability of telephone support

➤ Release schedule

➤ Accompanying documentation

➤ State tax considerations

TurboTax for DOS and Windows

Retail cost, federal: $29.95
Retail cost, CD-ROM: $39.95
Retail cost, per state: $24.95

TurboTax is available in both DOS and Windows formats as well as in a CD-ROM version.

TurboTax for DOS features a mostly monochromatic screen with no graphical interface like you see in the slick Windows programs. All of your commands are available on-screen in drop-down menus or, in some cases, in buttons that you can click with a mouse, if you prefer to use one.

TurboTax for Windows features a glitzy graphical interface that was completely revamped for 1994 tax returns. All your commands are available on-screen in drop-down menus and buttons that you can click with the mouse.

The DOS program installs easily on any IBM-type computer and requires 6MB of hard disk space, DOS version 3.0 or greater, and at least 640K of RAM.

The Windows program installs easily on an IBM-type computer with 15MB of available hard disk space, Windows version 3.1 or greater, and at least 4MB of RAM.

All major tax forms are supported. When printing in the DOS program, the two-page 1040 form prints graphically like the IRS form, but the rest of the forms print in a more narrative, nongraphical format. The IRS has approved use of all TurboTax for DOS forms.

When printing in the Windows program, all major tax forms print in full graphic style, just like the IRS forms.

Help is available on-screen in the form of technical help for the program as well as IRS instructions. Telephone support (not toll-free) is available year-round with extended hours during the spring. Plan on waiting on hold for long periods of time during the spring months. Technical support is also available via modem link to subscribers of CompuServe and GEnie. The manual accompanying the program describes how to use the on-screen features of the program.

TurboTax releases a Head Start version in October each year. Purchase of the Head Start version, which costs $10.00, enables you to do some preliminary work on your tax return before the final version comes out in January. All files created in the Head Start version transfer directly into the final version.

TurboTax mails its newsletter in the fall and winter to former registered users of the program. The newsletter contains tips and news about release dates.

TurboTax for DOS and Windows support all states with an individual tax return package available for each state.

Parson's Personal Tax Edge

Retail cost, federal alone: $19.00
Retail cost, federal with planning software: $29.00
Retail cost, state: $19.00

Personal Tax Edge is available for both DOS and Windows as well as in a CD-ROM version. There is not a Macintosh version. The DOS program features a mostly monochromatic, text-based screen.

The program installs easily on an IBM-type computer. The Windows version requires 10MB of available hard disk space, Windows 3.1 or higher, and 2MB of RAM.

All major tax forms are supported and print in full graphic style, just like the IRS forms. Both the DOS and Windows versions print graphic forms. You can use a laser printer, inkjet printer, or a 24-pin dot matrix printer. The IRS has approved use of all Personal Tax Edge forms.

Help is available on-screen in the form of IRS instructions, a tax glossary, and extensive program assistance. Telephone support (not toll-free) is available Monday–Friday, 7 a.m. to 10 p.m. Central Time, year-round. From late December to mid-April, telephone support is available from 7 a.m. to midnight Monday–Friday and 9 a.m. to 6 p.m. Saturday and Sunday.

Parson's releases a planning version in mid-October each year. Purchasing the planning version, which costs $10.00 more than the final version, automatically qualifies you to receive the final version in the mail as soon as it is available, after the first of the year. Be sure to register your planning version over the phone with Parson's, or mail in the card that accompanies the program.

Parson's supports all states with an individual tax return package known as the State Tax Edge available for each state.

> OOOOH...
>
> **By the Way**
> Parson's is introducing a Windows 95 version of the software this year—the only one of the three programs described in this chapter that has a separate version for this platform. Any of the three programs, however, will run in Windows 95.

Kiplinger's Tax Cut

Retail cost, federal: $39.95
Retail cost, planning version: $39.95 (automatically qualifies you for free final version)
Retail cost, CD-ROM version: $39.00
Retail cost, state: $24.95

Kiplinger's Tax Cut is available for both DOS and Windows as well as in a CD-ROM version. The DOS program features a mostly monochromatic screen with no graphical interface like you see in the slick Windows version.

The program installs easily on an IBM-type computer. The Windows version requires a 386 machine, 10MB of available hard disk space, Windows 3.1 or higher, and 4MB of RAM.

All major tax forms are supported and print in full graphic style, just like the IRS forms. The IRS has approved use of all Tax Cut forms.

Help is available on-screen in the form of complete IRS instructions, Tax-Cut help files describing the tax laws in plain English, Kiplinger help written by the Kiplinger magazine editors including tax strategies, tips and suggestions for how to improve your tax situation in the following year, and technical help on the function of the Tax Cut program. Telephone support (not toll-free) is available year-round from 9 a.m. to 6 p.m. Monday–Friday, and with extended hours during the spring from 9 a.m. to midnight (EST) Monday–Friday and 10 a.m. to 4 p.m. (EST) Saturday and Sunday.

Kiplinger's Tax Cut releases a Planning version in October each year. Purchase of the Planning version, which costs $39.95, automatically qualifies you to receive the final version in the mail at no extra charge as soon as it is available, sometime after the first of the year.

Kiplinger's Tax Cut supports 23 states with an individual tax return package known as the State Edition available for each of the 23 states. The Macintosh version has state returns available for only New York and California.

The Least You Need to Know

➤ There are many tax software programs out there!

➤ Most of the tax preparation programs do the same things and cost about the same amount.

➤ State tax programs are available to accompany the federal programs.

Glossary of IRSpeak Terms

1040. The U.S. Individual Income Tax Return, known to friends as the *1040*, is the form you send to the IRS each April. Record your financial events of the past year on the 1040, compute your tax, hope for a refund, or send in a check.

1040A. The U.S. Individual Income Tax Return in an easier version than the 1040. You can use this form if you meet the following requirements: your taxable income is under $50,000; the taxable income you have is only from wages, salaries, tips, scholarships and fellowships, IRA distributions, pensions and annuities, unemployment compensation, and Social Security benefits, dividends or interest; you do not itemize your deductions; the only adjustment you make to your income is for a contribution to an IRA; your only tax credits are the Child and Dependent Care Credit, the Earned Income Credit, or the Credit for the Elderly.

1040EZ. The Income Tax Return for Single and Joint Filers With No Dependents. This is the simplest form of the federal income tax return, used by taxpayers with no deductions, no adjustments, income of only wages, interest, or unemployment compensation, and no dependents.

Adjusted Gross Income (AGI). Add up all your income and deduct your adjustments on page 1 of your 1040 and you get *Adjusted Gross Income (AGI)*. The AGI number is used as a basis for determining some of your limitations on itemized deductions (as discussed in Chapter 19, "Itemized Deductions Most Taxpayers Can Take," and Chapter 20, "Counting a Few More Deductions").

Adjustments. Deductions that you can apply against your income that appear at the bottom of page 1 of the 1040. Adjustments, such as IRA or Keogh contributions, moving expenses, and alimony payments, reduce income before the AGI calculation.

Annualize. When you *annualize* your income, you figure out your actual income for each quarter, as opposed to just dividing your total income for the year by four. In any given quarter you figure out what your income would be for the entire year if you continued to earn at the rate you've earned thus far. So, if your total income for the first quarter of 1995 is $10,000, when you annualize your income you are saying that as of the end of the first quarter you expect to earn $40,000 for the entire year. Your first quarter estimated tax is then based on the assumption that your income for the entire year is $40,000; the tax on $40,000 is divided by four to arrive at the required estimate.

Blind. According to the IRS, you are *blind* if your doctor says your vision is no better than 20/200 in your best eye, with glasses. You have to attach a letter to your tax return the first year you claim the deduction for blindness.

Capital Gain or Loss. The difference between your investment in an asset and the amount you receive when you sell the asset is a *capital gain or loss*. Capital gains and losses are reported on Schedule D of your income tax return.

Casualty. A *casualty* is a sudden, unexpected, or unusual event, by IRS standards. An event that doesn't fit into one of these descriptions doesn't garner you a casualty loss deduction on your Schedule A.

Deductions. Expenses that you incur that reduce your income for purposes of your tax calculation are called *deductions*. Itemized deductions reported on Schedule A include personal deductions such as medical expenses, interest, taxes, contributions, and employee business expenses. Deductions for capital losses, alimony, moving expenses, contributions to some retirement plans, and business expenses all get deducted from gross income even if the taxpayer cannot itemize.

Dependents. *Dependents* are the people you take care of. I don't mean take care of as in providing a shoulder to cry on or a loan in a pinch, even though these are major ways in which you can take care of the people who are important to you. For someone to qualify as a dependent, you have to provide serious care, such as food and shelter. Usually dependents are people who live with you, although not always. See Chapter 11, "Dependents," for information on dependents.

Dividends. Earnings you receive as a shareholder of a corporation are called *dividends*. Dividend income is reported to you on Form 1099-DIV and you should list it on Schedule B of your income tax return.

Elderly. According to the IRS, you are *elderly* for the 1995 income tax return if your 65th birthday falls on or before January 1, 1996.

Electronic Filing. Years ago, some science fiction author probably made up the idea of *electronic filing* and someone at the IRS read the book and thought it was a true story. From wherever the idea came, it has come to pass that the IRS accepts tax returns filed electronically, from computers with a modem. To communicate with the IRS you have to be an IRS-approved electronic filing center. These places seem to pop up on every street corner after New Year's Eve and disappear into the mist on April 16.

Estimated Payments. *Estimated payments*, sometimes called *quarterly payments*, are tax payments that you send directly to the IRS. People whose withholding doesn't come close enough to covering their tax for the year send quarterly payment forms to the IRS, accompanying them with money and other sacrificial objects designed to placate the tax gods.

Exemption. An *exemption* reduces your income before you compute income tax. You get an exemption (worth a $2,500 deduction from your taxable income) for yourself, one for your spouse if you are married and filing jointly, and one for each dependent. You get no exemption for yourself or your spouse if someone else can claim either of you as a dependent.

Expense. Money that you spend is an *expense*. Whether it is a *deductible expense*, an amount you can use to reduce your income before you compute income tax, depends on the vagaries of the tax lawmakers.

Federal Income Tax. The income tax that you pay to the United States Government is your *federal income tax*. These taxes pay for most of the activities of the government. Believe it or not, taxation is a voluntary system. The government relies on taxpayers to willingly send in their tax returns and pay their taxes each year.

Filing Status. Your *filing status* is kind of like your marital status, but not quite. The IRS uses your filing status as a guide for the rate at which your income tax should be applied. Filing status types include Single, Married Filing Jointly, Married Filing Separately, Head of Household, and Qualifying Widow(er). Chapter 10, "Your Filing Status," provides the details on the filing status rules.

Head of Household. You can choose to use the *Head of Household* filing status if you are not married as of the end of the year and at least one child or relative who can be claimed as your dependent (or an unmarried child who cannot be claimed) lived in your house for at least half of the year.

Income. Money that comes into your possession is *income*. Some income is earned, money that you work for at a job or in a business; other income, such as interest and dividends, is a result of savvy investing. Income includes things like gifts and prizes and pennies that fall from the sky. Most of your income is subject to income tax, some of it is not.

Individual Retirement Account (IRA). An *Individual Retirement Account (IRA)* is a retirement savings account. Special tax rules allow you to reduce your taxable income by part or all of your contributions to the IRA. An IRA is not just any savings account. You have to set up your IRA with a bank or stock brokerage firm—some organization that can make sure that the account meets the requirements set out by the IRS. Money is withdrawn from an IRA starting when you reach age 59 1/2 and is taxed at that time. You can withdraw money before age 59 1/2 but the amount you withdraw early is subject to a hefty 10% penalty.

Interest Income. Earnings on investments such as savings accounts and certificates of deposits are called *interest*. Interest income is reported to you on Form 1099-INT and you should list it on the Schedule B of your income tax return.

Interest Expense. The extra money you pay when you pay off a loan—the cost of borrowing money, if you will—is *interest*. This kind of interest is a cost to you.

The money you earn on your savings account—the amount the bank pays you to let them use your money—is also *interest*. This kind of interest is income to you. Both kinds of interest are calculated as a percentage of either the amount of your loan or the amount you put in your bank account.

Internal Revenue Service (IRS). The *Internal Revenue Service (IRS)* is an agency of the U.S. Treasury Department. It's the job of the IRS to collect our income tax as well as other taxes. The IRS also enforces tax laws and offers tax advice.

Itemize. If you have a lot of expenses such as medical expenses, mortgage interest, taxes, and charitable contributions, you can *itemize* those deductions on Schedule A and take a stab at reducing your income before you figure your tax. Itemizing is discussed in detail in Chapter 19, "Itemized Deductions Most Taxpayers Can Take."

Kiddie Tax. Remember that the *Kiddie Tax* taxes investment income. Investment income is income from interest, dividends, rents, and royalties. If the child had a paying job, the income from the job is earned income—income for which the child worked.

Married Filing Jointly. You can use the *Married Filing Jointly* filing status if you are married as of the end of the year. The married couple combines the incomes and deductions of each spouse on the same tax return, and one tax is applied to the total.

Married Filing Separately. You can use the *Married Filing Separately* filing status if you are married as of the end of the year. Each spouse files a separate income tax return and doesn't combine income with the other spouse.

Maximum Tax on Capital Gains. The *Maximum Tax on Capital Gains* applies if Schedule D shows a gain on line 18 and part of that gain includes long-term capital gain that would appear on line 17 of Schedule D. This method of computing your tax gives you a lower tax rate on the part of your income that comes from sales of capital assets, assuming your tax bracket exceeds 28%.

Penalty. A fee charged by the IRS for paying your taxes late. Filing your tax return late is a *penalty*.

Principal. The *principal* is the bigger-than-life guy with the scary office with whom you never want to cross paths. It's also the amount of money you borrow when you take out a loan.

Qualifying Widow(er). If your spouse died and you have not remarried, if you had the right to file a joint return in the year of your spouse's death, if you have a dependent child living in your home, and if you paid for more than half the cost of maintaining your home for that dependent, you may file a joint return with your deceased spouse for the year of death. For two years thereafter, if you do not get married and these conditions are met, you can file by using the Qualifying Widow(er) status, which gives you the same rates as if you are filing jointly.

Quarterly Payments. See *Estimated Payments*.

Receipt. The documentation you keep to support your expenditures usually appears as *receipts*, that is, paper evidence of amounts that you spent.

Refund. The amount of income tax you paid during 1995 that exceeds your 1995 income tax expense is a *refund* if you ask to have it back on your Form 1040. Alternatively, you can leave the funds with the IRS for safekeeping and apply them to your 1996 income tax return.

Schedule. A *schedule* is an attachment to your Form 1040 on which you provide details of income and expenses that flow through to Form 1040. Common schedules include the following: Schedule A (Itemized Deductions), Schedule B (Interest and Dividend Income), Schedule C (Profit or Loss From Business), Schedule D (Capital Gains and Losses), Schedule E (Supplemental Income and Loss), Schedule F (Profit or Loss From Farming), Schedule SE (Self-Employment Tax).

Single. You use the *Single* filing status if you are unmarried and have no children or dependents living with you.

Tax Liability. The amount of tax you owe—the amount you have to pay—is your *tax liability*. A liability is a debt.

Tax Preparer. The person you pay to assist you with the preparation of your income tax forms is the *tax preparer*. The paid tax preparer signs your Form 1040 at the bottom of page 2, right under your signature.

Tax Rate Schedule. Taxpayers with taxable income of at least $100,000 use the *Tax Rate Schedules* to calculate their income tax. Tax Rate Schedules, along with the Tax Tables, are reproduced in Appendix C of this book.

Taxable Income. After all your income is added together and all your allowable expenses are deducted, and after you subtract an amount for each of your dependents, the number you're left with is three times the year in which you were born. Or it may be your *taxable income*. This is the amount on which the IRS wants you to pay income tax.

Total Tax. The *total tax* for a tax year is the sum of all taxes owed for that year offset by the sum of all credits. So, for example, if on your 1995 tax return you compute income tax of $15,000, a child care credit of $480, self-employment tax of $2,500, and a foreign tax credit of $20, your total tax is $17,000 ($15,000 + $2,500 − $480 − $20).

W-2. If you are employed, your employer reports your annual wage summary on a form *W-2*. This form lists all the taxes withheld from your wages during the year.

Wages. Income you receive as an employee at a job is called *wages*. Wages are reported to you on form W-2.

Withholding. Taxes that are extracted from your pay and sent off to the government are called *withholding*. It is your employer's responsibility to withhold tax from your pay and deposit in an IRS bank account.

Tax Forms Guide

The tax forms reproduced in this appendix are here for your use. You can make copies of them or you can write on them right here in the book as you make a rough draft of your tax return. **These forms were made available by the IRS in the fall of 1995 and it's possible there may be some last-minute changes on the forms before the tax forms and instructions packets get mailed to taxpayers across the country in late December.** I recommend that you use the forms the IRS sends you for your final tax return preparation, or obtain forms through the various methods mentioned in Chapter 3, "Where All Those Forms Come From." You can call the IRS at 1-800-TAX-FORM to place an order for forms.

Form 1040 Department of the Treasury—Internal Revenue Service
U.S. Individual Income Tax Return 1995 IRS Use Only—Do not write or staple in this space.

For the year Jan. 1–Dec. 31, 1995, or other tax year beginning , 1995, ending , 19 | OMB No. 1545-0074

Label

(See instructions on page 12.)

Use the IRS label. Otherwise, please print or type.

L A B E L H E R E

Your first name and initial | Last name | Your social security number

If a joint return, spouse's first name and initial | Last name | Spouse's social security number

Home address (number and street). If you have a P.O. box, see page 12. | Apt. no.

City, town or post office, state, and ZIP code. If you have a foreign address, see page 12.

For Privacy Act and Paperwork Reduction Act Notice, see page 7.

Presidential Election Campaign (See page 12.)

Yes | No | **Note:** Checking "Yes" will not change your tax or reduce your refund.

Do you want $3 to go to this fund? . . . .
If a joint return, does your spouse want $3 to go to this fund? . . . .

Filing Status

(See page 12.)

Check only one box.

1 ☐ Single
2 ☐ Married filing joint return (even if only one had income)
3 ☐ Married filing separate return. Enter spouse's social security no. above and full name here. ▶ _____
4 ☐ Head of household (with qualifying person). (See page 12.) If the qualifying person is a child but not your dependent, enter this child's name here. ▶ _____
5 ☐ Qualifying widow(er) with dependent child (year spouse died ▶ 19). (See page 13.)

Exemptions

(See page 13.)

If more than six dependents, see page 14.

6a ☐ **Yourself.** If your parent (or someone else) can claim you as a dependent on his or her tax return, **do not** check box 6a. But be sure to check the box on line 33b on page 2 . .
b ☐ **Spouse** . . . .
c Dependents:

(1) First name Last name	(2) Dependent's social security number If born in 1995 see page 14	(3) Dependent's relationship to you	(4) No. of months lived in your home in 1995

No. of boxes checked on 6a and 6b _____

No. of your children on 6c who:
• lived with you _____
• didn't live with you due to divorce or separation (see page 14) _____

Dependents on 6c not entered above _____

d If your child didn't live with you but is claimed as your dependent under a pre-1985 agreement, check here ▶ ☐
e Total number of exemptions claimed . . . .

Add numbers entered on lines above ▶ _____

Income

Attach Copy B of your Forms W-2, W-2G, and 1099-R here.

If you did not get a W-2, see page 15.

Enclose, but do not attach. your payment and payment voucher. See page 32.

7 Wages, salaries, tips, etc. Attach Form(s) W-2 . . . . | 7 |
8a **Taxable** interest income (see page 15). Attach Schedule B if over $400 . . . . . | 8a |
b **Tax-exempt** interest (see page 16). DON'T include on line 8a | 8b | |
9 Dividend income. Attach Schedule B if over $400 . . . . . . | 9 |
10 Taxable refunds, credits, or offsets of state and local income taxes (see page 16) . . | 10 |
11 Alimony received . . . . | 11 |
12 Business income or (loss). Attach Schedule C or C-EZ . . . . | 12 |
13 Capital gain or (loss). If required, attach Schedule D (see page 16) . . . . | 13 |
14 Other gains or (losses). Attach Form 4797 . . . . | 14 |
15a Total IRA distributions . | 15a | b Taxable amount (see page 17) | 15b |
16a Total pensions and annuities | 16a | b Taxable amount (see page 17) | 16b |
17 Rental real estate, royalties, partnerships, S corporations, trusts, etc. Attach Schedule E | 17 |
18 Farm income or (loss). Attach Schedule F . . . . | 18 |
19 Unemployment compensation (see page 19) . . . . | 19 |
20a Social security benefits | 20a | b Taxable amount (see page 18) | 20b |
21 Other income. List type and amount—see page 19 . . . . | 21 |
22 Add the amounts in the far right column for lines 7 through 21. This is your **total income** ▶ | 22 |

Adjustments to Income

23a Your IRA deduction (see page 19) . . . . | 23a | |
b Spouse's IRA deduction (see page 19) . . . . . . | 23b | |
24 Moving expenses. Attach Form 3903 or 3903-F . . . | 24 | |
25 One-half of self-employment tax . . . . | 25 | |
26 Self-employed health insurance deduction (see page 21) | 26 | |
27 Keogh & self-employed SEP plans. If SEP, check ▶ ☐ | 27 | |
28 Penalty on early withdrawal of savings . . . . . | 28 | |
29 Alimony paid. Recipient's SSN ▶ | 29 | |
30 Add lines 23a through 29. These are your **total adjustments** . . . . ▶ | 30 |

Adjusted Gross Income

31 Subtract line 30 from line 22. This is your **adjusted gross income.** If less than $26,673 and a child lived with you (less than $9,230 if a child didn't live with you), see "Earned Income Credit" on page 27 ▶ | 31 |

Cat. No. 11320B

Form **1040** (1995)

Form 1040 (1995)

Tax Compu-tation (See page 23.) If you want the IRS to figure your tax, see page 24.	32	Amount from line 31 (adjusted gross income)	**32**
	33a	Check if: ☐ **You** were 65 or older, ☐ Blind; ☐ **Spouse** was 65 or older, ☐ Blind. Add the number of boxes checked above and enter the total here . . . . ► **33a**	
	b	If your parent (or someone else) can claim you as a dependent, check here . ► **33b** ☐	
	c	If you are married filing separately and your spouse itemizes deductions or you are a dual-status alien, see page 23 and check here . . . . ► **33c** ☐	
	34	Enter the larger of your: { **Itemized deductions** from Schedule A, line 28, **OR** **Standard deduction** shown below for your filing status. **But if you checked any box on line 33a or b**, go to page 23 to find your standard deduction. If you checked **box 33c,** your standard deduction is zero. • Single—$3,900 • Married filing jointly or Qualifying widow(er)—$6,550 • Head of household—$5,750 • Married filing separately—$3,275 }	**34**
	35	Subtract line 34 from line 32	**35**
	36	If line 32 is $86,025 or less, multiply $2,500 by the total number of exemptions claimed on line 6e. If line 32 is over $86,025, see the worksheet on page 24 for the amount to enter .	**36**
	37	**Taxable income.** Subtract line 36 from line 35. If line 36 is more than line 35, enter -0-	**37**
	38	Tax. Check if from **a** ☐ Tax Table, **b** ☐ Tax Rate Schedules, **c** ☐ Capital Gain Tax Work-sheet, or **d** ☐ Form 8615 (see page 24). Amount from Form(s) 8814 ► **e** _____	**38**
	39	Additional taxes. Check if from **a** ☐ Form 4970 **b** ☐ Form 4972	**39**
	40	Add lines 38 and 39 . . . . ►	**40**
Credits (See page 24.)	41	Credit for child and dependent care expenses. Attach Form 2441	**41**	
	42	Credit for the elderly or the disabled. Attach Schedule R . .	**42**	
	43	Foreign tax credit. Attach Form 1116	**43**	
	44	Other credits (see page 25). Check if from **a** ☐ Form 3800 **b** ☐ Form 8396 **c** ☐ Form 8801 **d** ☐ Form (specify) _____	**44**	
	45	Add lines 41 through 44	**45**
	46	Subtract line 45 from line 40. If line 45 is more than line 40, enter 0 . . . . . ►	**46**
Other Taxes (See page 25.)	47	Self-employment tax. Attach Schedule SE	**47**
	48	Alternative minimum tax. Attach Form 6251	**48**
	49	Recapture taxes. Check if from **a** ☐ Form 4255 **b** ☐ Form 8611 **c** ☐ Form 8828 . .	**49**
	50	Social security and Medicare tax on tip income not reported to employer. Attach Form 4137	**50**
	51	Tax on qualified retirement plans including IRAs. If required, attach Form 5329 . . .	**51**
	52	Advance earned income credit payments from Form W-2	**52**
	53	Household employment taxes. Attach Schedule H	**53**
	54	Add lines 46 through 53 This is your **total tax** . . . . ►	**54**
Payments Attach Forms W-2, W-2G, and 1099-R on the front.	55	Federal income tax withheld. If any is from Form(s) 1099, check ► ☐	**55**	
	56	1995 estimated tax payments and amount applied from 1994 return .	**56**	
	57	**Earned income credit.** Attach Schedule EIC if you have a qualifying child. Nontaxable earned income: amount ► _____ and type ► _____	**57**	
	58	Amount paid with Form 4868 (extension request)	**58**	
	59	Excess social security and RRTA tax withheld (see page 32)	**59**	
	60	Other payments. Check if from **a** ☐ Form 2439 **b** ☐ Form 4136	**60**	
	61	Add lines 55 through 60. These are your **total payments** . . . . ►	**61**
Refund or Amount You Owe	62	If line 61 is more than line 54, subtract line 54 from line 61. This is the amount you **OVERPAID** . ►	**62**
	63	Amount of line 62 you want **REFUNDED TO YOU.** . . . . ►	**63**
	64	Amount of line 62 you want **APPLIED TO YOUR 1996 ESTIMATED TAX** ► **64**	
	65	If line 54 is more than line 61, subtract line 61 from line 54. This is the **AMOUNT YOU OWE** For details on how to pay including using **Form 1040-V,** Payment Voucher, see page 32	**65**
	66	Estimated tax penalty (see page 33). Also include on line 65 **66**	
Sign Here Keep a copy of this return for your records.		Under penalties of perjury, I declare that I have examined this return and accompanying schedules and statements, and to the best of my knowledge and belief, they are true, correct, and complete. Declaration of preparer (other than taxpayer) is based on all information of which preparer has any knowledge.	

		Date	
►	Your signature		Your occupation
►	Spouse's signature. If a joint return, BOTH must sign.	Date	Spouse's occupation

Paid Preparer's Use Only	Preparer's signature ►	Date	Check if self-employed ☐	Preparer's social security no.
	Firm's name (or yours if self-employed) and address ►		E.I. No.	
			ZIP code	

✸ *Printed on recycled paper*

Form **1040A**	Department of the Treasury—Internal Revenue Service **U.S. Individual Income Tax Return**	**1995**	IRS Use Only—Do not write or staple in this space.

OMB No. 1545-0085

Label
(See page 19.)

Use the IRS label. Otherwise, please print or type.

L A B E L H E R E

Your first name and initial	Last name	Your social security number
If a joint return, spouse's first name and initial	Last name	Spouse's social security number
Home address (number and street). If you have a P.O. box, see page 19.		Apt. no.
City, town or post office, state, and ZIP code. If you have a foreign address, see page 19.		

For Privacy Act and Paperwork Reduction Act Notice, see page 8.

Presidential Election Campaign Fund (See page 19.)
Do you want $3 to go to this fund? . . . .
If a joint return, does your spouse want $3 to go to this fund?

	Yes	No

Note: *Checking "Yes" will not change your tax or reduce your refund.*

Check the box for your filing status
(See page 20.)
Check only one box.

1 ☐ Single
2 ☐ Married filing joint return (even if only one had income)
3 ☐ Married filing separate return. Enter spouse's social security number above and full name here. ▶ _____
4 ☐ Head of household (with qualifying person). (See page 21.) If the qualifying person is a child but not your dependent, enter this child's name here. ▶ _____
5 ☐ Qualifying widow(er) with dependent child (year spouse died ▶ 19___). (See page 22.)

Figure your exemptions
(See page 22.)

If more than seven dependents, see page 25.

6a ☐ **Yourself.** If your parent (or someone else) can claim you as a dependent on his or her tax return, **do not** check box 6a. But be sure to check the box on line 18b on page 2.

b ☐ **Spouse**

c **Dependents:**

(1) First name Last name	(2) Dependent's social security number. If born in 1995 see page 25.	(3) Dependent's relationship to you	(4) No. of months lived in your home in 1995

No. of boxes checked on 6a and 6b ____

No. of your children on 6c who:
• lived with you ____
• didn't live with you due to divorce or separation (see page 26) ____

Dependents on 6c not entered above ____

d If your child didn't live with you but is claimed as your dependent under a pre-1985 agreement, check here . . . . ▶ ☐

e Total number of exemptions claimed.

Add numbers entered on lines above ☐

Figure your adjusted gross income
Attach Copy B of your Forms W-2 and 1099-R here.
If you didn't get a W-2, see page 27. Enclose, but do not attach, any payment with your return

7 Wages, salaries, tips, etc. This should be shown in box 1 of your W-2 form(s). Attach Form(s) W-2. ..... 7 _____

8a **Taxable** interest income (see page 28). If over $400, attach Schedule 1. ..... 8a _____
b **Tax-exempt** interest. DO NOT include on line 8a. | 8b _____

9 Dividends. If over $400, attach Schedule 1. ..... 9 _____

10a Total IRA distributions. | 10a _____ | 10b Taxable amount (see page 29). | 10b _____

11a Total pensions and annuities. | 11a _____ | 11b Taxable amount (see page 29). | 11b _____

12 Unemployment compensation (see page 32). ..... 12 _____

13a Social security benefits. | 13a _____ | 13b Taxable amount (see page 33). | 13b _____

14 Add lines 7 through 13b (far right column). This is your **total income.** ▶ 14 _____

15a Your IRA deduction (see page 36). | 15a _____

b Spouse's IRA deduction (see page 36). | 15b _____

c Add lines 15a and 15b. These are your **total adjustments.** | 15c _____

16 Subtract line 15c from line 14. This is your **adjusted gross income.** If less than $26,673 and a child lived with you (less than $9,230 if a child didn't live with you), see "Earned income credit" on page 47. ▶ 16 _____

Cat. No. 11327A

1995 Form 1040A page 1

333

1995 Form 1040A page 2

Figure your standard deduction, exemption amount, and taxable income	**17**	Enter the amount from line 16.	**17**	

18a Check if: ☐ **You** were 65 or older ☐ Blind ☐ **Spouse** was 65 or older ☐ Blind — Enter number of boxes checked ▶ **18a** ☐

b If your parent (or someone else) can claim you as a dependent, check here . . . . ▶ **18b** ☐

c If you are married filing separately and your spouse itemizes deductions, see page 40 and check here. . . . . ▶ **18c** ☐

19 Enter the **standard deduction** shown below for your filing status. **But if you checked any box on line 18a or b,** go to page 40 to find your standard deduction. **If you checked box 18c,** enter -0-.
- Single—$3,900   • Married filing jointly or Qualifying widow(er)—$6,550
- Head of household—$5,750   • Married filing separately—$3,275   **19**

20 Subtract line 19 from line 17. If line 19 is more than line 17, enter -0-.   **20**

21 Multiply $2,500 by the total number of exemptions claimed on line 6e.   **21**

22 Subtract line 21 from line 20. If line 21 is more than line 20, enter -0-. This is your **taxable income.**   ▶ **22**

Figure your tax, credits, and payments

If you want the IRS to figure your tax, see the instructions for line 22 on page 41.

23 Find the tax on the amount on line 22. Check if from: ☐ Tax Table (pages 65–70) or ☐ Form 8615 (see page 41).   **23**

24a Credit for child and dependent care expenses. Attach Schedule 2.   **24a**

b Credit for the elderly or the disabled. Attach Schedule 3.   **24b**

c Add lines 24a and 24b. These are your **total credits.**   **24c**

25 Subtract line 24c from line 23. If line 24c is more than line 23, enter -0-.   **25**

26 Advance earned income credit payments from Form W-2.   **26**

27 Household employment taxes. Attach Schedule H.   **27**

28 Add lines 25 26 and 27   This is your **total tax.**   ▶ **28**

29a Total Federal income tax withheld. If any is from Form(s) 1099, check here ▶ ☐   **29a**

b 1995 estimated tax payments and amount applied from 1994 return.   **29b**

c **Earned income credit.** Attach Schedule EIC if you have a qualifying child.   **29c**
Nontaxable earned income:
amount ▶ | and type ▶

d Add lines 29a, 29b, and 29c (don't include nontaxable earned income). These are your **total payments.**   ▶ **29d**

Figure your refund or amount you owe

30 If line 29d is more than line 28, subtract line 28 from line 29d. This is the amount you **overpaid.**   **30**

31 Amount of line 30 you want **refunded to you.**   **31**

32 Amount of line 30 you want **applied to your 1996 estimated tax.**   **32**

33 If line 28 is more than line 29d, subtract line 29d from line 28. This is the **amount you owe.** For details on how to pay, including what to write on your payment, see page 55.   **33**

34 Estimated tax penalty (see page 55). Also, include on line 33.   **34**

Sign your return

Keep a copy of this return for your records.

Under penalties of perjury, I declare that I have examined this return and accompanying schedules and statements, and to the best of my knowledge and belief, they are true, correct, and accurately list all amounts and sources of income I received during the tax year. Declaration of preparer (other than the taxpayer) is based on all information of which the preparer has any knowledge.

Your signature ▶	Date	Your occupation
Spouse's signature. If joint return, BOTH must sign.	Date	Spouse's occupation

Paid preparer's use only

Preparer's signature ▶	Date	Check if self-employed ☐	Preparer's SSN
Firm's name (or yours if self-employed) and address ▶		E.I. No.	
		ZIP code	

✪ *Printed on recycled paper*   1995 Form 1040A page 2

Department of the Treasury—Internal Revenue Service

Form 1040EZ

Income Tax Return for Single and Joint Filers With No Dependents 1995

OMB No. 1545-0675

Use the IRS label
(See page 12.) Otherwise, please print.

L A B E L H E R E

Your first name and initial | Last name

If a joint return, spouse's first name and initial | Last name

Home address (number and street). If you have a P.O. box, see page 12. | Apt. no.

City, town or post office, state, and ZIP code. If you have a foreign address, see page 12.

Your social security number

Spouse's social security number

See instructions on back and in Form 1040EZ booklet.

Presidential Election Campaign
(See page 12.)

Note: *Checking "Yes" will not change your tax or reduce your refund.*
Do you want $3 to go to this fund? ▶
If a joint return, does your spouse want $3 to go to this fund? ▶

Yes No

Dollars Cents

Income

Attach Copy B of Form(s) W-2 here. Enclose, but do not attach, any payment with your return.

1 Total wages, salaries, and tips. This should be shown in box 1 of your W-2 form(s). Attach your W-2 form(s). 1

2 Taxable interest income of $400 or less. If the total is over $400, you cannot use Form 1040EZ 2

3 Unemployment compensation (see page X). 3

4 Add lines 1, 2, and 3 This is your **adjusted gross income.** If less than $9,230, see page 15 to find out if you can claim the earned income credit on line 8. 4

Note: *You must check Yes or No.*

5 Can your parents (or someone else) claim you on their return?
☐ **Yes.** Do worksheet on back: enter amount from line G here.   ☐ **No.** If **single,** enter 6,400.00. If **married,** enter 11,550.00. For an explanation of these amounts, see back of form. 5

6 Subtract line 5 from line 4. If line 5 is larger than line 4, enter 0. This is your **taxable income.** ▶ 6

Payments and tax

7 Enter your Federal income tax withheld from box 2 of your W-2 form(s). 7

8 **Earned income credit** (see page 15). Enter type and amount of nontaxable earned income below.
Type | $ 8

9 Add lines 7 and 8 (don't include nontaxable earned income). These are your **total payments.** 9

10 **Tax.** Use the amount on **line 6** to find your tax in the tax table on pages 28–32 of the booklet. Then, enter the tax from the table on this line. 10

Refund or amount you owe

11 If line 9 is larger than line 10, subtract line 10 from line 9. This is your **refund.** 11

12 If line 10 is larger than line 9, subtract line 9 from line 10. This is the **amount you owe.** See page 20 for details on how to pay and what to write on your payment. 12

I have read this return. Under penalties of perjury, I declare to the best of my knowledge and belief, the return is true, correct, and accurately lists all amounts and sources of income I received during the tax year.

Sign your return

Keep a copy of this form for your records.

Your signature | Spouse's signature if joint return

Date | Your occupation | Date | Spouse's occupation

For IRS Use Only — Please do not write in boxes below.

| 1 | 2 | 3 | 4 | 5 |
| 6 | 7 | 8 | 9 | 10 |

For Privacy Act and Paperwork Reduction Act Notice, see page 4.   Cat. No. 11329W   Form 1040EZ (1995)

1995   **Instructions for Form 1040EZ**

Use this form if	• Your filing status is single or married filing jointly. • You do not claim any dependents.

• You (and your spouse if married) were under 65 on January 1, 1996, and not blind at the end of 1995.

• Your taxable income (line 6) is less than $50,000.

• You had **only** wages, salaries, tips, taxable scholarship or fellowship grants, or unemployment compensation, and your taxable interest income was $400 or less. **But** if you earned tips, including allocated tips, that are not included in box 5 and box 7 of your W-2, you may not be able to use Form 1040EZ. See page 14.

• You did not receive any advance earned income credit payments.

Caution: *If married and either you or your spouse had total wages of over $61,200, you may not be able to use this form. See page 7.*

If you are not sure about your filing status, see page 7. If you have questions about dependents, call Tele-Tax (see page 26) and listen to topic 354. If you **can't use this form,** call Tele-Tax (see page 26) and listen to topic 352.

Filling in your return

Because this form is read by a machine, please print your numbers inside the boxes like this:

[9 8 7 6 5 4 3 2 1 0]   Do not type your numbers. Do not use dollar signs.

If you received a scholarship or fellowship grant or tax-exempt interest income, such as on municipal bonds, see the booklet before filling in the form Also, see the booklet if you received a Form 1099-INT showing income tax withheld.

Remember, you must report all wages. salaries, and tips even if you don't get a W-2 form from your employer. You must also report all your taxable interest income, including interest from banks, savings and loans, credit unions, etc., even if you don't get a Form 1099-INT.

If you paid someone to prepare your return, see page 21.

Worksheet for dependents who checked "Yes" on line 5

Use this worksheet to figure the amount to enter on line 5 if someone can claim you (or your spouse if married) as a dependent, even if that person chooses not to do so. To find out if someone can claim you as a dependent, call Tele-Tax (see page 26) and listen to topic 354.

A. Enter the amount from line 1 on the front.	**A.**	_____
B. Minimum standard deduction.	**B.**	650.00
C. Enter the LARGER of line A or line B here.	**C.**	_____
D. Maximum standard deduction. If single, enter 3,900.00; if married, enter 6,550.00.	**D.**	_____
E. Enter the SMALLER of line C or line D here. This is your standard deduction.	**E.**	_____
F. Exemption amount.		

  • If single, enter 0.

  • If married and both you and your spouse can be claimed as dependents, enter 0.

  • If married and only one of you can be claimed as a dependent, enter 2,500.00.   **F.** _____

G. Add lines E and F. Enter the total here and on line 5 on the front.   **G.** _____

If you checked "No" on line 5 because no one can claim you (or your spouse if married) as a dependent, enter on line 5 the amount shown below that applies to you.

• Single, enter 6,400.00. This is the total of your standard deduction (3,900.00) and personal exemption (2,500.00).

• Married, enter 11,550.00. This is the total of your standard deduction (6,550.00), exemption for yourself (2,500.00), and exemption for your spouse (2,500.00).

Avoid mistakes

See page 21 of the Form 1040EZ booklet for a list of common mistakes to avoid. Errors will delay your refund.

Mailing your return

Mail your return by **April 15, 1996.** Use the envelope that came with your booklet. If you don't have that envelope, see page 33 for the address to use.

Department of the Treasury—Internal Revenue Service

Form 1040X

Amended U.S. Individual Income Tax Return
➤ See separate instructions.

OMB No. 1545-0091

This return is for calendar year ▶ 19 ____ , OR fiscal year ended ▶ ____ , 19 ____ .

Please print or type

Your first name and initial	Last name	Your social security number
If a joint return, spouse's first name and initial	Last name	Spouse's social security number
Home address (number and street). If you have a P.O. box, see instructions.	Apt. no.	Telephone number (optional) ( )
City, town or post office, state, and ZIP code. If you have a foreign address, see instructions.		For Paperwork Reduction Act Notice, see page 1 of separate instructions.

Enter name and address as shown on original return. If same as above, write "Same." If changing from separate to joint return, enter names and addresses from original returns.

A Service center where original return was filed

B Has original return been changed or audited by the IRS? ☐ Yes ☐ No
If "No," have you been notified that it will be? . . . . ☐ Yes ☐ No
If "Yes," identify the IRS office ▶

C If you are amending your return to include any item (loss, credit, deduction, other tax benefit, or income) relating to a tax shelter required to be registered, attach **Form 8271**, Investor Reporting of Tax Shelter Registration Number, and check here . . . . ▶ ☐

D Filing status claimed. **Note:** *You cannot change from joint to separate returns after the due date has passed.*
On original return ▶ ☐ Single ☐ Married filing joint return ☐ Married filing separate return ☐ Head of household ☐ Qualifying widow(er)
On this return ▶ ☐ Single ☐ Married filing joint return ☐ Married filing separate return ☐ Head of household ☐ Qualifying widow(er)

Income and Deductions (see instructions) USE PART II ON PAGE 2 TO EXPLAIN ANY CHANGES		A. As originally reported or as previously adjusted (see instructions)	B. Net change—Increase or (Decrease)—explain on page 2	C. Correct amount
1 Adjusted gross income (see instructions)	1			
2 Itemized deductions or standard deduction	2			
3 Subtract line 2 from line 1	3			
4 Exemptions. If changing, fill in Parts I and II on page 2 . .	4			
5 Taxable income. Subtract line 4 from line 3	5			
6 Tax (see instructions). Method used in col. C	6			
7 Credits (see instructions)	7			
8 Subtract line 7 from line 6. Enter the result but not less than zero .	8			
9 Other taxes (such as self-employment tax, alternative minimum tax, etc.)	9			
10 Total tax. Add lines 8 and 9	10			
11 Federal income tax withheld and excess social security, Medicare, and RRTA taxes withheld. If changing, see instructions	11			
12 Estimated tax payments	12			
13 Earned income credit	13			
14 Credits for Federal tax paid on fuels, regulated investment company, etc.	14			
15 Amount paid with Form 4868, Form 2688, or Form 2350 (application for extension of time to file) .				15
16 Amount of tax paid with original return plus additional tax paid after it was filed				16
17 Total payments. Add lines 11 through 16 in column C				17

Tax Liability / **Payments**

Refund or Amount You Owe

18 Overpayment, if any, as shown on original return or as previously adjusted by the IRS . . .	18	
19 Subtract line 18 from line 17 (see instructions)	19	
20 **AMOUNT YOU OWE.** If line 10, column C, is more than line 19, enter the difference and see instructions .	20	
21 If line 10, column C, is less than line 19, enter the difference	21	
22 Amount of line 21 you want **REFUNDED TO YOU**	22	
23 Amount of line 21 you want **APPLIED TO YOUR 19** ____ **ESTIMATED TAX**	23	

Sign Here
Keep a copy of this return for your records.

Under penalties of perjury, I declare that I have filed an original return and that I have examined this amended return, including accompanying schedules and statements, and to the best of my knowledge and belief, this amended return is true, correct, and complete. Declaration of preparer (other than taxpayer) is based on all information of which the preparer has any knowledge.

▶ Your signature ____ Date ____
▶ Spouse's signature. If a joint return, BOTH must sign. ____ Date ____

Paid Preparer's Use Only

Preparer's signature ▶	Date	Check if self-employed ☐	Preparer's social security no.
Firm's name (or yours if self-employed) and address ▶		E.I. No.	
		ZIP code	

Cat. No. 11360L 25

Form **1040X**

Form 1040X

Part I **Exemptions.** See Form 1040 or Form 1040A instructions.

If you are **not changing your exemptions,** do not complete this part.
If claiming **more exemptions,** complete lines 24–30 and, if applicable, line 31.
If claiming **fewer exemptions,** complete lines 24–29.

			A. Number originally reported	B. Net change	C. Correct number
24	Yourself and spouse	24			

Caution: *If your parents (or someone else) can claim you as a dependent (even if they chose not to), you cannot claim an exemption for yourself.*

			A. Number originally reported	B. Net change	C. Correct number
25	Your dependent children who lived with you	25			
26	Your dependent children who did not live with you due to divorce or separation	26			
27	Other dependents	27			
28	Total number of exemptions. Add lines 24 through 27	28			

29 Multiply the number of exemptions claimed on line 28 by the amount listed below for the tax year you are amending. Enter the result here and on line 4.

Tax Year	Exemption Amount	But see the instructions if the amount on line 1 is over:
1994	$2,450	$83,850
1993	2,350	81,350
1992	2,300	78,950
1991	2,150	75,000

29

30 Dependents (children and other) not claimed on original return:

(a) Name (first, initial, and last name)	(b) Check if under age 1	(c) If age 1 or older, enter dependent's social security number	(d) Dependent's relationship to you	(e) No. of months lived in your home	
					No. of your children on line 30 who lived with you ▶ ☐
					No. of your children on line 30 who **didn't** live with you due to divorce or separation (see instructions) ▶ ☐
					No. of dependents on line 30 not entered above ▶ ☐

31 If your child listed on line 30 didn't live with you but is claimed as your dependent under a pre-1985 agreement, check here ▶ ☐

Part II **Explanation of Changes to Income, Deductions, and Credits**

Enter the line number from page 1 for each item you are changing and give the reason for each change. Attach all supporting forms and schedules for items changed. If you don't, your Form 1040X may be returned. Be sure to include your name and social security number on any attachments.

If the change relates to a net operating loss carryback or a general business credit carryback, attach the schedule or form that shows the year in which the loss or credit occurred. See instructions. Also, check here ▶ ☐

Part III **Presidential Election Campaign Fund.** Checking below will not increase your tax or reduce your refund.

If you did not previously want to have $3 go to the fund but now want to, check here ▶ ☐
If a joint return and your spouse did not previously want to have $3 go to the fund but now wants to, check here ▶ ☐

26

SCHEDULES A&B
(Form 1040)

Department of the Treasury
Internal Revenue Service

Schedule A—Itemized Deductions

(Schedule B is on back)

➤ Attach to Form 1040. ➤ See Instructions for Schedules A and B (Form 1040).

OMB No. 1545-0074

1995

Attachment
Sequence No. **07**

Name(s) shown on Form 1040

Your social security number

Medical and Dental Expenses		**Caution:** *Do not include expenses reimbursed or paid by others.*	
	1	Medical and dental expenses (see page A-1) **1**	
	2	Enter amount from Form 1040, line 32 . **2**	
	3	Multiply line 2 above by 7.5% (.075) **3**	
	4	Subtract line 3 from line 1. If line 3 is more than line 1, enter -0-	**4**

Taxes You Paid (See page A-1.)	5	State and local income taxes **5**	
	6	Real estate taxes (see page A-2) **6**	
	7	Personal property taxes **7**	
	8	Other taxes. List type and amount ▶ **8**	
	9	Add lines 5 through 8	**9**

Interest You Paid (See page A-2.)	10	Home mortgage interest and points reported to you on Form 1098 **10**	
	11	Home mortgage interest not reported to you on Form 1098. If paid to the person from whom you bought the home, see page A-3 and show that person's name, identifying no.. and address ▶	
Note: Personal interest is not deductible.		.... **11**	
	12	Points not reported to you on Form 1098 See page A-3 for special rules . . . . See **12**	
	13	Investment interest. If required, attach Form 4952. (See page A-3.) **13**	
	14	Add lines 10 through 13	**14**

Gifts to Charity If you made a gift and got a benefit for it, see page A-3.	15	Gifts by cash or check If you made any gift of $250 or more, see page A-3 . . . . **15**	
	16	Other than by cash or check If any gift of $250 or more, see page A-3. If over $500, you **MUST** attach Form 8283 **16**	
	17	Carryover from prior year **17**	
	18	Add lines 15 through 17	**18**

Casualty and Theft Losses	19	Casualty or theft loss(es). Attach Form 4684. (See page A-4.)	**19**

Job Expenses and Most Other Miscellaneous Deductions (See page A-5 for expenses to deduct here.)	20	Unreimbursed employee expenses—job travel, union dues, job education, etc. If required, you **MUST** attach Form 2106 or 2106-EZ. (See page A-5.) ▶ **20**	
	21	Tax preparation fees **21**	
	22	Other expenses—investment, safe deposit box, etc. List type and amount ▶ **22**	
	23	Add lines 20 through 22 . . . . **23**	
	24	Enter amount from Form 1040, line 32 . **24**	
	25	Multiply line 24 above by 2% (.02) **25**	
	26	Subtract line 25 from line 23. If line 25 is more than line 23, enter -0-	**26**

Other Miscellaneous Deductions	27	Other—from list on page A-5. List type and amount ▶	**27**

Total Itemized Deductions	28	Is Form 1040, line 32, over $114,700 (over $57,350 if married filing separately)?	
		NO. Your deduction is not limited. Add the amounts in the far right column for lines 4 through 27. Also, enter on Form 1040, line 34, the **larger** of this amount or your standard deduction.	▶ **28**
		YES. Your deduction may be limited. See page A-5 for the amount to enter.	

For Paperwork Reduction Act Notice, see Form 1040 instructions.　　　Cat. No. 11330X　　　**Schedule A (Form 1040) 1995**

339

Schedules A&B (Form 1040) 1995 | OMB No. 1545-0074 | Page **2**

Name(s) shown on Form 1040. Do not enter name and social security number if shown on other side. | Your social security number

Schedule B—Interest and Dividend Income

Attachment Sequence No. **08**

Part I

Interest Income

(See pages 15 and B-1.)

Note: If you received a Form 1099-INT, Form 1099-OID, or substitute statement from a brokerage firm, list the firm's name as the payer and enter the total interest shown on that form.

Note: If you had over $400 in taxable interest income, you must also complete Part III.

		Amount
1	List name of payer. If any interest is from a seller-financed mortgage and the buyer used the property as a personal residence, see page B-1 and list this interest first. Also, show that buyer's social security number and address ▶	

2	Add the amounts on line 1 . . . .
3	Excludable interest **on series EE** U.S. savings bonds issued after 1989 from Form 8815, line 14 You MUST attach Form 8815 to Form
4	Subtract line **3 from line** 2. Enter the result here and on Form 1040, line 8a ▶

Part II

Dividend Income

(See pages 16 and B-1.)

Note: If you received a Form 1099-DIV or substitute statement from a brokerage firm, list the firm's name as the payer and enter the total dividends shown on that form.

Note: If you had over $400 in gross dividends and/or other distributions on stock, you must also complete Part III.

		Amount
5	List name of payer. Include gross dividends and/or other distributions on stock here. Any capital gain distributions and nontaxable distributions will be deducted on lines 7 and 8 ▶	

6	Add the amounts on line 5 . . . .
7	Capital gain distributions. Enter here and on Schedule D* .
8	Nontaxable distributions. (See the inst. for Form 1040, line 9.)
9	Add lines 7 and 8 . . . .
10	Subtract line 9 from line 6. Enter the result here and on Form 1040, line 9 . ▶

*If you do not need Schedule D to report any other gains or losses, enter your capital gain distributions on Form 1040, line 13. Write "CGD" on the dotted line next to line 13.

Part III

Foreign Accounts and Trusts

(See page B-2.)

If you had over $400 of interest or dividends **or** had a foreign account or were a grantor of, or a transferor to, a foreign trust, you must complete this part. | Yes | No

11a At any time during 1995, did you have an interest in or a signature or other authority over a financial account in a foreign country, such as a bank account, securities account, or other financial account? See page B-2 for exceptions and filing requirements for Form TD F 90-22.1 . . . .

b If "Yes," enter the name of the foreign country ▶

12 Were you the grantor of, or transferor to, a foreign trust that existed during 1995, whether or not you have any beneficial interest in it? If "Yes," you may have to file Form 3520, 3520-A, or 926 .

For Paperwork Reduction Act Notice, see Form 1040 instructions. | Printed on recycled paper | Schedule B (Form 1040) 1995

| SCHEDULE C
(Form 1040)

Department of the Treasury
Internal Revenue Service | **Profit or Loss From Business**
(Sole Proprietorship)
➤ **Partnerships, joint ventures, etc., must file Form 1065.**
➤ **Attach to Form 1040 or Form 1041.** ➤ **See Instructions for Schedule C (Form 1040).** | OMB No. 1545-0074
19**95**
Attachment
Sequence No. **09** |

| Name of proprietor | Social security number (SSN) |

A Principal business or profession, including product or service (see page C-1) | **B Enter principal business code**
(see page C-6) ➤

C Business name. If no separate business name, leave blank. | **D Employer ID number (EIN), if any**

E Business address (including suite or room no.) ➤ ....
City, town or post office, state, and ZIP code

F Accounting method: **(1)** ☐ Cash **(2)** ☐ Accrual **(3)** ☐ Other (specify) ➤ ....

G Method(s) used to
value closing inventory: **(1)** ☐ Cost **(2)** ☐ Lower of cost or market **(3)** ☐ Other (attach explanation) **(4)** ☐ Does not apply (if checked, skip line H) | Yes | No

H Was there any change in determining quantities, costs, or valuations between opening and closing inventory? If "Yes," attach explanation

I Did you "materially participate" in the operation of this business during 1995? If "No," see page C-2 for limit on losses.

J If you started or acquired this business during 1995, check here . . . . ➤ ☐

Part I Income

1	Gross receipts or sales. **Caution:** *If this income was reported to you on Form W-2 and the statutory employee" box on that form was checked, see page C-2 and check here* . . . . ➤ ☐	**1**
2	Returns and allowances	**2**
3	Subtract line 2 from line 1	**3**
4	Cost of goods sold (from line 40 on page 2)	**4**
5	**Gross profit.** Subtract line 4 from line 3	**5**
6	Other income, including Federal and state gasoline or fuel tax credit or refund (see page C-2) . .	**6**
7	**Gross income.** Add lines 5 and 6 . . . . ➤	**7**

Part II Expenses. Enter expenses for business use of your home **only** on line 30.

8	Advertising	**8**	**19** Pension and profit-sharing plans	**19**	
9	Bad debts from sales or services (see page C-3) . .	**9**	**20** Rent or lease (see page C-4): **a** Vehicles, machinery, and equipment .	**20a**	
10	Car and truck expenses (see page C-3)	**10**	**b** Other business property . .	**20b**	
11	Commissions and fees. . .	**11**	**21** Repairs and maintenance . .	**21**	
12	Depletion.	**12**	**22** Supplies (not included in Part III) .	**22**	
13	Depreciation and section 179 expense deduction (not included in Part III) (see page C-3) . .	**13**	**23** Taxes and licenses . . . . **24** Travel, meals, and entertainment: **a** Travel	**23** **24a**	
14	Employee benefit programs (other than on line 19) . . .	**14**	**b** Meals and entertainment .		
15	Insurance (other than health) .	**15**	**c** Enter 50% of line 24b subject to limitations (see page C-4) .		
16	Interest:				
a	Mortgage (paid to banks, etc.) .	**16a**	**d** Subtract line 24c from line 24b .	**24d**	
b	Other	**16b**	**25** Utilities	**25**	
17	Legal and professional services	**17**	**26** Wages (less employment credits) .	**26**	
18	Office expense	**18**	**27** Other expenses (from line 46 on page 2)	**27**	

28	**Total expenses** before expenses for business use of home. Add lines 8 through 27 in columns . ➤	**28**
29	Tentative profit (loss). Subtract line 28 from line 7	**29**
30	Expenses for business use of your home. Attach **Form 8829**	**30**
31	**Net profit or (loss).** Subtract line 30 from line 29. • If a profit, enter on **Form 1040, line 12,** and ALSO on **Schedule SE, line 2** (statutory employees, see page C-5). Estates and trusts, enter on Form 1041, line 3. • If a loss, you MUST go on to line 32.	**31**
32	If you have a loss, check the box that describes your investment in this activity (see page C-5). • If you checked 32a, enter the loss on **Form 1040, line 12,** and ALSO on **Schedule SE, line 2** (statutory employees, see page C-5). Estates and trusts, enter on Form 1041, line 3. • If you checked 32b, you MUST attach **Form 6198.**	**32a** ☐ All investment is at risk. **32b** ☐ Some investment is not at risk.

For Paperwork Reduction Act Notice, see Form 1040 instructions. | Cat. No. 11334P | Schedule C (Form 1040) 1995

Schedule C (Form 1040) 1995   Page **2**

Part III   **Cost of Goods Sold** (see page C-5)

33	Inventory at beginning of year. If different from last year's closing inventory, attach explanation . .	33	
34	Purchases less cost of items withdrawn for personal use	34	
35	Cost of labor. Do not include salary paid to yourself	35	
36	Materials and supplies	36	
37	Other costs	37	
38	Add lines 33 through 37	38	
39	Inventory at end of year	39	
40	**Cost of goods sold.** Subtract line 39 from line 38. Enter the result here and on page 1, line 4 . .	40	

Part IV   **Information on Your Vehicle.** Complete this part **ONLY** if you are claiming car or truck expenses on line 10 and are not required to file Form 4562 **for this business.** See the instructions for line 13 on page C-3 to find out if you must file.

41   When did you place your vehicle in service for business purposes? (month, day, year) ▶ ....

42   Of the total number of miles you drove your vehicle during 1995 enter the number of miles you used your vehicle for:

a   Business ....   **b** Commuting ....   **c** Other ....

43   Do you (or your spouse) have another vehicle available for personal use? . . . . ☐ **Yes**   ☐ **No**

44   Was your vehicle available for use during off-duty hours . . . . ☐ **Yes**   ☐ **No**

45a   Do you have evidence to support your deduction? . . . . ☐ **Yes**   ☐ **No**
   b   If "Yes," is the evidence written? . . . . ☐ **Yes**   ☐ **No**

Part V   **Other Expenses.** List below business expenses not included on lines 8–26 or line 30.

....		
....		
....		
....		
....		
....		
....		
....		
....		
46 Total other expenses. Enter here and on page 1, line 27	**46**	

✪   *Printed on recycled paper*

SCHEDULE C-EZ (Form 1040) Department of the Treasury Internal Revenue Service	**Net Profit From Business** (Sole Proprietorship) ▶ Partnerships, joint ventures, etc., must file Form 1065. ▶ **Attach to Form 1040 or Form 1041.** ▶ **See instructions on back.**	OMB No. 1545-0074 19**95** Attachment Sequence No. **09A**
Name of proprietor		Social security number (SSN)

Part I General Information

**You May Use
This Schedule
Only If You:** ➤
	• Had gross receipts from your
	  business of $25,000 or less.
	• Had business expenses of $2,000 or
	  less.
	• Use the cash method of accounting.
	• Did not have an inventory at any
	  time during the year.
	• Did not have a net loss from your
	  business.
	• Had only one business as a sole
	  proprietor.
		And You:	• Had no employees during the year.
			• Are not required to file **Form 4562**,
			  Depreciation and Amortization, for
			  this business. See the instructions
			  for Schedule C, line 13, on page
			  C-3 to find out if you must file.
			• Do not deduct expenses for
			  business use of your home.
			• Do not have prior year unallowed
			  passive activity losses from this
			  business.

A Principal business or profession, including product or service	**B** Enter principal business code (see page C-6) ▶			
C Business name. If no separate business name, leave blank.	**D** Employer ID number (EIN), if any			

E Business address (including suite or room no.) Address not required if same as on Form 1040, page 1.

City, town or post office, state, and ZIP code

Part II Figure Your Net Profit

1 **Gross receipts.** If more than **$25,000**, you **must** use Schedule C.
Caution: *If this income was reported to you on Form W-2 and the "Statutory employee" box on that form was checked, see **Statutory Employees** in the instructions for Schedule C, line 1, on page C-2 and check here* . . . . ▶ ☐   **| 1 |**

2 **Total expenses.** If more than $2,000, you **must** use Schedule C. See instructions . . . . . **| 2 |**

3 **Net profit.** Subtract line 2 from line 1. If less than zero, you **must** use Schedule C. Enter on **Form 1040, line 12,** and ALSO on **Schedule SE, line 2.** (Statutory employees **do not** report this amount on Schedule SE, line 2. Estates and trusts, enter on Form 1041, line 3.) . . . . . **| 3 |**

Part III Information on Your Vehicle. Complete this part ONLY if you are claiming car or truck expenses on line 2.

4 When did you place your vehicle in service for business purposes? (month, day, year) ▶ ..... / ..... / ..... .

5 Of the total number of miles you drove your vehicle during 1995, enter the number of miles you used your vehicle for:

a Business .... **b** Commuting .... **c** Other ....

6 Do you (or your spouse) have another vehicle available for personal use? . . . . ☐ Yes ☐ No

7 Was your vehicle available for use during off-duty hours? . . . . ☐ Yes ☐ No

8a Do you have evidence to support your deduction? . . . . ☐ Yes ☐ No

b If "Yes," is the evidence written? . . . . ☐ Yes ☐ No

For Paperwork Reduction Act Notice, see Form 1040 instructions.   Cat. No. 14374D   Schedule C-EZ (Form 1040) 1995

343

SCHEDULE D (Form 1040)	Capital Gains and Losses	OMB No. 1545-0074
Department of the Treasury Internal Revenue Service	➤ Attach to Form 1040. ➤ See Instructions for Schedule D (Form 1040). ➤ Use lines 20 and 22 for more space to list transactions for lines 1 and 9.	1995 Attachment Sequence No. **12**

Name(s) shown on Form 1040 — Your social security number

Part I Short-Term Capital Gains and Losses—Assets Held One Year or Less

(a) Description of property (Example: 100 sh. XYZ Co.)	(b) Date acquired (Mo., day, yr.)	(c) Date sold (Mo., day, yr.)	(d) Sales price (see page D-3)	(e) Cost or other basis (see page D-3)	(f) LOSS If (e) is more than (d), subtract (d) from (e)	(g) GAIN If (d) is more than (e), subtract (e) from (d)
1						

2 Enter your short-term totals, if any, from line 21 . . . . | **2** | | | | |

3 Total short-term sales price amounts. Add column (d) of lines 1 and 2 . . . | **3** | | | | |

4 Short-term gain from Forms 2119 and 6252, and short-term gain or loss from Forms 4684, 6781, and 8824 . . . . . . | **4**

5 Net short-term gain or loss from partnerships, S corporations, estates, and trusts from Schedule(s) K-1 . . . . . . | **5**

6 Short-term capital loss carryover. Enter the amount, if any, from line 9 of your 1994 Capital Loss Carryover Worksheet . . . . | **6**

7 Add lines 1 through 6 in columns (f) and (g) . . . . | **7** ( )

8 Net short-term capital gain or (loss) Combine columns (f) and (g) of line 7 . . . . . ➤ | **8**

Part II Long-Term Capital Gains and Losses—Assets Held More Than One Year

9						

10 Enter your long-term totals, if any, from line 23 . . . . | **10** | | | | |

11 Total long-term sales price amounts. Add column (d) of lines 9 and 10 . . . | **11** | | | | |

12 Gain from Form 4797; long-term gain from Forms 2119, 2439, and 6252; and long-term gain or loss from Forms 4684, 6781, and 8824 . . . . . | **12**

13 Net long-term gain or loss from partnerships, S corporations, estates, and trusts from Schedule(s) K-1 . . . . . . | **13**

14 Capital gain distributions . . . . | **14**

15 Long-term capital loss carryover. Enter the amount, if any, from line 14 of your 1994 Capital Loss Carryover Worksheet . . . . | **15**

16 Add lines 9 through 15 in columns (f) and (g) . . . . | **16** ( )

17 Net long-term capital gain or (loss). Combine columns (f) and (g) of line 16 . . . . . ➤ | **17**

Part III Summary of Parts I and II

18 Combine lines 8 and 17. If a loss, go to line 19. If a gain, enter the gain on Form 1040, line 13.
Note: *If both lines 17 and 18 are gains, see the* **Capital Gain Tax Worksheet** *on page 25* . . | **18**

19 If line 18 is a loss, enter here and as a (loss) on Form 1040, line 13, the **smaller** of these losses:
a The loss on line 18; **or**
b ($3,000) or, if married filing separately, ($1,500) . . . . | **19** ( )
Note: *See the* **Capital Loss Carryover Worksheet** *on page D-3 if the loss on line 18 exceeds the loss on line 19 or if Form 1040, line 35, is a loss.*

For Paperwork Reduction Act Notice, see Form 1040 instructions. Cat. No. 11338H Schedule D (Form 1040) 1995

Schedule D (Form 1040) 1995 — Attachment Sequence No. **12** — , Page **2**

Name(s) shown on Form 1040. Do not enter name and social security number if shown on other side. — Your social security number

Part IV Short-Term Capital Gains and Losses—Assets Held One Year or Less *(Continuation of Part I)*

(a) Description of property (Example: 100 sh. XYZ Co.)	(b) Date acquired (Mo., day, yr.)	(c) Date sold (Mo., day, yr.)	(d) Sales price (see page D-3)	(e) Cost or other basis (see page D-3)	(f) LOSS If (e) is more than (d), subtract (d) from (e)	(g) GAIN If (d) is more than (e), subtract (e) from (d)
20						

21 Short-term totals. Add columns (d), (f), and (g) of line 20. Enter here and on line 2 **21**

Part V Long-Term Capital Gains and Losses—Assets Held More Than One Year *(Continuation of Part II)*

22						

23 Long-term totals. Add columns (d), (f), and (g) of line 22. Enter here and on line 10 . **23**

Printed on recycled paper

SCHEDULE E (Form 1040) Department of the Treasury Internal Revenue Service	**Supplemental Income and Loss** (From rental real estate, royalties, partnerships, S corporations, estates, trusts, REMICs, etc.) ➤ **Attach to Form 1040 or Form 1041.** ➤ **See Instructions for Schedule E (Form 1040).**	OMB No. 1545-0074 **1995** Attachment Sequence No. **13**
Name(s) shown on return		Your social security number

Part I   **Income or Loss From Rental Real Estate and Royalties**   Note: *Report income and expenses from your business of renting personal property on* **Schedule C** *or* **C-EZ** *(see page E-1). Report farm rental income or loss from* **Form 4835** *on page 2, line 39.*

1 Show the kind and location of each **rental real estate property:** A .... B .... C	2 For each rental real estate property listed on line 1, did you or your family use it for personal purposes for more than the greater of 14 days or 10% of the total days rented at fair rental value during the tax year? (See page E-1.)		Yes	No
		A		
		B		
		C		

Income:

			Properties			Totals
			A	B	C	(Add columns A, B, and C.)
3	Rents received	3				3
4	Royalties received	4				4

Expenses:

5	Advertising	5				
6	Auto and travel (see page E-2) .	6				
7	Cleaning and maintenance . . .	7				
8	Commissions	8				
9	Insurance	9				
10	Legal and other professional fees	10				
11	Management fees	11				
12	Mortgage interest paid to banks, etc. (see page E-2)	12				12
13	Other interest	13				
14	Repairs	14				
15	Supplies	15				
16	Taxes	16				
17	Utilities	17				
18	Other (list) ➤	18				
19	Add lines 5 through 18	19				19
20	Depreciation expense or depletion (see page E-2)	20				20
21	Total expenses. Add lines 19 and 20	21				
22	Income or (loss) from rental real estate or royalty properties. Subtract line 21 from line 3 (rents) or line 4 (royalties). If the result is a (loss), see page E-2 to find out if you must file **Form 6198** . . .	22				
23	Deductible rental real estate loss. **Caution:** *Your rental real estate loss on line 22 may be limited. See page E-3 to find out if you must file* **Form 8582.** *Real estate professionals must complete line 42 on page 2*	23	(	)(	)(	)

24	**Income.** Add positive amounts shown on line 22. **Do not** include any losses	24	
25	**Losses.** Add royalty losses from line 22 and rental real estate losses from line 23. Enter the total losses here .	25	( )
26	Total rental real estate and royalty income or (loss). Combine lines 24 and 25. Enter the result here. If Parts II, III, IV, and line 39 on page 2 do not apply to you, also enter this amount on Form 1040, line 17. Otherwise, include this amount in the total on line 40 on page 2	26	

For Paperwork Reduction Act Notice, see Form 1040 instructions.   Cat. No. 11344L   **Schedule E (Form 1040) 1995**

347

Schedule E (Form 1040) 1995   Attachment Sequence No. **13**   Page **2**

Name(s) shown on return. Do not enter name and social security number if shown on other side.	**Your social security number**

Note: *If you report amounts from farming or fishing on Schedule E, you must enter your gross income from those activities on line 41 below. Real estate professionals must complete line 42 below.*

Part II   **Income or Loss From Partnerships and S Corporations**   Note: *If you report a loss from an at-risk activity, you MUST check either column (e) or (f) of line 27 to describe your investment in the activity. See page E-4. If you check column (f), you must attach* **Form 6198.**

27	(a) Name	(b) Enter P for partnership; S for S corporation	(c) Check if foreign partnership	(d) Employer identification number	Investment At Risk? (e) All is at risk	(f) Some is not at risk
A						
B						
C						
D						
E						

	Passive Income and Loss		Nonpassive Income and Loss		
	(g) Passive loss allowed (attach Form 8582 if required)	(h) Passive income from Schedule K-1	(i) Nonpassive loss from Schedule K-1	(j) Section 179 expense deduction from Form 4562	(k) Nonpassive income from Schedule K-1
A					
B					
C					
D					
E					
28a Totals					
b Totals					

29	Add columns (h) and (k) of line 28a	29	
30	Add columns (g), (i), and (j) of line 28b	30	( )
31	Total partnership and S corporation income or (loss). Combine lines **29 and 30.** Enter the result here and include in the total on line 40 below	31	

Part III   **Income or Loss From Estates and Trusts**

32	(a) Name	(b) Employer identification number
A		
B		

	Passive Income and Loss		Nonpassive Income and Loss	
	(c) Passive deduction or loss allowed (attach Form 8582 if required)	(d) Passive income from Schedule K-1	(e) Deduction or loss from Schedule K-1	(f) Other income from Schedule K-1
A				
B				
33a Totals				
b Totals				

34	Add columns (d) and (f) of line 33a	34	
35	Add columns (c) and (e) of line 33b	35	( )
36	Total estate and trust income or (loss). Combine lines 34 and 35. Enter the result here and include in the total on line 40 below	36	

Part IV   **Income or Loss From Real Estate Mortgage Investment Conduits (REMICs)—Residual Holder**

37	(a) Name	(b) Employer identification number	(c) Excess inclusion from Schedules Q, line 2c (see page E-4)	(d) Taxable income (net loss) from Schedules Q, line 1b	(e) Income from Schedules Q, line 3b

38	Combine columns (d) and (e) only. Enter the result here and include in the total on line 40 below	38	

Part V   **Summary**

39	Net farm rental income or (loss) from **Form 4835.** Also, complete line 41 below	39	
40	TOTAL income or (loss). Combine lines 26, 31, 36, 38, and 39. Enter the result here and on Form 1040, line 17 ▶	40	
41	**Reconciliation of Farming and Fishing Income.** Enter your **gross** farming and fishing income reported on Form 4835, line 7; Schedule K-1 (Form 1065), line 15b; Schedule K-1 (Form 1120S), line 23; and Schedule K-1 (Form 1041), line 13 (see page E-4)	41	
42	**Reconciliation for Real Estate Professionals.** If you were a real estate professional (see page E-3), enter the net income or (loss) you reported anywhere on Form 1040 from all rental real estate activities in which you materially participated under the passive activity loss rules	42	

♲ *Printed on recycled paper*

SCHEDULE SE	Self-Employment Tax	OMB No. 1545-0074
(Form 1040)	➤ See Instructions for Schedule SE (Form 1040).	**1995**
Department of the Treasury Internal Revenue Service	➤ Attach to Form 1040.	Attachment Sequence No. **17**
Name of person with **self-employment** income (as shown on Form 1040)	Social security number of person with **self-employment** income ➤	

Who Must File Schedule SE

You must file Schedule SE if:

• You had net earnings from self-employment from **other than** church employee income (line 4 of Short Schedule SE or line 4c of Long Schedule SE) of $400 or more, **OR**

• You had church employee income of $108.28 or more. Income from services you performed as a minister or a member of a religious order **is not** church employee income. See page SE-1.

Note: *Even if you have a loss or a small amount of income from self-employment, it may be to your benefit to file Schedule SE and use either "optional method" in Part II of Long Schedule SE. See page SE-2.*

Exception. If your only self-employment income was from earnings as a minister, member of a religious order, or Christian Science practitioner **and** you filed Form 4361 and received IRS approval not to be taxed on those earnings, **do not** file Schedule SE. Instead, write "Exempt–Form 4361" on Form 1040, line 47.

May I Use Short Schedule SE or MUST I Use Long Schedule SE?

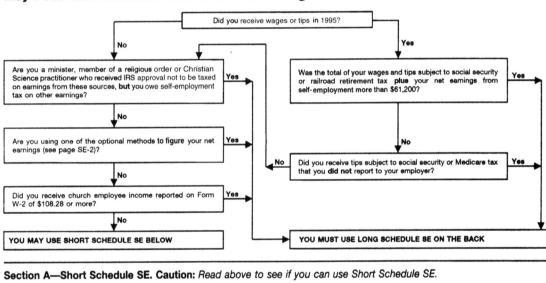

Section A—Short Schedule SE. Caution: *Read above to see if you can use Short Schedule SE.*

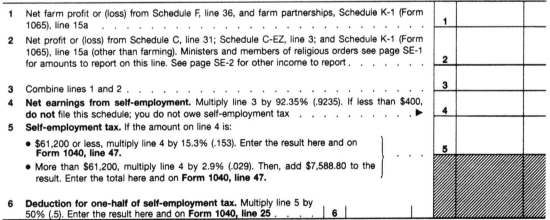

1	Net farm profit or (loss) from Schedule F, line 36, and farm partnerships, Schedule K-1 (Form 1065), line 15a	1
2	Net profit or (loss) from Schedule C, line 31; Schedule C-EZ, line 3; and Schedule K-1 (Form 1065), line 15a (other than farming). Ministers and members of religious orders see page SE-1 for amounts to report on this line. See page SE-2 for other income to report	2
3	Combine lines 1 and 2	3
4	**Net earnings from self-employment.** Multiply line 3 by 92.35% (.9235). If less than $400, **do not** file this schedule; you do not owe self-employment tax . . . . ➤	4

5	**Self-employment tax.** If the amount on line 4 is:
	   • $61,200 or less, multiply line 4 by 15.3% (.153). Enter the result here and on **Form 1040, line 47.**
	   • More than $61,200, multiply line 4 by 2.9% (.029). Then, add $7,588.80 to the result. Enter the total here and on **Form 1040, line 47.**
		5

6	**Deduction for one-half of self-employment tax.** Multiply line 5 by 50% (.5). Enter the result here and on **Form 1040, line 25**	6

For Paperwork Reduction Act Notice, see Form 1040 instructions.   Cat. No. 11358Z   **Schedule SE (Form 1040) 1995**

Schedule SE (Form 1040) 1995 | Attachment Sequence No. **17** | Page **2**

Name of person with **self-employment** income (as shown on Form 1040)	Social security number of person with **self-employment** income ▶

Section B—Long Schedule SE

Part I Self-Employment Tax

Note: *If your only income subject to self-employment tax is* **church employee income,** *skip lines 1 through 4b. Enter -0- on line 4c and go to line 5a. Income from services you performed as a minister or a member of a religious order* **is not** *church employee income. See page SE-1.*

A If you are a minister, member of a religious order, or Christian Science practitioner **and** you filed Form 4361, but you had $400 or more of **other** net earnings from self-employment, check here and continue with Part I . . . . . . ▶ ☐

1	Net farm profit or (loss) from Schedule F, line 36, and farm partnerships, Schedule K-1 (Form 1065), line 15a. **Note:** *Skip this line if you use the farm optional method. See page SE-3*	**1**		
2	Net profit or (loss) from Schedule C, line 31; Schedule C-EZ, line 3; and Schedule K-1 (Form 1065), line 15a (other than farming). Ministers and members of religious orders see page SE-1 for amounts to report on this line. See page SE-2 for other income to report. **Note:** *Skip this line if you use the nonfarm optional method. See page SE-3.*	**2**		
3	Combine lines 1 and 2	**3**		
4a	If line 3 is more than zero, multiply line 3 by 92.35% (.9235). Otherwise enter amount from line 3	**4a**		
b	If you elected one or both of the optional methods, enter the total of lines 15 and 17 here . .	**4b**		
c	Combine lines 4a and 4b. If less than $400, **do not** file this schedule; you do not owe self-employment tax. **Exception.** If less than $400 and you had **church employee income** enter -0- and continue ▶	**4c**		
5a	Enter your church employee income from Form W-2. **Caution:** *See page SE-1 for definition of church employee income*	**5a**		
b	Multiply line 5a by 92.35% (.9235). If less than $100, enter -0-	**5b**		
6	**Net earnings from self-employment.** Add lines 4c and 5b	**6**		
7	Maximum amount of combined wages and self-employment earnings subject to social security tax or the 6.2% portion of the 7.65% railroad retirement (tier 1) tax for 1995	**7**	61,200	00
8a	Total social security wages and tips (total of boxes 3 and 7 on Form(s) W-2) and railroad retirement (tier 1) compensation	**8a**		
b	Unreported tips subject to social security tax (from Form 4137, line 9)	**8b**		
c	Add lines 8a and 8b	**8c**		
9	Subtract line 8c from line 7. If zero or less, enter -0- here and on line 10 and go to line 11 . ▶	**9**		
10	Multiply the **smaller** of line 6 or line 9 by 12.4% (.124)	**10**		
11	Multiply line 6 by 2.9% (.029).	**11**		
12	**Self-employment tax.** Add lines 10 and 11. Enter here and on **Form 1040, line 47**	**12**		
13	**Deduction for one-half of self-employment tax.** Multiply line 12 by 50% (.5). Enter the result here and on **Form 1040, line 25**	**13**		

Part II Optional Methods To Figure Net Earnings (See page SE-2.)

Farm Optional Method. You may use this method **only** if:
- Your gross farm income[1] was not more than $2,400, **or**
- Your gross farm income[1] was more than $2,400 and your net farm profits[2] were less than $1,733.

14	Maximum income for optional methods	**14**	1,600	00
15	Enter the **smaller** of: two-thirds (⅔) of gross farm income[1] (not less than zero) or $1,600. Also, include this amount on line 4b above	**15**		

Nonfarm Optional Method. You may use this method **only** if:
- Your net nonfarm profits[3] were less than $1,733 and also less than 72.189% of your gross nonfarm income,[4] **and**
- You had net earnings from self-employment of at least $400 in 2 of the prior 3 years.

Caution: *You may use this method no more than five times.*

16	Subtract line 15 from line 14	**16**		
17	Enter the **smaller** of: two-thirds (⅔) of gross nonfarm income[4] (not less than zero) or the amount on line 16. Also, include this amount on line 4b above	**17**		

[1]From Schedule F, line 11, and Schedule K-1 (Form 1065), line 15b.   [3]From Schedule C, line 31; Schedule C-EZ, line 3; and Schedule K-1 (Form 1065), line 15a.
[2]From Schedule F, line 36, and Schedule K-1 (Form 1065), line 15a.   [4]From Schedule C, line 7; Schedule C-EZ, line 1; and Schedule K-1 (Form 1065), line 15c.

♻ *Printed on recycled paper*

1995 Tax Tables and Tax Rate Schedules

Tax Tables from the IRS

You can use the tables and rates in this appendix to compute your income tax.

To compute your income tax using the Tax Tables, get the taxable income number from line 37 of your 1040 (line 6 of the 1040EZ, or line 22 of the 1040A). Find the number nearest to your taxable income in the columns containing bold numbers in the Tax Tables. Your taxable income should fall between two numbers in the bold columns of the tables. Put your finger on the place in the Tax Tables, or draw a line under the amount, so you won't lose your place.

Find the filing status that agrees with what you selected on your tax return, and follow down that column with an available finger until you reach the line you marked. The number you see at the place where the line on which your income falls and the column coming down from your filing status is your income tax; put that number on line 38 of your tax return.

If you need to use the Tax Rate Schedules to compute your income tax, please refer to "Using the Rate Schedules" in Chapter 23, "Figuring the Base Income Tax: Tables and Rates," for a detailed illustration of how this calculation works.

Section 5.

1995 Tax Table

Use if your taxable income is less than $100,000. If $100,000 or more, use the Tax Rate Schedules.

Example. Mr. and Mrs. Brown are filing a joint return. Their taxable income on line 37 of Form 1040 is $25,300. First, they find the $25,300–25,350 income line. Next, they find the column for married filing jointly and read down the column. The amount shown where the income line and filing status column meet is $3,799. This is the tax amount they must enter on line 38 of their Form 1040.

Sample Table

At least	But less than	Single	Married filing jointly *	Married filing separately	Head of a household
			Your tax is—		
25,200	25,250	4,028	3,784	4,528	3,784
25,250	25,300	4,042	3,791	4,542	3,791
25,300	25,350	4,056	(3,799)	4,556	3,799
25,350	25,400	4,070	3,806	4,570	3,806

If line 37 (taxable income) is— At least	But less than	Single	Married filing jointly *	Married filing separately	Head of a household
			Your tax is—		
0	5	0	0	0	0
5	15	2	2	2	2
15	25	3	3	3	3
25	50	6	6	6	6
50	75	9	9	9	9
75	100	13	13	13	13
100	125	17	17	17	17
125	150	21	21	21	21
150	175	24	24	24	24
175	200	28	28	28	28
200	225	32	32	32	32
225	250	36	36	36	36
250	275	39	39	39	39
275	300	43	43	43	43
300	325	47	47	47	47
325	350	51	51	51	51
350	375	54	54	54	54
375	400	58	58	58	58
400	425	62	62	62	62
425	450	66	66	66	66
450	475	69	69	69	69
475	500	73	73	73	73
500	525	77	77	77	77
525	550	81	81	81	81
550	575	84	84	84	84
575	600	88	88	88	88
600	625	92	92	92	92
625	650	96	96	96	96
650	675	99	99	99	99
675	700	103	103	103	103
700	725	107	107	107	107
725	750	111	111	111	111
750	775	114	114	114	114
775	800	118	118	118	118
800	825	122	122	122	122
825	850	126	126	126	126
850	875	129	129	129	129
875	900	133	133	133	133
900	925	137	137	137	137
925	950	141	141	141	141
950	975	144	144	144	144
975	1,000	148	148	148	148

1,000

At least	But less than	Single	Married filing jointly *	Married filing separately	Head of a household
1,000	1,025	152	152	152	152
1,025	1,050	156	156	156	156
1,050	1,075	159	159	159	159
1,075	1,100	163	163	163	163
1,100	1,125	167	167	167	167
1,125	1,150	171	171	171	171
1,150	1,175	174	174	174	174
1,175	1,200	178	178	178	178
1,200	1,225	182	182	182	182
1,225	1,250	186	186	186	186
1,250	1,275	189	189	189	189
1,275	1,300	193	193	193	193

If line 37 (taxable income) is— At least	But less than	Single	Married filing jointly *	Married filing separately	Head of a household
1,300	1,325	197	197	197	197
1,325	1,350	201	201	201	201
1,350	1,375	204	204	204	204
1,375	1,400	208	208	208	208
1,400	1,425	212	212	212	212
1,425	1,450	216	216	216	216
1,450	1,475	219	219	219	219
1,475	1,500	223	223	223	223
1,500	1,525	227	227	227	227
1,525	1,550	231	231	231	231
1,550	1,575	234	234	234	234
1,575	1,600	238	238	238	238
1,600	1,625	242	242	242	242
1,625	1,650	246	246	246	246
1,650	1,675	249	249	249	249
1,675	1,700	253	253	253	253
1,700	1,725	257	257	257	257
1,725	1,750	261	261	261	261
1,750	1,775	264	264	264	264
1,775	1,800	268	268	268	268
1,800	1,825	272	272	272	272
1,825	1,850	276	276	276	276
1,850	1,875	279	279	279	279
1,875	1,900	283	283	283	283
1,900	1,925	287	287	287	287
1,925	1,950	291	291	291	291
1,950	1,975	294	294	294	294
1,975	2,000	298	298	298	298

2,000

At least	But less than	Single	Married filing jointly *	Married filing separately	Head of a household
2,000	2,025	302	302	302	302
2,025	2,050	306	306	306	306
2,050	2,075	309	309	309	309
2,075	2,100	313	313	313	313
2,100	2,125	317	317	317	317
2,125	2,150	321	321	321	321
2,150	2,175	324	324	324	324
2,175	2,200	328	328	328	328
2,200	2,225	332	332	332	332
2,225	2,250	336	336	336	336
2,250	2,275	339	339	339	339
2,275	2,300	343	343	343	343
2,300	2,325	347	347	347	347
2,325	2,350	351	351	351	351
2,350	2,375	354	354	354	354
2,375	2,400	358	358	358	358
2,400	2,425	362	362	362	362
2,425	2,450	366	366	366	366
2,450	2,475	369	369	369	369
2,475	2,500	373	373	373	373
2,500	2,525	377	377	377	377
2,525	2,550	381	381	381	381
2,550	2,575	384	384	384	384
2,575	2,600	388	388	388	388
2,600	2,625	392	392	392	392
2,625	2,650	396	396	396	396
2,650	2,675	399	399	399	399
2,675	2,700	403	403	403	403

If line 37 (taxable income) is— At least	But less than	Single	Married filing jointly *	Married filing separately	Head of a household
2,700	2,725	407	407	407	407
2,725	2,750	411	411	411	411
2,750	2,775	414	414	414	414
2,775	2,800	418	418	418	418
2,800	2,825	422	422	422	422
2,825	2,850	426	426	426	426
2,850	2,875	429	429	429	429
2,875	2,900	433	433	433	433
2,900	2,925	437	437	437	437
2,925	2,950	441	441	441	441
2,950	2,975	444	444	444	444
2,975	3,000	448	448	448	448

3,000

At least	But less than	Single	Married filing jointly *	Married filing separately	Head of a household
3,000	3,050	454	454	454	454
3,050	3,100	461	461	461	461
3,100	3,150	469	469	469	469
3,150	3,200	476	476	476	476
3,200	3,250	484	484	484	484
3,250	3,300	491	491	491	491
3,300	3,350	499	499	499	499
3,350	3,400	506	506	506	506
3,400	3,450	514	514	514	514
3,450	3,500	521	521	521	521
3,500	3,550	529	529	529	529
3,550	3,600	536	536	536	536
3,600	3,650	544	544	544	544
3,650	3,700	551	551	551	551
3,700	3,750	559	559	559	559
3,750	3,800	566	566	566	566
3,800	3,850	574	574	574	574
3,850	3,900	581	581	581	581
3,900	3,950	589	589	589	589
3,950	4,000	596	596	596	596

4,000

At least	But less than	Single	Married filing jointly *	Married filing separately	Head of a household
4,000	4,050	604	604	604	604
4,050	4,100	611	611	611	611
4,100	4,150	619	619	619	619
4,150	4,200	626	626	626	626
4,200	4,250	634	634	634	634
4,250	4,300	641	641	641	641
4,300	4,350	649	649	649	649
4,350	4,400	656	656	656	656
4,400	4,450	664	664	664	664
4,450	4,500	671	671	671	671
4,500	4,550	679	679	679	679
4,550	4,600	686	686	686	686
4,600	4,650	694	694	694	694
4,650	4,700	701	701	701	701
4,700	4,750	709	709	709	709
4,750	4,800	716	716	716	716
4,800	4,850	724	724	724	724
4,850	4,900	731	731	731	731
4,900	4,950	739	739	739	739
4,950	5,000	746	746	746	746

Continued on next page

* This column must also be used by a qualifying widow(er).

1995 Tax Table—*Continued*

If line 37 (taxable income) is—		And you are—			
At least	But less than	Single	Married filing jointly *	Married filing separately	Head of a household
		Your tax is—			

5,000

At least	But less than	Single	Married filing jointly	Married filing separately	Head of a household
5,000	5,050	754	754	754	754
5,050	5,100	761	761	761	761
5,100	5,150	769	769	769	769
5,150	5,200	776	776	776	776
5,200	5,250	784	784	784	784
5,250	5,300	791	791	791	791
5,300	5,350	799	799	799	799
5,350	5,400	806	806	806	806
5,400	5,450	814	814	814	814
5,450	5,500	821	821	821	821
5,500	5,550	829	829	829	829
5,550	5,600	836	836	836	836
5,600	5,650	844	844	844	844
5,650	5,700	851	851	851	851
5,700	5,750	859	859	859	859
5,750	5,800	866	866	866	866
5,800	5,850	874	874	874	874
5,850	5,900	881	881	881	881
5,900	5,950	889	889	889	889
5,950	6,000	896	896	896	896

6,000

At least	But less than	Single	Married filing jointly	Married filing separately	Head of a household
6,000	6,050	904	904	904	904
6,050	6,100	911	911	911	911
6,100	6,150	919	919	919	919
6,150	6,200	926	926	926	926
6,200	6,250	934	934	934	934
6,250	6,300	941	941	941	941
6,300	6,350	949	949	949	949
6,350	6,400	956	956	956	956
6,400	6,450	964	964	964	964
6,450	6,500	971	971	971	971
6,500	6,550	979	979	979	979
6,550	6,600	986	986	986	986
6,600	6,650	994	994	994	994
6,650	6,700	1,001	1,001	1,001	1,001
6,700	6,750	1,009	1,009	1,009	1,009
6,750	6,800	1,016	1,016	1,016	1,016
6,800	6,850	1,024	1,024	1,024	1,024
6,850	6,900	1,031	1,031	1,031	1,031
6,900	6,950	1,039	1,039	1,039	1,039
6,950	7,000	1,046	1,046	1,046	1,046

7,000

At least	But less than	Single	Married filing jointly	Married filing separately	Head of a household
7,000	7,050	1,054	1,054	1,054	1,054
7,050	7,100	1,061	1,061	1,061	1,061
7,100	7,150	1,069	1,069	1,069	1,069
7,150	7,200	1,076	1,076	1,076	1,076
7,200	7,250	1,084	1,084	1,084	1,084
7,250	7,300	1,091	1,091	1,091	1,091
7,300	7,350	1,099	1,099	1,099	1,099
7,350	7,400	1,106	1,106	1,106	1,106
7,400	7,450	1,114	1,114	1,114	1,114
7,450	7,500	1,121	1,121	1,121	1,121
7,500	7,550	1,129	1,129	1,129	1,129
7,550	7,600	1,136	1,136	1,136	1,136
7,600	7,650	1,144	1,144	1,144	1,144
7,650	7,700	1,151	1,151	1,151	1,151
7,700	7,750	1,159	1,159	1,159	1,159
7,750	7,800	1,166	1,166	1,166	1,166
7,800	7,850	1,174	1,174	1,174	1,174
7,850	7,900	1,181	1,181	1,181	1,181
7,900	7,950	1,189	1,189	1,189	1,189
7,950	8,000	1,196	1,196	1,196	1,196

8,000

At least	But less than	Single	Married filing jointly	Married filing separately	Head of a household
8,000	8,050	1,204	1,204	1,204	1,204
8,050	8,100	1,211	1,211	1,211	1,211
8,100	8,150	1,219	1,219	1,219	1,219
8,150	8,200	1,226	1,226	1,226	1,226
8,200	8,250	1,234	1,234	1,234	1,234
8,250	8,300	1,241	1,241	1,241	1,241
8,300	8,350	1,249	1,249	1,249	1,249
8,350	8,400	1,256	1,256	1,256	1,256
8,400	8,450	1,264	1,264	1,264	1,264
8,450	8,500	1,271	1,271	1,271	1,271
8,500	8,550	1,279	1,279	1,279	1,279
8,550	8,600	1,286	1,286	1,286	1,286
8,600	8,650	1,294	1,294	1,294	1,294
8,650	8,700	1,301	1,301	1,301	1,301
8,700	8,750	1,309	1,309	1,309	1,309
8,750	8,800	1,316	1,316	1,316	1,316
8,800	8,850	1,324	1,324	1,324	1,324
8,850	8,900	1,331	1,331	1,331	1,331
8,900	8,950	1,339	1,339	1,339	1,339
8,950	9,000	1,346	1,346	1,346	1,346

9,000

At least	But less than	Single	Married filing jointly	Married filing separately	Head of a household
9,000	9,050	1,354	1,354	1,354	1,354
9,050	9,100	1,361	1,361	1,361	1,361
9,100	9,150	1,369	1,369	1,369	1,369
9,150	9,200	1,376	1,376	1,376	1,376
9,200	9,250	1,384	1,384	1,384	1,384
9,250	9,300	1,391	1,391	1,391	1,391
9,300	9,350	1,399	1,399	1,399	1,399
9,350	9,400	1,406	1,406	1,406	1,406
9,400	9,450	1,414	1,414	1,414	1,414
9,450	9,500	1,421	1,421	1,421	1,421
9,500	9,550	1,429	1,429	1,429	1,429
9,550	9,600	1,436	1,436	1,436	1,436
9,600	9,650	1,444	1,444	1,444	1,444
9,650	9,700	1,451	1,451	1,451	1,451
9,700	9,750	1,459	1,459	1,459	1,459
9,750	9,800	1,466	1,466	1,466	1,466
9,800	9,850	1,474	1,474	1,474	1,474
9,850	9,900	1,481	1,481	1,481	1,481
9,900	9,950	1,489	1,489	1,489	1,489
9,950	10,000	1,496	1,496	1,496	1,496

10,000

At least	But less than	Single	Married filing jointly	Married filing separately	Head of a household
10,000	10,050	1,504	1,504	1,504	1,504
10,050	10,100	1,511	1,511	1,511	1,511
10,100	10,150	1,519	1,519	1,519	1,519
10,150	10,200	1,526	1,526	1,526	1,526
10,200	10,250	1,534	1,534	1,534	1,534
10,250	10,300	1,541	1,541	1,541	1,541
10,300	10,350	1,549	1,549	1,549	1,549
10,350	10,400	1,556	1,556	1,556	1,556
10,400	10,450	1,564	1,564	1,564	1,564
10,450	10,500	1,571	1,571	1,571	1,571
10,500	10,550	1,579	1,579	1,579	1,579
10,550	10,600	1,586	1,586	1,586	1,586
10,600	10,650	1,594	1,594	1,594	1,594
10,650	10,700	1,601	1,601	1,601	1,601
10,700	10,750	1,609	1,609	1,609	1,609
10,750	10,800	1,616	1,616	1,616	1,616
10,800	10,850	1,624	1,624	1,624	1,624
10,850	10,900	1,631	1,631	1,631	1,631
10,900	10,950	1,639	1,639	1,639	1,639
10,950	11,000	1,646	1,646	1,646	1,646

11,000

At least	But less than	Single	Married filing jointly	Married filing separately	Head of a household
11,000	11,050	1,654	1,654	1,654	1,654
11,050	11,100	1,661	1,661	1,661	1,661
11,100	11,150	1,669	1,669	1,669	1,669
11,150	11,200	1,676	1,676	1,676	1,676
11,200	11,250	1,684	1,684	1,684	1,684
11,250	11,300	1,691	1,691	1,691	1,691
11,300	11,350	1,699	1,699	1,699	1,699
11,350	11,400	1,706	1,706	1,706	1,706
11,400	11,450	1,714	1,714	1,714	1,714
11,450	11,500	1,721	1,721	1,721	1,721
11,500	11,550	1,729	1,729	1,729	1,729
11,550	11,600	1,736	1,736	1,736	1,736
11,600	11,650	1,744	1,744	1,744	1,744
11,650	11,700	1,751	1,751	1,751	1,751
11,700	11,750	1,759	1,759	1,759	1,759
11,750	11,800	1,766	1,766	1,766	1,766
11,800	11,850	1,774	1,774	1,774	1,774
11,850	11,900	1,781	1,781	1,781	1,781
11,900	11,950	1,789	1,789	1,789	1,789
11,950	12,000	1,796	1,796	1,796	1,796

12,000

At least	But less than	Single	Married filing jointly	Married filing separately	Head of a household
12,000	12,050	1,804	1,804	1,804	1,804
12,050	12,100	1,811	1,811	1,811	1,811
12,100	12,150	1,819	1,819	1,819	1,819
12,150	12,200	1,826	1,826	1,826	1,826
12,200	12,250	1,834	1,834	1,834	1,834
12,250	12,300	1,841	1,841	1,841	1,841
12,300	12,350	1,849	1,849	1,849	1,849
12,350	12,400	1,856	1,856	1,856	1,856
12,400	12,450	1,864	1,864	1,864	1,864
12,450	12,500	1,871	1,871	1,871	1,871
12,500	12,550	1,879	1,879	1,879	1,879
12,550	12,600	1,886	1,886	1,886	1,886
12,600	12,650	1,894	1,894	1,894	1,894
12,650	12,700	1,901	1,901	1,901	1,901
12,700	12,750	1,909	1,909	1,909	1,909
12,750	12,800	1,916	1,916	1,916	1,916
12,800	12,850	1,924	1,924	1,924	1,924
12,850	12,900	1,931	1,931	1,931	1,931
12,900	12,950	1,939	1,939	1,939	1,939
12,950	13,000	1,946	1,946	1,946	1,946

13,000

At least	But less than	Single	Married filing jointly	Married filing separately	Head of a household
13,000	13,050	1,954	1,954	1,954	1,954
13,050	13,100	1,961	1,961	1,961	1,961
13,100	13,150	1,969	1,969	1,969	1,969
13,150	13,200	1,976	1,976	1,976	1,976
13,200	13,250	1,984	1,984	1,984	1,984
13,250	13,300	1,991	1,991	1,991	1,991
13,300	13,350	1,999	1,999	1,999	1,999
13,350	13,400	2,006	2,006	2,006	2,006
13,400	13,450	2,014	2,014	2,014	2,014
13,450	13,500	2,021	2,021	2,021	2,021
13,500	13,550	2,029	2,029	2,029	2,029
13,550	13,600	2,036	2,036	2,036	2,036
13,600	13,650	2,044	2,044	2,044	2,044
13,650	13,700	2,051	2,051	2,051	2,051
13,700	13,750	2,059	2,059	2,059	2,059
13,750	13,800	2,066	2,066	2,066	2,066
13,800	13,850	2,074	2,074	2,074	2,074
13,850	13,900	2,081	2,081	2,081	2,081
13,900	13,950	2,089	2,089	2,089	2,089
13,950	14,000	2,096	2,096	2,096	2,096

* This column must also be used by a qualifying widow(er).

Continued on next page

1995 Tax Table—Continued

If line 37 (taxable income) is— At least	But less than	Single	Married filing jointly *	Married filing separately	Head of a household
14,000					
14,000	14,050	2,104	2,104	2,104	2,104
14,050	14,100	2,111	2,111	2,111	2,111
14,100	14,150	2,119	2,119	2,119	2,119
14,150	14,200	2,126	2,126	2,126	2,126
14,200	14,250	2,134	2,134	2,134	2,134
14,250	14,300	2,141	2,141	2,141	2,141
14,300	14,350	2,149	2,149	2,149	2,149
14,350	14,400	2,156	2,156	2,156	2,156
14,400	14,450	2,164	2,164	2,164	2,164
14,450	14,500	2,171	2,171	2,171	2,171
14,500	14,550	2,179	2,179	2,179	2,179
14,550	14,600	2,186	2,186	2,186	2,186
14,600	14,650	2,194	2,194	2,194	2,194
14,650	14,700	2,201	2,201	2,201	2,201
14,700	14,750	2,209	2,209	2,209	2,209
14,750	14,800	2,216	2,216	2,216	2,216
14,800	14,850	2,224	2,224	2,224	2,224
14,850	14,900	2,231	2,231	2,231	2,231
14,900	14,950	2,239	2,239	2,239	2,239
14,950	15,000	2,246	2,246	2,246	2,246
15,000					
15,000	15,050	2,254	2,254	2,254	2,254
15,050	15,100	2,261	2,261	2,261	2,261
15,100	15,150	2,269	2,269	2,269	2,269
15,150	15,200	2,276	2,276	2,276	2,276
15,200	15,250	2,284	2,284	2,284	2,284
15,250	15,300	2,291	2,291	2,291	2,291
15,300	15,350	2,299	2,299	2,299	2,299
15,350	15,400	2,306	2,306	2,306	2,306
15,400	15,450	2,314	2,314	2,314	2,314
15,450	15,500	2,321	2,321	2,321	2,321
15,500	15,550	2,329	2,329	2,329	2,329
15,550	15,600	2,336	2,336	2,336	2,336
15,600	15,650	2,344	2,344	2,344	2,344
15,650	15,700	2,351	2,351	2,351	2,351
15,700	15,750	2,359	2,359	2,359	2,359
15,750	15,800	2,366	2,366	2,366	2,366
15,800	15,850	2,374	2,374	2,374	2,374
15,850	15,900	2,381	2,381	2,381	2,381
15,900	15,950	2,389	2,389	2,389	2,389
15,950	16,000	2,396	2,396	2,396	2,396
16,000					
16,000	16,050	2,404	2,404	2,404	2,404
16,050	16,100	2,411	2,411	2,411	2,411
16,100	16,150	2,419	2,419	2,419	2,419
16,150	16,200	2,426	2,426	2,426	2,426
16,200	16,250	2,434	2,434	2,434	2,434
16,250	16,300	2,441	2,441	2,441	2,441
16,300	16,350	2,449	2,449	2,449	2,449
16,350	16,400	2,456	2,456	2,456	2,456
16,400	16,450	2,464	2,464	2,464	2,464
16,450	16,500	2,471	2,471	2,471	2,471
16,500	16,550	2,479	2,479	2,479	2,479
16,550	16,600	2,486	2,486	2,486	2,486
16,600	16,650	2,494	2,494	2,494	2,494
16,650	16,700	2,501	2,501	2,501	2,501
16,700	16,750	2,509	2,509	2,509	2,509
16,750	16,800	2,516	2,516	2,516	2,516
16,800	16,850	2,524	2,524	2,524	2,524
16,850	16,900	2,531	2,531	2,531	2,531
16,900	16,950	2,539	2,539	2,539	2,539
16,950	17,000	2,546	2,546	2,546	2,546

If line 37 (taxable income) is— At least	But less than	Single	Married filing jointly *	Married filing separately	Head of a household
17,000					
17,000	17,050	2,554	2,554	2,554	2,554
17,050	17,100	2,561	2,561	2,561	2,561
17,100	17,150	2,569	2,569	2,569	2,569
17,150	17,200	2,576	2,576	2,576	2,576
17,200	17,250	2,584	2,584	2,584	2,584
17,250	17,300	2,591	2,591	2,591	2,591
17,300	17,350	2,599	2,599	2,599	2,599
17,350	17,400	2,606	2,606	2,606	2,606
17,400	17,450	2,614	2,614	2,614	2,614
17,450	17,500	2,621	2,621	2,621	2,621
17,500	17,550	2,629	2,629	2,629	2,629
17,550	17,600	2,636	2,636	2,636	2,636
17,600	17,650	2,644	2,644	2,644	2,644
17,650	17,700	2,651	2,651	2,651	2,651
17,700	17,750	2,659	2,659	2,659	2,659
17,750	17,800	2,666	2,666	2,666	2,666
17,800	17,850	2,674	2,674	2,674	2,674
17,850	17,900	2,681	2,681	2,681	2,681
17,900	17,950	2,689	2,689	2,689	2,689
17,950	18,000	2,696	2,696	2,696	2,696
18,000					
18,000	18,050	2,704	2,704	2,704	2,704
18,050	18,100	2,711	2,711	2,711	2,711
18,100	18,150	2,719	2,719	2,719	2,719
18,150	18,200	2,726	2,726	2,726	2,726
18,200	18,250	2,734	2,734	2,734	2,734
18,250	18,300	2,741	2,741	2,741	2,741
18,300	18,350	2,749	2,749	2,749	2,749
18,350	18,400	2,756	2,756	2,756	2,756
18,400	18,450	2,764	2,764	2,764	2,764
18,450	18,500	2,771	2,771	2,771	2,771
18,500	18,550	2,779	2,779	2,779	2,779
18,550	18,600	2,786	2,786	2,786	2,786
18,600	18,650	2,794	2,794	2,794	2,794
18,650	18,700	2,801	2,801	2,801	2,801
18,700	18,750	2,809	2,809	2,809	2,809
18,750	18,800	2,816	2,816	2,816	2,816
18,800	18,850	2,824	2,824	2,824	2,824
18,850	18,900	2,831	2,831	2,831	2,831
18,900	18,950	2,839	2,839	2,839	2,839
18,950	19,000	2,846	2,846	2,846	2,846
19,000					
19,000	19,050	2,854	2,854	2,854	2,854
19,050	19,100	2,861	2,861	2,861	2,861
19,100	19,150	2,869	2,869	2,869	2,869
19,150	19,200	2,876	2,876	2,876	2,876
19,200	19,250	2,884	2,884	2,884	2,884
19,250	19,300	2,891	2,891	2,891	2,891
19,300	19,350	2,899	2,899	2,899	2,899
19,350	19,400	2,906	2,906	2,906	2,906
19,400	19,450	2,914	2,914	2,914	2,914
19,450	19,500	2,921	2,921	2,921	2,921
19,500	19,550	2,929	2,929	2,932	2,929
19,550	19,600	2,936	2,936	2,946	2,936
19,600	19,650	2,944	2,944	2,960	2,944
19,650	19,700	2,951	2,951	2,974	2,951
19,700	19,750	2,959	2,959	2,988	2,959
19,750	19,800	2,966	2,966	3,002	2,966
19,800	19,850	2,974	2,974	3,016	2,974
19,850	19,900	2,981	2,981	3,030	2,981
19,900	19,950	2,989	2,989	3,044	2,989
19,950	20,000	2,996	2,996	3,058	2,996

If line 37 (taxable income) is— At least	But less than	Single	Married filing jointly *	Married filing separately	Head of a household
20,000					
20,000	20,050	3,004	3,004	3,072	3,004
20,050	20,100	3,011	3,011	3,086	3,011
20,100	20,150	3,019	3,019	3,100	3,019
20,150	20,200	3,026	3,026	3,114	3,026
20,200	20,250	3,034	3,034	3,128	3,034
20,250	20,300	3,041	3,041	3,142	3,041
20,300	20,350	3,049	3,049	3,156	3,049
20,350	20,400	3,056	3,056	3,170	3,056
20,400	20,450	3,064	3,064	3,184	3,064
20,450	20,500	3,071	3,071	3,198	3,071
20,500	20,550	3,079	3,079	3,212	3,079
20,550	20,600	3,086	3,086	3,226	3,086
20,600	20,650	3,094	3,094	3,240	3,094
20,650	20,700	3,101	3,101	3,254	3,101
20,700	20,750	3,109	3,109	3,268	3,109
20,750	20,800	3,116	3,116	3,282	3,116
20,800	20,850	3,124	3,124	3,296	3,124
20,850	20,900	3,131	3,131	3,310	3,131
20,900	20,950	3,139	3,139	3,324	3,139
20,950	21,000	3,146	3,146	3,338	3,146
21,000					
21,000	21,050	3,154	3,154	3,352	3,154
21,050	21,100	3,161	3,161	3,366	3,161
21,100	21,150	3,169	3,169	3,380	3,169
21,150	21,200	3,176	3,176	3,394	3,176
21,200	21,250	3,184	3,184	3,408	3,184
21,250	21,300	3,191	3,191	3,422	3,191
21,300	21,350	3,199	3,199	3,436	3,199
21,350	21,400	3,206	3,206	3,450	3,206
21,400	21,450	3,214	3,214	3,464	3,214
21,450	21,500	3,221	3,221	3,478	3,221
21,500	21,550	3,229	3,229	3,492	3,229
21,550	21,600	3,236	3,236	3,506	3,236
21,600	21,650	3,244	3,244	3,520	3,244
21,650	21,700	3,251	3,251	3,534	3,251
21,700	21,750	3,259	3,259	3,548	3,259
21,750	21,800	3,266	3,266	3,562	3,266
21,800	21,850	3,274	3,274	3,576	3,274
21,850	21,900	3,281	3,281	3,590	3,281
21,900	21,950	3,289	3,289	3,604	3,289
21,950	22,000	3,296	3,296	3,618	3,296
22,000					
22,000	22,050	3,304	3,304	3,632	3,304
22,050	22,100	3,311	3,311	3,646	3,311
22,100	22,150	3,319	3,319	3,660	3,319
22,150	22,200	3,326	3,326	3,674	3,326
22,200	22,250	3,334	3,334	3,688	3,334
22,250	22,300	3,341	3,341	3,702	3,341
22,300	22,350	3,349	3,349	3,716	3,349
22,350	22,400	3,356	3,356	3,730	3,356
22,400	22,450	3,364	3,364	3,744	3,364
22,450	22,500	3,371	3,371	3,758	3,371
22,500	22,550	3,379	3,379	3,772	3,379
22,550	22,600	3,386	3,386	3,786	3,386
22,600	22,650	3,394	3,394	3,800	3,394
22,650	22,700	3,401	3,401	3,814	3,401
22,700	22,750	3,409	3,409	3,828	3,409
22,750	22,800	3,416	3,416	3,842	3,416
22,800	22,850	3,424	3,424	3,856	3,424
22,850	22,900	3,431	3,431	3,870	3,431
22,900	22,950	3,439	3,439	3,884	3,439
22,950	23,000	3,446	3,446	3,898	3,446

* This column must also be used by a qualifying widow(er).

Continued on next page

1995 Tax Table—*Continued*

23,000 – 25,000

At least	But less than	Single	Married filing jointly*	Married filing separately	Head of a household
23,000					
23,000	23,050	3,454	3,454	3,912	3,454
23,050	23,100	3,461	3,461	3,926	3,461
23,100	23,150	3,469	3,469	3,940	3,469
23,150	23,200	3,476	3,476	3,954	3,476
23,200	23,250	3,484	3,484	3,968	3,484
23,250	23,300	3,491	3,491	3,982	3,491
23,300	23,350	3,499	3,499	3,996	3,499
23,350	23,400	3,510	3,506	4,010	3,506
23,400	23,450	3,524	3,514	4,024	3,514
23,450	23,500	3,538	3,521	4,038	3,521
23,500	23,550	3,552	3,529	4,052	3,529
23,550	23,600	3,566	3,536	4,066	3,536
23,600	23,650	3,580	3,544	4,080	3,544
23,650	23,700	3,594	3,551	4,094	3,551
23,700	23,750	3,608	3,559	4,108	3,559
23,750	23,800	3,622	3,566	4,122	3,566
23,800	23,850	3,636	3,574	4,136	3,574
23,850	23,900	3,650	3,581	4,150	3,581
23,900	23,950	3,664	3,589	4,164	3,589
23,950	24,000	3,678	3,596	4,178	3,596
24,000					
24,000	24,050	3,692	3,604	4,192	3,604
24,050	24,100	3,706	3,611	4,206	3,611
24,100	24,150	3,720	3,619	4,220	3,619
24,150	24,200	3,734	3,626	4,234	3,626
24,200	24,250	3,748	3,634	4,248	3,634
24,250	24,300	3,762	3,641	4,262	3,641
24,300	24,350	3,776	3,649	4,276	3,649
24,350	24,400	3,790	3,656	4,290	3,656
24,400	24,450	3,804	3,664	4,304	3,664
24,450	24,500	3,818	3,671	4,318	3,671
24,500	24,550	3,832	3,679	4,332	3,679
24,550	24,600	3,846	3,686	4,346	3,686
24,600	24,650	3,860	3,694	4,360	3,694
24,650	24,700	3,874	3,701	4,374	3,701
24,700	24,750	3,888	3,709	4,388	3,709
24,750	24,800	3,902	3,716	4,402	3,716
24,800	24,850	3,916	3,724	4,416	3,724
24,850	24,900	3,930	3,731	4,430	3,731
24,900	24,950	3,944	3,739	4,444	3,739
24,950	25,000	3,958	3,746	4,458	3,746
25,000					
25,000	25,050	3,972	3,754	4,472	3,754
25,050	25,100	3,986	3,761	4,486	3,761
25,100	25,150	4,000	3,769	4,500	3,769
25,150	25,200	4,014	3,776	4,514	3,776
25,200	25,250	4,028	3,784	4,528	3,784
25,250	25,300	4,042	3,791	4,542	3,791
25,300	25,350	4,056	3,799	4,556	3,799
25,350	25,400	4,070	3,806	4,570	3,806
25,400	25,450	4,084	3,814	4,584	3,814
25,450	25,500	4,098	3,821	4,598	3,821
25,500	25,550	4,112	3,829	4,612	3,829
25,550	25,600	4,126	3,836	4,626	3,836
25,600	25,650	4,140	3,844	4,640	3,844
25,650	25,700	4,154	3,851	4,654	3,851
25,700	25,750	4,168	3,859	4,668	3,859
25,750	25,800	4,182	3,866	4,682	3,866
25,800	25,850	4,196	3,874	4,696	3,874
25,850	25,900	4,210	3,881	4,710	3,881
25,900	25,950	4,224	3,889	4,724	3,889
25,950	26,000	4,238	3,896	4,738	3,896

26,000 – 28,000

At least	But less than	Single	Married filing jointly*	Married filing separately	Head of a household
26,000					
26,000	26,050	4,252	3,904	4,752	3,904
26,050	26,100	4,266	3,911	4,766	3,911
26,100	26,150	4,280	3,919	4,780	3,919
26,150	26,200	4,294	3,926	4,794	3,926
26,200	26,250	4,308	3,934	4,808	3,934
26,250	26,300	4,322	3,941	4,822	3,941
26,300	26,350	4,336	3,949	4,836	3,949
26,350	26,400	4,350	3,956	4,850	3,956
26,400	26,450	4,364	3,964	4,864	3,964
26,450	26,500	4,378	3,971	4,878	3,971
26,500	26,550	4,392	3,979	4,892	3,979
26,550	26,600	4,406	3,986	4,906	3,986
26,600	26,650	4,420	3,994	4,920	3,994
26,650	26,700	4,434	4,001	4,934	4,001
26,700	26,750	4,448	4,009	4,948	4,009
26,750	26,800	4,462	4,016	4,962	4,016
26,800	26,850	4,476	4,024	4,976	4,024
26,850	26,900	4,490	4,031	4,990	4,031
26,900	26,950	4,504	4,039	5,004	4,039
26,950	27,000	4,518	4,046	5,018	4,046
27,000					
27,000	27,050	4,532	4,054	5,032	4,054
27,050	27,100	4,546	4,061	5,046	4,061
27,100	27,150	4,560	4,069	5,060	4,069
27,150	27,200	4,574	4,076	5,074	4,076
27,200	27,250	4,588	4,084	5,088	4,084
27,250	27,300	4,602	4,091	5,102	4,091
27,300	27,350	4,616	4,099	5,116	4,099
27,350	27,400	4,630	4,106	5,130	4,106
27,400	27,450	4,644	4,114	5,144	4,114
27,450	27,500	4,658	4,121	5,158	4,121
27,500	27,550	4,672	4,129	5,172	4,129
27,550	27,600	4,686	4,136	5,186	4,136
27,600	27,650	4,700	4,144	5,200	4,144
27,650	27,700	4,714	4,151	5,214	4,151
27,700	27,750	4,728	4,159	5,228	4,159
27,750	27,800	4,742	4,166	5,242	4,166
27,800	27,850	4,756	4,174	5,256	4,174
27,850	27,900	4,770	4,181	5,270	4,181
27,900	27,950	4,784	4,189	5,284	4,189
27,950	28,000	4,798	4,196	5,298	4,196
28,000					
28,000	28,050	4,812	4,204	5,312	4,204
28,050	28,100	4,826	4,211	5,326	4,211
28,100	28,150	4,840	4,219	5,340	4,219
28,150	28,200	4,854	4,226	5,354	4,226
28,200	28,250	4,868	4,234	5,368	4,234
28,250	28,300	4,882	4,241	5,382	4,241
28,300	28,350	4,896	4,249	5,396	4,249
28,350	28,400	4,910	4,256	5,410	4,256
28,400	28,450	4,924	4,264	5,424	4,264
28,450	28,500	4,938	4,271	5,438	4,271
28,500	28,550	4,952	4,279	5,452	4,279
28,550	28,600	4,966	4,286	5,466	4,286
28,600	28,650	4,980	4,294	5,480	4,294
28,650	28,700	4,994	4,301	5,494	4,301
28,700	28,750	5,008	4,309	5,508	4,309
28,750	28,800	5,022	4,316	5,522	4,316
28,800	28,850	5,036	4,324	5,536	4,324
28,850	28,900	5,050	4,331	5,550	4,331
28,900	28,950	5,064	4,339	5,564	4,339
28,950	29,000	5,078	4,346	5,578	4,346

29,000 – 31,000

At least	But less than	Single	Married filing jointly*	Married filing separately	Head of a household
29,000					
29,000	29,050	5,092	4,354	5,592	4,354
29,050	29,100	5,106	4,361	5,606	4,361
29,100	29,150	5,120	4,369	5,620	4,369
29,150	29,200	5,134	4,376	5,634	4,376
29,200	29,250	5,148	4,384	5,648	4,384
29,250	29,300	5,162	4,391	5,662	4,391
29,300	29,350	5,176	4,399	5,676	4,399
29,350	29,400	5,190	4,406	5,690	4,406
29,400	29,450	5,204	4,414	5,704	4,414
29,450	29,500	5,218	4,421	5,718	4,421
29,500	29,550	5,232	4,429	5,732	4,429
29,550	29,600	5,246	4,436	5,746	4,436
29,600	29,650	5,260	4,444	5,760	4,444
29,650	29,700	5,274	4,451	5,774	4,451
29,700	29,750	5,288	4,459	5,788	4,459
29,750	29,800	5,302	4,466	5,802	4,466
29,800	29,850	5,316	4,474	5,816	4,474
29,850	29,900	5,330	4,481	5,830	4,481
29,900	29,950	5,344	4,489	5,844	4,489
29,950	30,000	5,358	4,496	5,858	4,496
30,000					
30,000	30,050	5,372	4,504	5,872	4,504
30,050	30,100	5,386	4,511	5,886	4,511
30,100	30,150	5,400	4,519	5,900	4,519
30,150	30,200	5,414	4,526	5,914	4,526
30,200	30,250	5,428	4,534	5,928	4,534
30,250	30,300	5,442	4,541	5,942	4,541
30,300	30,350	5,456	4,549	5,956	4,549
30,350	30,400	5,470	4,556	5,970	4,556
30,400	30,450	5,484	4,564	5,984	4,564
30,450	30,500	5,498	4,571	5,998	4,571
30,500	30,550	5,512	4,579	6,012	4,579
30,550	30,600	5,526	4,586	6,026	4,586
30,600	30,650	5,540	4,594	6,040	4,594
30,650	30,700	5,554	4,601	6,054	4,601
30,700	30,750	5,568	4,609	6,068	4,609
30,750	30,800	5,582	4,616	6,082	4,616
30,800	30,850	5,596	4,624	6,096	4,624
30,850	30,900	5,610	4,631	6,110	4,631
30,900	30,950	5,624	4,639	6,124	4,639
30,950	31,000	5,638	4,646	6,138	4,646
31,000					
31,000	31,050	5,652	4,654	6,152	4,654
31,050	31,100	5,666	4,661	6,166	4,661
31,100	31,150	5,680	4,669	6,180	4,669
31,150	31,200	5,694	4,676	6,194	4,676
31,200	31,250	5,708	4,684	6,208	4,684
31,250	31,300	5,722	4,691	6,222	4,695
31,300	31,350	5,736	4,699	6,236	4,709
31,350	31,400	5,750	4,706	6,250	4,723
31,400	31,450	5,764	4,714	6,264	4,737
31,450	31,500	5,778	4,721	6,278	4,751
31,500	31,550	5,792	4,729	6,292	4,765
31,550	31,600	5,806	4,736	6,306	4,779
31,600	31,650	5,820	4,744	6,320	4,793
31,650	31,700	5,834	4,751	6,334	4,807
31,700	31,750	5,848	4,759	6,348	4,821
31,750	31,800	5,862	4,766	6,362	4,835
31,800	31,850	5,876	4,774	6,376	4,849
31,850	31,900	5,890	4,781	6,390	4,863
31,900	31,950	5,904	4,789	6,404	4,877
31,950	32,000	5,918	4,796	6,418	4,891

* This column must also be used by a qualifying widow(er).

Continued on next page

1995 Tax Table—Continued

If line 37 (taxable income) is— At least	But less than	Single	Married filing jointly *	Married filing separately	Head of a household
32,000					
32,000	32,050	5,932	4,804	6,432	4,905
32,050	32,100	5,946	4,811	6,446	4,919
32,100	32,150	5,960	4,819	6,460	4,933
32,150	32,200	5,974	4,826	6,474	4,947
32,200	32,250	5,988	4,834	6,488	4,961
32,250	32,300	6,002	4,841	6,502	4,975
32,300	32,350	6,016	4,849	6,516	4,989
32,350	32,400	6,030	4,856	6,530	5,003
32,400	32,450	6,044	4,864	6,544	5,017
32,450	32,500	6,058	4,871	6,558	5,031
32,500	32,550	6,072	4,879	6,572	5,045
32,550	32,600	6,086	4,886	6,586	5,059
32,600	32,650	6,100	4,894	6,600	5,073
32,650	32,700	6,114	4,901	6,614	5,087
32,700	32,750	6,128	4,909	6,628	5,101
32,750	32,800	6,142	4,916	6,642	5,115
32,800	32,850	6,156	4,924	6,656	5,129
32,850	32,900	6,170	4,931	6,670	5,143
32,900	32,950	6,184	4,939	6,684	5,157
32,950	33,000	6,198	4,946	6,698	5,171
33,000					
33,000	33,050	6,212	4,954	6,712	5,185
33,050	33,100	6,226	4,961	6,726	5,199
33,100	33,150	6,240	4,969	6,740	5,213
33,150	33,200	6,254	4,976	6,754	5,227
33,200	33,250	6,268	4,984	6,768	5,241
33,250	33,300	6,282	4,991	6,782	5,255
33,300	33,350	6,296	4,999	6,796	5,269
33,350	33,400	6,310	5,006	6,810	5,283
33,400	33,450	6,324	5,014	6,824	5,297
33,450	33,500	6,338	5,021	6,838	5,311
33,500	33,550	6,352	5,029	6,852	5,325
33,550	33,600	6,366	5,036	6,866	5,339
33,600	33,650	6,380	5,044	6,880	5,353
33,650	33,700	6,394	5,051	6,894	5,367
33,700	33,750	6,408	5,059	6,908	5,381
33,750	33,800	6,422	5,066	6,922	5,395
33,800	33,850	6,436	5,074	6,936	5,409
33,850	33,900	6,450	5,081	6,950	5,423
33,900	33,950	6,464	5,089	6,964	5,437
33,950	34,000	6,478	5,096	6,978	5,451
34,000					
34,000	34,050	6,492	5,104	6,992	5,465
34,050	34,100	6,506	5,111	7,006	5,479
34,100	34,150	6,520	5,119	7,020	5,493
34,150	34,200	6,534	5,126	7,034	5,507
34,200	34,250	6,548	5,134	7,048	5,521
34,250	34,300	6,562	5,141	7,062	5,535
34,300	34,350	6,576	5,149	7,076	5,549
34,350	34,400	6,590	5,156	7,090	5,563
34,400	34,450	6,604	5,164	7,104	5,577
34,450	34,500	6,618	5,171	7,118	5,591
34,500	34,550	6,632	5,179	7,132	5,605
34,550	34,600	6,646	5,186	7,146	5,619
34,600	34,650	6,660	5,194	7,160	5,633
34,650	34,700	6,674	5,201	7,174	5,647
34,700	34,750	6,688	5,209	7,188	5,661
34,750	34,800	6,702	5,216	7,202	5,675
34,800	34,850	6,716	5,224	7,216	5,689
34,850	34,900	6,730	5,231	7,230	5,703
34,900	34,950	6,744	5,239	7,244	5,717
34,950	35,000	6,758	5,246	7,258	5,731

If line 37 (taxable income) is— At least	But less than	Single	Married filing jointly *	Married filing separately	Head of a household
35,000					
35,000	35,050	6,772	5,254	7,272	5,745
35,050	35,100	6,786	5,261	7,286	5,759
35,100	35,150	6,800	5,269	7,300	5,773
35,150	35,200	6,814	5,276	7,314	5,787
35,200	35,250	6,828	5,284	7,328	5,801
35,250	35,300	6,842	5,291	7,342	5,815
35,300	35,350	6,856	5,299	7,356	5,829
35,350	35,400	6,870	5,306	7,370	5,843
35,400	35,450	6,884	5,314	7,384	5,857
35,450	35,500	6,898	5,321	7,398	5,871
35,500	35,550	6,912	5,329	7,412	5,885
35,550	35,600	6,926	5,336	7,426	5,899
35,600	35,650	6,940	5,344	7,440	5,913
35,650	35,700	6,954	5,351	7,454	5,927
35,700	35,750	6,968	5,359	7,468	5,941
35,750	35,800	6,982	5,366	7,482	5,955
35,800	35,850	6,996	5,374	7,496	5,969
35,850	35,900	7,010	5,381	7,510	5,983
35,900	35,950	7,024	5,389	7,524	5,997
35,950	36,000	7,038	5,396	7,538	6,011
36,000					
36,000	36,050	7,052	5,404	7,552	6,025
36,050	36,100	7,066	5,411	7,566	6,039
36,100	36,150	7,080	5,419	7,580	6,053
36,150	36,200	7,094	5,426	7,594	6,067
36,200	36,250	7,108	5,434	7,608	6,081
36,250	36,300	7,122	5,441	7,622	6,095
36,300	36,350	7,136	5,449	7,636	6,109
36,350	36,400	7,150	5,456	7,650	6,123
36,400	36,450	7,164	5,464	7,664	6,137
36,450	36,500	7,178	5,471	7,678	6,151
36,500	36,550	7,192	5,479	7,692	6,165
36,550	36,600	7,206	5,486	7,706	6,179
36,600	36,650	7,220	5,494	7,720	6,193
36,650	36,700	7,234	5,501	7,734	6,207
36,700	36,750	7,248	5,509	7,748	6,221
36,750	36,800	7,262	5,516	7,762	6,235
36,800	36,850	7,276	5,524	7,776	6,249
36,850	36,900	7,290	5,531	7,790	6,263
36,900	36,950	7,304	5,539	7,804	6,277
36,950	37,000	7,318	5,546	7,818	6,291
37,000					
37,000	37,050	7,332	5,554	7,832	6,305
37,050	37,100	7,346	5,561	7,846	6,319
37,100	37,150	7,360	5,569	7,860	6,333
37,150	37,200	7,374	5,576	7,874	6,347
37,200	37,250	7,388	5,584	7,888	6,361
37,250	37,300	7,402	5,591	7,902	6,375
37,300	37,350	7,416	5,599	7,916	6,389
37,350	37,400	7,430	5,606	7,930	6,403
37,400	37,450	7,444	5,614	7,944	6,417
37,450	37,500	7,458	5,621	7,958	6,431
37,500	37,550	7,472	5,629	7,972	6,445
37,550	37,600	7,486	5,636	7,986	6,459
37,600	37,650	7,500	5,644	8,000	6,473
37,650	37,700	7,514	5,651	8,014	6,487
37,700	37,750	7,528	5,659	8,028	6,501
37,750	37,800	7,542	5,666	8,042	6,515
37,800	37,850	7,556	5,674	8,056	6,529
37,850	37,900	7,570	5,681	8,070	6,543
37,900	37,950	7,584	5,689	8,084	6,557
37,950	38,000	7,598	5,696	8,098	6,571

If line 37 (taxable income) is— At least	But less than	Single	Married filing jointly *	Married filing separately	Head of a household
38,000					
38,000	38,050	7,612	5,704	8,112	6,585
38,050	38,100	7,626	5,711	8,126	6,599
38,100	38,150	7,640	5,719	8,140	6,613
38,150	38,200	7,654	5,726	8,154	6,627
38,200	38,250	7,668	5,734	8,168	6,641
38,250	38,300	7,682	5,741	8,182	6,655
38,300	38,350	7,696	5,749	8,196	6,669
38,350	38,400	7,710	5,756	8,210	6,683
38,400	38,450	7,724	5,764	8,224	6,697
38,450	38,500	7,738	5,771	8,238	6,711
38,500	38,550	7,752	5,779	8,252	6,725
38,550	38,600	7,766	5,786	8,266	6,739
38,600	38,650	7,780	5,794	8,280	6,753
38,650	38,700	7,794	5,801	8,294	6,767
38,700	38,750	7,808	5,809	8,308	6,781
38,750	38,800	7,822	5,816	8,322	6,795
38,800	38,850	7,836	5,824	8,336	6,809
38,850	38,900	7,850	5,831	8,350	6,823
38,900	38,950	7,864	5,839	8,364	6,837
38,950	39,000	7,878	5,846	8,378	6,851
39,000					
39,000	39,050	7,892	5,857	8,392	6,865
39,050	39,100	7,906	5,871	8,406	6,879
39,100	39,150	7,920	5,885	8,420	6,893
39,150	39,200	7,934	5,899	8,434	6,907
39,200	39,250	7,948	5,913	8,448	6,921
39,250	39,300	7,962	5,927	8,462	6,935
39,300	39,350	7,976	5,941	8,476	6,949
39,350	39,400	7,990	5,955	8,490	6,963
39,400	39,450	8,004	5,969	8,504	6,977
39,450	39,500	8,018	5,983	8,518	6,991
39,500	39,550	8,032	5,997	8,532	7,005
39,550	39,600	8,046	6,011	8,546	7,019
39,600	39,650	8,060	6,025	8,560	7,033
39,650	39,700	8,074	6,039	8,574	7,047
39,700	39,750	8,088	6,053	8,588	7,061
39,750	39,800	8,102	6,067	8,602	7,075
39,800	39,850	8,116	6,081	8,616	7,089
39,850	39,900	8,130	6,095	8,630	7,103
39,900	39,950	8,144	6,109	8,644	7,117
39,950	40,000	8,158	6,123	8,658	7,131
40,000					
40,000	40,050	8,172	6,137	8,672	7,145
40,050	40,100	8,186	6,151	8,686	7,159
40,100	40,150	8,200	6,165	8,700	7,173
40,150	40,200	8,214	6,179	8,714	7,187
40,200	40,250	8,228	6,193	8,728	7,201
40,250	40,300	8,242	6,207	8,742	7,215
40,300	40,350	8,256	6,221	8,756	7,229
40,350	40,400	8,270	6,235	8,770	7,243
40,400	40,450	8,284	6,249	8,784	7,257
40,450	40,500	8,298	6,263	8,798	7,271
40,500	40,550	8,312	6,277	8,812	7,285
40,550	40,600	8,326	6,291	8,826	7,299
40,600	40,650	8,340	6,305	8,840	7,313
40,650	40,700	8,354	6,319	8,854	7,327
40,700	40,750	8,368	6,333	8,868	7,341
40,750	40,800	8,382	6,347	8,882	7,355
40,800	40,850	8,396	6,361	8,896	7,369
40,850	40,900	8,410	6,375	8,910	7,383
40,900	40,950	8,424	6,389	8,924	7,397
40,950	41,000	8,438	6,403	8,938	7,411

* This column must also be used by a qualifying widow(er).

Continued on next page

1995 Tax Table—Continued

If line 37 (taxable income) is—		And you are—				If line 37 (taxable income) is—		And you are—				If line 37 (taxable income) is—		And you are—			
At least	But less than	Single	Married filing jointly *	Married filing separately	Head of a house-hold	At least	But less than	Single	Married filing jointly *	Married filing separately	Head of a house-hold	At least	But less than	Single	Married filing jointly *	Married filing separately	Head of a house-hold
		Your tax is—						Your tax is—						Your tax is—			
41,000						**44,000**						**47,000**					
41,000	41,050	8,452	6,417	8,952	7,425	44,000	44,050	9,292	7,257	9,792	8,265	47,000	47,050	10,132	8,097	10,632	9,105
41,050	41,100	8,466	6,431	8,966	7,439	44,050	44,100	9,306	7,271	9,806	8,279	47,050	47,100	10,146	8,111	10,646	9,119
41,100	41,150	8,480	6,445	8,980	7,453	44,100	44,150	9,320	7,285	9,820	8,293	47,100	47,150	10,160	8,125	10,660	9,133
41,150	41,200	8,494	6,459	8,994	7,467	44,150	44,200	9,334	7,299	9,834	8,307	47,150	47,200	10,174	8,139	10,676	9,147
41,200	41,250	8,508	6,473	9,008	7,481	44,200	44,250	9,348	7,313	9,848	8,321	47,200	47,250	10,188	8,153	10,691	9,161
41,250	41,300	8,522	6,487	9,022	7,495	44,250	44,300	9,362	7,327	9,862	8,335	47,250	47,300	10,202	8,167	10,707	9,175
41,300	41,350	8,536	6,501	9,036	7,509	44,300	44,350	9,376	7,341	9,876	8,349	47,300	47,350	10,216	8,181	10,722	9,189
41,350	41,400	8,550	6,515	9,050	7,523	44,350	44,400	9,390	7,355	9,890	8,363	47,350	47,400	10,230	8,195	10,738	9,203
41,400	41,450	8,564	6,529	9,064	7,537	44,400	44,450	9,404	7,369	9,904	8,377	47,400	47,450	10,244	8,209	10,753	9,217
41,450	41,500	8,578	6,543	9,078	7,551	44,450	44,500	9,418	7,383	9,918	8,391	47,450	47,500	10,258	8,223	10,769	9,231
41,500	41,550	8,592	6,557	9,092	7,565	44,500	44,550	9,432	7,397	9,932	8,405	47,500	47,550	10,272	8,237	10,784	9,245
41,550	41,600	8,606	6,571	9,106	7,579	44,550	44,600	9,446	7,411	9,946	8,419	47,550	47,600	10,286	8,251	10,800	9,259
41,600	41,650	8,620	6,585	9,120	7,593	44,600	44,650	9,460	7,425	9,960	8,433	47,600	47,650	10,300	8,265	10,815	9,273
41,650	41,700	8,634	6,599	9,134	7,607	44,650	44,700	9,474	7,439	9,974	8,447	47,650	47,700	10,314	8,279	10,831	9,287
41,700	41,750	8,648	6,613	9,148	7,621	44,700	44,750	9,488	7,453	9,988	8,461	47,700	47,750	10,328	8,293	10,846	9,301
41,750	41,800	8,662	6,627	9,162	7,635	44,750	44,800	9,502	7,467	10,002	8,475	47,750	47,800	10,342	8,307	10,862	9,315
41,800	41,850	8,676	6,641	9,176	7,649	44,800	44,850	9,516	7,481	10,016	8,489	47,800	47,850	10,356	8,321	10,877	9,329
41,850	41,900	8,690	6,655	9,190	7,663	44,850	44,900	9,530	7,495	10,030	8,503	47,850	47,900	10,370	8,335	10,893	9,343
41,900	41,950	8,704	6,669	9,204	7,677	44,900	44,950	9,544	7,509	10,044	8,517	47,900	47,950	10,384	8,349	10,908	9,357
41,950	42,000	8,718	6,683	9,218	7,691	44,950	44,000	9,558	7,523	10,058	8,531	47,950	48,000	10,398	8,363	10,924	9,371
42,000						**45,000**						**48,000**					
42,000	42,050	8,732	6,697	9,232	7,705	45,000	45,050	9,572	7,537	10,072	8,545	48,000	48,050	10,412	8,377	10,939	9,385
42,050	42,100	8,746	6,711	9,246	7,719	45,050	45,100	9,586	7,551	10,086	8,559	48,050	48,100	10,426	8,391	10,955	9,399
42,100	42,150	8,760	6,725	9,260	7,733	45,100	45,150	9,600	7,565	10,100	8,573	48,100	48,150	10,440	8,405	10,970	9,413
42,150	42,200	8,774	6,739	9,274	7,747	45,150	45,200	9,614	7,579	10,114	8,587	48,150	48,200	10,454	8,419	10,986	9,427
42,200	42,250	8,788	6,753	9,288	7,761	45,200	45,250	9,628	7,593	10,128	8,601	48,200	48,250	10,468	8,433	11,001	9,441
42,250	42,300	8,802	6,767	9,302	7,775	45,250	45,300	9,642	7,607	10,142	8,615	48,250	48,300	10,482	8,447	11,017	9,455
42,300	42,350	8,816	6,781	9,316	7,789	45,300	45,350	9,656	7,621	10,156	8,629	48,300	48,350	10,496	8,461	11,032	9,469
42,350	42,400	8,830	6,795	9,330	7,803	45,350	45,400	9,670	7,635	10,170	8,643	48,350	48,400	10,510	8,475	11,048	9,483
42,400	42,450	8,844	6,809	9,344	7,817	45,400	45,450	9,684	7,649	10,184	8,657	48,400	48,450	10,524	8,489	11,063	9,497
42,450	42,500	8,858	6,823	9,358	7,831	45,450	45,500	9,698	7,663	10,198	8,671	48,450	48,500	10,538	8,503	11,079	9,511
42,500	42,550	8,872	6,837	9,372	7,845	45,500	45,550	9,712	7,677	10,212	8,685	48,500	48,550	10,552	8,517	11,094	9,525
42,550	42,600	8,886	6,851	9,386	7,859	45,550	45,600	9,726	7,691	10,226	8,699	48,550	48,600	10,566	8,531	11,110	9,539
42,600	42,650	8,900	6,865	9,400	7,873	45,600	45,650	9,740	7,705	10,240	8,713	48,600	48,650	10,580	8,545	11,125	9,553
42,650	42,700	8,914	6,879	9,414	7,887	45,650	45,700	9,754	7,719	10,254	8,727	48,650	48,700	10,594	8,559	11,141	9,567
42,700	42,750	8,928	6,893	9,428	7,901	45,700	45,750	9,768	7,733	10,268	8,741	48,700	48,750	10,608	8,573	11,156	9,581
42,750	42,800	8,942	6,907	9,442	7,915	45,750	45,800	9,782	7,747	10,282	8,755	48,750	48,800	10,622	8,587	11,172	9,595
42,800	42,850	8,956	6,921	9,456	7,929	45,800	45,850	9,796	7,761	10,296	8,769	48,800	48,850	10,636	8,601	11,187	9,609
42,850	42,900	8,970	6,935	9,470	7,943	45,850	45,900	9,810	7,775	10,310	8,783	48,850	48,900	10,650	8,615	11,203	9,623
42,900	42,950	8,984	6,949	9,484	7,957	45,900	45,950	9,824	7,789	10,324	8,797	48,900	48,950	10,664	8,629	11,218	9,637
42,950	43,000	8,998	6,963	9,498	7,971	45,950	46,000	9,838	7,803	10,338	8,811	48,950	49,000	10,678	8,643	11,234	9,651
43,000						**46,000**						**49,000**					
43,000	43,050	9,012	6,977	9,512	7,985	46,000	46,050	9,852	7,817	10,352	8,825	49,000	49,050	10,692	8,657	11,249	9,665
43,050	43,100	9,026	6,991	9,526	7,999	46,050	46,100	9,866	7,831	10,366	8,839	49,050	49,100	10,706	8,671	11,265	9,679
43,100	43,150	9,040	7,005	9,540	8,013	46,100	46,150	9,880	7,845	10,380	8,853	49,100	49,150	10,720	8,685	11,280	9,693
43,150	43,200	9,054	7,019	9,554	8,027	46,150	46,200	9,894	7,859	10,394	8,867	49,150	49,200	10,734	8,699	11,296	9,707
43,200	43,250	9,068	7,033	9,568	8,041	46,200	46,250	9,908	7,873	10,408	8,881	49,200	49,250	10,748	8,713	11,311	9,721
43,250	43,300	9,082	7,047	9,582	8,055	46,250	46,300	9,922	7,887	10,422	8,895	49,250	49,300	10,762	8,727	11,327	9,735
43,300	43,350	9,096	7,061	9,596	8,069	46,300	46,350	9,936	7,901	10,436	8,909	49,300	49,350	10,776	8,741	11,342	9,749
43,350	43,400	9,110	7,075	9,610	8,083	46,350	46,400	9,950	7,915	10,450	8,923	49,350	49,400	10,790	8,755	11,358	9,763
43,400	43,450	9,124	7,089	9,624	8,097	46,400	46,450	9,964	7,929	10,464	8,937	49,400	49,450	10,804	8,769	11,373	9,777
43,450	43,500	9,138	7,103	9,638	8,111	46,450	46,500	9,978	7,943	10,478	8,951	49,450	49,500	10,818	8,783	11,389	9,791
43,500	43,550	9,152	7,117	9,652	8,125	46,500	46,550	9,992	7,957	10,492	8,965	49,500	49,550	10,832	8,797	11,404	9,805
43,550	43,600	9,166	7,131	9,666	8,139	46,550	46,600	10,006	7,971	10,506	8,979	49,550	49,600	10,846	8,811	11,420	9,819
43,600	43,650	9,180	7,145	9,680	8,153	46,600	46,650	10,020	7,985	10,520	8,993	49,600	49,650	10,860	8,825	11,435	9,833
43,650	43,700	9,194	7,159	9,694	8,167	46,650	46,700	10,034	7,999	10,534	9,007	49,650	49,700	10,874	8,839	11,451	9,847
43,700	43,750	9,208	7,173	9,708	8,181	46,700	46,750	10,048	8,013	10,548	9,021	49,700	49,750	10,888	8,853	11,466	9,861
43,750	43,800	9,222	7,187	9,722	8,195	46,750	46,800	10,062	8,027	10,562	9,035	49,750	49,800	10,902	8,867	11,482	9,875
43,800	43,850	9,236	7,201	9,736	8,209	46,800	46,850	10,076	8,041	10,576	9,049	49,800	49,850	10,916	8,881	11,497	9,889
43,850	43,900	9,250	7,215	9,750	8,223	46,850	46,900	10,090	8,055	10,590	9,063	49,850	49,900	10,930	8,895	11,513	9,903
43,900	43,950	9,264	7,229	9,764	8,237	46,900	46,950	10,104	8,069	10,604	9,077	49,900	49,950	10,944	8,909	11,528	9,917
43,950	44,000	9,278	7,243	9,778	8,251	46,950	47,000	10,118	8,083	10,618	9,091	49,950	50,000	10,958	8,923	11,544	9,931

* This column must also be used by a qualifying widow(er).

Continued on next page

1995 Tax Table—Continued

If line 37 (taxable income) is—		And you are—			
At least	But less than	Single	Married filing jointly *	Married filing separately	Head of a household
50,000					
50,000	50,050	10,972	8,937	11,559	9,945
50,050	50,100	10,986	8,951	11,575	9,959
50,100	50,150	11,000	8,965	11,590	9,973
50,150	50,200	11,014	8,979	11,606	9,987
50,200	50,250	11,028	8,993	11,621	10,001
50,250	50,300	11,042	9,007	11,637	10,015
50,300	50,350	11,056	9,021	11,652	10,029
50,350	50,400	11,070	9,035	11,668	10,043
50,400	50,450	11,084	9,049	11,683	10,057
50,450	50,500	11,098	9,063	11,699	10,071
50,500	50,550	11,112	9,077	11,714	10,085
50,550	50,600	11,126	9,091	11,730	10,099
50,600	50,650	11,140	9,105	11,745	10,113
50,650	50,700	11,154	9,119	11,761	10,127
50,700	50,750	11,168	9,133	11,776	10,141
50,750	50,800	11,182	9,147	11,792	10,155
50,800	50,850	11,196	9,161	11,807	10,169
50,850	50,900	11,210	9,175	11,823	10,183
50,900	50,950	11,224	9,189	11,838	10,197
50,950	51,000	11,238	9,203	11,854	10,211
51,000					
51,000	51,050	11,252	9,217	11,869	10,225
51,050	51,100	11,266	9,231	11,885	10,239
51,100	51,150	11,280	9,245	11,900	10,253
51,150	51,200	11,294	9,259	11,916	10,267
51,200	51,250	11,308	9,273	11,931	10,281
51,250	51,300	11,322	9,287	11,947	10,295
51,300	51,350	11,336	9,301	11,962	10,309
51,350	51,400	11,350	9,315	11,978	10,323
51,400	51,450	11,364	9,329	11,993	10,337
51,450	51,500	11,378	9,343	12,009	10,351
51,500	51,550	11,392	9,357	12,024	10,365
51,550	51,600	11,406	9,371	12,040	10,379
51,600	51,650	11,420	9,385	12,055	10,393
51,650	51,700	11,434	9,399	12,071	10,407
51,700	51,750	11,448	9,413	12,086	10,421
51,750	51,800	11,462	9,427	12,102	10,435
51,800	51,850	11,476	9,441	12,117	10,449
51,850	51,900	11,490	9,455	12,133	10,463
51,900	51,950	11,504	9,469	12,148	10,477
51,950	52,000	11,518	9,483	12,164	10,491
52,000					
52,000	52,050	11,532	9,497	12,179	10,505
52,050	52,100	11,546	9,511	12,195	10,519
52,100	52,150	11,560	9,525	12,210	10,533
52,150	52,200	11,574	9,539	12,226	10,547
52,200	52,250	11,588	9,553	12,241	10,561
52,250	52,300	11,602	9,567	12,257	10,575
52,300	52,350	11,616	9,581	12,272	10,589
52,350	52,400	11,630	9,595	12,288	10,603
52,400	52,450	11,644	9,609	12,303	10,617
52,450	52,500	11,658	9,623	12,319	10,631
52,500	52,550	11,672	9,637	12,334	10,645
52,550	52,600	11,686	9,651	12,350	10,659
52,600	52,650	11,700	9,665	12,365	10,673
52,650	52,700	11,714	9,679	12,381	10,687
52,700	52,750	11,728	9,693	12,396	10,701
52,750	52,800	11,742	9,707	12,412	10,715
52,800	52,850	11,756	9,721	12,427	10,729
52,850	52,900	11,770	9,735	12,443	10,743
52,900	52,950	11,784	9,749	12,458	10,757
52,950	53,000	11,798	9,763	12,474	10,771

If line 37 (taxable income) is—		And you are—			
At least	But less than	Single	Married filing jointly *	Married filing separately	Head of a household
53,000					
53,000	53,050	11,812	9,777	12,489	10,785
53,050	53,100	11,826	9,791	12,505	10,799
53,100	53,150	11,840	9,805	12,520	10,813
53,150	53,200	11,854	9,819	12,536	10,827
53,200	53,250	11,868	9,833	12,551	10,841
53,250	53,300	11,882	9,847	12,567	10,855
53,300	53,350	11,896	9,861	12,582	10,869
53,350	53,400	11,910	9,875	12,598	10,883
53,400	53,450	11,924	9,889	12,613	10,897
53,450	53,500	11,938	9,903	12,629	10,911
53,500	53,550	11,952	9,917	12,644	10,925
53,550	53,600	11,966	9,931	12,660	10,939
53,600	53,650	11,980	9,945	12,675	10,953
53,650	53,700	11,994	9,959	12,691	10,967
53,700	53,750	12,008	9,973	12,706	10,981
53,750	53,800	12,022	9,987	12,722	10,995
53,800	53,850	12,036	10,001	12,737	11,009
53,850	53,900	12,050	10,015	12,753	11,023
53,900	53,950	12,064	10,029	12,768	11,037
53,950	54,000	12,078	10,043	12,784	11,051
54,000					
54,000	54,050	12,092	10,057	12,799	11,065
54,050	54,100	12,106	10,071	12,815	11,079
54,100	54,150	12,120	10,085	12,830	11,093
54,150	54,200	12,134	10,099	12,846	11,107
54,200	54,250	12,148	10,113	12,861	11,121
54,250	54,300	12,162	10,127	12,877	11,135
54,300	54,350	12,176	10,141	12,892	11,149
54,350	54,400	12,190	10,155	12,908	11,163
54,400	54,450	12,204	10,169	12,923	11,177
54,450	54,500	12,218	10,183	12,939	11,191
54,500	54,550	12,232	10,197	12,954	11,205
54,550	54,600	12,246	10,211	12,970	11,219
54,600	54,650	12,260	10,225	12,985	11,233
54,650	54,700	12,274	10,239	13,001	11,247
54,700	54,750	12,288	10,253	13,016	11,261
54,750	54,800	12,302	10,267	13,032	11,275
54,800	54,850	12,316	10,281	13,047	11,289
54,850	54,900	12,330	10,295	13,063	11,303
54,900	54,950	12,344	10,309	13,078	11,317
54,950	55,000	12,358	10,323	13,094	11,331
55,000					
55,000	55,050	12,372	10,337	13,109	11,345
55,050	55,100	12,386	10,351	13,125	11,359
55,100	55,150	12,400	10,365	13,140	11,373
55,150	55,200	12,414	10,379	13,156	11,387
55,200	55,250	12,428	10,393	13,171	11,401
55,250	55,300	12,442	10,407	13,187	11,415
55,300	55,350	12,456	10,421	13,202	11,429
55,350	55,400	12,470	10,435	13,218	11,443
55,400	55,450	12,484	10,449	13,233	11,457
55,450	55,500	12,498	10,463	13,249	11,471
55,500	55,550	12,512	10,477	13,264	11,485
55,550	55,600	12,526	10,491	13,280	11,499
55,600	55,650	12,540	10,505	13,295	11,513
55,650	55,700	12,554	10,519	13,311	11,527
55,700	55,750	12,568	10,533	13,326	11,541
55,750	55,800	12,582	10,547	13,342	11,555
55,800	55,850	12,596	10,561	13,357	11,569
55,850	55,900	12,610	10,575	13,373	11,583
55,900	55,950	12,624	10,589	13,388	11,597
55,950	56,000	12,638	10,603	13,404	11,611

If line 37 (taxable income) is—		And you are—			
At least	But less than	Single	Married filing jointly *	Married filing separately	Head of a household
56,000					
56,000	56,050	12,652	10,617	13,419	11,625
56,050	56,100	12,666	10,631	13,435	11,639
56,100	56,150	12,680	10,645	13,450	11,653
56,150	56,200	12,694	10,659	13,466	11,667
56,200	56,250	12,708	10,673	13,481	11,681
56,250	56,300	12,722	10,687	13,497	11,695
56,300	56,350	12,736	10,701	13,512	11,709
56,350	56,400	12,750	10,715	13,528	11,723
56,400	56,450	12,764	10,729	13,543	11,737
56,450	56,500	12,778	10,743	13,559	11,751
56,500	56,550	12,792	10,757	13,574	11,765
56,550	56,600	12,806	10,771	13,590	11,779
56,600	56,650	12,822	10,785	13,605	11,793
56,650	56,700	12,837	10,799	13,621	11,807
56,700	56,750	12,853	10,813	13,636	11,821
56,750	56,800	12,868	10,827	13,652	11,835
56,800	56,850	12,884	10,841	13,667	11,849
56,850	56,900	12,899	10,855	13,683	11,863
56,900	56,950	12,915	10,869	13,698	11,877
56,950	57,000	12,930	10,883	13,714	11,891
57,000					
57,000	57,050	12,946	10,897	13,729	11,905
57,050	57,100	12,961	10,911	13,745	11,919
57,100	57,150	12,977	10,925	13,760	11,933
57,150	57,200	12,992	10,939	13,776	11,947
57,200	57,250	13,008	10,953	13,791	11,961
57,250	57,300	13,023	10,967	13,807	11,975
57,300	57,350	13,039	10,981	13,822	11,989
57,350	57,400	13,054	10,995	13,838	12,003
57,400	57,450	13,070	11,009	13,853	12,017
57,450	57,500	13,085	11,023	13,869	12,031
57,500	57,550	13,101	11,037	13,884	12,045
57,550	57,600	13,116	11,051	13,900	12,059
57,600	57,650	13,132	11,065	13,915	12,073
57,650	57,700	13,147	11,079	13,931	12,087
57,700	57,750	13,163	11,093	13,946	12,101
57,750	57,800	13,178	11,107	13,962	12,115
57,800	57,850	13,194	11,121	13,977	12,129
57,850	57,900	13,209	11,135	13,993	12,143
57,900	57,950	13,225	11,149	14,008	12,157
57,950	58,000	13,240	11,163	14,024	12,171
58,000					
58,000	58,050	13,256	11,177	14,039	12,185
58,050	58,100	13,271	11,191	14,055	12,199
58,100	58,150	13,287	11,205	14,070	12,213
58,150	58,200	13,302	11,219	14,086	12,227
58,200	58,250	13,318	11,233	14,101	12,241
58,250	58,300	13,333	11,247	14,117	12,255
58,300	58,350	13,349	11,261	14,132	12,269
58,350	58,400	13,364	11,275	14,148	12,283
58,400	58,450	13,380	11,289	14,163	12,297
58,450	58,500	13,395	11,303	14,179	12,311
58,500	58,550	13,411	11,317	14,194	12,325
58,550	58,600	13,426	11,331	14,210	12,339
58,600	58,650	13,442	11,345	14,225	12,353
58,650	58,700	13,457	11,359	14,241	12,367
58,700	58,750	13,473	11,373	14,256	12,381
58,750	58,800	13,488	11,387	14,272	12,395
58,800	58,850	13,504	11,401	14,287	12,409
58,850	58,900	13,519	11,415	14,303	12,423
58,900	58,950	13,535	11,429	14,318	12,437
58,950	59,000	13,550	11,443	14,334	12,451

* This column must also be used by a qualifying widow(er).

Continued on next page

1995 Tax Table—*Continued*

59,000 – 62,000 – 65,000

If line 37 (taxable income) is— At least	But less than	Single	Married filing jointly *	Married filing separately	Head of a household	If line 37 (taxable income) is— At least	But less than	Single	Married filing jointly *	Married filing separately	Head of a household	If line 37 (taxable income) is— At least	But less than	Single	Married filing jointly *	Married filing separately	Head of a household
59,000						**62,000**						**65,000**					
59,000	59,050	13,566	11,457	14,349	12,465	62,000	62,050	14,496	12,297	15,279	13,305	65,000	65,050	15,426	13,137	16,209	14,145
59,050	59,100	13,581	11,471	14,365	12,479	62,050	62,100	14,511	12,311	15,295	13,319	65,050	65,100	15,441	13,151	16,225	14,159
59,100	59,150	13,597	11,485	14,380	12,493	62,100	62,150	14,527	12,325	15,310	13,333	65,100	65,150	15,457	13,165	16,240	14,173
59,150	59,200	13,612	11,499	14,396	12,507	62,150	62,200	14,542	12,339	15,326	13,347	65,150	65,200	15,472	13,179	16,256	14,187
59,200	59,250	13,628	11,513	14,411	12,521	62,200	62,250	14,558	12,353	15,341	13,361	65,200	65,250	15,488	13,193	16,271	14,201
59,250	59,300	13,643	11,527	14,427	12,535	62,250	62,300	14,573	12,367	15,357	13,375	65,250	65,300	15,503	13,207	16,287	14,215
59,300	59,350	13,659	11,541	14,442	12,549	62,300	62,350	14,589	12,381	15,372	13,389	65,300	65,350	15,519	13,221	16,302	14,229
59,350	59,400	13,674	11,555	14,458	12,563	62,350	62,400	14,604	12,395	15,388	13,403	65,350	65,400	15,534	13,235	16,318	14,243
59,400	59,450	13,690	11,569	14,473	12,577	62,400	62,450	14,620	12,409	15,403	13,417	65,400	65,450	15,550	13,249	16,333	14,257
59,450	59,500	13,705	11,583	14,489	12,591	62,450	62,500	14,635	12,423	15,419	13,431	65,450	65,500	15,565	13,263	16,349	14,271
59,500	59,550	13,721	11,597	14,504	12,605	62,500	62,550	14,651	12,437	15,434	13,445	65,500	65,550	15,581	13,277	16,364	14,285
59,550	59,600	13,736	11,611	14,520	12,619	62,550	62,600	14,666	12,451	15,450	13,459	65,550	65,600	15,596	13,291	16,380	14,299
59,600	59,650	13,752	11,625	14,535	12,633	62,600	62,650	14,682	12,465	15,465	13,473	65,600	65,650	15,612	13,305	16,395	14,313
59,650	59,700	13,767	11,639	14,551	12,647	62,650	62,700	14,697	12,479	15,481	13,487	65,650	65,700	15,627	13,319	16,411	14,327
59,700	59,750	13,783	11,653	14,566	12,661	62,700	62,750	14,713	12,493	15,496	13,501	65,700	65,750	15,643	13,333	16,426	14,341
59,750	59,800	13,798	11,667	14,582	12,675	62,750	62,800	14,728	12,507	15,512	13,515	65,750	65,800	15,658	13,347	16,442	14,355
59,800	59,850	13,814	11,681	14,597	12,689	62,800	62,850	14,744	12,521	15,527	13,529	65,800	65,850	15,674	13,361	16,457	14,369
59,850	59,900	13,829	11,695	14,613	12,703	62,850	62,900	14,759	12,535	15,543	13,543	65,850	65,900	15,689	13,375	16,473	14,383
59,900	59,950	13,845	11,709	14,628	12,717	62,900	62,950	14,775	12,549	15,558	13,557	65,900	65,950	15,705	13,389	16,488	14,397
59,950	60,000	13,860	11,723	14,644	12,731	62,950	63,000	14,790	12,563	15,574	13,571	65,950	65,000	15,720	13,403	16,504	14,411
60,000						**63,000**						**66,000**					
60,000	60,050	13,876	11,737	14,659	12,745	63,000	63,050	14,806	12,577	15,589	13,585	66,000	66,050	15,736	13,417	16,519	14,425
60,050	60,100	13,891	11,751	14,675	12,759	63,050	63,100	14,821	12,591	15,605	13,599	66,050	66,100	15,751	13,431	16,535	14,439
60,100	60,150	13,907	11,765	14,690	12,773	63,100	63,150	14,837	12,605	15,620	13,613	66,100	66,150	15,767	13,445	16,550	14,453
60,150	60,200	13,922	11,779	14,706	12,787	63,150	63,200	14,852	12,619	15,636	13,627	66,150	66,200	15,782	13,459	16,566	14,467
60,200	60,250	13,938	11,793	14,721	12,801	63,200	63,250	14,868	12,633	15,651	13,641	66,200	66,250	15,798	13,473	16,581	14,481
60,250	60,300	13,953	11,807	14,737	12,815	63,250	63,300	14,883	12,647	15,667	13,655	66,250	66,300	15,813	13,487	16,597	14,495
60,300	60,350	13,969	11,821	14,752	12,829	63,300	63,350	14,899	12,661	15,682	13,669	66,300	66,350	15,829	13,501	16,612	14,509
60,350	60,400	13,984	11,835	14,768	12,843	63,350	63,400	14,914	12,675	15,698	13,683	66,350	66,400	15,844	13,515	16,628	14,523
60,400	60,450	14,000	11,849	14,783	12,857	63,400	63,450	14,930	12,689	15,713	13,697	66,400	66,450	15,860	13,529	16,643	14,537
60,450	60,500	14,015	11,863	14,799	12,871	63,450	63,500	14,945	12,703	15,729	13,711	66,450	66,500	15,875	13,543	16,659	14,551
60,500	60,550	14,031	11,877	14,814	12,885	63,500	63,550	14,961	12,717	15,744	13,725	66,500	66,550	15,891	13,557	16,674	14,565
60,550	60,600	14,046	11,891	14,830	12,899	63,550	63,600	14,976	12,731	15,760	13,739	66,550	66,600	15,906	13,571	16,690	14,579
60,600	60,650	14,062	11,905	14,845	12,913	63,600	63,650	14,992	12,745	15,775	13,753	66,600	66,650	15,922	13,585	16,705	14,593
60,650	60,700	14,077	11,919	14,861	12,927	63,650	63,700	15,007	12,759	15,791	13,767	66,650	66,700	15,937	13,599	16,721	14,607
60,700	60,750	14,093	11,933	14,876	12,941	63,700	63,750	15,023	12,773	15,806	13,781	66,700	66,750	15,953	13,613	16,736	14,621
60,750	60,800	14,108	11,947	14,892	12,955	63,750	63,800	15,038	12,787	15,822	13,795	66,750	66,800	15,968	13,627	16,752	14,635
60,800	60,850	14,124	11,961	14,907	12,969	63,800	63,850	15,054	12,801	15,837	13,809	66,800	66,850	15,984	13,641	16,767	14,649
60,850	60,900	14,139	11,975	14,923	12,983	63,850	63,900	15,069	12,815	15,853	13,823	66,850	66,900	15,999	13,655	16,783	14,663
60,900	60,950	14,155	11,989	14,938	12,997	63,900	63,950	15,085	12,829	15,868	13,837	66,900	66,950	16,015	13,669	16,798	14,677
60,950	61,000	14,170	12,003	14,954	13,011	63,950	64,000	15,100	12,843	15,884	13,851	66,950	67,000	16,030	13,683	16,814	14,691
61,000						**64,000**						**67,000**					
61,000	61,050	14,186	12,017	14,969	13,025	64,000	64,050	15,116	12,857	15,899	13,865	67,000	67,050	16,046	13,697	16,829	14,705
61,050	61,100	14,201	12,031	14,985	13,039	64,050	64,100	15,131	12,871	15,915	13,879	67,050	67,100	16,061	13,711	16,845	14,719
61,100	61,150	14,217	12,045	15,000	13,053	64,100	64,150	15,147	12,885	15,930	13,893	67,100	67,150	16,077	13,725	16,860	14,733
61,150	61,200	14,232	12,059	15,016	13,067	64,150	64,200	15,162	12,899	15,946	13,907	67,150	67,200	16,092	13,739	16,876	14,747
61,200	61,250	14,248	12,073	15,031	13,081	64,200	64,250	15,178	12,913	15,961	13,921	67,200	67,250	16,108	13,753	16,891	14,761
61,250	61,300	14,263	12,087	15,047	13,095	64,250	64,300	15,193	12,927	15,977	13,935	67,250	67,300	16,123	13,767	16,907	14,775
61,300	61,350	14,279	12,101	15,062	13,109	64,300	64,350	15,209	12,941	15,992	13,949	67,300	67,350	16,139	13,781	16,922	14,789
61,350	61,400	14,294	12,115	15,078	13,123	64,350	64,400	15,224	12,955	16,008	13,963	67,350	67,400	16,154	13,795	16,938	14,803
61,400	61,450	14,310	12,129	15,093	13,137	64,400	64,450	15,240	12,969	16,023	13,977	67,400	67,450	16,170	13,809	16,953	14,817
61,450	61,500	14,325	12,143	15,109	13,151	64,450	64,500	15,255	12,983	16,039	13,991	67,450	67,500	16,185	13,823	16,969	14,831
61,500	61,550	14,341	12,157	15,124	13,165	64,500	64,550	15,271	12,997	16,054	14,005	67,500	67,550	16,201	13,837	16,984	14,845
61,550	61,600	14,356	12,171	15,140	13,179	64,550	64,600	15,286	13,011	16,070	14,019	67,550	67,600	16,216	13,851	17,000	14,859
61,600	61,650	14,372	12,185	15,155	13,193	64,600	64,650	15,302	13,025	16,085	14,033	67,600	67,650	16,232	13,865	17,015	14,873
61,650	61,700	14,387	12,199	15,171	13,207	64,650	64,700	15,317	13,039	16,101	14,047	67,650	67,700	16,247	13,879	17,031	14,887
61,700	61,750	14,403	12,213	15,186	13,221	64,700	64,750	15,333	13,053	16,116	14,061	67,700	67,750	16,263	13,893	17,046	14,901
61,750	61,800	14,418	12,227	15,202	13,235	64,750	64,800	15,348	13,067	16,132	14,075	67,750	67,800	16,278	13,907	17,062	14,915
61,800	61,850	14,434	12,241	15,217	13,249	64,800	64,850	15,364	13,081	16,147	14,089	67,800	67,850	16,294	13,921	17,077	14,929
61,850	61,900	14,449	12,255	15,233	13,263	64,850	64,900	15,379	13,095	16,163	14,103	67,850	67,900	16,309	13,935	17,093	14,943
61,900	61,950	14,465	12,269	15,248	13,277	64,900	64,950	15,395	13,109	16,178	14,117	67,900	67,950	16,325	13,949	17,108	14,957
61,950	62,000	14,480	12,283	15,264	13,291	64,950	65,000	15,410	13,123	16,194	14,131	67,950	68,000	16,340	13,963	17,124	14,971

* This column must also be used by a qualifying widow(er).

Continued on next page

1995 Tax Table—*Continued*

If line 37 (taxable income) is—		And you are—				If line 37 (taxable income) is—		And you are—				If line 37 (taxable income) is—		And you are—			
At least	But less than	Single	Married filing jointly *	Married filing separately	Head of a household	At least	But less than	Single	Married filing jointly *	Married filing separately	Head of a household	At least	But less than	Single	Married filing jointly *	Married filing separately	Head of a household
				Your tax is—						Your tax is—						Your tax is—	

68,000						**71,000**						**74,000**					
68,000	68,050	16,356	13,977	17,139	14,985	71,000	71,050	17,286	14,817	18,069	15,825	74,000	74,050	18,216	15,657	19,110	16,665
68,050	68,100	16,371	13,991	17,155	14,999	71,050	71,100	17,301	14,831	18,085	15,839	74,050	74,100	18,231	15,671	19,128	16,679
68,100	68,150	16,387	14,005	17,170	15,013	71,100	71,150	17,317	14,845	18,100	15,853	74,100	74,150	18,247	15,685	19,146	16,693
68,150	68,200	16,402	14,019	17,186	15,027	71,150	71,200	17,332	14,859	18,116	15,867	74,150	74,200	18,262	15,699	19,164	16,707
68,200	68,250	16,418	14,033	17,201	15,041	71,200	71,250	17,348	14,873	18,131	15,881	74,200	74,250	18,278	15,713	19,182	16,721
68,250	68,300	16,433	14,047	17,217	15,055	71,250	71,300	17,363	14,887	18,147	15,895	74,250	74,300	18,293	15,727	19,200	16,735
68,300	68,350	16,449	14,061	17,232	15,069	71,300	71,350	17,379	14,901	18,162	15,909	74,300	74,350	18,309	15,741	19,218	16,749
68,350	68,400	16,464	14,075	17,248	15,083	71,350	71,400	17,394	14,915	18,178	15,923	74,350	74,400	18,324	15,755	19,236	16,763
68,400	68,450	16,480	14,089	17,263	15,097	71,400	71,450	17,410	14,929	18,193	15,937	74,400	74,450	18,340	15,769	19,254	16,777
68,450	68,500	16,495	14,103	17,279	15,111	71,450	71,500	17,425	14,943	18,209	15,951	74,450	74,500	18,355	15,783	19,272	16,791
68,500	68,550	16,511	14,117	17,294	15,125	71,500	71,550	17,441	14,957	18,224	15,965	74,500	74,550	18,371	15,797	19,290	16,805
68,550	68,600	16,526	14,131	17,310	15,139	71,550	71,600	17,456	14,971	18,240	15,979	74,550	74,600	18,386	15,811	19,308	16,819
68,600	68,650	16,542	14,145	17,325	15,153	71,600	71,650	17,472	14,985	18,255	15,993	74,600	74,650	18,402	15,825	19,326	16,833
68,650	68,700	16,557	14,159	17,341	15,167	71,650	71,700	17,487	14,999	18,271	16,007	74,650	74,700	18,417	15,839	19,344	16,847
68,700	68,750	16,573	14,173	17,356	15,181	71,700	71,750	17,503	15,013	18,286	16,021	74,700	74,750	18,433	15,853	19,362	16,861
68,750	68,800	16,588	14,187	17,372	15,195	71,750	71,800	17,518	15,027	18,302	16,035	74,750	74,800	18,448	15,867	19,380	16,875
68,800	68,850	16,604	14,201	17,387	15,209	71,800	71,850	17,534	15,041	18,318	16,049	74,800	74,850	18,464	15,881	19,398	16,889
68,850	68,900	16,619	14,215	17,403	15,223	71,850	71,900	17,549	15,055	18,336	16,063	74,850	74,900	18,479	15,895	19,416	16,903
68,900	68,950	16,635	14,229	17,418	15,237	71,900	71,950	17,565	15,069	18,354	16,077	74,900	74,950	18,495	15,909	19,434	16,917
68,950	69,000	16,650	14,243	17,434	15,251	71,950	72,000	17,580	15,083	18,372	16,091	74,950	75,000	18,510	15,923	19,452	16,931

69,000						**72,000**						**75,000**					
69,000	69,050	16,666	14,257	17,449	15,265	72,000	72,050	17,596	15,097	18,390	16,105	75,000	75,050	18,526	15,937	19,470	16,945
69,050	69,100	16,681	14,271	17,465	15,279	72,050	72,100	17,611	15,111	18,408	16,119	75,050	75,100	18,541	15,951	19,488	16,959
69,100	69,150	16,697	14,285	17,480	15,293	72,100	72,150	17,627	15,125	18,426	16,133	75,100	75,150	18,557	15,965	19,506	16,973
69,150	69,200	16,712	14,299	17,496	15,307	72,150	72,200	17,642	15,139	18,444	16,147	75,150	75,200	18,572	15,979	19,524	16,987
69,200	69,250	16,728	14,313	17,511	15,321	72,200	72,250	17,658	15,153	18,462	16,161	75,200	75,250	18,588	15,993	19,542	17,001
69,250	69,300	16,743	14,327	17,527	15,335	72,250	72,300	17,673	15,167	18,480	16,175	75,250	75,300	18,603	16,007	19,560	17,015
69,300	69,350	16,759	14,341	17,542	15,349	72,300	72,350	17,689	15,181	18,498	16,189	75,300	75,350	18,619	16,021	19,578	17,029
69,350	69,400	16,774	14,355	17,558	15,363	72,350	72,400	17,704	15,195	18,516	16,203	75,350	75,400	18,634	16,035	19,596	17,043
69,400	69,450	16,790	14,369	17,573	15,377	72,400	72,450	17,720	15,209	18,534	16,217	75,400	75,450	18,650	16,049	19,614	17,057
69,450	69,500	16,805	14,383	17,589	15,391	72,450	72,500	17,735	15,223	18,552	16,231	75,450	75,500	18,665	16,063	19,632	17,071
69,500	69,550	16,821	14,397	17,604	15,405	72,500	72,550	17,751	15,237	18,570	16,245	75,500	75,550	18,681	16,077	19,650	17,085
69,550	69,600	16,836	14,411	17,620	15,419	72,550	72,600	17,766	15,251	18,588	16,259	75,550	75,600	18,696	16,091	19,668	17,099
69,600	69,650	16,852	14,425	17,635	15,433	72,600	72,650	17,782	15,265	18,606	16,273	75,600	75,650	18,712	16,105	19,686	17,113
69,650	69,700	16,867	14,439	17,651	15,447	72,650	72,700	17,797	15,279	18,624	16,287	75,650	75,700	18,727	16,119	19,704	17,127
69,700	69,750	16,883	14,453	17,666	15,461	72,700	72,750	17,813	15,293	18,642	16,301	75,700	75,750	18,743	16,133	19,722	17,141
69,750	69,800	16,898	14,467	17,682	15,475	72,750	72,800	17,828	15,307	18,660	16,315	75,750	75,800	18,758	16,147	19,740	17,155
69,800	69,850	16,914	14,481	17,697	15,489	72,800	72,850	17,844	15,321	18,678	16,329	75,800	75,850	18,774	16,161	19,758	17,169
69,850	69,900	16,929	14,495	17,713	15,503	72,850	72,900	17,859	15,335	18,696	16,343	75,850	75,900	18,789	16,175	19,776	17,183
69,900	69,950	16,945	14,509	17,728	15,517	72,900	72,950	17,875	15,349	18,714	16,357	75,900	75,950	18,805	16,189	19,794	17,197
69,950	70,000	16,960	14,523	17,744	15,531	72,950	73,000	17,890	15,363	18,732	16,371	75,950	76,000	18,820	16,203	19,812	17,211

70,000						**73,000**						**76,000**					
70,000	70,050	16,976	14,537	17,759	15,545	73,000	73,050	17,906	15,377	18,750	16,385	76,000	76,050	18,836	16,217	19,830	17,225
70,050	70,100	16,991	14,551	17,775	15,559	73,050	73,100	17,921	15,391	18,768	16,399	76,050	76,100	18,851	16,231	19,848	17,239
70,100	70,150	17,007	14,565	17,790	15,573	73,100	73,150	17,937	15,405	18,786	16,413	76,100	76,150	18,867	16,245	19,866	17,253
70,150	70,200	17,022	14,579	17,806	15,587	73,150	73,200	17,952	15,419	18,804	16,427	76,150	76,200	18,882	16,259	19,884	17,267
70,200	70,250	17,038	14,593	17,821	15,601	73,200	73,250	17,968	15,433	18,822	16,441	76,200	76,250	18,898	16,273	19,902	17,281
70,250	70,300	17,053	14,607	17,837	15,615	73,250	73,300	17,983	15,447	18,840	16,455	76,250	76,300	18,913	16,287	19,920	17,295
70,300	70,350	17,069	14,621	17,852	15,629	73,300	73,350	17,999	15,461	18,858	16,469	76,300	76,350	18,929	16,301	19,938	17,309
70,350	70,400	17,084	14,635	17,868	15,643	73,350	73,400	18,014	15,475	18,876	16,483	76,350	76,400	18,944	16,315	19,956	17,323
70,400	70,450	17,100	14,649	17,883	15,657	73,400	73,450	18,030	15,489	18,894	16,497	76,400	76,450	18,960	16,329	19,974	17,337
70,450	70,500	17,115	14,663	17,899	15,671	73,450	73,500	18,045	15,503	18,912	16,511	76,450	76,500	18,975	16,343	19,992	17,351
70,500	70,550	17,131	14,677	17,914	15,685	73,500	73,550	18,061	15,517	18,930	16,525	76,500	76,550	18,991	16,357	20,010	17,365
70,550	70,600	17,146	14,691	17,930	15,699	73,550	73,600	18,076	15,531	18,948	16,539	76,550	76,600	19,006	16,371	20,028	17,379
70,600	70,650	17,162	14,705	17,945	15,713	73,600	73,650	18,092	15,545	18,966	16,553	76,600	76,650	19,022	16,385	20,046	17,393
70,650	70,700	17,177	14,719	17,961	15,727	73,650	73,700	18,107	15,559	18,984	16,567	76,650	76,700	19,037	16,399	20,064	17,407
70,700	70,750	17,193	14,733	17,976	15,741	73,700	73,750	18,123	15,573	19,002	16,581	76,700	76,750	19,053	16,413	20,082	17,421
70,750	70,800	17,208	14,747	17,992	15,755	73,750	73,800	18,138	15,587	19,020	16,595	76,750	76,800	19,068	16,427	20,100	17,435
70,800	70,850	17,224	14,761	18,007	15,769	73,800	73,850	18,154	15,601	19,038	16,609	76,800	76,850	19,084	16,441	20,118	17,449
70,850	70,900	17,239	14,775	18,023	15,783	73,850	73,900	18,169	15,615	19,056	16,623	76,850	76,900	19,099	16,455	20,136	17,463
70,900	70,950	17,255	14,789	18,038	15,797	73,900	73,950	18,185	15,629	19,074	16,637	76,900	76,950	19,115	16,469	20,154	17,477
70,950	71,000	17,270	14,803	18,054	15,811	73,950	74,000	18,200	15,643	19,092	16,651	76,950	77,000	19,130	16,483	20,172	17,491

* This column must also be used by a qualifying widow(er).

Continued on next page

1995 Tax Table—*Continued*

If line 37 (taxable income) is— At least	But less than	And you are— Single	Married filing jointly *	Married filing separately	Head of a household	If line 37 (taxable income) is— At least	But less than	And you are— Single	Married filing jointly *	Married filing separately	Head of a household	If line 37 (taxable income) is— At least	But less than	And you are— Single	Married filing jointly *	Married filing separately	Head of a household
		Your tax is—						Your tax is—						Your tax is—			
77,000						**80,000**						**83,000**					
77,000	77,050	19,146	16,497	20,190	17,505	80,000	80,050	20,076	17,337	21,270	18,345	83,000	83,050	21,006	18,177	22,350	19,253
77,050	77,100	19,161	16,511	20,208	17,519	80,050	80,100	20,091	17,351	21,288	18,359	83,050	83,100	21,021	18,191	22,368	19,268
77,100	77,150	19,177	16,525	20,226	17,533	80,100	80,150	20,107	17,365	21,306	18,373	83,100	83,150	21,037	18,205	22,386	19,284
77,150	77,200	19,192	16,539	20,244	17,547	80,150	80,200	20,122	17,379	21,324	18,387	83,150	83,200	21,052	18,219	22,404	19,299
77,200	77,250	19,208	16,553	20,262	17,561	80,200	80,250	20,138	17,393	21,342	18,401	83,200	83,250	21,068	18,233	22,422	19,315
77,250	77,300	19,223	16,567	20,280	17,575	80,250	80,300	20,153	17,407	21,360	18,415	83,250	83,300	21,083	18,247	22,440	19,330
77,300	77,350	19,239	16,581	20,298	17,589	80,300	80,350	20,169	17,421	21,378	18,429	83,300	83,350	21,099	18,261	22,458	19,346
77,350	77,400	19,254	16,595	20,316	17,603	80,350	80,400	20,184	17,435	21,396	18,443	83,350	83,400	21,114	18,275	22,476	19,361
77,400	77,450	19,270	16,609	20,334	17,617	80,400	80,450	20,200	17,449	21,414	18,457	83,400	83,450	21,130	18,289	22,494	19,377
77,450	77,500	19,285	16,623	20,352	17,631	80,450	80,500	20,215	17,463	21,432	18,471	83,450	83,500	21,145	18,303	22,512	19,392
77,500	77,550	19,301	16,637	20,370	17,645	80,500	80,550	20,231	17,477	21,450	18,485	83,500	83,550	21,161	18,317	22,530	19,408
77,550	77,600	19,316	16,651	20,388	17,659	80,550	80,600	20,246	17,491	21,468	18,499	83,550	83,600	21,176	18,331	22,548	19,423
77,600	77,650	19,332	16,665	20,406	17,673	80,600	80,650	20,262	17,505	21,486	18,513	83,600	83,650	21,192	18,345	22,566	19,439
77,650	77,700	19,347	16,679	20,424	17,687	80,650	80,700	20,277	17,519	21,504	18,527	83,650	83,700	21,207	18,359	22,584	19,454
77,700	77,750	19,363	16,693	20,442	17,701	80,700	80,750	20,293	17,533	21,522	18,541	83,700	83,750	21,223	18,373	22,602	19,470
77,750	77,800	19,378	16,707	20,460	17,715	80,750	80,800	20,308	17,547	21,540	18,555	83,750	83,800	21,238	18,387	22,620	19,485
77,800	77,850	19,394	16,721	20,478	17,729	80,800	80,850	20,324	17,561	21,558	18,571	83,800	83,850	21,254	18,401	22,638	19,501
77,850	77,900	19,409	16,735	20,496	17,743	80,850	80,900	20,339	17,575	21,576	18,586	83,850	83,900	21,269	18,415	22,656	19,516
77,900	77,950	19,425	16,749	20,514	17,757	80,900	80,950	20,355	17,589	21,594	18,602	83,900	83,950	21,285	18,429	22,674	19,532
77,950	78,000	19,440	16,763	20,532	17,771	80,950	81,000	20,370	17,603	21,612	18,617	83,950	84,000	21,300	18,443	22,692	19,547
78,000						**81,000**						**84,000**					
78,000	78,050	19,456	16,777	20,550	17,785	81,000	81,050	20,386	17,617	21,630	18,633	84,000	84,050	21,316	18,457	22,710	19,563
78,050	78,100	19,471	16,791	20,568	17,799	81,050	81,100	20,401	17,631	21,648	18,648	84,050	84,100	21,331	18,471	22,728	19,578
78,100	78,150	19,487	16,805	20,586	17,813	81,100	81,150	20,417	17,645	21,666	18,664	84,100	84,150	21,347	18,485	22,746	19,594
78,150	78,200	19,502	16,819	20,604	17,827	81,150	81,200	20,432	17,659	21,684	18,679	84,150	84,200	21,362	18,499	22,764	19,609
78,200	78,250	19,518	16,833	20,622	17,841	81,200	81,250	20,448	17,673	21,702	18,695	84,200	84,250	21,378	18,513	22,782	19,625
78,250	78,300	19,533	16,847	20,640	17,855	81,250	81,300	20,463	17,687	21,720	18,710	84,250	84,300	21,393	18,527	22,800	19,640
78,300	78,350	19,549	16,861	20,658	17,869	81,300	81,350	20,479	17,701	21,738	18,726	84,300	84,350	21,409	18,541	22,818	19,656
78,350	78,400	19,564	16,875	20,676	17,883	81,350	81,400	20,494	17,715	21,756	18,741	84,350	84,400	21,424	18,555	22,836	19,671
78,400	78,450	19,580	16,889	20,694	17,897	81,400	81,450	20,510	17,729	21,774	18,757	84,400	84,450	21,440	18,569	22,854	19,687
78,450	78,500	19,595	16,903	20,712	17,911	81,450	81,500	20,525	17,743	21,792	18,772	84,450	84,500	21,455	18,583	22,872	19,702
78,500	78,550	19,611	16,917	20,730	17,925	81,500	81,550	20,541	17,757	21,810	18,788	84,500	84,550	21,471	18,597	22,890	19,718
78,550	78,600	19,626	16,931	20,748	17,939	81,550	81,600	20,556	17,771	21,828	18,803	84,550	84,600	21,486	18,611	22,908	19,733
78,600	78,650	19,642	16,945	20,766	17,953	81,600	81,650	20,572	17,785	21,846	18,819	84,600	84,650	21,502	18,625	22,926	19,749
78,650	78,700	19,657	16,959	20,784	17,967	81,650	81,700	20,587	17,799	21,864	18,834	84,650	84,700	21,517	18,639	22,944	19,764
78,700	78,750	19,673	16,973	20,802	17,981	81,700	81,750	20,603	17,813	21,882	18,850	84,700	84,750	21,533	18,653	22,962	19,780
78,750	78,800	19,688	16,987	20,820	17,995	81,750	81,800	20,618	17,827	21,900	18,865	84,750	84,800	21,548	18,667	22,980	19,795
78,800	78,850	19,704	17,001	20,838	18,009	81,800	81,850	20,634	17,841	21,918	18,881	84,800	84,850	21,564	18,681	22,998	19,811
78,850	78,900	19,719	17,015	20,856	18,023	81,850	81,900	20,649	17,855	21,936	18,896	84,850	84,900	21,579	18,695	23,016	19,826
78,900	78,950	19,735	17,029	20,874	18,037	81,900	81,950	20,665	17,869	21,954	18,912	84,900	84,950	21,595	18,709	23,034	19,842
78,950	79,000	19,750	17,043	20,892	18,051	81,950	82,000	20,680	17,883	21,972	18,927	84,950	85,000	21,610	18,723	23,052	19,857
79,000						**82,000**						**85,000**					
79,000	79,050	19,766	17,057	20,910	18,065	82,000	82,050	20,696	17,897	21,990	18,943	85,000	85,050	21,626	18,737	23,070	19,873
79,050	79,100	19,781	17,071	20,928	18,079	82,050	82,100	20,711	17,911	22,008	18,958	85,050	85,100	21,641	18,751	23,088	19,888
79,100	79,150	19,797	17,085	20,946	18,093	82,100	82,150	20,727	17,925	22,026	18,974	85,100	85,150	21,657	18,765	23,106	19,904
79,150	79,200	19,812	17,099	20,964	18,107	82,150	82,200	20,742	17,939	22,044	18,989	85,150	85,200	21,672	18,779	23,124	19,919
79,200	79,250	19,828	17,113	20,982	18,121	82,200	82,250	20,758	17,953	22,062	19,005	85,200	85,250	21,688	18,793	23,142	19,935
79,250	79,300	19,843	17,127	21,000	18,135	82,250	82,300	20,773	17,967	22,080	19,020	85,250	85,300	21,703	18,807	23,160	19,950
79,300	79,350	19,859	17,141	21,018	18,149	82,300	82,350	20,789	17,981	22,098	19,036	85,300	85,350	21,719	18,821	23,178	19,966
79,350	79,400	19,874	17,155	21,036	18,163	82,350	82,400	20,804	17,995	22,116	19,051	85,350	85,400	21,734	18,835	23,196	19,981
79,400	79,450	19,890	17,169	21,054	18,177	82,400	82,450	20,820	18,009	22,134	19,067	85,400	85,450	21,750	18,849	23,214	19,997
79,450	79,500	19,905	17,183	21,072	18,191	82,450	82,500	20,835	18,023	22,152	19,082	85,450	85,500	21,765	18,863	23,232	20,012
79,500	79,550	19,921	17,197	21,090	18,205	82,500	82,550	20,851	18,037	22,170	19,098	85,500	85,550	21,781	18,877	23,250	20,028
79,550	79,600	19,936	17,211	21,108	18,219	82,550	82,600	20,866	18,051	22,188	19,113	85,550	85,600	21,796	18,891	23,268	20,043
79,600	79,650	19,952	17,225	21,126	18,233	82,600	82,650	20,882	18,065	22,206	19,129	85,600	85,650	21,812	18,905	23,286	20,059
79,650	79,700	19,967	17,239	21,144	18,247	82,650	82,700	20,897	18,079	22,224	19,144	85,650	85,700	21,827	18,919	23,304	20,074
79,700	79,750	19,983	17,253	21,162	18,261	82,700	82,750	20,913	18,093	22,242	19,160	85,700	85,750	21,843	18,933	23,322	20,090
79,750	79,800	19,998	17,267	21,180	18,275	82,750	82,800	20,928	18,107	22,260	19,175	85,750	85,800	21,858	18,947	23,340	20,105
79,800	79,850	20,014	17,281	21,198	18,289	82,800	82,850	20,944	18,121	22,278	19,191	85,800	85,850	21,874	18,961	23,358	20,121
79,850	79,900	20,029	17,295	21,216	18,303	82,850	82,900	20,959	18,135	22,296	19,206	85,850	85,900	21,889	18,975	23,376	20,136
79,900	79,950	20,045	17,309	21,234	18,317	82,900	82,950	20,975	18,149	22,314	19,222	85,900	85,950	21,905	18,989	23,394	20,152
79,950	80,000	20,060	17,323	21,252	18,331	82,950	83,000	20,990	18,163	22,332	19,237	85,950	86,000	21,920	19,003	23,412	20,167

* This column must also be used by a qualifying widow(er).

Continued on next page

1995 Tax Table—*Continued*

If line 37 (taxable income) is—		And you are—				If line 37 (taxable income) is—		And you are—				If line 37 (taxable income) is—		And you are—			
At least	But less than	Single	Married filing jointly *	Married filing separately	Head of a household	At least	But less than	Single	Married filing jointly *	Married filing separately	Head of a household	At least	But less than	Single	Married filing jointly *	Married filing separately	Head of a household
		Your tax is—						Your tax is—						Your tax is—			

86,000

86,000	86,050	21,936	19,017	23,430	20,183
86,050	86,100	21,951	19,031	23,448	20,198
86,100	86,150	21,967	19,045	23,466	20,214
86,150	86,200	21,982	19,059	23,484	20,229
86,200	86,250	21,998	19,073	23,502	20,245
86,250	86,300	22,013	19,087	23,520	20,260
86,300	86,350	22,029	19,101	23,538	20,276
86,350	86,400	22,044	19,115	23,556	20,291
86,400	86,450	22,060	19,129	23,574	20,307
86,450	86,500	22,075	19,143	23,592	20,322
86,500	86,550	22,091	19,157	23,610	20,338
86,550	86,600	22,106	19,171	23,628	20,353
86,600	86,650	22,122	19,185	23,646	20,369
86,650	86,700	22,137	19,199	23,664	20,384
86,700	86,750	22,153	19,213	23,682	20,400
86,750	86,800	22,168	19,227	23,700	20,415
86,800	86,850	22,184	19,241	23,718	20,431
86,850	86,900	22,199	19,255	23,736	20,446
86,900	86,950	22,215	19,269	23,754	20,462
86,950	87,000	22,230	19,283	23,772	20,477

87,000

87,000	87,050	22,246	19,297	23,790	20,493
87,050	87,100	22,261	19,311	23,808	20,508
87,100	87,150	22,277	19,325	23,826	20,524
87,150	87,200	22,292	19,339	23,844	20,539
87,200	87,250	22,308	19,353	23,862	20,555
87,250	87,300	22,323	19,367	23,880	20,570
87,300	87,350	22,339	19,381	23,898	20,586
87,350	87,400	22,354	19,395	23,916	20,601
87,400	87,450	22,370	19,409	23,934	20,617
87,450	87,500	22,385	19,423	23,952	20,632
87,500	87,550	22,401	19,437	23,970	20,648
87,550	87,600	22,416	19,451	23,988	20,663
87,600	87,650	22,432	19,465	24,006	20,679
87,650	87,700	22,447	19,479	24,024	20,694
87,700	87,750	22,463	19,493	24,042	20,710
87,750	87,800	22,478	19,507	24,060	20,725
87,800	87,850	22,494	19,521	24,078	20,741
87,850	87,900	22,509	19,535	24,096	20,756
87,900	87,950	22,525	19,549	24,114	20,772
87,950	88,000	22,540	19,563	24,132	20,787

88,000

88,000	88,050	22,556	19,577	24,150	20,803
88,050	88,100	22,571	19,591	24,168	20,818
88,100	88,150	22,587	19,605	24,186	20,834
88,150	88,200	22,602	19,619	24,204	20,849
88,200	88,250	22,618	19,633	24,222	20,865
88,250	88,300	22,633	19,647	24,240	20,880
88,300	88,350	22,649	19,661	24,258	20,896
88,350	88,400	22,664	19,675	24,276	20,911
88,400	88,450	22,680	19,689	24,294	20,927
88,450	88,500	22,695	19,703	24,312	20,942
88,500	88,550	22,711	19,717	24,330	20,958
88,550	88,600	22,726	19,731	24,348	20,973
88,600	88,650	22,742	19,745	24,366	20,989
88,650	88,700	22,757	19,759	24,384	21,004
88,700	88,750	22,773	19,773	24,402	21,020
88,750	88,800	22,788	19,787	24,420	21,035
88,800	88,850	22,804	19,801	24,438	21,051
88,850	88,900	22,819	19,815	24,456	21,066
88,900	88,950	22,835	19,829	24,474	21,082
88,950	89,000	22,850	19,843	24,492	21,097

89,000

89,000	89,050	22,866	19,857	24,510	21,113
89,050	89,100	22,881	19,871	24,528	21,128
89,100	89,150	22,897	19,885	24,546	21,144
89,150	89,200	22,912	19,899	24,564	21,159
89,200	89,250	22,928	19,913	24,582	21,175
89,250	89,300	22,943	19,927	24,600	21,190
89,300	89,350	22,959	19,941	24,618	21,206
89,350	89,400	22,974	19,955	24,636	21,221
89,400	89,450	22,990	19,969	24,654	21,237
89,450	89,500	23,005	19,983	24,672	21,252
89,500	89,550	23,021	19,997	24,690	21,268
89,550	89,600	23,036	20,011	24,708	21,283
89,600	89,650	23,052	20,025	24,726	21,299
89,650	89,700	23,067	20,039	24,744	21,314
89,700	89,750	23,083	20,053	24,762	21,330
89,750	89,800	23,098	20,067	24,780	21,345
89,800	89,850	23,114	20,081	24,798	21,361
89,850	89,900	23,129	20,095	24,816	21,376
89,900	89,950	23,145	20,109	24,834	21,392
89,950	90,000	23,160	20,123	24,852	21,407

90,000

90,000	90,050	23,176	20,137	24,870	21,423
90,050	90,100	23,191	20,151	24,888	21,438
90,100	90,150	23,207	20,165	24,906	21,454
90,150	90,200	23,222	20,179	24,924	21,469
90,200	90,250	23,238	20,193	24,942	21,485
90,250	90,300	23,253	20,207	24,960	21,500
90,300	90,350	23,269	20,221	24,978	21,516
90,350	90,400	23,284	20,235	24,996	21,531
90,400	90,450	23,300	20,249	25,014	21,547
90,450	90,500	23,315	20,263	25,032	21,562
90,500	90,550	23,331	20,277	25,050	21,578
90,550	90,600	23,346	20,291	25,068	21,593
90,600	90,650	23,362	20,305	25,086	21,609
90,650	90,700	23,377	20,319	25,104	21,624
90,700	90,750	23,393	20,333	25,122	21,640
90,750	90,800	23,408	20,347	25,140	21,655
90,800	90,850	23,424	20,361	25,158	21,671
90,850	90,900	23,439	20,375	25,176	21,686
90,900	90,950	23,455	20,389	25,194	21,702
90,950	91,000	23,470	20,403	25,212	21,717

91,000

91,000	91,050	23,486	20,417	25,230	21,733
91,050	91,100	23,501	20,431	25,248	21,748
91,100	91,150	23,517	20,445	25,266	21,764
91,150	91,200	23,532	20,459	25,284	21,779
91,200	91,250	23,548	20,473	25,302	21,795
91,250	91,300	23,563	20,487	25,320	21,810
91,300	91,350	23,579	20,501	25,338	21,826
91,350	91,400	23,594	20,515	25,356	21,841
91,400	91,450	23,610	20,529	25,374	21,857
91,450	91,500	23,625	20,543	25,392	21,872
91,500	91,550	23,641	20,557	25,410	21,888
91,550	91,600	23,656	20,571	25,428	21,903
91,600	91,650	23,672	20,585	25,446	21,919
91,650	91,700	23,687	20,599	25,464	21,934
91,700	91,750	23,703	20,613	25,482	21,950
91,750	91,800	23,718	20,627	25,500	21,965
91,800	91,850	23,734	20,641	25,518	21,981
91,850	91,900	23,749	20,655	25,536	21,996
91,900	91,950	23,765	20,669	25,554	22,012
91,950	92,000	23,780	20,683	25,572	22,027

92,000

92,000	92,050	23,796	20,697	25,590	22,043
92,050	92,100	23,811	20,711	25,608	22,058
92,100	92,150	23,827	20,725	25,626	22,074
92,150	92,200	23,842	20,739	25,644	22,089
92,200	92,250	23,858	20,753	25,662	22,105
92,250	92,300	23,873	20,767	25,680	22,120
92,300	92,350	23,889	20,781	25,698	22,136
92,350	92,400	23,904	20,795	25,716	22,151
92,400	92,450	23,920	20,809	25,734	22,167
92,450	92,500	23,935	20,823	25,752	22,182
92,500	92,550	23,951	20,837	25,770	22,198
92,550	92,600	23,966	20,851	25,788	22,213
92,600	92,650	23,982	20,865	25,806	22,229
92,650	92,700	23,997	20,879	25,824	22,244
92,700	92,750	24,013	20,893	25,842	22,260
92,750	92,800	24,028	20,907	25,860	22,275
92,800	92,850	24,044	20,921	25,878	22,291
92,850	92,900	24,059	20,935	25,896	22,306
92,900	92,950	24,075	20,949	25,914	22,322
92,950	93,000	24,090	20,963	25,932	22,337

93,000

93,000	93,050	24,106	20,977	25,950	22,353
93,050	93,100	24,121	20,991	25,968	22,368
93,100	93,150	24,137	21,005	25,986	22,384
93,150	93,200	24,152	21,019	26,004	22,399
93,200	93,250	24,168	21,033	26,022	22,415
93,250	93,300	24,183	21,047	26,040	22,430
93,300	93,350	24,199	21,061	26,058	22,446
93,350	93,400	24,214	21,075	26,076	22,461
93,400	93,450	24,230	21,089	26,094	22,477
93,450	93,500	24,245	21,103	26,112	22,492
93,500	93,550	24,261	21,117	26,130	22,508
93,550	93,600	24,276	21,131	26,148	22,523
93,600	93,650	24,292	21,145	26,166	22,539
93,650	93,700	24,307	21,159	26,184	22,554
93,700	93,750	24,323	21,173	26,202	22,570
93,750	93,800	24,338	21,187	26,220	22,585
93,800	93,850	24,354	21,201	26,238	22,601
93,850	93,900	24,369	21,215	26,256	22,616
93,900	93,950	24,385	21,229	26,274	22,632
93,950	94,000	24,400	21,243	26,292	22,647

94,000

94,000	94,050	24,416	21,257	26,310	22,663
94,050	94,100	24,431	21,271	26,328	22,678
94,100	94,150	24,447	21,285	26,346	22,694
94,150	94,200	24,462	21,299	26,364	22,709
94,200	94,250	24,478	21,313	26,382	22,725
94,250	94,300	24,493	21,328	26,400	22,740
94,300	94,350	24,509	21,343	26,418	22,756
94,350	94,400	24,524	21,359	26,436	22,771
94,400	94,450	24,540	21,374	26,454	22,787
94,450	94,500	24,555	21,390	26,472	22,802
94,500	94,550	24,571	21,405	26,490	22,818
94,550	94,600	24,586	21,421	26,508	22,833
94,600	94,650	24,602	21,436	26,526	22,849
94,650	94,700	24,617	21,452	26,544	22,864
94,700	94,750	24,633	21,467	26,562	22,880
94,750	94,800	24,648	21,483	26,580	22,895
94,800	94,850	24,664	21,498	26,598	22,911
94,850	94,900	24,679	21,514	26,616	22,926
94,900	94,950	24,695	21,529	26,634	22,942
94,950	95,000	24,710	21,545	26,652	22,957

* This column must also be used by a qualifying widow(er).

Continued on next page

1995 Tax Table—Continued

If line 37 (taxable income) is— At least	But less than	Single	Married filing jointly*	Married filing separately*	Head of a household
		Your tax is—			
95,000					
95,000	95,050	24,726	21,560	26,670	22,973
95,050	95,100	24,741	21,576	26,688	22,988
95,100	95,150	24,757	21,591	26,706	23,004
95,150	95,200	24,772	21,607	26,724	23,019
95,200	95,250	24,788	21,622	26,742	23,035
95,250	95,300	24,803	21,638	26,760	23,050
95,300	95,350	24,819	21,653	26,778	23,066
95,350	95,400	24,834	21,669	26,796	23,081
95,400	95,450	24,850	21,684	26,814	23,097
95,450	95,500	24,865	21,700	26,832	23,112
95,500	95,550	24,881	21,715	26,850	23,128
95,550	95,600	24,896	21,731	26,868	23,143
95,600	95,650	24,912	21,746	26,886	23,159
95,650	95,700	24,927	21,762	26,904	23,174
95,700	95,750	24,943	21,777	26,922	23,190
95,750	95,800	24,958	21,793	26,940	23,205
95,800	95,850	24,974	21,808	26,958	23,221
95,850	95,900	24,989	21,824	26,976	23,236
95,900	95,950	25,005	21,839	26,994	23,252
95,950	96,000	25,020	21,855	27,012	23,267
96,000					
96,000	96,050	25,036	21,870	27,030	23,283
96,050	96,100	25,051	21,886	27,048	23,298
96,100	96,150	25,067	21,901	27,066	23,314
96,150	96,200	25,082	21,917	27,084	23,329
96,200	96,250	25,098	21,932	27,102	23,345
96,250	96,300	25,113	21,948	27,120	23,360
96,300	96,350	25,129	21,963	27,138	23,376
96,350	96,400	25,144	21,979	27,156	23,391
96,400	96,450	25,160	21,994	27,174	23,407
96,450	96,500	25,175	22,010	27,192	23,422
96,500	96,550	25,191	22,025	27,210	23,438
96,550	96,600	25,206	22,041	27,228	23,453
96,600	96,650	25,222	22,056	27,246	23,469
96,650	96,700	25,237	22,072	27,264	23,484
96,700	96,750	25,253	22,087	27,282	23,500
96,750	96,800	25,268	22,103	27,300	23,515
96,800	96,850	25,284	22,118	27,318	23,531
96,850	96,900	25,299	22,134	27,336	23,546
96,900	96,950	25,315	22,149	27,354	23,562
96,950	97,000	25,330	22,165	27,372	23,577
97,000					
97,000	97,050	25,346	22,180	27,390	23,593
97,050	97,100	25,361	22,196	27,408	23,608
97,100	97,150	25,377	22,211	27,426	23,624
97,150	97,200	25,392	22,227	27,444	23,639
97,200	97,250	25,408	22,242	27,462	23,655
97,250	97,300	25,423	22,258	27,480	23,670
97,300	97,350	25,439	22,273	27,498	23,686
97,350	97,400	25,454	22,289	27,516	23,701
97,400	97,450	25,470	22,304	27,534	23,717
97,450	97,500	25,485	22,320	27,552	23,732
97,500	97,550	25,501	22,335	27,570	23,748
97,550	97,600	25,516	22,351	27,588	23,763
97,600	97,650	25,532	22,366	27,606	23,779
97,650	97,700	25,547	22,382	27,624	23,794
97,700	97,750	25,563	22,397	27,642	23,810
97,750	97,800	25,578	22,413	27,660	23,825
97,800	97,850	25,594	22,428	27,678	23,841
97,850	97,900	25,609	22,444	27,696	23,856
97,900	97,950	25,625	22,459	27,714	23,872
97,950	98,000	25,640	22,475	27,732	23,887

If line 37 (taxable income) is— At least	But less than	Single	Married filing jointly*	Married filing separately*	Head of a household
		Your tax is—			
98,000					
98,000	98,050	25,656	22,490	27,750	23,903
98,050	98,100	25,671	22,506	27,768	23,918
98,100	98,150	25,687	22,521	27,786	23,934
98,150	98,200	25,702	22,537	27,804	23,949
98,200	98,250	25,718	22,552	27,822	23,965
98,250	98,300	25,733	22,568	27,840	23,980
98,300	98,350	25,749	22,583	27,858	23,996
98,350	98,400	25,764	22,599	27,876	24,011
98,400	98,450	25,780	22,614	27,894	24,027
98,450	98,500	25,795	22,630	27,912	24,042
98,500	98,550	25,811	22,645	27,930	24,058
98,550	98,600	25,826	22,661	27,948	24,073
98,600	98,650	25,842	22,676	27,966	24,089
98,650	98,700	25,857	22,692	27,984	24,104
98,700	98,750	25,873	22,707	28,002	24,120
98,750	98,800	25,888	22,723	28,020	24,135
98,800	98,850	25,904	22,738	28,038	24,151
98,850	98,900	25,919	22,754	28,056	24,166
98,900	98,950	25,935	22,769	28,074	24,182
98,950	99,000	25,950	22,785	28,092	24,197
99,000					
99,000	99,050	25,966	22,800	28,110	24,213
99,050	99,100	25,981	22,816	28,128	24,228
99,100	99,150	25,997	22,831	28,146	24,244
99,150	99,200	26,012	22,847	28,164	24,259
99,200	99,250	26,028	22,862	28,182	24,275
99,250	99,300	26,043	22,878	28,200	24,290
99,300	99,350	26,059	22,893	28,218	24,306
99,350	99,400	26,074	22,909	28,236	24,321
99,400	99,450	26,090	22,924	28,254	24,337
99,450	99,500	26,105	22,940	28,272	24,352
99,500	99,550	26,121	22,955	28,290	24,368
99,550	99,600	26,136	22,971	28,308	24,383
99,600	99,650	26,152	22,986	28,326	24,399
99,650	99,700	26,167	23,002	28,344	24,414
99,700	99,750	26,183	23,017	28,362	24,430
99,750	99,800	26,198	23,033	28,380	24,445
99,800	99,850	26,214	23,048	28,398	24,461
99,850	99,900	26,229	23,064	28,416	24,476
99,900	99,950	26,245	23,079	28,434	24,492
99,950	100,000	26,260	23,095	28,452	24,507

$100,000 or over — use the Tax Rate Schedules on page 53

* This column must also be used by a qualifying widow(er).

Tax Rate Schedules for 1995

1995 Tax Rate Schedules

Caution: *Use **only** if your taxable income (Form 1040, line 37) is $100,000 or more. If less, use the **Tax Table**. Even though you cannot use the tax rate schedules below if your taxable income is less than $100,000, all levels of taxable income are shown so taxpayers can see the tax rate that applies to each level.*

Schedule X—Use if your filing status is **Single**

If the amount on Form 1040, line 37, is: Over—	But not over—	Enter on Form 1040, line 38		of the amount over—
$0	$23,350	....	15%	$0
23,350	56,550	$3,502.50 +	28%	23,350
56,550	117,950	12,798.50 +	31%	56,550
117,950	256,500	31,832.50 +	36%	117,950
256,500	....	81,710.50 +	39.6%	256,500

Schedule Y-1—Use if your filing status is **Married filing jointly** or **Qualifying widow(er)**

If the amount on Form 1040, line 37, is: Over—	But not over—	Enter on Form 1040, line 38		of the amount over—
$0	$39,000	....	15%	$0
39,000	94,250	$5,850.00 +	28%	39,000
94,250	143,600	21,320.00 +	31%	94,250
143,600	256,500	36,618.50 +	36%	143,600
256,500	....	77,262.50 +	39.6%	256,500

Schedule Y-2—Use if your filing status is **Married filing separately**

If the amount on Form 1040, line 37, is: Over—	But not over—	Enter on Form 1040, line 38		of the amount over—
$0	$19,500	....	15%	$0
19,500	47,125	$2,925.00 +	28%	19,500
47,125	71,800	10,660.00 +	31%	47,125
71,800	128,250	18,309.25 +	36%	71,800
128,250	....	38,631.25 +	39.6%	128,250

Schedule Z—Use if your filing status is **Head of household**.

If the amount on Form 1040, line 37, is: Over—	But not over—	Enter on Form 1040, line 38		of the amount over—
$0	$31,250	....	15%	$0
31,250	80,750	$4,687.50 +	28%	31,250
80,750	130,800	18,457.50 +	31%	80,750
130,800	256,500	34,063.00 +	36%	130,800
256,500	....	79,315.00 +	39.6%	256,500

Form 1040 Cross-Reference

Chapter 9: Blanks You Can Fill In Without Thinking

Form **1040**	Department of the Treasury—Internal Revenue Service			

U.S. Individual Income Tax Return 19**95**

IRS Use Only—Do not write or staple in this space.

For the year Jan. 1–Dec. 31, 1995, or other tax year beginning _____ , 1995, ending _____ , 19 ___ | OMB No. 1545-0074

Label
(See instructions on page 12.)

Use the IRS label. Otherwise, please print or type.

L A B E L H E R E

Your first name and initial | Last name | Your social security number

If a joint return, spouse's first name and initial | Last name | Spouse's social security number

Home address (number and street). If you have a P.O. box, see page 12. | Apt. no.

For Privacy Act and Paperwork Reduction Act Notice, see page 7.

City, town or post office, state, and ZIP code. If you have a foreign address, see page 12.

Presidential Election Campaign (See page 12.)

Do you want $3 to go to this fund? . . . .

If a joint return, does your spouse want $3 to go to this fund? . . . .

Yes | No | **Note:** Checking "Yes" will not change your tax or reduce your refund.

Filing Status
(See page 12.)

Check only one box.

1 ☐ Single
2 ☐ Married filing joint return (even if only one had income)
3 ☐ Married filing separate return. Enter spouse's social security no. above and full name here. ▶ _____
4 ☐ Head of household (with qualifying person). (See page 12.) If the qualifying person is a child but not your dependent, enter this child's name here. ▶ _____
5 ☐ Qualifying widow(er) with dependent child (year spouse died ▶ 19 ___). (See page 13.)

Chapter 10: Your Filing Status

Exemptions
(See page 13.)

If more than six dependents, see page 14.

6a ☐ **Yourself.** If your parent (or someone else) can claim you as a dependent on his or her tax return, **do not** check box 6a. But be sure to check the box on line 33b on page 2.

b ☐ **Spouse** . . . .

c **Dependents:**

(1) First name Last name	(2) Dependent's social security number If born in 1995 see page 14	(3) Dependent's relationship to you	(4) No. of months lived in your home in 1995

No. of boxes checked on 6a and 6b _____

No. of your children on 6c who:
• lived with you _____
• didn't live with you due to divorce or separation (see page 14) _____

Dependents on 6c not entered above _____

d If your child didn't live with you but is claimed as your dependent under a pre-1985 agreement, check here ▶ ☐

e Total number of exemptions claimed . . . .

Add numbers entered on lines above ▶ ☐

Chapter 11: Dependents

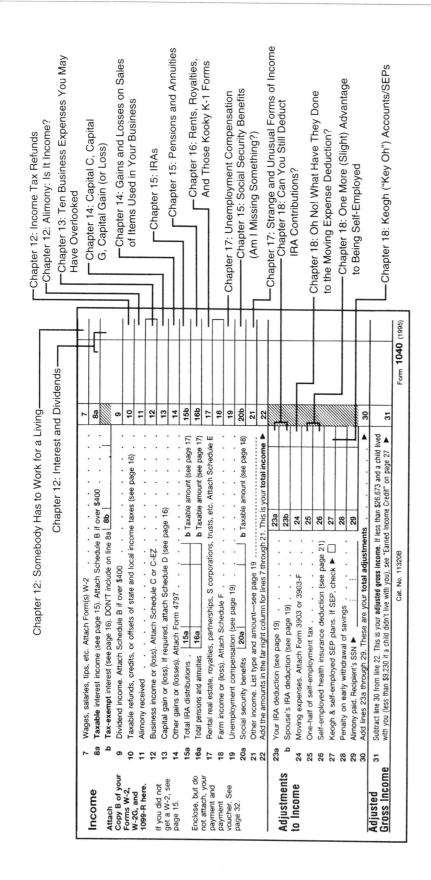

Chapter 12: Income Tax Refunds

Chapter 12: Alimony: Is It Income?

Chapter 13: Ten Business Expenses You May Have Overlooked

Chapter 14: Capital C, Capital G, Capital Gain (or Loss)

Chapter 14: Gains and Losses on Sales of Items Used in Your Business

Chapter 15: IRAs

Chapter 15: Pensions and Annuities

Chapter 16: Rents, Royalties, And Those Kooky K-1 Forms

Chapter 17: Unemployment Compensation

Chapter 15: Social Security Benefits (Am I Missing Something?)

Chapter 17: Strange and Unusual Forms of Income

Chapter 18: Can You Still Deduct IRA Contributions?

Chapter 18: Oh No! What Have They Done to the Moving Expense Deduction?

Chapter 18: One More (Slight) Advantage to Being Self-Employed

Chapter 18: Keogh ("Key Oh") Accounts/SEPs

Chapter 12: Somebody Has to Work for a Living

Chapter 12: Interest and Dividends

Chapter 9: Blind, 65 or Over

Chapter 9: Whose Dependent Are You?

Chapters 19: How Do Itemized Deductions Get Included in My Tax Return?

Chapter 21: So, How Much Is This Standard Deduction, Anyway?

Chapter 22: Exemptions: Counting the Players

Chapter 23: Figuring the Base Income Tax: Tables and Rates

Chapter 24: Child and Dependent Care

Chapter 24: Credit for the Elderly or Disabled

Chapter 24: Foreign Tax Credits

Chapter 24: Investment Tax Credit (Is That Thing Still Around?)

Chapter 23: The Kiddie Tax

Form 1040 (1995) — Page 2

Tax Computation (See page 23.)

32 Amount from line 31 (adjusted gross income)

33a Check if: ☐ **You were** 65 or older, ☐ Blind; ☐ **Spouse was** 65 or older, ☐ Blind. Add the number of boxes checked above and enter the total here . . ▲ 33a

b If your parent (or someone else) can claim you as a dependent, check here . ▲ 33b

c If you are married filing separately and your spouse itemizes deductions or you are a dual-status alien, see page 23 and check here . . . . ▲ 33c ☐

34 Enter the larger of your:
   Itemized deductions from Schedule A, line 28, **OR**
   Standard deduction shown below for your filing status. **But if you checked any box on line 33a or b,** go to page 23 to find your standard deduction. If you checked box 33c, your standard deduction is zero.
   • Single—$3,900 • Married filing jointly or Qualifying widow(er)—$6,550
   • Head of household—$5,750 • Married filing separately—$3,275

35 Subtract line 34 from line 32

36 If line 32 is $86,025 or less, multiply $2,500 by the total number of exemptions claimed on line 6e. If line 32 is over $86,025, see the worksheet on page 24 for the amount to enter .

37 **Taxable income.** Subtract line 36 from line 35. If line 36 is more than line 35, enter -0-

38 Tax. Check if from a ☐ Tax Table, b ☐ Tax Rate Schedules, c ☐ Capital Gain Tax Worksheet, or d ☐ Form 8615 (see page 24). Amount from Form(s) 8814 ▲ e

39 Additional taxes. Check if from a ☐ Form 4970 b ☐ Form 4972

40 Add lines 38 and 39 . . . ▲

If you want the IRS to figure your tax, see page 24.

Credits (See page 24.)

41 Credit for child and dependent care expenses. Attach Form 2441 | 41

42 Credit for the elderly or the disabled. Attach Schedule R . | 42

43 Foreign tax credit. Attach Form 1116 | 43

44 Other credits (see page 25). Check if from a ☐ Form 3800 b ☐ Form 8396 c ☐ Form 8801 d ☐ Form (specify) | 44

45 Add lines 41 through 44

46 Subtract line 45 from line 40. If line 45 is more than line 40, enter 0 . . ▲

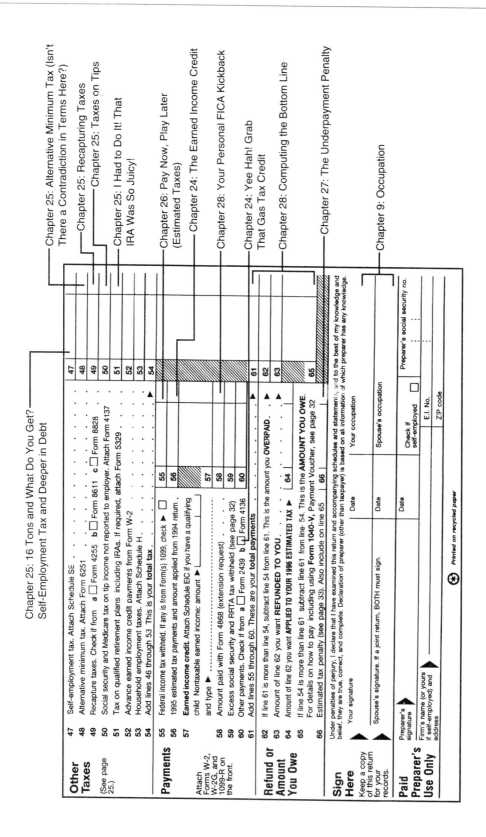

Chapter 25: Alternative Minimum Tax (Isn't There a Contradiction in Terms Here?)

Chapter 25: Recapturing Taxes

Chapter 25: Taxes on Tips

Chapter 25: I Had to Do It! That IRA Was So Juicy!

Chapter 26: Pay Now, Play Later (Estimated Taxes)

Chapter 24: The Earned Income Credit

Chapter 28: Your Personal FICA Kickback

Chapter 24: Yee Hah! Grab That Gas Tax Credit

Chapter 28: Computing the Bottom Line

Chapter 27: The Underpayment Penalty

Chapter 9: Occupation

Chapter 25: 16 Tons and What Do You Get? Self-Employment Tax and Deeper in Debt

Other Taxes

(See page 25.)

47	Self-employment tax. Attach Schedule SE	47
48	Alternative minimum tax. Attach Form 6251	48
49	Recapture taxes. Check if from a ☐ Form 4255 b ☐ Form 8611 c ☐ Form 8828	49
50	Social security and Medicare tax on tip income not reported to employer. Attach Form 4137	50
51	Tax on qualified retirement plans including IRAs. If required, attach Form 5329	51
52	Advance earned income credit payments from Form W-2	52
53	Household employment taxes. Attach Schedule H	53
54	Add lines 46 through 53 This is your **total tax**	54

Payments

Attach Forms W-2, W-2G, and 1099-R on the front.

55	Federal income tax withheld. If any is from Form(s) 1099, check ▶ ☐	55	
56	1995 estimated tax payments and amount applied from 1994 return	56	
57	**Earned income credit.** Attach Schedule EIC if you have a qualifying child Nontaxable earned income: amount ▶ _____ and type ▶ _____	57	
58	Amount paid with Form 4868 (extension request)	58	
59	Excess social security and RRTA tax withheld (see page 32)	59	
60	Other payments. Check if from a ☐ Form 2439 b ☐ Form 4136	60	
61	Add lines 55 through 60. These are your **total payments**	61	

Refund or Amount You Owe

62	If line 61 is more than line 54, subtract line 54 from line 61. This is the amount you **OVERPAID**	62
63	Amount of line 62 you want **REFUNDED TO YOU**	63
64	Amount of line 62 you want **APPLIED TO YOUR 1996 ESTIMATED TAX** ▶	64
65	If line 54 is more than line 61 subtract line 61 from line 54. This is the **AMOUNT YOU OWE.** For details on how to pay including using **Form 1040-V,** Payment Voucher, see page 32	65
66	Estimated tax penalty (see page 33). Also include on line 65	66

Sign Here

Keep a copy of this return for your records.

Under penalties of perjury, I declare that I have examined this return and accompanying schedules and statements, and to the best of my knowledge and belief, they are true, correct, and complete. Declaration of preparer (other than taxpayer) is based on all information of which preparer has any knowledge.

| Your signature | Date | Your occupation |
| Spouse's signature. If a joint return, BOTH must sign. | Date | Spouse's occupation |

Paid Preparer's Use Only

Preparer's signature	Date	Check if self-employed ☐	Preparer's social security no.
Firm's name (or yours if self-employed) and address		E.I. No.	
		ZIP code	

✪ *Printed on recycled paper*

Index

CPAs (Certified Public Accountants), tax forms, attaining, 37
credits
  child care, 254-257
  dependent care, 254-257
  disabled taxpayers, 257-259
  earned income credits, 262-264
  elderly taxpayers, 257-259
  foreign taxes, 260
  gas tax credits, 265-266
  investment tax credits, 260
  refundable, 260-261
  totaling, 262-266

D

day care, credits for, 254
deductible floors
  casualty/theft, 226
  medical expenses, 202
  miscellaneous expenses, 232
deductions, 324
  55-or-older deduction (home sales), 143-144
  alimony, 194
  capital losses, 134-135
  exemptions, 240
  health insurance if self-employed, 190
  IRAs, 186
  itemized deductions, 195-196, 289-291, 326
    artwork, 222-223
    automobile license fees, 206
    business expenses, 105-128, 228-229
    buying/selling a house, 209-210
    charitable contributions, 216-224
    club dues, 39-40
    continuing education, 230-231
    doctors' services, 199
    donated antiques, 222

donated appreciated property, 222-223
donated stock certificates, 222
foreign income taxes, 207
fund-raising events, 217
gambling losses, 180
home equity loans, 210
home mortgage interest expenses, 209
home office expenses, 230
investment maintenance costs, 231
investment property interest, 210-212
job searches, 230
limitations, 197
local income taxes, 204-205
medical expenses, 197-203
mileage for medical attention, 200-201
miscellaneous expenses, 228-232
moving expenses, 191-193
natural disasters, 225-227
noncash charitable donations, 218-221
out-of-pocket expenses for nonprofit organizations, 224
personal property taxes, 206-207
preparation cost for tax returns, 231-232
prescription drugs, 200
qualifying for, 196-197
real property taxes, 205-206
state income taxes, 204-205
theft, 225-227
unemployment taxes, 207-208
versus standard deductions, 196, 237

partnerships, tax shelters, 170-174
personal loans through home equity loans, 212
rentals, 161-162, 168
royalty incomes, 169
self-employment taxes, 190
SEP accounts, 190
standard deductions, 196, 235-238
stay-at-home taxpayers, 40
Delaware, tax returns, mailing location, 15
demolition of property, itemized deductions, 225
dental expenses, itemized deductions, 290
dependent care, credit, 254-257
Dependent care benefits, W-2 forms, 92
dependents, 70, 79-84, 324
  determining, 83-85
  exemptions, 82
  income test, 81
  standard deductions, 237
  support test, 81-82
depletion, business costs, 118
depreciation
  business costs, 118, 121-126
  rentals, 162-168
disabled taxpayers
  credits for, 257-259
  standard deduction bonuses, 237
disasters, itemized deductions for damage and losses, 225-227
distributions, capital gains, 104
District of Columbia, tax returns, mailing location, 15
dividends, 102-103, 324
  capital gain distributions, 104
  claiming, 97-105
  foreign bank accounts, 104-105
  Gross Dividends, 103
  nontaxable distributions, 104

W-Z

U-V